THE BARBARIANS OF ANCIENT EUROPE

The Barbarians of Ancient Europe deals with the reality of the indigenous peoples of Europe, in contrast to many publications that explore these peoples in the context of the Greek idea of "barbarians" as the "Other." These varied groups – Thracians, Scythians, Celts, Germans, Etruscans, and other peoples of Italy, the Alps, and beyond – had contact with one another and with Greek culture during its flowering. Images on the spectacular gold and silver objects buried in royal tombs show how the horse-riding nomads and the barbarian women warriors known in antiquity as Amazons saw themselves. Archaeological discoveries show how these "barbarian" peoples dressed, what they ate and drank, where they lived, and how they honored their dead kings with barbaric splendor and human sacrifices, allowing us to change, correct, or confirm the picture given in Greek and Roman literature.

Larissa Bonfante is Professor of Classics Emerita at New York University. A member of the American Philosophical Society and the German Archaeological Institute and President of the U.S. Section of the Istituto di Studi Etruschi, she is the author of *Etruscan Dress, Etruscan Life and Afterlife: A Handbook of Etruscan Studies*, and *The Etruscan Language: An Introduction* (with Giuliano Bonfante); coeditor of *The World of Roman Costume*; and coauthor of *Etruscan Myths*.

THE BARBARIANS OF ANCIENT EUROPE

Realities and Interactions

Edited by

LARISSA BONFANTE
New York University

CAMBRIDGE
UNIVERSITY PRESS

CAMBRIDGE
UNIVERSITY PRESS

University Printing House, Cambridge CB2 8BS, United Kingdom

One Liberty Plaza, 20th Floor, New York, NY 10006, USA

477 Williamstown Road, Port Melbourne, VIC 3207, Australia

4843/24, 2nd Floor, Ansari Road, Daryaganj, Delhi - 110002, India

79 Anson Road, #06-04/06, Singapore 079906

Cambridge University Press is part of the University of Cambridge.

It furthers the University's mission by disseminating knowledge in the pursuit of education, learning and research at the highest international levels of excellence.

www.cambridge.org
Information on this title: www.cambridge.org/9781107692404

© Cambridge University Press 2011

First published 2011
Reprinted 2011, 2012
First paperback edition 2014

A catalogue record for this publication is available from the British Library

Library of Congress Cataloging in Publication data
The barbarians of ancient Europe : realities and interactions / edited by Larissa Bonfante.
    p. cm.
"The articles here were first presented as papers at a conference held at the University of Richmond in March 2003" – Pref.
Includes bibliographical references and index.
ISBN 978-0-521-19404-4
1. Indo-Europeans – History – Congresses.   2. Indo-Europeans – Cultural assimilation – Congresses.   3. Indo-Europeans – Antiquities – Congresses.
4. Acculturation – Europe – History – Congresses.   5. Social change – Europe – History – Congresses.   6. Ethnohistory – Europe – Congresses.
7. Ethnoarchaeology – Europe – Congresses.   8. Europe – Civilization – Greek influences – Congresses.
I. Bonfante, Larissa.   II. Title.
GN539.B27   2011
936–dc22   2010026372

ISBN 978-0-521-19404-4 Hardback
ISBN 978-1-107-69240-4 Paperback

The publication of this volume was supported in part by a grant from the Institute for the Study of the Ancient World, from funds provided by the Leon Levy Foundation. Funds were also provided by the National Endowment for the Humanities, with the additional support of the Classics Department of the University of Richmond.

CONTENTS

ILLUSTRATIONS

COLOR PLATES

Color plates follow page xxiv.

MAPS

CONTRIBUTORS

LARISSA BONFANTE, Professor of Classics Emerita at New York University, is a member of the Archaeological Institute of America, the Istituto di Studi Etruschi ed Italici, the Société des Etudes Latines, the German Archaeological Institute, and the American Philosophical Society. Her publications include *The Etruscan Language: An Introduction*, with Giuliano Bonfante; *Out of Etruria*; *Etruscan Mirrors: The Metropolitan Museum of Art*; *The World of Roman Costume*; *Etruscan Dress*; and *Etruscan Life and Afterlife*. She is the founder and coeditor, with Jane Whitehead, of *Etruscan News*, the bulletin of the U.S. Section of the Istituto di Studi Etruschi ed Italici. In 2007 she was awarded the Gold Medal of the Archaeological Institute of America.

BARRY CUNLIFFE was knighted in 2006. A Professor of European Archaeology at the University of Oxford, he has been President of the Council for British Archaeology, member of the Advisory Committee of the Discovery Programme (Ireland), Governor of the Museum of London, President of the Society of Antiquaries of London, and Fellow of the British Academy. He has excavated at important British sites, including Fishbourne. His publications on the archaeology of Iron Age Europe and British archaeology include *Rome and the Barbarians*; *Greeks, Romans and Barbarians: Spheres of Interaction*; *Iron Age Communities in Britain*; *L'Univers des Celtes*; *The Ancient Celts*; *Facing the Ocean: The Atlantic and Its Peoples, 8000 BC–AD 1500*; and, most recently, *Europe between the Oceans: 9000 BC–AD 1000*.

NANCY THOMSON DE GRUMMOND, M. Lynette Thompson Distinguished Research Professor of Classics at Florida State University, Tallahassee, specializes in Etruscan, Roman, and Hellenistic art and archaeology, with a concentration on Etruscan myth and religion. She is director of the FSU excavations at the Sanctuary of the Etruscan Artisans at Cetamura del Chianti. She has published numerous books, including *A Guide to Etruscan Mirrors* and *Etruscan Myth, Sacred History, and Legend*. She edited *The Religion of the Etruscans*, with Erika Simon, and *An Encyclopedia of the History of Classical Archaeology*. Her many articles have appeared in a variety of classical, art historical, and archaeological journals and collections.

ANN E. FARKAS is Professor Emerita, of the Department of Anthropology and Archaeology, Brooklyn College, The City University of New York. She has written on the Scythians and other nomads and is interested in nomads and barbarism, style and visual perception, and Minerva's Owl, or the impossibility of interpreting the past.

OTTO-HERMAN FREY, formerly Professor at the University of Hamburg and Chair of Pre- and Protohistoric Archaeology in Marburg, is the author of *Die Entstehung der Situlenkunst, Studien zur figürlich verzierten Toreutik von Este*, the basic study for the subject of situla art. His publications also deal with Celtic art and its distribution and with new finds of Iron Age art in Germany. A member of the German Archaeological Institute, the British Academy, the Royal Irish Academy, and the Istituto di Studi Etruschi ed Italici, he has carried out excavations in Spain, Italy, Slovenia, Hungary, Austria, and Germany.

ASKOLD I. IVANTCHIK, an international authority on the history and cultures of the Cimmerians and Scythians, is Scientific Director of the Center for Comparative Studies of Ancient Civilizations of the Russian Academy of Sciences in Moscow and Directeur de Recherches of the Centre National de la Recherche Scientifique (CNRS) at the Institute *Ausonius* in Bordeaux, as well as a corresponding member of the Russian Academy of Sciences, of the German Archaeological Insitute (DAI), and of the Istituto Italiano par Africa et l'Oriente (IsIAO). A former Member of the Institute for Advanced Study in Princeton, New Jersey, he is chief editor of the *Journal of Ancient History* (*Vestnik drevney istorii*), Moscow, and of *Ancient Civilizations from Scythia to Siberia*, Leiden; author of *Les Cimmériens au Proche-Orient* (1993), *The Cimmerians: Ancient Oriental Civilizations and Steppe Nomads in the 8th–7th Centuries* BC (1996), *Kimmerier und Skythen* (2001), and *Am Vorabend der Kolonisation* (2005).

PAUL T. KEYSER, an independent scholar, holds PhD degrees in physics and classics and works at IBM's Watson Research Center in Hawthorne, New York. A former Junior Fellow at the Center for Hellenic Studies, he has published on Greek tragedy, stylometry, ancient science, gravitational physics, and computer science. He is the coeditor and author of two books on ancient science, *Greek Science of the Hellenistic Era* (2002) and *Biographical Encyclopedia of Ancient Natural Sciences: The Greek Tradition and Its Many Heirs* (2008), and he is at work on a third, edited with John Scarborough, *Oxford Handbook of Science and Medicine in the Classical World*.

IVAN MARAZOV is the former Director of the Graduate Program in the History of Art, History of Culture Department, New Bulgarian University, Sofia, and Minister of Culture of the Republic of Bulgaria. He is the editor and author of numerous books, including *Ancient Gold: The Wealth of the Thracians: Treasures from the Republic of Bulgaria*; *Thrace and the Thracians* (with Alexander Fol); *Myth, Ritual and Art in Ancient Thrace*; *The Visual Myth*; *Mythology of Gold*; *The Rogozen Treasure*; *Thracians and Wine*; *Rhytons in Ancient Thrace*; *Thracian Mythology*, *Thracian Warrior*; and, most recently, *Saved Treasures from V. Bojkov Collection* and *The Mysteries of the Kabeiroi in Ancient Thrace*.

JOHN MARINCOLA, Leon Golden Professor of Classics at Florida State University, Tallahassee, is well known for his work on ancient Greek and Roman historiography. He is the editor of *A Companion to Greek and Roman Historiography*; the author of *Greek Historians* and *Authority and Tradition in Ancient Historiography*; coauthor of a commentary on *Herodotus: Book IX*; coeditor of *The Cambridge Companion to Herodotus*; and editor of *A Companion to Greek and Roman Historiography* and the revised Penguin edition of *Herodotus: The Histories*, translated by A. de Sélincourt. He is currently at work on books entitled *Plutarch's Persian Wars: Myth, History and Identity in Roman Greece* and *Hellenistic Historiography*.

RENATE ROLLE, Professor Emerita of Archaeology at the Archaeological Institute of the University of Hamburg, and formerly head of the
Division of Eastern Europe and Central Asia Archaeology, is a member
of the German Archaeological Institute and of the National Academy
of Ukraine. A renowned authority on the archaeology of the horse
and Scythian archaeology, she directed the excavations at the Scythian
hill fortress of Bel'sk, in eastern Ukraine, which modified the view of
the Scythian nomadic way of life as described by Herodotus. She has
directed or participated in many other excavations, including Tolstaja
Mogila, Zeltokamenka, and Čhertomlÿk. She has published *The World
of the Scythians*; *Gold of the Steppes: Archaeology of the Ukraine*; *Totenkult
der Skythen*; and *Archäologische Studien in Kontaktzonen der antiken Welt*.
Further scholarly projects involve exhibits on Scythians and Amazons
and experimental archaeology.

WALTER STEVENSON teaches Greek and Latin literature and Roman
history in the Department of Classical Studies at the University of
Richmond. He has been Visiting Professor at the Lviv State University
and Lviv Theological Academy in Ukraine, and he continues his scholarly involvement with archaeological and historical studies of the region.
His research interests lie in the social history of the late Roman Empire
and the historiography of the early Byzantine Empire. Selected publications include "Eunuchs and Early Christianity" in *Eunuchs in Antiquity
and Beyond*; "Sozomen, Barbarians and Early Byzantine Historiography"
in *Greek, Roman, and Byzantine Studies*; and "John Chrysostom, Maruthas
and Christian Evangelism in Sasanian Iran," *Studia Patristica* 47 (2010)
301–306.

PETER S. WELLS is Professor in the Department of Anthropology at
the University of Minnesota. His principal interests are in later European
prehistory and Europe just before, during, and after the Roman conquests.
His books include *The Barbarians Speak: How the Conquered Peoples Shaped
Roman Europe*; *Beyond Celts, Germans and Scythians: Archaeology and Identity
in Iron Age Europe*; *The Battle That Stopped Rome: Emperor Augustus, Arminius,
and the Slaughter of the Legions in the Teutoburg Forest*; and, most recently,
Barbarians to Angels: The Dark Ages Reconsidered.

PREFACE AND ACKNOWLEDGMENTS

The present volume had its origins in a conference that took place at the University of Richmond, Virginia, in 2003, made possible by a generous grant from the National Endowment for the Humanities and hosted by the Classics Department of the University of Richmond during the spring semester of 2003. The subject of the conference, the barbarian peoples of ancient Europe, with its specific geographical and chronological focus, allowed for comparisons and contrasts of barbarians with their Greek and Etruscan neighbors and with each other and provided scholars specializing in these subjects – often used to working in isolation – with an opportunity to collaborate more closely and perhaps even come to some conclusions.

The enthusiastic response of the participants, all of them specialists in their fields, resulted in an exhilarating meeting of minds. In spite of the difficult moment of our recent history, the beginning of the current Iraq war, they came down from the cold North to the sunny climes of the South, like the European barbarians of old, and for one magical weekend we all traveled back into the past together. Later, during the long publication process, they graciously answered queries and put up with delays. It has been an honor and a pleasure to work with them.

I am deeply grateful for the advice and constant support of Ann E. Farkas throughout the conference and period of publication. She was the spirit behind the splendid Scythian exhibit at the Metropolitan Museum of Art in 2000, and her non-Hellenocentric view of barbarians has helped to keep the book on an even keel. Included in this volume are her notes on Delacroix's beautiful painting, *Ovid among the Scythians* (Plate XXIII).

Not everyone who participated at the conference is represented in this volume. Guenter Kopcke's paper on Hellenism, which contributed much to the discussions, is absent, as is Gocha Tsetskhladze's report on the Iberians. Nor could the Barbarian Fashion Show produced by Bernard and Norma Goldman and modeled by student volunteers be included. We mourn the death of Bernard Goldman.

Also sadly missing from the volume and from the Richmond he loved is Stuart Wheeler, co-organizer of the conference and chief of protocol, at that time the Chairman of the Department of Classics. He was a native Virginian whose deep knowledge of the history and the world of Richmond enriched our stay in many ways.

During the course of the semester, my former student and longtime friend Julie Laskaris, and Erica Longenbach, my student assistant, cheerfully and efficiently steered me through schedules and snowstorms. Dean June Aprille and Margaret Mayo at the Virginia Museum of Fine Arts did much to make the original conference a success, as did the bureaucratic savvy and care of Stella Jones, administrative assistant of the Classics Department.

The book owes its existence and present form to the generosity and patience of many friends and colleagues. The present chairman of the Department of Classical Studies at the University of Richmond, Dean Simpson, helped support this publication in several ways. Ingrid Rowland and Laurie Schneider Adams read all or part of the manuscript and made useful suggestions, as did several anonymous reviewers, most of whose advice I followed. Paul T. Keyser earned my gratitude by acting as Map Editor for the volume, while Susanne Ebbinghaus, Margarita Gleba, Maya Muratov, Walter Stevenson, and Maya Vassileva helped with the Russian and Bulgarian languages, Thracian rhyta, and Ukrainian kurgans. The early stages of the alchemical transformation of loose pages of texts and images into a book are due to Mary Knight, my mentor in matters of publication, and to the graceful efficiency of my assistant, Lyneve Quiles. At the Press, I am grateful for the assistance of Amanda J. Smith, and of the copy editor, Helen Greenberg, and the production editor, Helen Wheeler. Finally, Beatrice Rehl, no stranger to acknowledgments of grateful authors, guided the book through its long initial journey and the reefs and hazards of the publication process. She deserves and receives my heartfelt thanks.

Larissa Bonfante

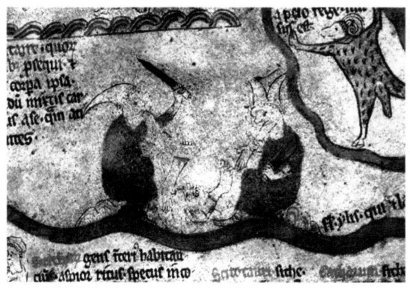

Plate I. Tribe of imaginary Scythians, the Issedone Sithe, cutting up and eating the bodies of their dead parents. Hereford Cathedral, medieval manuscript, ca. 1300. (Courtesy the Dean and Chapter of Hereford and the Hereford Mappa Mundi Trust.)

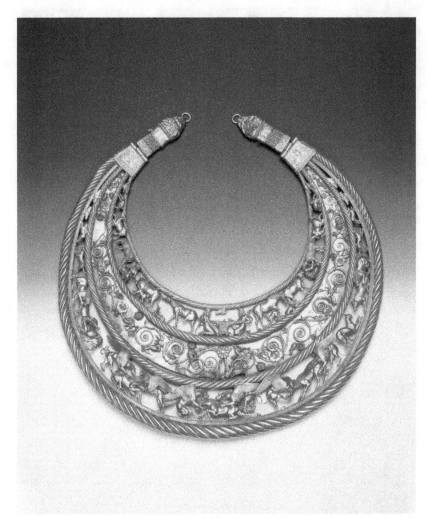

Plate II. Scythian way of life. Top register: Two Scythian warriors sewing a shirt made of skins while other nomads tend their horses, cows, and sheep. Lower register: Combats of griffins and various wild and domestic animals. Details of Scythian gold pectoral commissioned from a Greek artist. (Luka Mjeda/Art Resource.)

Plate III. Mutilation of mourners. Wall painting in Pyandzhikent (II, B), seventh century AD. (After Yakubovskiy and D'yakonov 1954, plate XX.)

Plate IV. Excavation on Chertomlÿk Kurgan, 1981. Original height of kurgan still standing (9 meters of the original 21 meters). Below, front, ancient level with horse burials. Main burial was 12 beneath this level. (Photo R. Rolle, W. Herz.)

Plate V. Scythian leader of Kurgan Solocha with typical armor. Reconstruction by M. Gorelik. (Rolle 1973, fig. 4.)

Plate VI. Reconstruction of Amazon and Scythian warrior, based on archaeological material from necropolis of Bel'sk. (From exhibition on "Scythian Warriors and Amazons." Photo M. Weigand.)

Plate VII. Borovo Treasure, first half of the fourth century BC. (Marazov 1998, 83–84, Cat. 173–177.)

Plate VIIIA. Deity confronting a dragon. Silver appliqué from the Letnitsa Treasure, second half of the fourth century BC. (Marazov 1998, 165–166, Cat. 95.)

Plate VIIIB. Silver helmet from Peretu, Romania, second half of the fourth century BC.

Plate IX. Detail of a pitcher rhyton from the Borovo Treasure, first half of the fourth century BC.

Plate X. Frescoes from the central chamber of the Kazanlak Tomb, first half of the third century BC. (Marazov 1998, 78, fig. 35.)

Plate XI. Gold helmet from Kotsofeneshti, Romania, second half of the fourth century BC. (Marazov 1998, 67, fig. 27.)

Plate XII. Boar hunt and hero on a golden horse. Detail of a fresco in the central chamber of the Alexandrovo Tomb, first half of the fourth century BC. (Photo Marazov.)

Plate XIII. Silver appliqué from the Loukovit Treasure, second half of the fourth century BC. (Marazov 1998, 124, Cat. 44a.)

Plate XIV. Two goddesses riding on lionesses, flanking a central animal group. Silver jug No. 155 from the Rogozen Treasure, second half of the fourth century BC. (Marazov 1998, 186, Cat. 123.)

Plate XV. Silver phiale from the Rogozen Treasure, second half of the fourth century BC. (Marazov 1998, 176, Cat. 107.)

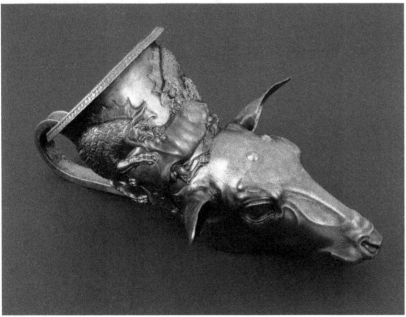

Plate XVI. Lion and griffin attacking a bull on a rhyton from the Malomirovo-Zlatinitsa tumulus mound. Second half of the fourth century BC.

Plate XVII. Gold and silver rhyton with a running stag protome from the Vassil Bojkov Collection. Last quarter of the fifth century BC.

Plate XVIII. Greave with an image of a goddess on the knee, from Malomirovo-Zlatinitsa tumulus-mound. Second half of the fourth century BC.

Plate XIX. Bird-shaped handle of a knife (*machaira*) from the Golyama Kosmatka tumulus mound. Second half of the fourth century BC.

Plate XX. Canopus from Dolciano. 650–600 BC. Chiusi, Museo Archeologico Nazionale. (Photo Courtesy Soprintendenza per i Beni Archeologici della Toscana.)

Plate XXI. Symplegma: female figure on the lap of a seated male figure, with a standing attendant holding a decorated vase and tree branch. Thracian silver-gilt plaque from Letnitsa. Fourth century BC. Lovech Museum of History. (Marazov 1998, 162–163, no. 92.)

Plate XXIIA. Etruscan scarab with a scene of Tages and Tarchon (?). Rome, Museo Nazionale di Villa Giulia. (Photo Courtesy Ministero per i Beni e le Attività Culturali, Soprintendenza per i Beni Archeologici dell'Etruria meridionale – Museo Nazionale di Villa Giulia.)

Plate XXIIB. Etruscan scarab with a scene of Turms and an oracular head in a bag. London, British Museum. (Photo © copyright by Trustees of the British Museum.)

Plate XXIII. F.-V.-E. Delacroix, *Ovid among the Scythians*

CHAPTER ONE

CLASSICAL AND BARBARIAN

Larissa Bonfante

In contrast to recent conferences and publications on the Greek idea of the barbarian, The Barbarians of Ancient Europe *deals with the indigenous peoples of Europe who had contact with Greek culture during its flowering – Thracians, Scythians, Celts, Germans, Etruscans, and other peoples of Italy, the Alps, and beyond (Map 1.1). The chapters in this book were first presented as papers at a conference held at the University of Richmond in March 2003. Since that time, there has been growing interest in the reality of the peoples who were long referred to as "barbarians" in the pejorative sense. In this chapter, I review some of the major themes and debates presented in this volume and lay out a framework to help the reader situate the arguments and conclusions of each contributing author.[1]*

The subtitle of this volume, *Realities and Interactions*, refers to two kinds of archaeology. The first is the classical "antiquarian" approach to prehistoric archaeology, which illustrates the life, manners, customs, and beliefs of ancient peoples. The second emphasizes technology, trade, connections, and interactions, and defines cultures as the product of an interaction between society and environment.[2] Both approaches are illustrated in the volume. Though the available evidence is the same for both, however, the focuses are different, as are the methodology and conclusions.

The evidence consists of references and descriptions in Greek and Roman literature as well as an ever-growing body of archaeological

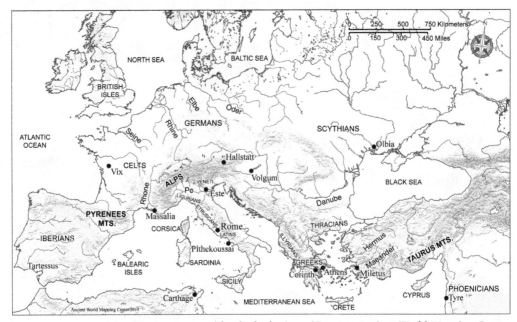

Map 1.1. Areas covered by the barbarians. (Courtesy Ancient World Mapping Center, copyright 2010; www.unc.edu/awmc.)

information. How do we understand the relationship between these two kinds of testimony, between the way classical authors represented these non-Greek peoples and the way we read their cultures today on the basis of their art and imagery, their burial practices, their homes, and their way of life? Which of the two has more authority and should be accorded priority? Can we reconcile archaeological discoveries with statements and narratives of literary sources that represent ancient perceptions of the nonclassical peoples of antiquity? We ourselves are necessarily bound by our own modern views of these cultures as we try to re-create the past and create new myths.

Challenging classical scholarship's dependence on the written word raises many questions. What kinds of histories can be written about peoples with no written historical traditions of their own? What did these different cultures have in common, aside from their geographical situations and their nonclassical status? And finally, how do we deal with questions of their chronology and historical change? Identity is not fixed, but changes for all of us, as it did for the Greeks and the various peoples around them.

The Evidence

We can try to learn about the life of the barbarians through the art and artifacts they have left behind, but this archaeological evidence must be translated. We must interpret it from its context, and we can never be sure that we understand it correctly. "No fact exists without an interpretation. For facts are like words in a dictionary; they are dead."[3] Though we feel on surer ground when we have classical texts that describe the appearance and culture of the peoples we are dealing with, classical texts tell us something of other peoples only when their history touches that of the Greeks and Romans, and their accounts tend to be biased, driven by their own agendas. Reflected in the various chapters of this volume are ongoing discussions and disagreements among modern scholars about the relative value of various kinds of evidence – linguistic, archaeological, philological, historical – while the inclusion of Russian, Bulgarian, and other specialized bibliographies makes available the results of new research and archaeological discoveries.

Askold Ivantchik illustrates a method for matching the historical information and archaeological data. For the Scythians, whom we know mainly through archaeology, a careful comparison of Herodotus's account of royal burials with the results of actual excavation brings out numerous convergences and surprising similarities, from the sacrificial horseback riders who stood guard around the royal mound to their tattoos.[4]

Renate Rolle's account illustrates a different method by which we can reach an understanding of aspects of the Scythian way of life. Her re-creation of the royal procession of the empress of Russia through her far-flung empire is reminiscent of the Scythian and Thracian royal round.[5] It includes a description of the luxurious little houses on golden runners of the empress's cortège, much like the ox-drawn wagons of the nomadic Scythians described by various authors of antiquity, which were inhabited by women and children as well as the old and the sick.

Herodotus (4.46) attributes to the Scythians the invention of taking their homes with them. "The advantage of this way of life was the fact that no one marching against them could escape them, while on the other hand no one was able to lay their hands on the Scythians unless they allowed themselves to be found." Rolle's excavations at Bel'sk, a site that was the destination of Greek traders with a rich supply of goods, also proves the existence of a different Scythian way of life, that of a population who lived in a nomadic or seminomadic way together with resident inhabitants.[6] Such a huge, complex structure, she points out, can only have been realized under the central direction and protection of Scythian kings – those same Scythian kings whose royal graves are found in the necropolis of Bel'sk.

Peter Wells likewise provides archaeological evidence for a previously unrecognized supracommunity political organization of the Germans in the pre-Roman Iron Age period. It includes the surprising discovery of the construction of wooden trackways across marshy areas, and of a deposit of weapons large enough to outfit eighty warriors and presumably warships, evidence of far more complex organized warfare than was thought possible before the arrival of Roman armies on the Rhine.[7]

Recent publications have emphasized the interpretation of images within a particular culture. In the case of the Greeks, the focus has been on the iconography of vase painting as evidence for the religion, society, myths, and customs of fifth-century Athenians,[8] for which Greek literary texts can provide social, historical, and literary contexts for the images. But for most other cultures, the rarity or total lack of written texts means that we must depend on purely visual and archaeological evidence. Several authors confront the problem of trying to understand the significance of local myths and iconography when there are no written texts to guide us.

Nancy de Grummond's analysis of the motif of the talking head in Etruscan and Thracian art brings out meanings and structural frameworks and provides an example of the way an iconographic motif can be interpreted. Analogous observations on the iconography of Thracian art by Ivan Marazov, who relies heavily on semiology, illustrate the way the Thracians chose images and situations of Greek myth that appeared to be most suitable for motivating power and then transformed them. The Thracians perceived the ordering of the world as a hierarchy, and in their art the powerful goddess who protects the king has a prominent place. The iconography makes clear the authority of the king in visual terms, focusing on the figure of the hero, the Thracian Horseman, and the sequence of the royal choice: trials, consecration, investiture, and marriage. Marazov's contribution serves to make us aware of the way these images were transformed and of the different meanings they had for the people for whom they were made.

Three contributions work together to give a picture of the complex interrelations of the richly diverse but related ancient cultures that developed and flourished in Europe between the international Orientalizing period and the fourth century. My chapter on the Etruscans as mediators, Frey's chapter on the situla art of the Alpine regions and beyond, and de Grummond's chapter on the motif of the severed heads illustrate artistic interconnections and seem to reflect similar features of the customs, society, and beliefs of the peoples involved.

My account of the Etruscans emphasizes interactions and their role in Europe as mediators by way of the conveniently funnel-shaped Italian peninsula, a crossroads between the Classical Greek cultures of the Mediterranean and the peoples beyond the Alps. Crossroads, as John Boardman noted, are busy and informative places.[9] The time is ripe for a discussion of the place of the Etruscans in ancient history and for an attempt to remove them from the isolation to which they have been condemned by much modern classical scholarship.

Were the Etruscans barbarians? Their Classical Greek contemporaries may have seen them as non-Greek barbarians, but in early times they looked more like the Homeric Phaeacians than the barbarous cannibal Cyclops.[10] For many peoples of Europe and the Mediterranean, they counted as a classical civilization. Keith DeVries coined a phrase, the "Nearly Other," for the Etruscans and the Latins of central Italy to the west, and the Phrygians and Lydians to the east, as peoples who belong to a Hellenizing penumbra beyond the Greek world.[11] Yet the role of the Etruscans as models and mediators, and the distinctiveness of their art, give them a place as a ranking classical civilization, along with the Greeks and Romans.[12]

Etruscan culture influenced the art of the Alpine regions north of Italy that we call *situla art*, which in turn mediated influences from the Mediterranean to the Celts of Europe. Otto-Herman Frey examines the art of these barbarians on the northern border of Italy and the Alpine regions of Switzerland, Austria, and Slovenia, who were influenced by classical art and customs mediated by Etruscan culture. He discusses chronological developments and mutual influences, including successive contacts and distinctions between situla art and the figural style of early Celtic art, and reveals something of the lives, societies, and beliefs of the people who made, decorated, and used these well-crafted objects. Frey explores a number of questions raised by their iconography, including the implications of images of women for their role in these societies. He also asks whether these peoples merely adopted earlier classical art forms as artistic motifs or whether, and to what extent, classical culture actually influenced and transformed life in the Alpine region.[13]

Finally, Barry Cunliffe confronts modern interpretations of the term "Celtic" and traces the history of the controversy that has led some modern authors to go so far as to question the very existence of such a people. His contribution makes clear the extent to which modern biases have determined the various views of these ancient peoples.

What happened to the barbarians? The chapters by Marincola and Stevenson bring glimpses of later developments and overturn some prevalent preconceptions. The Romans, who adopted Greek culture, could define themselves as non-Greek "barbarians" – an intriguing idea for us, accustomed as we are to a Greco-Roman view of the Classical. Closely related to one of principal themes of this volume is Stevenson's view of the construction of an independent identity for the Goths, based on their participation in the classical culture of wine drinking and translation of the Bible, and ultimately on religion and language.

Identity

Modern scholars, and modern nations, often disagree on who the barbarian peoples were in antiquity and who their descendants are today. There is much debate over questions of identity and eventually of that most explosive issue, national identity.

Identity as a label that others apply to a group is the topic of the chapter by Paul Keyser, which illustrates the shifting nature of a vision of the barbarians of Europe in antiquity and of the successive structures in which the ancients placed the peoples on the fringe of their world in their mental maps. Ancients tended to see the world in East–West terms rather than divided between North and South, and it is not surprising that the Romans illustrated the extent of imperial gains from East to West.[14] This concept colored their view of barbarian geography over time, including the way they saw distinctions between the more sophisticated barbarians of the East and the mostly less "civilized" barbarians of the West.

The vast bibliography that has grown up today on identity – ethnic, racial, religious, linguistic, gender – and the related concept of alterity sees modern "Others" as those who are marginalized in terms of economy, race, gender, society, or religion. For an Athenian of the Classical period, the "Others" included barbarians, women, slaves, Amazons, and satyrs – anyone who was not a Greek, usually meaning a male citizen of fifth-century Athens.[15] Yet as Otto Brendel once put it: "We take the Greeks as our model, forgetting that the Greeks did everything differently from everybody else."[16] It was the Greeks of the Classical period who were the "Others," for they did things differently from all other peoples around them.

The concept of the barbarian as the "Other" crystallized with the sharp break between the archaic past and the post–Persian War period of the fifth century. At the same time, there also developed a consciousness of the otherness of their own past in relation to the Classical period. They distinguished themselves both from contemporary barbarians and from their own barbarian past. Herodotus, Thucydides, Aeschylus, and Euripides all indicate that Athenians felt that they had left their archaic past behind after their victory over the Persians and that their ancestors were as different from them as were the non-Greek barbarians of their own days.[17] To these Classical descendants, the Greeks of the archaic period were indeed a "foreign country," similar in many ways to the barbarians of their own times.[18] Because they saw otherness in chronological terms, they equated barbarian customs with those of their ancestors, who were not yet the "real" Greeks of Classical times.

Among the barbarians, on the other hand, earlier customs were held to be more genuine, purer characteristics of a people. Herodotus's description of Scythian royal burials shows a preference for attributing to the Scythians certain archaic traditions, as Ivantchik points out in this volume. According to Marazov and de Grummond, too, the Thracians, though contemporary with the Greeks, belonged to a different epoch in the process of history and exhibited social, political, and religious patterns not unlike those of the early Greeks of preclassical Homeric times.[19]

Fifth-century Athenians saw themselves as more Greek than their ancestors because Greekness was moving from an ethnic to a cultural identity. You could eventually become Greek by speaking Greek; you could be more or less Greek.[20] And foreigners could become more or less barbaric, sliding up and down the barbarian meter, from almost Greek, like Alexander, to fully barbarian, like a Scythian.[21]

Race, language, and culture have all been taken as markers of the Other. But in an important article, "Race, Language and Culture,"[22] whose date of publication in 1938 is deeply significant, Franz Boas explains how the bloodline, physical type, language, geography, customs, and culture of a group or nation rarely if ever remain permanent or work together all at the same time. Extended changes in language and culture often occur without corresponding changes in physical type, and there are many instances of permanence of "blood, or ethnic identity," along with far-reaching modifications of language and culture.

According to descriptions in Greek texts, barbarians spoke non-Greek languages and practiced non-Greek customs such as human sacrifice. In the eyes of the Greeks, they were set apart by their physical appearance, their dress and attitude to nudity, their *truphe* – conspicuous consumption, lust and luxury, the symbolism of gold as a status symbol – and the different role of women in society.

Differences and distinctions of language, dress, hair, housing, gender, and religion set groups apart from one another in the ancient world, as they have in every place and time. There were rules governing such distinctions, but they were more often unspoken assumptions than clearly delineated differences.[23] Such questions of identity constitute an anthropological problem that we try to understand through archaeological and written evidence. But what in the archaeological evidence, or in the texts, elucidates the attitude of a particular culture at a particular moment toward women's roles in society, illustrates its attitudes toward the dead, or illuminates the writer's or narrator's perception of the Other?

Names

Basic to the identity of any group is its name.[24] It carries messages of identity and self-presentation, nicely illustrating the distinction between the way people see themselves and how others see them. Even today, we call the inhabitants of the Peloponnese Greeks, while they call themselves Hellenes. The country we call Switzerland is Helvetia to the Swiss. The citizens of Germany call their homeland Deutschland. The names of the Gallic tribes inscribed on the Augustan Trophée des Alpes at la Turbie are taken to define the beginning of French identity.[25]

Modern countries and groups have used names according to nationalistic biases in order to exalt their own ancestors or to claim an area or a group as their own. Descendants tend to idealize those they consider to be their ancestors:[26] Romantics and nationalists have maintained that the Druids were philosophers, never involved in human sacrifice,[27] while the Hungarian scholar Janos Szilágyi documents a case of a nineteenth-century search for imaginary ancestors.[28] The most infamous example is that of the mythical "Aryans," the nineteenth-century term for Indo-Europeans that was polluted by Nazi propaganda when the concept of Indo-European identity led to the aberrant abuse of the concept of an Aryan race.[29]

The names as well as the presumed locations of barbarian nations are fluid. But such fluidity is by no means limited to barbarians. When we speak of the ancient Greeks, we usually mean those of fifth-century Athens. "Rome" can mean many things, including the whole Roman Empire.[30] The names of the Celts, the Germans, or the Scythians meant different things at different times according to who was using the term and when: they could refer to different peoples or to different stages in the history of the same people. We do not always know whether the names we use actually correspond to particular ethnic groups. What did each one call itself? What did other people call them and when? How did the names of the geographical areas they inhabited reflect their history and the languages spoken there before the coming of the Greeks and Romans?

Ancient and modern authors have applied these names arbitrarily, with different meanings. The names we use here – Germans, Celts or Gauls, Thracians, Scythians, Etruscans – are innocent enough if we understand them to be a conventional, convenient way of recognizing a certain group of people with similar characteristics during a certain time.[31] We need names to work with: "I've got to use words when I talk to you."[32]

The situation with the names of the peoples dealt with in this volume varies. Classical authors gave the name "Scythians" to many different tribes. Medieval authors, knowing nothing of these faraway peoples, located them in the snowy North; on late maps various Sithe appear, including, from the East, the Hunni Sithe, the Issedone Sithe, and others.[33]

Greek authors called the Etruscans of central Italy, long their wealthy rivals in the Mediterranean, Tyrrhenians, and named the sea they controlled the Tyrrhenian Sea, while the Romans, for whom the Tarquin dynasty was part of their own early history, knew the people to the north of their borders as Tusci. Etruscans used the name Rasna to refer to their people as a whole. But a citizen of Tarquinia, Chiusi, or Volterra depended on his or her own city for identity rather than on the larger linguistic and religious entity.[34] Because Greek and Roman historians did not record them, however, we have no ancient names for the peoples of northern Italy and beyond who represented details of their lives and ideals in the art of their situlas or bronze vessels, decorated in a narrative style they had learned from their southern neighbors the Etruscans.

"Who were the Germans?" "Who were the Celts?" These questions are asked repeatedly in publications dealing with these peoples and in this book. According to Caesar, as every schoolboy used to know, Gaul was divided into three parts: southwest of the Garonne were the Aquitani; north of the Seine and Marne was the territory of the Belgae; and in the vast area lying between are "the people we call Gauls, though in their own language they are called Celts."[35] But the name, origin, and identity of these Celts have recently been the subject of much controversy. Some modern authors have even suggested that the concept of the Celts, or Kelts, was invented in later times. Indeed, it was antiquarians studying the indigenous languages of the Atlantic fringe of Europe who chose to call them Celtic and who went on to pose the question "When did the Celts arrive here?"[36]

This question of origins, closely related to language, is also regularly asked of the Etruscans and accounts for their so-called mystery. The fact that the Etruscan language is unrelated to that of their neighbors naturally brings up the question "Where did the people who spoke this language come from?"[37] It is a valid question for linguists, who ask why the Etruscan language is non-Indo-European and different from that of any of its neighbors, as well as any other language known to us today. Archaeologists, however, do not consider that Etruscan origins are a problem, for we can trace the Etruscans' continuous development in situ in central Italy from as early as 1200 BC. This fact has not stopped the popular press from announcing at regular intervals a solution to the problem of Etruscan origins on the basis of a revelation of the actual nature of their language or, more recently, their DNA, that is, their race. The origin of the Indo-Europeans (see the later section "Indo-Europeans"), originally a language group, has become an archaeological problem. As Boas understood, there is a desire to see race, language, and culture as inseparable rather than as aspects of a people subject to changes in their history.

Language

According to the ancients, two institutions identified a nation: language and dress.[38] The languages spoken by the barbarians were a fundamental aspect of their identity, but this is too large a subject to be included here. Yet, as we have just seen, the question of language cannot be ignored.

We know something of the languages of the peoples we are dealing with, in some cases because they were written down using versions of the Semitic alphabet the Greeks had adapted.[39] These people all spoke with each other. The very interaction – trade, migration, exogamy – that brings people in contact and transmits ideas among societies implies bilingualism, even multilingualism. Evidence of this phenomenon from the early period, however, is almost completely lost to us. A rare instance is that of a sixth-century Celtic funerary inscription found in Italy in the Veneto region recording the name of a man who was *pompeteguaios*, meaning that he knew five languages; these could have been Celtic, Venetic, Etruscan, Illyrian, and Greek.[40] Certainly various peoples could speak one another's languages and communicated freely at various times in history, though at vastly different levels, ranging from the pidgin *koine* of merchants to the sophisticated language of philosophers and priests. Eventually, Greek and Latin won out. Unlike the languages of the barbarian peoples, ancient Greek and Latin literature survived because of their cultural and political prestige; they allowed easier communication, and became the international lingua francas.[41]

Greeks and Romans differed in their relations with the barbarians and their ways of seeing – and acting in – the world around them. In their own times, as Arnaldo Momigliano noted, the Greeks normally ignored languages other than their own, while the Romans used their knowledge of Greek culture to create a common Italian culture in the Latin language.[42] Only in very distant barbarian lands was Latin not spoken. Ovid among the Scythians claimed that he did not know their language and made himself understood with his hands. The tables are turned, he complained. It is he who is the barbarian, and his hosts laugh at him:

> barbarus hic ego sum, qui non intellegat ulli
> et rident stolidi verba Latina Getae.

> "Here I am a barbarian, understood by nobody,
> and the Getae laugh stupidly at my Latin." (Tristia V.10.37–38).

Indo-Europeans

Related to the question of language, origins, and identity is the Indo-European background of most of the peoples of Europe. The barbarians of Europe we are dealing with all shared aspects of language. They also shared, to some extent, aspects of religion and society. According to Georges Dumézil's influential theory, a deeply rooted structure held true in Indo-European society as it did in the world of imagination, ritual, and myth.[43] His work, at one point downgraded to the level of fantasy scholarship like Bachofen's matriarchy, has recently stimulated interesting discussions and controversies.[44] Dumézil could successfully compare Indian, Celtic, and ancient Roman myth and language because of the remarkably conservative character of their institutions in general, which jealously preserved ancient forms. In contrast, the innovative character of Greek language and culture proved to be more resistant to such comparisons.[45]

There were naturally mutual influences among neighbors, especially in the aptly named Orientalizing period, when the influence of the civilizations of the Near East and the Semitic peoples became overwhelming.[46] Language and religion, however, tend to retain their own character throughout many generations and provide the basis for the identity of a people. Celtic myths long preserved aspects of ancient customs and traditions, helped by the oral tradition that flourished among the Druids, and continued to be practiced by poets well into Christian times. Bernard Sergent examined elements of the Indo-European background of Celtic and Greek and found striking similarities between the characters of Achilles and Cuchulainn.[47] The Etruscans long retained their own language and religion in the face of outside influences. Their non-Indo-European character probably accounts for distinctions that can still be traced in historical times between the beliefs of Etruscans and those of their Indo-European neighbors. The importance of Etruscan mother goddesses, which was never diminished under the influence of the dominant paternalistic Indo-European religion, helps to explain the character of two female goddesses in Etruria: Uni, whose image is far more central than that of her Greek counterpart, Hera, and Menrva, whose maternal character offers a striking contrast to that of the Greek Athena.

Though comparisons are helpful in understanding something about the complexity of the ancient history of Europe, however, we must guard against accepting exaggerated distinctions between Indo-European and non-Indo-European, male and female, patriarchy and matriarchy, heaven and earth, Olympian and chthonic, intellect and instinct.[48]

Human Sacrifice

A custom taken to be characteristic of barbarians was the practice of human sacrifice. The available archaeological evidence has shown that such a custom existed and that it was shared by pre-Classical Greeks and barbarians.[49] The Greeks and the Hebrews – and the Romans, who participated in Classical Greco-Roman civilization – had consciously renounced this practice, and considered this to be a sign of the moral superiority of their cultures and religions over those of their forefathers and their neighbors. In their myths, the Greeks relegated the practice to the dark times of their early history, when Agamemnon could sacrifice his own daughter Iphigeneia, just as Abraham had contemplated sacrificing his son Isaac.

Archaeological evidence in fact shows that these practices existed almost everywhere in antiquity from the time of the Neanderthals – and they are still practiced in some civilized countries today.[50] The Minoans, Phoenicians, Etruscans, and Celts all practiced some form of human sacrifice without reference to the level of their civilizations.[51] Such ritual practices are not comparable to the casual cruelty of war: Achilles's slaughter of twelve Trojan prisoners at the tomb of his dead comrade (*Iliad* 23.175–184) was a gruesome deed, perhaps appropriate for his character, but a measure of his extreme mental anguish and likely frowned on by readers of Homer. It was different in kind from killing in battle. Yet this reference to human sacrifice may well have reflected an early custom.[52] There has been a reluctance among scholars to admit that such practices actually existed, because the religious sphere to which such rituals belonged is the hardest of all to imagine, and it is difficult for us to understand the beliefs that would have accompanied practices and customs that seem so foreign.

There were different types of human sacrifice, but they all had a social function. Much of our archaeological evidence comes from burials, where traces of sacrificial rituals appear in the cult of the dead and in practices related to the preeminent role of the warrior. Remnants of human skeletons of the "death riders" whom the Scythians sacrificed at the graves of high-ranking individuals were found along with their horses in situ at the base of impressive burial mounds or kurgans.[53] The Etruscans, who needed blood for the dead, depicted scenes of bloody battles and sacrifices in their funerary art and are said to have sacrificed prisoners of war. Evidence of another function of human sacrifice was recently revealed in central Italy when the existence of early Etruscan foundation rites involving human sacrifice was confirmed by the excavation of the sacred area at a ninth- to seventh-century BC site at Tarquinia.[54]

A frequent trophy of the sacrifice of enemies was the severed head, which figures prominently in the art and literature of a number of non-classical cultures. Celtic warriors cut off the heads of their enemies and exhibited these severed heads in a variety of contexts. Their priests, or Druids, oversaw the human sacrifices that were carried out even in Roman times[55] (Fig. 1.1). Herodotus (4.64–66) tells of the Scythian habit of taking the scalps of enemies and making them into handkerchiefs, and of using the skulls as drinking cups, sometimes with gilding added.[56] The presence of the severed heads of enemies killed in battle in Scythian and Thracian art thus seems to reflect an actual custom.

Today there is a push to deny the image of Carthage as the site of child sacrifice and of the *tophets* where they were buried, which testify

1.1. "The Wicker Image." Celtic human sacrifice, "The Burning Man." Engraving from Aylett Sammes, *Britannia Antiqua Illustrata*, 1676. Inspired by the description in Caesar, *Gallic Wars* 6.16. (From Piggott 1985, 111, fig. 78.)

to the practice.[57] But we know that even the Romans of the historical period practiced human sacrifice in times of danger: in the course of the Punic Wars and conflicts against the Celts,[58] they may have decided to try a system of placating the gods that seemed to be working for their enemies.

The proverbial cruelty of the Thracians, manifested in the form of human sacrifices, was one of the "barbaric" behavioral norms and customs that fifth-century Greeks could no longer understand. A much later example of the mutual incomprehension that existed with reference to such customs can be seen in a nomad ruler's statement in his correspondence with the pope (1246): "It is said in your letter that the slaughter of men ... puzzled and embarrassed you. We can simply reply that we are not able to understand this."[59]

It was often assumed, in antiquity and later, that far-off, uncivilized peoples normally carried on cannibalistic practices. There is at present no evidence to support such a claim for the peoples with which we are dealing. Homer attributes such behavior to the barbarous Cyclops. The medieval Hereford map of ca. 1300 shows the Issedone Sithe – supposedly a tribe of Scythians, according to the thinking of the time – cutting up and eating the bodies of their dead parents, with a Latin caption explaining that the Issedones thought this practice preferable to allowing worms to eat their deceased family members (Plate I).[60]

The Role of Women

Women represented a kind of seismograph of the condition of a civilization or society in Herodotus's *Histories*,[61] as well as in various historical accounts, including our own. The views of Greek philosophers varied on the place of women in society. For Aristotle, a civilized people such as the Greeks held the female and the slave to be two distinct and specialized types of human beings, neither of whom is quite equal to the free male citizen.

> Now the female is distinguished by nature from the slave. For nature makes nothing in an economizing spirit ... but one thing with a view to one thing; and each instrument would perform more finely if it served one task rather than many. The barbarians, though, have the same arrangement for female and slave. The reason for this is that they have no naturally ruling element: with them, the partnership [of man and woman] is that of female slave and male slave. That is why the poets say "it is fitting for Greeks to rule barbarians," the assumption being that barbarian and slave are the same thing. (Aristotle, *Politics* 1252b 1–9)[62]

According to Aristotle, barbarians were therefore inferior to the Greeks because they failed to recognize these natural categories. Aristotle's

Greek audience evidently saw the leveling effect of barbarian marriage as something bizarre and distasteful,[63] because their division into male and female was an unimportant detail in contrast to the complex dynamic of specialization and hierarchy of the Greeks, who saw the division between men and women as not only natural, but much more sharply distinguished than the one between Greek and barbarian, which, as we saw, admitted of gradations, and which according to Plato was not a natural division.[64]

Yet the Greeks held barbarians and women to have much in common, including a primitive lack of self-control, the *sophrosyne* of which the Greeks were so proud. Greek myth situated the shocking murder of Orpheus and his decapitation, carried out by Thracian women, in a foreign context. In Scythian society and others related to it, women actively participated in funerals, mourning and inflicting damage on their bodies, hair, and clothing. (Ivantchik, Figs. 3.4 and 3.5, and Plate III).[65]

Recent works have explained deviant aspects of various groups of female Others, including Amazons, as well as Etruscan and Spartan women, as resulting from male fear of women, which fantasized and distorted perceptions of the "Other."[66] But the tide in modern scholarship is turning, and Amazons are attaining a higher degree of historical respectability. The fact that "Amazonian" female warriors are to be found in the legends and literature of widely differing peoples does not mean that such armed female guardians did not actually exist, and in fact archaeological discoveries show many aspects of the mythical Amazons to have been historical. All of the legends about Amazons are reflected in the grave goods of excavated Scythian tombs,[67] and it has been suggested that in Greek thought, "Amazon" could signify martial prowess rather than being a label of ethnicity.[68]

Archaeological evidence has indeed revealed much about the role of women in barbarian societies. A picture of the life of Scythian women derived from archaeology tells us a great deal about their social status and the importance of children in Scythian society. Much of this agrees with Greek accounts, though these often attempt to rationalize observed resemblances, or to explain them in historical or mythological terms. The Sauromatae, for example, were said to be the offspring of Scythians who had mated with Amazons, whose female descendants continued to observe the ancient customs of Amazon warrior women, hunting on horseback with their husbands, taking part in war, and wearing the same dress as the men; no girl could be married until she had killed a man in battle. "They spoke the same language as the Scythians, but they never talked it correctly, because the Amazons had learned it imperfectly" (Herodotus 4.110–117).[69]

In Greek accounts, too, Celtic women fit the classical world's stereotype of the Celt as the antithesis of the civilized man, who was controlled, steadfast, and sober.[70] Celts were war mad, excitable, easily dispirited, loud, and boastful. Artistic monuments like the statue of the Gaul killing himself beside his wife reinforced the Celtic stereotype, though it also celebrated the courage of the noble enemy.

For the importance of women among the Germans, we have the testimony of Tacitus:

> An especially powerful incitement to courage is the fact that the squadrons and divisions are not made up at random by the mustering of chance comers, but are each composed of men of one family or clan. Close by them, too, are their nearest and dearest, so that they can hear the wailing of their women-folk and the cry of their children. They believe that there resides in women an element of holiness and a gift of prophecy; and so they do not scorn to ask their advice, or lightly disregard their replies.[71]

This passage implies a stark contrast with the contemporary situation in Rome and the Classical world. Athenian authors tended to find stories of the great respect paid to women by the barbarians of the West incredible or at best unlikely, and indeed, many stories they relate are of the topsy-turvy, "world upside down" variety, turning the convention around to make the story seem more marvelous. The farther west one went, the more marvelous the tale. On certain islands near Iberia, men were said to have prized women to such an extent that they ransomed them at three times or more the price of men.[72]

But in real life, women determined much of the identity of a group based on the family. In Etruscan society, the ubiquitous figures of Etruscan couples show the importance of the married couple and the past and future families they represent. Erotic scenes in situla art stand for the marriage that defines the family unit and the alliance of families. The warrior Goths created an identity for themselves when they settled down with their wives and children.

Barbarian Customs

Their appearance set the barbarians apart in the eyes of the classical world. Ethnographic works describe northern peoples as paler and taller than those around the Mediterranean basin. The Germans were tall, with fierce blue eyes and red hair, and wore skins.

But it was dress that marked the clearest visual contrast between classical and barbarian and that identified foreigners. In many cases, their way of dressing was seen as a sign of the *truphe* or luxurious excess that was typical of tyrants, women, and barbarians. The ostentatious display of gold, the purple carpet on which Agamemnon walked to his doom, the image of the *obesus etruscus* lying on his symposium couch – all these were symbols immediately understood by a citizen of Rome or by an Athenian audience as a sign of barbarian *truphe*.[73] Typical of Etruscan *truphe* were the expensive Etruscan sandals, luxury items worn by fashionable fifth-century BC Athenian ladies.

Etruscan men wore a rounded mantle, or *tebenna*, the forerunner of the toga, the solemnly draped costume that eventually distinguished Roman male citizens from both the Greeks, who wore the square himation, and the pants-wearing barbarians.[74]

Celts wore oddly cut clothes, riding breeches, and brightly colored plaid mantles fastened with buckles. Images of Celts in battle show them as tall and well built; they fought naked, wearing only belts around their waists. Tribes on the coast of Persia were said to dress in skins or to lack clothes altogether. In Spain, women wore veils draped over iron frames, the modern mantilla headdress of Spanish women.[75] Tacitus's description of the Germans includes remarks on the ritual dress of their priests.[76]

Greek artists often illustrated the motley-colored long pants characteristic of barbarians, Amazons, and Asiatic mythological figures.[77] Their close-fitting, long-sleeved woolen shirts and warm trousers were practical garments that served to protect the northern barbarians from the cold and against chafing when they rode on horseback.[78] These nomadic pastoral tribes sewed them together from smaller pieces of animal skins (Fig. 1.2 and Plate II),[79] in contrast to the draped mantles and simple tunics of the Classical period, made from wide, uncut lengths

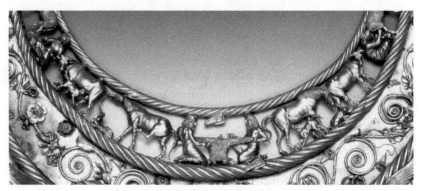

1.2. Scythian way of life. Top register: Two Scythian warriors sewing a shirt made of skins while other nomads tend their horses, cows, and sheep. Detail of Scythian gold pectoral commissioned from a Greek artist. (Luka Mjeda/Art Resource.)

of woven woolen or linen fabrics. It is interesting to note that literary accounts attributed the invention of barbarian pants to women: according to Diodorus of Sicily, Semiramis invented pants; Herodotus says that Tomyris invented them, while others credit Medea with the invention.[80]

Such barbarian dress items as Phrygian hats and the heavy, patterned woolen Thracian mantles also often appear in Greek art. In fact, colorful foreign costumes could be seen all around Athens, worn by Scythian slaves employed as policemen and represented in the theater, on temple sculpture, and on symposium ware at private parties. Athenian men adopted the warm fur hats and the heavy Thracian mantle as practical attire for travel and horseback riding.[81] Shirts with sewn, fitted sleeves and long pants were seen on the streets of Athens and of Rome, and were eventually adopted in late imperial times as comfortable everyday wear, marking the transformation from Classical to modern clothing.[82]

But in the Classical period, it was the "costume" of nudity that most clearly set the Greeks apart from the barbarians. According to Thucydides, the custom of athletic male nudity separated the Greeks of his time from both their own ancestors and contemporary barbarians. The innovation of athletic male nudity had transformed an age-old taboo, and the costume of nudity, which distinguished citizens from slaves and women,[83] was adopted by the same democracy that had brought about the separation of the lives of men and women.

Nudity, originally a ritual costume used in the initiation of Greek youths in transition from adolescence to manhood, became the athletic costume worn by ephebes who exercised in the aptly named "gymnasium," as citizens who served in the army and had to be in fighting shape. This civic nudity came to be seen as the badge of citizenship that marked the difference between civilized Greeks and primitive barbarians, as well as old-fashioned ancestors and vulnerable women. The Spartan general Agesilaos once ordered Persian prisoners to be stripped naked so that the sight of the contrast between the tanned bodies of the Greek men and the white, feminine flabbiness of the Persians would encourage his troops.[84] Descriptions of the tall, blond Gauls who fought naked but did not exercise like the Greeks emphasized the striking appearance of the red blood that flowed from the wounds on their white bodies (Livy 28.21.9).

Male nudity as practiced in Athens and other Greek cities remained an isolated phenomenon: even East Greek kouroi were often draped,[85] and male nudity was only reluctantly adopted outside Greece proper. People who embraced classical culture eventually accepted male nudity in art, along with the nude female figure that entered the artistic repertoire in the fourth century. But it was never again to be accepted as a normal custom in daily life.[86]

The visual impact of the gold trappings and brightly shining armor and weapons of barbarian warriors emphasized the *truphe* attributed to tyrants, women, and barbarians by the Greeks, who accused the barbarians of adorning themselves with gold like women (Diodorus Siculus 10.43). In contrast to the Greeks and the Romans, barbarians had no sumptuary laws limiting the ostentation of chieftains, kings, and princes.[87] In Rome, the construction of the huge temple of Jupiter Optimus Maximus in the sixth century marks a shift from private to public expenditure. Probably at the same time the earliest written Roman laws, the Twelve Tables, dating from the fourth century, though its provisions are from an earlier period, expressly forbade the use of gold in burials or placing gold objects on the funeral pyre.[88] Also forbidden was excessive ostentation in the expression of mourning. "The women shall not tear their faces nor wail on account of the funeral."

But it was just such ostentation that marked the lavish Scythian and Thracian funerals and burials. The rituals observed for the burial of a Scythian king showed the prevalence of self-mutilation (Chapter 3, Figs. 3.4 and 3.5 and Plate III). As for the gold, Thracian ideology and mythology and Scythian royal burials of the fifth and fourth centuries all emphasize its function as a royal symbol.[89] The dazzling appearance of the Thracian king wearing splendid gold armor and a beautifully decorated shield, and riding a horse decorated with gold trappings, as described by Herodotus (1.215), explains why the Thracians referred to their nobility as brilliant and shining. We are once again reminded of pre-Classical archaic Greek customs, Achilles's extravagant mourning at the grave of Patroclus, the splendid armor of Homeric heroes, and the rich gifts exchanged by the princely houses.

A story related by Herodotus (4.5) confirms the royal connotations of gold among the barbarian nobility.[90] Targitaus had three sons, who divided the rule of the kingdom of the Scythians among themselves. During their reign a collection of golden objects – a plough, a yoke, a battle-axe, and a cup – came down from heaven and fell in the Scythian land. Only the third and youngest was allowed to come near them; the other two were driven away by blazing fire. The elder brothers acknowledged the meaning of this divine sign and handed over their kingly power to him.[91] Like these kingly symbols, his articles of adornment, sets of drinking ware, protective armor, and horse trappings accompanied the deceased king to the grave. They were political insignia, signs of divine favor capable of restoring his royal rank in the world beyond.

A warrior on horseback, the familiar image of the Thracian Horseman, represented the king.[92] The barbarians had a special relationship with their horses, the faithful companions of the nomadic warriors, which accompanied them in life, were represented in their art, and were buried with them in their graves.[93] They felt close to the other animals that lived with them. Nomads cared for the sheep and herds that provided them with food and clothing (Fig. 1.2, Plate II). The affection that the otherwise savage, isolated Polyphemus of the *Odyssey* exhibits for his sheep reflects this closeness between man and animal. So does the animal style, which came in from the Near East and became the hallmark of the art of the Scythians and other nomads. Used to decorate small objects, it became a favorite of many of these peoples and persisted in the arts of Europe, where it found a home on Greek vases, in Romanesque art, and into modern times.[94]

Like their way of dressing, the food and drink typical of barbarians resulted from their style of life. These customs account for their adoption the three B's – butter, breeches, and beer. Breeches, or trousers, were practical garments for cold climates and horseback riders and became the stereotypically barbarian dress. A diet of meat, butter, cheese, and milk was likewise typical of the nomadic pastoral tribes that tended their herds of cattle and made skin garments.[95] The gold pectoral commissioned from Greek artists and the painting by Delacroix (frontispiece) show scenes of their daily life: a mare with a foal nursing, a cow with a calf nursing, and nearby a man milking a sheep (Fig. 1.2 and Plate II).[96] It was their use of dairy products that early on earned the Scythians and other barbarians the reputation of being curd eaters and milk drinkers: Homer's *Iliad* (13.5–6) mentions the "mare-milkers," the *hippomolgoi galaktophagoi*, a nomadic Scythian tribe who drink mares' milk.[97]

The drinking of beer rather than wine also characterized barbarian people in ways that even language could not.[98] The importing of wine and symposium ware or drinking equipment and the Greek social convention of the symposium characterized groups who wanted to share in the cultural and aristocratic prestige of this sophisticated custom of the classical world.[99] Gallic chieftains had Greek wine and symposium ware brought into Gaul by way of the Greek colony at Marseilles. Farther east, across the Alps, it was the Etruscans who taught the French, who were then the Gauls, to appreciate wine: Livy (5.32–35) tells us that the Gauls who first came into northern and central Italy as mercenaries then stayed on, like so many northerners before and since, because of the wine and the sweetness of the fruit. The drinking of wine was the mark of a cultured group, as against the beer- and milk-drinking barbarians. Its social prestige was such that even rabbinic prohibitions against the mixing of meat and dairy products may have been connected with the desire of Jews of the Hellenistic and Roman periods to distance themselves from barbarian practices, as earlier they had wanted to distance themselves from their neighbors the Canaanites, who boiled a kid in its mother's milk.[100]

These were some of the contrasts between the way of life of northern Europe in language, dress and food, appearance, religious practices, and social customs that set them apart from the "civilized" classical cultures of the Greeks and later of the Romans. Why, though, did the Greeks establish this long-lasting distinction between civilized and barbarian, a distinction that we still follow in our language, even if we do not always accept its pejorative significance? Michel de Montaigne, noting that "barbarian" simply means "strange," declared, "I think there is nothing barbarous and savage, ... except that each man calls barbarism whatever is not his own practice; for indeed it seems we have no other test of truth and reason than the example and pattern of the opinions and customs of the country we live in."[101]

For his part, Herodotus illustrates the relativity of barbarian customs with the story of Darius, king of Persia, who summoned the Greeks present at his court and asked them what price would persuade them to eat the dead bodies of their fathers. They replied that they would not do it for any price. He then asked some Indians of the tribe called Callatiae, who did in fact eat their parents' dead bodies, what would persuade them to burn their fathers at death. They uttered a cry of horror and forbade him to mention such a dreadful thing. His conclusion says it best: "For if anyone ... were given the opportunity of choosing from amongst all the nations in the world the set of beliefs which he thought best, he would inevitably ... choose that of his own country" (Herodotus 3.38). Here Herodotus describes a deeper truth than a merely factual one. Not all representations of the Greeks as the opposite of the "Others" were so enlightened.[102]

Remarkable parallels are to be found between the attitudes of the ancient Greeks and Chinese and their relationship to the nomadic barbarian tribes surrounding them.[103] Both the Greeks and the Chinese recognized their own superior culture in opposition to those of the barbarians. Both were literate societies that observed those foreign worlds and recorded their impressions of them. The animal imagery of the steppe tribes was adopted by both Chinese artists and the Greek craftsmen who used the Near Eastern animal style to decorate the remarkable gold vessels and jewelry they made for their northern clients.[104] The Greeks noticed the special relationship with the world of animals that existed among the nomads, though their observations often showed a lack of understanding of foreign customs and beliefs. What the Chinese did not share with the Greeks, and later the Romans, was their tendency to idealize the uprightness and simple lifestyle of these northern barbarians.[105]

Barbarian ancestors have long provided the peoples of Europe with an identity, as is clear from the Celtic and Germanic models. Marinetti declared, in the *Futurist Manifesto*, "I am a barbarian."[106] More recently, in his book on the barbarians of Europe, Karol Modzelewski,[107] formerly a child of socialism, imprisoned dissident, leader of Solidarnosc, and now a citizen of Poland, hails the "return to Europe" of his country. But he reminds us that this Europe has a Classical past and also a past of barbarians who had their own traditions, ways of life, leadership, beliefs, and worldviews, and warns that we must not idealize either past at the expense of the other. In our own book on the barbarians of ancient Europe we look for the reality and relationships of the lives, beliefs and customs of these ancestors, and along the way we often encounter our own world.

Notes

1. Our focus is on the earlier, pre-Roman barbarians of Western Europe, in contrast to the exhibition at Palazzo Grassi in Venice on *Rome and the Barbarians* (Aillagon et al. 2008). Elias Bickerman's *Origines gentium* (1952) and Arnaldo Momigliano's *Alien Wisdom* (1975) have been both inspiring and influential for our understanding of Greek and Roman views of the barbarians. Both historians, I believe, would have appreciated the surveys of archaeological material as well as the imaginative historical reconstructions included in this volume.
2. Kaeser 2002, 171–172. I have adopted his description and terminology because of its clarity, reference to the question of nationalism, and recent date; many other references are equally relevant to our study.
3. Linderski 1984, 140.
4. A recent survey of the scholarship of the last forty years on Herodotus focuses on the reliability of Herodotus's accounts: Cartledge 2009, 371–382.
5. See Ivantchik, Chapter 3, and Marazov, Chapter 5, in this volume.
6. For a discussion of later nomadism, see Batty 2008.
7. Wells, Chapter 7, in this volume. His discussion of excavated material includes the surprising mention among the weapons of the earliest example of chain mail.
8. Ferrari 1983, 2002; Lissarague 1984; Marconi 2004; Schroer 2006.
9. Boardman 2009. There was an enduring contrast between the Greek cities and those of the Etruscans and, more generally, between the peoples of ancient Greece and Italy, whose geography and diversity of cultures brought about a different kind of contact.
10. Bonfante 2011.
11. De Vries 2000, 338–363.
12. Brendel 1995, 15.
13. Frey, Chapter 9, in this volume.
14. Bowersock 2005, 167–178. Today conflict with the Islamic East has modified this orientation. See Horace, *Odes* 2.20.13–20, and Smith 1988, 72, for the boundaries of the Roman world.
15. Cohen 2000; Davidson 2002, 13–14.
16. Personal communication.
17. Hall 1989.
18. The title *The Past Is a Foreign Country* (Lowenthal 1985) is a quote from Leslie Poles Hartley, *The Go-Between* (1953): "The past is a foreign country: they do things differently there."

19. Sherratt and Sherratt 1992. "Homeric" is used as a chronological term, describing the world of the Scythian lords in the royal burials, the kings of the Thracians, the princes of the elite society of the Etruscans, and the tribal chiefs represented in situla art.
20. Hall 2002; Price 2003, 303–304.
21. See the story in Plutarch, *Pyrrhus*, about the kings of the ancient Molossians, who "became barbarous" in the course of time. But an ancestor of Pyrrhus, Tharrhypas, introduced Greek customs, literature, and humane laws into his cities and made them less barbarous again.
22. Boas 1938, 144–158; for the "Aryan problem," see p. 151. For a discussion of the influence of politics on ideas about migrations, see Härke 1998, 19–45; Gruen 2005. I owe the reference to Walter Stevenson.
23. Edwards and McCollough 2007.
24. Personal names also tell a story; see the recent studies of personal names as evidence for the history and society of the Thracians and the Etruscans by Dimitrov 2004 and Morandi Taramella 2004.
25. Formigé 1949; Lamboglia 1964; Pliny, *NH* 3.136–137. For a visual representation of the barbarian *ethne* of the Roman Empire, see Smith 1988: 52–77.
26. For the example of Greece, see Damaskos and Plantzos 2008.
27. See Cunliffe, Chapter 6, note 10, in this volume; Piggott 1985, 110–112. Cf. Euripides, *IT* 40: Iphigeneia, the Greek priestess, does not participate actively in the human sacrifice practiced by the barbarian Taurians.
28. Szilágyi 2004, 216: "On the Ethnicity of the Scythians," by Antal Csengery (1822–1880).
29. Boas 1938, 253–272, "The Race Problem in Modern Society." See also Stevenson, Chapter 12 in this volume, on the image of the Goths.
30. On the many meanings of Rome see Brendel 1979, 3.
31. Witness the changing racial terms in the United States: from "colored" to "Negro," "Black," "Afro-American," and "African American."
32. Sweeney, in T. S. Eliot, "Fragment of an Agon."
33. Keyser, Chapter 2, in this volume.
34. Ridgway 2002.
35. *B.G.* 1.1; Wells 2001, 111–113, and Chapter 7 in this volume.
36. Cunliffe, Chapter 6, in this volume.
37. Bonfante and Bonfante 2002, 3–5.
38. Vergil, *Aen.* 8.722–723, *gentes quam variae linguis, habitu tam vestis et armis*. Cf. Polybius 2.17: "The Egyptians call everyone a barbarian who does not speak the same language as themselves." Benardete 1969, 65, on Herodotus 2.158.5.
39. Morandi 1982; Markoe 2000, 111–113; Bonfante and Bonfante 2002, 52–56, 117–120.
40. Bonfante 2001, 3: Celtic was his native language, Venetic the language of the area where the inscription was found and where he lived and died. For trade and the development of a lingua franca see Cunliffe, Chapter 6, in this volume. On the important subject of languages, communication, and trade in the Roman Empire see Bang 2008.
41. On these questions of communication, see Bang 2008.
42. Momigliano 1975, 149.
43. Including a special form of Indo-European social organization with a tripartite structure of priests, warriors, and farmers. Dumézil 1970; Benveniste 1973; Renfrew 1987, 20–28, 145–154.

44. Bachofen 1967, written in 1861. See the criticism by Momigliano 1984, 312–330. Scholars influenced by Dumézil include Sergent 2005, Woodard 2006, and Anthony 2007. Attempts to integrate evidence from historical linguistics and archaeology have generally not been convincing for the reasons given by Boas 1938, cited in note 23.
45. Roman institutions were deeply conservative and Latin was the most conservative of the Indo-European languages, in contrast to Greek, which was the most innovative, as demonstrated, for example, by the Greek innovation of the word *adelphos*, as against Latin *frater*, related to Romance and Germanic languages ("brother," *Bruder, frère,* etc.) and deriving from Indo-European.
46. Burkert 1992.
47. Sergent 2005. Severed heads frequently appear in *The Táin* 2002, ix.
48. Burkert 1985, 15–19. See also Boas 1938.
49. For human sacrifice see Keyser, Chapter 2, in this volume. According to Herodotus, the gods, because of their human shape, do not allow human sacrifice, which is practiced by both the uncultivated Scythians and the civilized Persians (4.71.4; 72.2; 7.114.2; 7.114.2; 180): Benardete 1969, 136. See also Miller 2000, 414–415.
50. Among most civilized cultures today, human sacrifice and cannibalism are taboo. This does not mean that they never occur, only that they are not socially accepted. Though illegal in India, suttee is still practiced in some rural communities.
51. The bibliography on human sacrifice is enormous. Rudhardt and Reverdin 1981; Burkert 1985, 27–28, 31, 37, 59, 65, 83, 151, 235, 248; Hughes 1991; Steel 1995, 18–27. See the historical survey in Acton 1863, 395–442. On cannibalism see Rives 1995, 65–85; White 2003, 86–93.
52. Hughes 1991, 49–56. In Etruscan art, Achilles's ambush and killing of Troilos is represented as a sacrifice: see Lowenstam 2008, 139–147; 201 for the earlier bibliography.
53. Ivantchik, Chapter 3, in this volume.
54. For Tarquinia, see Bonghi Jovino 2010, 161–180, with the previous bibliography. For Etruscan iconography showing human sacrifice, see Bonfante 1978, 136–162.
55. See Piggott 1985, 108–112, for Druids and Celtic human sacrifice. For their presence in Celtic literature of the eighth century, see *The Táin* 2002. For Etruscan and Thracian severed heads, see de Grummond, Chapter 10, in this volume. See also Bonfante 1984a, 1984b; Knauer 2001, 283–332.
56. Knauer 2001, 283–332. A fragment of an Attic vase by Onesimus in the J. Paul Getty Museum (86.AE.311) shows a Greek soldier wearing a helmet decorated with a scalp, probably that of a Persian enemy: Moore 1998, 31–32, No. 46; plate 417, 1–2. For Greek representations of severed heads see Vermeule 1979, 107. For archaeological evidence of scalping see Mednikova 2000; Murphy et al. 2002; Ivantchik 2008.
57. Markoe 2000, 132–136; Higgins 2005.
58. Rives 1995, 65–85.
59. Piggott 1965, 357. I thank Guenter Kopcke for this reference. For the Thracians see Marazov, Chapter 5, in this volume.
60. Bevan and Phillott 1969; Westrem 2001.
61. Blok 2002, 225–242, esp. 226; Fisher 2002, 199–224.
62. Aristotle, *Politics* 1252b 1–9, Carnes Lord translation; Joshel and Murnaghan 1998, 1–2.

63. Cited by Fantham et al. 1994, 123; Joshel and Murnaghan 1998, 1–2.
64. Plato's Eleatic Stranger says that dividing the human race into Greeks and barbarians is not a natural division, because barbarians do not form a natural kind: *Politicus* 262d. I owe this reference to David Murphy.
65. Ivantchik, Chapter 3, in this volume.
66. Cohen 2000. On the mythical Amazons see Blok 1994; Fantham et al. 1994, 128–135 (but see 134, at the end). On Spartan women see Pomeroy 2002, and Fantham et al. 1994, 56–67. On Etruscan women, see Bonfante 1986, 234–237; 1994, 248–259. Theopompos's description of the scandalous way of life of Etruscan women must be read in the context of the Greek idea of barbarian *truphe* and the conservative Greek fourth-century views of women: Flower 1994.
67. Rolle, Chapter 4, in this volume.
68. Penrose 2006; Ivantchik 2008, 201.
69. Blok 1994, 86–89; 2002, 225; Frohnhaus et al. 1998.
70. Cunliffe, Chapter 6, and Keyser, Chapter 2, in this volume.
71. Tacitus, *Germania* 78. Translation adapted from Mattingly-Handford 1970.
72. Keyser, Chapter 2 in this volume. For a topsy-turvy view in Herodotus's accounts, see Benardete 1969.
73. Nenci 1983, 1019–1031; Blum 1998.
74. Bonfante 2003, 48–49, 59, 130 (notes 3–6); Stone 1994, 13, 38.
75. Keyser, Chapter 2, in this volume. Tacitus, *Germania* 4, Caesar *BG* 6.21–22; Strabo, 3.4.17, 4.4.3. D.S. 5.30.1.
76. Tacitus 43.4.3 on the female dress of priests.
77. See Koda 2003 for classical dress. The Barbarian Fashion Show organized by Norma and Bernard Goldman in Richmond in 2003 illustrated the contrast between these solemnly draped Greek and Roman robes and the colorful fitted garments of northern barbarians.
78. Todd 1972, 81–95, for the later barbarians; Cunliffe 1993, 24, for Celtic male dress; Reeder 1999, 329, and Rolle, Chapter 4, in this volume, for Scythian dress.
79. Two Scythians sewing a shirt made of skins appear on a gold pectoral commissioned from a Greek, artist. Reeder 1999, 326–331, No. 172; Savostina 2001, 304–323.
80. Gera 1997; Daina Shobrys, personal communication.
81. Cohen 2001, 242–251. A recent study of color in Greek sculpture has brought out the hues of the Eastern dress of Paris as a Trojan archer from the Temple of Aphaia in Aegina, now in Munich, his legs covered by strikingly harlequin-patterned long pants or hose: Brinkman 2004.
82. Marrou 1979, 18–22.
83. Bonfante 1989, 543–570.
84. Xen. *Agesilaos* 1.28.
85. Thucydides 1.5–6. "And even in the present day many parts of Hellas still follow the old fashion...."
86. Boardman 1994, 316–337; Bonfante 1989, 543–570; 1999, 20–25; 2000, 271–293.
87. For *truphe*, see Nenci 1983, 1019–1031. The bibliography on sumptuary laws is enormous. For Greece, see Frisone 2000, 124–125, 72–273; Figuera 2003.
88. Table X: "But if his teeth are held together with gold, and are buried or burnt with him, it shall be with impunity." For the Twelve Tables, see Watson 1975. See Capogrosso Colognesi 2009, 73, on the sumptuary legislation codified in the later Twelve Tables. For the temple of Jupiter Optimus Maximus, see Cifani 2008, 80–109, 298–305.

89. On the huge amounts of gold from Kazakhstan for the production of Scythian ornaments, see Bilde 1993, 95. On the myth of the Golden Ram, which comes from the region of the Black Sea, see Gantz 1993, 358-362. For the symbolic meaning of gold in the tombs of the Orientalizing period, see Sannibale 2008, 348-349.
90. See Ivantchik, Chapter 3, in this volume, note 71, on the gold insignia of royalty.
91. See Marazov, Chapter 5, in this volume.
92. Farkas 1982, 46.
93. Ivantchik, Chapter 3, and de Grummond, Chapter 10, in this volume: horses were thought to be able to prophesy.
94. Knauer 1998; Aruz et al. 2006.
95. Scientists consider the lactose tolerance found in many northern Europeans – the descendants of an ancient cattle-rearing culture that emerged in the region some 6,000 years ago – to be evidence for culture as a selective force. Lactose tolerance is now recognized as a case in which a cultural practice – drinking raw milk – has caused an evolutionary change in the human genome. Wade 2010.
96. Savostina 2001. Reeder 1999, 326, No. 172. In the *Odyssey* (9, 216-223), the pastoral Cyclops Polyphemus tends his flocks of sheep, milks them, and makes cheeses. See Keyser, Chapter 2, in this volume, and Romm 1992, 60-67.
97. Ivantchik 2005, 18-66.
98. Stevenson, Chapter 12, in this volume. For the value of the wine imported into Europe, see Cunliffe, Chapter 13, in this volume.
99. Though it did not necessarily substitute for the drinking of beer, which Tacitus, *Germania* 23, describes as "a sort of wine made from fermented barley," and which Dionysius of Halicarnassus (13.10) calls a "foul smelling drink."
100. Nelson 2005, 41, 74; Kraemer 2007, 53.
101. Montaigne (1533-1592), 1958 translation, 152. Cited by Farkas, "Barbarians and Barbarism," unpublished paper.
102. Cartledge 2009, 377, 379-380.
103. Knauer 1998, 12-16, 139. I am grateful for a stimulating discussion of this topic with Elfriede (Kezia) Knauer at the meeting of the American Philosophical Society in November 2009.
104. Barr-Sharrar 2008, 7, 160-161.
105. Knauer 1998, 13-14.
106. The Futurist Manifesto was published in French on the front page of *Le Figaro*, February 20, 1909.
107. Modzelewski 2006, "Introduction."

Bibliography

Acton, Lord. 1863. "Human Sacrifice." In Fears 1988, 395-442.

Aillagon, J.J., U. Roberto, and Y. Rivière, eds. 2008. *Roma e i Barbari/Rome et les Barbares*. Exhibition Catalogue, Venice, Palazzo Grassi. Milan.

Anthony, David W. 2007. *The Horse, the Wheel, and Language: How Bronze-Age Riders from the Eurasian Steppes Shaped the Modern World*. Princeton, NJ. Reviewed by Christine Kenneally, *New York Times*, March 2, 2008.

Aruz, Joan, Ann Farkas, and Elizabeth Vatz Fino. 2006. *The Golden Deer of Eurasia: Perspectives on the Steppe Nomads of the Ancient World*. New York and New Haven, CT.

Asheri, David, Alan B. Lloyd, and Aldo Corcella. 2007. *A Commentary on Herodotus I–IV*, ed. Oswyn Murray and Alfonso Moreno. Oxford.

Bachofen, Johann Jakob. 1967. *Myth, Religion, and Mother Right: Selected Writings of J. J. Bachofen.* Bollingen Series 84. Translation of *Mutterrecht*, 1861. Princeton, NJ.

Bakker, Egbert J., Irene J. F. De Jong, and Hans Van Weer. 2002. *Brill's Companion to Herodotus.* Leiden.

Bang, Peter F. 2008. *The Roman Bazaar: A Comparative Study of Trade and Markets in a Tributary Empire.* Cambridge.

Barfield, Lawrence. 1998. "Gender Issues in North Italian Prehistory." In Whitehouse 1998, 143–179.

Barr-Sharrar, Beryl. 2008. *The Derveni Krater: Masterpiece of Classical Greek Metalwork.* Athens.

Batty, Roger. 2008. *Rome and the Nomads: The Pontic-Danubian Realm in Antiquity.* Oxford.

Benardete, Seth. 1969. *Herodotean Inquiries.* The Hague.

Benveniste, Émile. 1973. *Indo-European Language and Society.* Miami Linguistics Series 12. Coral Gables, FL. Translation of *Le vocabulaire des institutions indo-européennes*, Paris, 1969.

Bevan, William Latham, and H. W. Phillott. 1969. *Mediaeval Geography: An Essay in Illustration of the Hereford Mappa Mundi.* Amsterdam.

Bianchi Bandinelli, Ranuccio. 1971. *The Late Empire: Roman Art A.D. 200–400.* Rome.

Bickerman, Elias J. 1952. "Origines gentium." *Classical Philology* 47: 65–81 = *Religions and Politics in the Hellenistic and Roman Periods*, ed. Emilio Gabba and Morton Smith, 401–417. Como, 1985.

Bilde, Per, Troels Engberg-Pedersen, Lise Hannestad, and Jan Zahle, eds. 1993. *Centre and Periphery in the Hellenistic World.* Aarhus.

Blok, Josine. 1994. *The Early Amazons: Modern and Ancient Perspectives on a Persistent Myth.* Leiden.

  2002. "Women in Herodotus' Histories." In Bakker et al. 2002.

Blum, Hartmut. 1998. *Purpur als Statussymbol in der griechischen Welt.* Bonn.

Boardman, John. 1994. *The Diffusion of Classical Art in Antiquity.* Princeton, NJ.

  2009. "Tillya Tepe and the Echoes of Greece and China." Unpublished lecture, Metropolitan Museum of Art, September 9.

Boas, Franz. 1938. *The Mind of Primitive Man*, rev. ed. New York. Originally published 1911.

Bonfante, Giuliano. 2001. "Pompeteguaios," *Linguistica* 42:3.

Bonfante, Giuliano, and Larissa Bonfante. 2002. *The Etruscan Language: An Introduction*, 2nd ed. Manchester, England.

Bonfante, Larissa. 1978. "Historical Art: Etruscan and Early Roman." *AJA* 3:136–162.

  1984a. "Human Sacrifice on an Etruscan Urn." *AJA* 88:531–539.

  1984b. "Un'urna etrusca a New York con têtes coupées." In *Studi di antichità in onore di G. Maetzke, Archaeologica* 49:143–150. Rome.

  1986. *Etruscan Life and Afterlife.* Detroit.

1989. "Nudity as a Costume in Classical Art." *AJA* 93:543–570.

1994. "Excursus: Etruscan Women." In Fantham et al. 1994, 243–259.

2000. "Classical Nudity in Italy and Greece." In *Ancient Italy in Its Mediterranean Setting*, ed. David Ridgway, Francesca R. Serra Ridgway, Mark Pearce, Edward Herring, Ruth D. Whitehouse, and John B. Wilkins, 271–293. London.

2003a. *Etruscan Dress*. Baltimore.

2003b. 'The Greeks in Etruria." In *The Greeks Beyond the Aegean: From Marseilles to Bactria*, ed. V. Karageorghis, 43–58. New York.

2011. "What Role for Etruscans?" In *ΑΜΙΛΛΑ: The Quest for Excellence: Studies in Honor of Guenter Kopcke*. Robert Koehl, ed. Philadelphia.

Bonghi Jovino, M. 2010. "The Tarquinia Project: A Summary of Twenty-Five Years of Excavation." *AJA* 114:161–180.

Bonnechère, Pierre. 1994. *Le sacrifice humain en Grèce ancienne*. Liège.

1998. "La Notion d' 'art collectif' dans le sacrifice humain grec." *Phoenix* 52:191–215.

Bowersock, Glen W. 1990. *Hellenism in Late Antiquity*. Ann Arbor, MI.

2005. "The East–West Orientation of Mediterranean Studies and the Meaning of North and South in Antiquity." In Harris 2005, 167–178.

Braund, David. 2005. *Scythians and Greeks: Cultural Interactions in Scythia, Athens and the Early Roman Empire, Sixth Century BC–First Century AD*. Exeter, England.

Brendel, Otto J. 1979. *Prolegomena to the Study of Roman Art*. New Haven, CT. Originally published as *Prolegomena to a Book on Roman Art*. Memoirs of the American Academy in Rome, 1953.

1995. *Etruscan Art*. New Haven and London.

Briggs, Daphne Nash. 2003. "Metals, Salt, and Slaves: Economic Links Between Gaul and Italy from the Eighth to the Late Sixth Centuries BC." *Oxford Journal of Archaeology* 22:243–259.

Brill's Companion to Herodotus. 2002. Leiden. See Bakker et al. 2002.

Brinkman, Vinzenz. 2004. *Bunte Götter: die Farbigkeit antiker Skulptur*. Munich.

Briquel, Dominique. 1993. *Les Etrusques, peuple de la différence*. Paris.

1997. *Le Regard des Autres: Les origines de Rome vues par ses ennemis*. Besançon.

Burkert, Walter. 1985. *Greek Religion*. Cambridge, MA.

1992. *The Orientalizing Revolution*. Cambridge, MA.

Capogrosso Colognesi, Luigi. 2009. *Storia di Roma tra diritto e potere*. Bologna.

Cartledge, Paul A. 2009. "Taking Herodotus Personally." *Classical World* 102: 371–382.

Cifani, Gabriele. 2008. *Architettura etrusca arcaica*. Rome.

Cohen, Beth, ed. 2000. *Not the Classical Ideal: Athens and the Construction of the Other in Greek Art. Part III, External Others: The Portrayal of Foreigners*, 18–20, 315–479. Leiden.

2001. "Ethnic Identity in Democratic Athens and the Visual Vocabulary of Male Costume." In Malkin 2001, 235–274.

Cunliffe, Barry. 1993. *The Celtic World*. London and New York.

1997. *The Ancient Celts*. Oxford and New York.

Damaskos, Dimitris, and Dimitris Plantzos, eds. 2008. *A Singular Antiquity: Archaeology and the Hellenic Identity in the Twentieth Century*. Athens.

Davidson, J. 2002. "Too Much Other? François Hartog and the Memories of Odysseus." Reviewed by Hartog, *Times Literary Supplement*, April 19, 2002, 13–14.

Le délit religieux dans la cité antique. 1981. Table Ronde, Rome 1978. Collection de l' Ecole Française de Rome 48. Rome.

De Vries, Keith. 2000. "The Nearly Other: The Attic Vision of Phrygians and Lydians." In Cohen 2000, 338–363.

Dimitrov, Peter A. 2004. "The Thracian Language: Inscriptions and Phonology." D. Litt. dissertation. Sofia, Bulgaria.

Donati, Luigi. 2004. "Il sacrificio umano." *ThesCRA* 1:136–139.

Dumézil, Georges. 1970. *Archaic Roman Religion. With an Appendix on the Religion of the Etruscans.* Chicago. Translation of *La religion romaine archaïque suivi d'un appendice sur la religion des Étrusques.* Paris 1966.

Edwards, Douglas R., and C. Thomas McCollough, eds. 2007. *The Archaeology of Difference: Gender, Ethnicity, Class, and the "Other" in Antiquity. Studies in Honor of Eric M. Meyers.* 2 vols. ASOR Annual 60 and 61. Boston.

Eicher, J. B., ed. 1995. *Dress and Ethnicity.* Oxford.

Fantham, Elaine, Helene Peet Foley, Natalie Boymel Kampen, Sarah. B. Pomeroy, and H. Alan Shapiro. 1994. *Women in the Classical World.* New York and Oxford.

Farkas, Ann E. 1982. "Style and Subject Matter in Native Thracian Art." *The Metropolitan Museum Journal* 16:33–48.

Farkas, Ann. n.d. [ca. 2003]. "Barbarians and Barbarism," unpublished paper.

Fears, J. Rufus, ed. 1988. *Essays in Religion, Politics, and Morality: Selected Writings of Lord Acton III.* Indianapolis, IN.

Ferrari Pinney, Gloria. 1983. "Achilles Lord of Scythia." In Moon 1983, 127–146.

Figuera, Thomas. 2003. "*Xenelasia* and Social Control in Classical Sparta." *CQ* 53:44–74.

Fisher, Nick. 2002. "Popular Morality in Herodotus." In Bakker et al. 2002, 199–224.

Flower, M. A. 1994. *Theopompus of Chios: History and Rhetoric in the Fourth Century BC.* Oxford.

Formigé, J. 1949. *Le trophée des Alpes (La Turbie).* Paris.

Fortson, Benjamin W., IV. 2004. *Indo-European Language and Culture: An Introduction.* Malden, MA.

Fraschetti, A. 1981. "Le sepolture rituali del Foro Boario." In *Délit religieux* 1981, 51–115.

Frisone, Flavia. 2000. *Leggi e regolamenti funerari nel mondo greco. 1. Le fonti epigrafiche.* Lecce.

Frohnhaus, Gabriele, Barbara Grotkamp-Schepers, and Renate Philipp, eds. 1998. *Schwert in Frauenhand: Weibliche Bewaffnung.* Essen.

Gantz, Timothy. 1993. *Early Greek Myth: A Guide to Literary and Artistic Sources.* Baltimore.

Gera, Deborah. 1997. *Warrior Women: The Anonymous Tractatus de Mulieribus.* Leiden.

Gruen, Erich, ed. 2005. *Cultural Borrowings and Ethnic Appropriations in Antiquity. Oriens et Occidens 8*. Stuttgart.

Hall, Edith. 1989. *Inventing the Barbarians: Greek Self-Definition through Tragedy*. Oxford.

Hall, Jonathan M. 2002. *Hellenicity: Between Ethnicity and Culture*. Chicago.

Härke, Heinrich. 1998. "Archaeologists and Migration: A Problem of Attitude?" With comments and reply. *Current Anthropology* 39:19–45.

Harris, W. V. 2005. *Rethinking the Mediterranean*. Oxford.

Hartley, Leslie Poles. 1953. *The Go-Between*. New York.

Higgins, Andrew. 2005. "Carthage Tries to Live Down Image as Site of Infanticide." *The Wall Street Journal*, May 26.

Hölscher, Tonio. 2003. "Körper, Handlung und Raum als Sinnfiguren in der griechischen Kunst und Kultur." In *Sinn (in) der Antike: Orientierungssysteme, Leitbilder und Wertkonzepte im Altertum*, ed. Karl-Joachim Hölkeskamp et al., 163–192. Mainz.

Hughes, Dennis D. 1991. *Human Sacrifice in Ancient Greece*. New York.

Ivantchik, A. I. 2005. *Das nördliche Schwarzmeergebiet und die Steppennomaden des 8.–7. Jhs. v. Chr. in der klassischen Literaturtradition: Mündliche Überlieferung, Literatur und Geschichte*. Berlin and Moscow.

    2008. Review of Asheri, Lloyd, Corcella 2007. *Ancient Civilizations from Scythia to Siberia* 14:193–220.

Jones, C. P. 1987. "Stigma: Tattooing and Branding in Graeco-Roman Antiquity." *Journal of Roman Studies* 77:139–155.

Joshel, Sandra R., and Sheila Murnaghan 1998. *Women and Slaves in Greco-Roman Culture: Differential Equations*. London and New York.

Kaeser, Marc-Antoine. 2002. "On the International Roots of Prehistory," ed. Simon Stoddart. *Antiquity* 76:170–177.

Knauer, Elfriede R. 1998. *The Camel's Load in Life and Death: Iconography and Ideology of Chinese Pottery Figurines from Ho Tang and Their Relevance to Trade Along the Silk Routes*. Zurich.

    2001. "Observations on the 'Barbarian' Custom of Suspending the Heads of Vanquished Enemies from the Neck of Horses." *Archäologisches Mitteilungen aus Iran und Turan* 33:283–332.

Koda, Harold, ed. 2003. *Goddess: The Classical Mode*. Catalogue of exhibit, Costume Institute, Metropolitan Museum of Art, New York.

Kraemer, David Charles. 2007. *Jewish Eating and Identity through the Ages*. New York

Lamboglia, N. 1964. *Le trophée d'Auguste à la Turbie*. Cuneo.

Linderski, Jerzy. 1984. "Si vis pacem, para bellum: Concepts of Defensive Imperialism." *Papers and Monographs of the American Academy in Rome*, 29, 132–164, 184–191.

Lissarrague, F., ed. 1984. *La cité des images: Religion et société en Grèce antique*. Lausanne.

Lowenstam, Steven. 2008. *As Witnessed by Images: The Trojan War Tradition in Greek and Etruscan Art*. Baltimore.

Lowenthal, David. 1985. *The Past Is a Foreign Country*. Cambridge.

Malkin, Irad, ed. 2001. *Ancient Perceptions of Greek Ethnicity*. Center for Hellenic Studies Colloquia 5. Cambridge, MA.

Marconi, Clemente, ed. 2004. *Greek Vases: Images, Contexts and Controversies*. Leiden and Boston.

Markoe, Glenn E. 2000. *Phoenicians*. London.

Marrou, Henri-Irénée. 1979. *Decadenza romana o tarda antichità?* Translation of *Décadence romaine ou antiquité tardive? IIIe–VIe siècle*. 1977. Milan.

Mattingley-Handford. See Tacitus 1970.

Mednikova, M. B. 2000. "Skal'pirovanie na Evraziiskom kontinente" ("Remains of Scalping in the Eurasian Continent"). *RA* No. 3, 59-68.

Miller, Margaret C. 2000. "The Myth of Bousiris: Ethnicity and Art." In Cohen 2000, 413–442.

Modzelewski, Karol. 2006. *L'Europe des Barbares: Germains et Slaves face aux héritiers de Rome*. Paris. Translation of *Barbarzyńska Europa*. Warsaw, 2004.

    2008. "Interview: Pagan Substratum." *Academia: The Magazine of the Polish Academy of Sciences* 2 (18): 40–43.

Momigliano, Arnaldo Dante. 1975. *Alien Wisdom: The Limits of Hellenization*. Cambridge. French translation, *Sagesses barbares*. Paris.

    1984. "Georges Dumézil and the Trifunctional Approach to Roman Civilization." *History and Theory* 23 (3): 312–330.

de Montaigne, Michel. 1958. "Of Cannibals," in *The Complete Essays of Montaigne*, translation by Donald M. Frame, 150–158. Stanford, CA.

Moon, Warren G., ed. 1983. *Ancient Greek Art and Iconography*. Madison, WI.

Moore, Mary B. 1998. *Corpus Vasorum Antiquorum*. The J. Paul Getty Museum 8 (USA 33), 31–32, no. 46; plate 417, 1–2. Los Angeles.

Morandi, Alessandro. 1982. *Epigrafia Italica*. Rome.

Morandi Taramella, Massimo 2004. *Prosopografia Etrusca I. Corpus. 1. Etruria meridionale*. Rome.

Murphy, E., I. Gokhman, Y. Chistov, and L. Barkova. 2002. "Prehistoric Old World Scalping: New Cases from the Cemetery of Aymyrlyg, South Siberia." *AJA* 106:1–10.

Nelson, Max. 2005. *The Barbarian's Beverage: A History of Beer in Ancient Europe*. London and New York.

Nenci, G. 1983. "Truphe e colonizzazione." In *Forme di contatto e processi di trasformazione nelle società antiche*. Atti del Convegno di Cortona, maggio 1981, 1019–1031. Pisa.

Nielsen, Marjatta. 1996. "The Symbolic and Ideological Significance of the Representation of the Barbarians in Classical Art." *XIII International Congress of Prehistoric and Protohistoric Sciences*, Forlí (Italy). Colloquium 25, Section 13, "The Roman Period (in the Provinces and the Barbaric World)." Forlí.

Penrose, Walter D. 2006. "Bold with Bow and Arrow: Amazons, Ethnicity, and the Ideology of Courage in Ancient Greek and Asian Cultures." PhD dissertation, CUNY.

Piggott, Stuart. 1965. *Ancient Europe*. Chicago.

    1985. *The Druids*. New York. (Originally published 1968.)

Pomeroy, Sarah P. 2002. *Spartan Women*. Oxford.

Price, Simon. 2003. Review of Hall 2002. *AJP* 124:303–306.

Pritchett, W. Kendrick. 1993. "Hartog and Skythia." In *The Liar School of Herodotos*, ed. W. Kendrick Pritchett, 191–226. Amsterdam.

Ratto, S. 1998. "Les Etrusques étaient-ils des Barbares?" In *Rome e les Barbares*, ed. S. Laigneu, 3–40. Dijon.

Reeder, Ellen D. 1999. *Scythian Gold*. New York, Baltimore, and San Antonio, TX.

Renfrew, Colin. 1987. *Archaeology and Language: The Puzzle of Indoeuropean Origins*. New York and Cambridge.

Reverdin, Olivier, and Jean Rudhardt, eds. 1981. *Le sacrifice dans l'antiquité. Huit exposés suivis de discussions. Entretiens sur l'antiquité classique 27*. Vandeouvres-Geneva.

Ridgway, David. 2002. *The World of the Early Etruscans*. Jonsered.

Rives, James. 1995. "Human Sacrifice among Pagans and Christians." *JRS* 85:65–85.

Romm, James S. 1992. *The Edges of the Earth in Ancient Thought: Geography, Exploration, and Fiction*. Princeton, NJ.

Rudhart, Jean, and Olivier Reverdin, eds. 1981. *Le sacrifice dans l'antiquité. Entretiens sur l'antiquité classique 28*. Vandeouvres-Geneva.

Sannibale, Maurizio. 2008. "Gli ori della Tomba Regolini-Galassi: tra tecnologia e simbolo." *MEFRA* 120:337–367.

Savostina, Elena. 2001. "The 'Bosporan Style' and Motifs from Herodotus in Plastic Arts from the Northern Pontic Area." In *Bosporan Battle Relief. Amazonomachia*, ed. E. Savostina, 304–323. Monograph on the Monument, vol. 2. Moscow and St. Petersburg.

Schroer, Silvia. 2006. *Images and Gender: Contributions to the Hermeneutics of Reading Ancient Art*. Orbis Biblicus et Orientalis 220. Göttingen.

Sebesta, Judith Lynn, and Larissa Bonfante. 1994. *The World of Roman Costume*. Madison, WI.

Sergent, Bernard. 2005. *Celti e Greci: Il libro degli eroi*. Rome. Translation of *Celtes et Grecs: Le livre des héros*. Paris, 1999.

Sherratt, Susan, and Andrew Sherratt. 1992. "The Growth of Mediterranean Economy in the Early First Millennium BC." *World Archaeology* 24 (3): 361–378.

Smith, R. R. R. 1988. "Simulacra Gentium: The Ethne from the Sebasteion at Aphrodisias." *JRS* 78:50–77.

Spencer, Nigel. 1995. *Time, Tradition and Society in Greek Archaeology: Bridging the "Great Divide."* New York.

Steel, Louise. 1995. "Challenging Preconceptions of Oriental 'Barbarity' and Greek 'Humanity': Human Sacrifice in the Ancient World." In Spencer 1995, 18–27.

Stone, Shelley. 1994. "The Toga: From National to Ceremonial Costume." In Sebesta and Bonfante 1994, 13–45.

Szilàgyi, Janos Gyorgy. 2004. *In Search of Pelasgian Ancestors*. Budapest.

Tacitus, 1970. *The Agricola and the Germania*. Trans. Harold Mattingly, rev. S. A. Handford. Harmondsworth, Middlesex, England.

The Táin. 2002. From the Irish epic *Táin Bó Cuailnge*, trans. Thomas Kinsella. Oxford.

Todd, Malcolm. 1972. *The Barbarians: Goths, Franks and Vandals*. London.

Torelli, Mario. 1981. "Delitto religioso: Qualche indizio sulla situazione in Etruria." In *Délit religieux* 1981, 1–7.

Vermeule, Emily. 1979. *Aspects of Death in Early Greek Art and Poetry*. Sather Classical Lectures. Berkeley, CA.

Wade, Nicholas. 2010. "Human Culture, an Evolutionary Force." *New York Times*, March 2, Science Section.

Watson, A. 1975. *Rome of the Twelve Tables*. Princeton, NJ.

Wells, Peter S. 1980. *Culture Contact and Culture Change: Early Iron Age Central Europe and the Mediterranean World*. Cambridge.

　　1984. *Farms, Villages, and Cities: Commerce and Urban Origins in Late Prehistoric Europe*. Ithaca, NY.

　　2001. *Beyond Celts, Germans and Scythians: Archaeology and Identity in Iron Age Europe*. London.

Westrem, Scott D. 2001. *The Hereford Map: A Transcription and Translation of the Legends with Commentary. Terrarum Orbis: History of the Representation of Space in Text and Image I*, ed. Patrick Gautier Dalche. Turhout, Belgium.

White, T. D. 2003. "Once We Were Cannibals" *Scientific American*. Special Edition: *New Look at Human Evolution*, 86–93.

Whitehouse, Ruth, ed. 1998. *Gender and Italian Archaeology: Challenging the Stereotypes*. London.

Woodard, Roger D. 2006. *Indo-European Sacred Space: Vedic and Roman Cult*. Chicago.

Zazoff, Peter. 1987. "Der neue thrakische Silberschatz von Rogozen in Bulgarien." *Antike Welt* 4:3–28.

CHAPTER TWO

GREEK GEOGRAPHY OF THE WESTERN BARBARIANS

Paul T. Keyser

This survey of ideas about barbarians living in the different areas of the known world explores the geographic peculiarities of the extreme West in Greek thought: Homer, who wrote of the mysterious, wealthy West, peopled by Phaeacians; and early tales, in the works of Herodotus and others, of the abundant amber and cattle, gold, tin, and silver to be found there. Ephorus depicted a tabular earth, delimited by four pillars at its corners and peopled by four races at its edges, with the Celts at the westernmost edge. The spherical earth preferred by Plato, Aristotle, and others privileged the directions north and south, but the daily path of the sun from east to west guaranteed a value to that axis. Peoples grew extreme at the edges of the earth, either in savagery or in the nobility of the uncivilized, and examples of both are frequent from the western front. These reports persisted later in the West than in the East; the coming of the Romans finally reduced the West from paradox and paradigm to province.

When Herodotus or Aeschylus or Pericles gazed at the setting sun, what did they see? Not, of course, the earth turning round into its own shadow and not even the sun going round the globe. Rather, they saw the sun descend behind the remote western edge of the flat earth, there to be quenched, or sleep, until at dawn it rose again above the fertile, far, and dew-bedizened East. These twin extremes lay most beneath the sun, which, fresh as spring, at dawn shone down on fertile lands that grew great plants and beasts, in India, and that, burning hot at setting, fell like autumn upon the western land or Ocean stream.

Later, when Eudoxus or Aristotle or Alexander observed a sunset, their sun orbited a spherical earth, and night was a cone of darkness racing away from the sun's rays. Still the West was an extreme, but only of the *oikoumene*, the inhabited landmasses, beyond which lay leagues of sea reaching to India, the fabled Sinae, or even perhaps the unknown land opposite the Hellas-centered *oikoumene*.

Those Greeks stood on an earth they regarded as central and unmoved, but we are able to conceive our perception of sunset as the earth turning round into its own cone of shadow, despite still using the geocentric metaphor "sunset." Our knowledge and comprehension of the reality of sunset have expanded, although language, as a shared behavior, must be conservative. Greek knowledge and perception of the earth and the peoples upon it also expanded, but did so most slowly in the lands west of Greece. Much of what the Greeks wrote about remote places and peoples was based in part on evidence: for example, the north of Europe was and is colder and wetter than the Mediterranean littoral, and the northern peoples are paler and taller than those around the Mediterranean basin. But it is on perceptions that I here focus my attention.

I survey how successive generations of Greeks, geographers and others, saw the far Western world, first in the early period through the end of the fourth century BC and the conquests of Alexander, then in the third and following centuries.[1] I consider Greek views of only the far west of Europe, not of Sicily and south Italy, and not of North Africa, all of which pose greater and different problems. Moreover, I rarely confront those Greek views of Western Europe with the reality on the ground – another very different problem. The survey shows how Greeks persistently schematized their world-picture, invoking notions of symmetry to impose order upon the data; the particular symmetries invoked changed over time, from an east–west axis, to an Ocean stream encircling the disk of the earth, to a flat earth whose edges grew extreme, and thence to a sphere. These notions of symmetry persisted longer in the Greek views of the West, primarily because of ignorance about facts on the ground. The early presence of such symmetries is a manifestation of a mode of thought common among societies operating according to traditional categories;[2] the later persistence of this mode among Greeks discussing the West provides evidence of how gradual was the transition from traditional to more open and evidential modes of thought, a transition much discussed by Lloyd and others.[3] Symmetric and schematized "geographies" form the world-pictures of societies operating according to traditional categories and are known from numerous cultures, such as Polynesia,[4] the Semitic milieu of the Hebrew scriptures,[5] and the ancient Persians.[6]

Early Greek geographers record little about the uttermost West – even the garrulous and catholic Herodotus, 3.115, admits that he cannot speak with any certainty about the extreme parts of the West. With rare exception, the western limits of Greek knowledge seem to have been Sicily and southern Italy. Only in the third century, in the works of Timaeus of Tauromenium or Eratosthenes of Cyrene, did observation replace myth in those parts. Greek writers often devoted works to the history of major Eastern or Southern peoples, such as the Persians, Ethiopians, Babylonians, or Egyptians, but almost never, and not until the Roman period, did they write monographs on Western peoples.[7]

Always the remote and unknown land was seen as rich, wild, and peopled with noble primitives or else with impolitic barbarians. Civilized peoples had history, but barbarians were static and ever the same.[8] Moreover, reports about Western peoples were fitted into the existing conceptual framework, whether of myth or history, in an attempt to appropriate their genealogies, migrations, and past for Greek tradition. Such political appropriation of the past was common in Greek thought and is found as early as the work of the Spartan poet Tyrtaeus.[9] The information on the West available to Greek writers was limited, however, probably because of their lack of access to the western Mediterranean, as it was controlled by the Carthaginian thalassocracy. Eratosthenes recorded an explicit Carthaginian ban on foreign navigation,[10] but no special ban was needed during the long Carthaginian wars against the Greeks of Sicily and the Etruscans in the fifth and fourth centuries (Diodorus of Sicily, 11.15), and then against the Romans in the third and second centuries BC.[11]

Early Greek Geographers: Western Lands

Well before Greeks gazed westward, Egyptians did, and saw in sunset lands the kingdom of the happy dead.[12] In the heroic tales of the *Odyssey*, Proteus of the Sea prophesied Menelaus's translation to the

Elysian Fields, where ever-pleasant Ocean breezes blew from the West, though surely no rhapsode knew or cared where lay Ogygia.[13] Hesiod in *The Catalogue of Women* told of the flight of the sons of the North Wind round the disk of the earth, passing over remote lands and peoples; his western landmarks were the Eridanos River (later identified with the Po), where amber is found, and Mount Aetna (i.e., Sicily), where the Laestrygonians dwell.[14] Tartessus in southwestern Iberia became known to Greeks sometimes as a prosperous land, sometimes as a city, in each case ruled by an aged, happy king, with people who rejoiced in written laws.[15] By the era of Hesiod and the Homeric epics, Phoenicians had planted a colony at Gaddir (from Punic "fortress"; modern Cadiz) and made Tartessus their own with the name Tarshish.[16]

Then Greeks came from Phocaea to found Massalia, which later had its own outposts farther west.[17] Probably a generation earlier, the trader Kolaios sailed by chance from Samos to the Phoenician ports of Spain and returned richer by talents of silver (Herodotus 4.152). At about that same time, Mimnermus of Smyrna sang of the sun's rays stored up at the edge of the Ocean – the same sun who asleep sails in his golden bowl around to the sunrise Ethiopians, starting from the sunset Hesperides,[18] whom Hesiod had called the daughters of Night (*Theogony* 213-216). Later, a now-nameless Massiliote captain sailed round Iberia to Finisterre, seeking tin fields.[19]

The early Greek worldview can be schematically represented as in Map 2.1, showing the geometrical symmetries imposed on the data. The cardinal directions have peoples and climes whose character is determined primarily by the action of the sun. The earth was thought to be flat, like a disk, with Greece near its middle.[20]

Such traditional myths and traders' reports coexisted peacefully in early Greek versions of the uttermost West, but neither cast much light upon those sunset lands. By the early fifth century BC, when Hellenic eyes were drawn eastward toward Persian predation, the Carthaginians sent Himilkon out along the north Atlantic coast to survey for prospective colonies and trade (perhaps in tin); his travel reports, including tales of shallow, congealed seas, are preserved in later Latin sources[21] and presumably reached some Greek ears. The Greeks had by now divided their world into two or three regions: Europe, Asia, and sometimes Libya.[22] But the Pillars of Heracles increasingly seemed a divine limit to westward

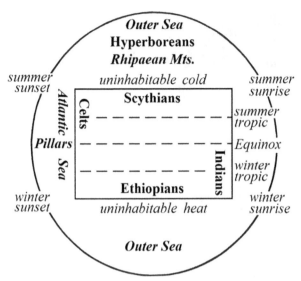

Map 2.1. The early Greek worldview: Ionian map. (Author's map, after Thomson 1948, 97, fig. 10.)

navigation beyond which one could not go.[23] They, or the Fountains of Night, marked the limit of the West; the other cardinal points too were primary – the North wind, the Unfoldings of Heaven in the East, and the ancient Garden of Phoebus in the South.[24] An alternate western terminus was Erytheia, the isle of the red sunset.[25] The far western reaches, however marked, seemed still the land of happiness, at least to the fugacious *choros* in Euripides's *Hippolytus* (732–751).

To many peoples who saw the earth as flat, the East and West seemed the primary *axis mundi*, determined by the sun. The Egyptians posited an eastern sunrise peak, Bachu, matched by the western sunset peak Manu.[26] Mesopotamian cosmic geography likewise often offered a pair of solar mountains in the East and West,[27] and the early Semitic context of the Hebrew scriptures also presupposes an east–west axis, so that the word for "north" means "left" and that for "south" means "right."[28] Early Greek epics seem to orient their world around the same east–west, or dawn–dusk axis, connecting right and light with east, and left and gloom with west (*Iliad* 12.238–240, *Odyssey* 13.239–241), and also (in *Odyssey* 10.80–86, 190–192, and Hesiod, *Theogony* 746–757) placing the paths of day and night adjacent.[29] Pindar records the myth that Zeus sent two eagles from the uttermost East and West who met at Delphi, thus demonstrating its utter centrality,[30] and the Europe/Asia dichotomy in Hecataeus and Herodotus seems to reflect the same view (see

Map 2.2. Hecataeus's map. (Author's map, after Thomson 1948, 99, fig. 11.)

the following discussion). Roman authors, and the late Hellenistic poet Agathyllos of Arcadia (known only from Dionysius of Halicarnassus), called the whole western region, or just Italy or just Spain, "Hesperia," apparently based on Apollonius of Rhodes, *Argonautica* 3.310–311, *hesperies eiso khthonos*, "into the western land."[31]

The earliest mapmaker whose picture we can reconstruct, Hecataeus of Miletus, synthesized the knowledge of his day as in Map 2.2.[32] The map of Hecataeus, and probably that of the first known Greek mapmaker, Anaximander, placed all lands within the fabulous disk-girdling Ocean. Hecataeus's work, whose title was perhaps *Trip around the Earth*, covered Europe in book 1 and Asia in book 2. Of the nearly 330 mostly very brief fragments, 158 concern Europe, of which only 20 (all mere names of coastal towns or peoples) refer to Spain, the Ligures, or the Celts.[33]

Herodotus sought to confute that schema of an earth-girdling Ocean (Map 2.3)[34] and offered his own schema, in which he portrayed some edges of the earth as desert land (*eremos* or *eremie*), but all edges as extreme in their produce (3.106.1). The far South was empty (4.185), the far North was desert (4.17, 5.9), and beyond those edges one could not inquire (2.32, 4.31). From Northern Europe came much gold, perhaps guarded by griffins (3.116, 4.27); from the far East, where the sun burns

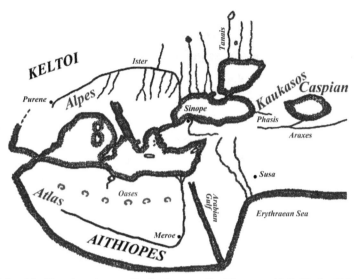

Map 2.3. Herodotus's map. (Author's map, after Thomson 1948, 99, fig. 12.)

close at dawn but cool at even (3.104), we have sand, and more gold, excavated by giant ants (3.98, 102); the South produced huge elephants, tall,
long-lived beauteous folk – and plentiful gold (3.114). Only the far West
was not empty and made the first Greek who traded there fabulously
wealthy (4.152). In the farthest North, even days and nights were said to
be extreme, lasting six months each, straining even Herodotus's credu-
lity (4.25). The historian's known and inhabited world was symmetrical
about its temperate central point, Greece: the Nile must resemble the
Danube, in mouths and course, and if there were Hyperboreans living
beyond the North wind, why then there would also be Hypernoteans
living beyond the South wind.[35]

Roughly contemporary with Herodotus, and deploying similar notions about geographical symmetry, is a medical writer in the
Hippocratic corpus, who sought to explain disease on the basis of direc-
tional exposure. He described the South as phlegmatic and moist, to
which the North was symmetrically opposed, bilious and cold. The East
was mild like spring, so that Asia was fertile, and the West was autum-
nal, while Greece, being centrally located, was moderate and best.[36]

By the end of the fifth century BC, certain sectarians had suggested a
spherical earth, a theory that gradually came to dominate geographical thinking in the fourth century (though Epicurus never caught on to
the idea). Not long before the end of the fifth century, the astronomer

Euctemon reported a submarine reef outside Gibraltar, which later led a
periplus-writer known as Scylax, as well as Plato and Aristotle, to believe
the outer sea to be largely shallow.[37] A little later than Euctemon, the
physician Ctesias of Cnidus traveled in the East and claimed that the sun
in India rose ten times the size it did in Greece to demonstrate how close
India lay to the edge.[38] Early in the fourth century, Ephorus of Cyme
made a map of the world as a table, flat, rectangular and regular, with
pillars at the four cardinal points, perhaps to hold up the sky: the pillars of Heracles to the west, a great northern one,[39] those at the mouth
of the Red Sea,[40] and probably those of Bacchus by the mouth of the
Ganges.[41] This rectangular portrait is remarkably similar in its outlines
to the Persian view of the world in the time of Darius, according to which
peoples lived at the corners of a rectangle whose center was Persia; the
peoples ruled by Darius are Lydians to the northwest, Skythians to the
northeast, Indians to the southeast, and the land of Kush to the southwest.[42] Shortly after Ephorus, the *Periplus* attributed to Scylax covered all
of Iberia and Gaul in three brief sentences that mainly mention ports,
and even to Italy gives only thrice that much text; for him, the peoples
out west are Iberes and Ligures, whereas the Celts live only in Italy.[43]

   The first geography founded on the spherical earth theory was that of
Eudoxus of Cnidus, who nonetheless divided the world into Asia (East)
and Europe (West).[44] The westernmost site among his fragments is the
Massalian colony Agathe (near Narbo), among the Ligures.[45] He treated
islands in a seventh book, as if not just the Blessed Isle, but all isles,
were situated in the interstices between Europe and Asia. Eudoxus's
near-contemporary, Plato, set his blessed isle Atlantis far west beyond
the Pillars of Heracles, but his very civilized yet warlike Atlanteans dwelt
in a fairyland, and his earth was a dimpled sphere in whose hollows air
and mist and water collected, and people gathered like ants or frogs
round a pond.[46] A little later, Pytheas sailed far out beyond the Pillars,
exploring the most remote regions of the West, likely seeking amber or
tin; and he was the first of the Greeks known to reach Britain,[47] con-
firming both the congealed sea of Himilkon[48] and the six-month days
and nights of Herodotus.[49] He even saw that the remarkable tides of the
Atlantic were linked to the moon,[50] thus balancing Herodotus's report
of tides in the remote eastern ocean.[51] But the Atlantic tides were titanic,
at times making certain coastal British islets into peninsulas.[52] Even

farther off lay the Royal Isle, where the sea cast up amber on the shore.[53] Pytheas's reports were accepted, or at least repeated, in the third century BC by Eratosthenes and Timaeus[54] but were rejected by Polybius, eager to depict himself as the first serious geographer on the West.[55]

Although Aristotle was convinced that the earth was a sphere, he spun a good yarn that the Mediterranean was a dimple fringed by lofty peaks whence mighty rivers flowed: in the West, these storied heights were Pyrene in the Celtic land, where the Ister rose, and to the north the Arkynian mountains, source of many nameless streams; thus he preserved as much as he could of Plato's picture of a dimpled earth. About those Western lands Aristotle told a few tales: the Rhone and one unnamed other were great navigable rivers;[56] quakes beset Liguria;[57] and Gaul lacked donkeys, because the Celtic country above Iberia was so cold.[58] Theophrastus reported nothing west of Italy and little enough even on that peninsula,[59] in contrast to his ample data on Cyrene, Crete, Asia, Cyprus, Egypt, Syria, Babylon, and India. Dicaearchus oriented his map along the old east-west axis, through Sardinia, Sicily, the Peloponnese, and east along the Taurus Mountains to the Himalayas. He identified the Pillars of Heracles with a pair of rocky islets in the straits, but his measurements fell short west of Sicily; moreover, he placed Sardinia and Sicily on the same latitude, a location not required by any tradition and not easy to explain unless he employed unreliable reports of sailing directions or of sun-height measurements.[60] Thus, even at the end of the fourth century BC, geographers grasped no more than traders.

Early Greek Geographers: Western Peoples

So much for the land. What of its people, uncivil or wild? For Hesiod, those of the South were all dark Ethiopians, those of the North were all Scythians, and those of the West were all Ligurians.[61] In the *Odyssey* and in Aeschylus's *Prometheus Unbound*, the far Westerners were labeled Ethiopians;[62] Herodotus agrees, and distinguishes the east and west Ethiopians only by hair and speech.[63] Ephorus's tabular world held Scythians in the North, in the South Ethiopians who crossed Libya as far as the Atlas Mountains, then Indians under the sunrise, and under the sunset, Celts.[64] Thus, although the label changes (Ethiopians or Ligurians or Celts), Greeks long saw all Westerners as one kind.

And what kind were those who dwelt in the remote West? Westerners were often written up in terms derived as much from what the Greek writers desired or feared as from what they knew. In the *Iliad* the remote tribes to the north and west are "mare-milkers, curd-eaters, and the Abioi" (*Abioi* seems to mean "warless"), called "most just" (*dikaiotatoi*); and the Ethiopians who dwell beneath the sun's setting are blameless (*amymones*).[65] Those are the earliest traces of a path many Greek thinkers followed, viewing remote and primitive peoples as noble and uncorrupted by civilization. Pindar praised the happy Hyperboreans,[66] whereas Herodotus argued that harsh climes make for tough folk in order to praise Greeks in contrast to Egyptians and Babylonians.[67] The author of the Hippocratic *Airs, Waters, Places* advanced similar notions to explain the toughness of Northern and Western European tribes,[68] and Ephorus believed that the Scythians were a tough, honorable folk.[69] Those who are remote and unknown are portrayed as either above us or below, but because they are remote, they must be unusual, and hence cannot be seen as like us.

Philosophers elevated these biases to hypotheses or even theories. Thus Plato insinuated that Westerners were spirited (*thumoeides*),[70] while Aristotle argued that it was natural for Europeans to be full of spirit (*thumos*) but a bit short of wit and skill, thus being free but unruly, just the reverse of Asiatics, who were clever weaklings.[71] To Aristotle, Celts were mindless braves[72] and, like Spartans or Scythians, lived only for war, toughened from infancy by exposure to cold.[73] Pytheas claimed that the never-mastered Brittani, dwelling humbly in log cabins, were simple of habit and modest of diet, lived peaceably with one another (Diodorus of Sicily, 5.21.5–6), and hospitably exported tin all the way to Massalia.[74] Theopompus of Chios contrived a tale about the blessed inhabitants of the landmass across the Ocean, who were so happy that they held even the Hyperboreans in contempt.[75]

The philosophical theories can be traced back to Democritus, who turned Hesiod's myth of divinely golden ancestors on its head and suggested that we humans had gradually created our own civilization, prompted by our natural sense of fellowship. He and those who followed in his track sought evidence of this behavior in reports of remote and simple tribes of men, still clinging to their olden ways.[76] Democritus's own exposition was not localized,[77] but its most salient features were regularly applied by geographers to reports about the West. Three notions are frequent: fertility, peace, and purity, all seen in Lucretius's version. For primitive humans, earth provided freely of its bounty, a fertile motherland, as for Hesiod's golden folk.[78] Small communities of early people were peaceful and cohesive.[79] Primitive folk, however, were corrupted when civilization infused enervating luxury.[80]

A few examples from various historians will show how these ideas percolated into their portraits of barbarians. Herodotus told how a nomad band of Scythians came to intermarry with exile warrior women of the Amazons (food and sex preceded talk).[81] Two early Alexander-historians did the same. The ambassador Megasthenes reported that the Indians once upon a time were wanderers, cityless, clothed in skins, and feeding on bark and raw game – until, that is, Dionysus imported wine and, with it, culture.[82] The admiral Nearchus claimed that he saw wild Oritans in Tomerus, along the coast of Persia, who had nails like claws, used no metal tools, and dressed in skins, while the Fish-eaters of that coast were supplied with food by nature itself when the tide brought in their fish.[83] That description was given more color in Agatharchides's work on the Red Sea; he added that they lacked clothes, had their women and children in common, and were naturally happy and uncorrupted by civilization.[84]

About the West as well, Greek writers responded to their desire for a life free of the defects of civilization, as well as to their fear of losing the restraints of society. Some Western tribes were so primitive as to seem subhuman; Strabo reported bizarre customs among the old Irish:[85] Cannibals all, they honored dead fathers by having them for dinner and dishonored live mothers and sisters by having them openly (*phaneros*). Besides that, they – or the Thulians – had no wine, only mead and beer.[86] Ephorus said that although some remote European barbarians were so cruel as to be cannibals, others excelled in justice (*dikaiosune*), because they lived modest lives without private property.[87] The Celts living on the Adriatic were brave enough to tell the recently crowned Alexander that they feared nothing except the sky falling.[88] Too much civilization would corrupt a man, however: Strabo claimed (7.3.7) that in his day the noble Scythians had descended to luxury and pleasure, in support of which they required trickery, greed, and even trade.

On the other hand, some Western peoples were reputed to show signs of civilization. Dionysius of Halicarnassus collected notes from Greek historians, from about 425 to 200 BC, that recorded the foundation of the city of Rome.[89] They based their tales on Hesiod's reference to the children of Circe and Odysseus, rulers of the Tyrsenoi, or Etruscans, and attributed the city's foundation to heroes on their way home from the Trojan War.[90] Heracleides of Pontus recorded an account in which not Celts but Hyperboreans sacked Rome (about 390 BC).[91] Even at the end of the third century BC, however, when Rome was already a Mediterranean power, Greek historians offered little on the history of that city.[92]

The Etruscans (Tyrsenoi or Tyrrhenoi in Greek) were more talked of and served as the Western counterparts to the Persians – rich and literate but luxurious and cruel.[93] In the very earliest Greek accounts, they were often connected with the Pelasgians, the people who preceded the Greeks.[94] From about 560 to about 300 BC, they were described as a seafaring nation, formidable opponents or useful allies;[95] who placed dedications at Delphi commemorating their naval victories.[96] By about 500 BC, however, they were also often portrayed as living a life of luxurious revelry[97] and as being cruel and inhumane. The latter characteristics they demonstrated by stoning prisoners of war (a punishment inflicted on the worst criminals) and torturing captives to death by binding them to corpses.[98] Although early Greeks had been pirates (Thuc. 1.5), the Etruscans' barbarity was made manifest by their persistence in the practice.[99] Most Greek writers portrayed them as autochthonous descendants of the ancient fabled Pelasgian people,[100] but they were so much like Easterners that Herodotus seems to have accepted, or contrived, a tale making them a Lydian people.[101] For Herodotus, the Lydians were hellenized eastern barbarians, inimical to Greeks, and congenitally prone to luxury.[102]

Hellenistic Geographers

Thus, up to the end of the fourth century BC, Greeks continued to be largely ignorant about the land and peoples of the far West, and geographers of the third century were only a little better informed; Polybius boasted that *all* of his predecessors were weak in their knowledge of the West.[103] In contrast to his copious data on Scythia, Ethiopia, and even India, Aristotle knew nothing of the beasts west of Sicily; likewise, Theophrastus knew of no plant from west of Sicily and Italy. Even

much later, when pharmacists had amply harvested in the West, Aelian's
Hellenistic sources on animals scarcely touched on the West, providing only four brief notes.[104] In 323 BC Alexander received as a novelty
emissaries from the Celts and the Iberians,[105] but after the invasions of
279/278 BC, the Celts who settled in what became Galatia were widely
valued as mercenaries.[106]

The geography in the first two books of Timaeus's history was best on
his native Sicily and nearby islets[107] and almost as thorough on Illyria and
Italy,[108] plus the large islands Sardo (Sardinia) and Kyrnos (Corsica).[109]
Kyrnos provided slaves and tribute to Tyrrhenians, although the Kyrnians
themselves lived on milk and honey and meat, more justly (*dikaios*) than
almost any other barbarians.[110] Timaeus recorded many wild animals on
Kyrnos, hunted by the natives, but a century or so later, Polybius would
only allow wild foxes, rabbits, and sheep; the cattle seemed wild only to
ignorant foreigners from Sicily who did not know that the native shep-
herds summoned their animals with trumpet blasts.[111] Sardo had been
partly conquered by Carthaginians, but according to Timaeus its pastoral natives, descendants of Heracles, survived in the highlands on milk
and cheese and meat, forever free of foreign rule.[112]

The farther west, the more marvelous. The women of Liguria, or perhaps Iberia, were so tough that they ceased fieldwork only long enough
to give birth, caching their babies beneath nearby bushes.[113] On certain
islands near Iberia, people went about naked all summer long,[114] and
men so prized women that they ransomed them at three times or more
the price of men; but they used no gold or silver, and at weddings the
new bride lay with every man.[115] Along the coast of Provence ran a road,
Heracles's highway, maintained by tolls and safe for all.[116] The ground
was rich enough in silver that a dinner campfire would smelt it out
during the course of the meal,[117] so one could sail back home on ships
fitted with solid silver anchors.[118] For Britain, Timaeus relied on Pytheas
alone, but he also knew that out beyond the Pillars lay the secret blessed
isle found by Carthaginians and desired in vain by Tyrrhenians.[119]

Eratosthenes of Cyrene believed that neither of the great islands,
Sardinia and Corsica, was visible from the mainland, that is, southern Italy,[120] but he did know of the great Northern European forest of
oak.[121] Eratosthenes also reported accurately enough – apparently from
Pytheas – about the portless coast of northern Iberia,[122] about the Celts

of the Atlantic coast, especially Brittany,[123] and even about the British Isles.[124] Eratosthenes reasserted the existence of the circumfluent Ocean in order to explain how tides could exist both far to the east and west,[125] and concluded, as Aristotle had, that[126] "the inhabited world forms a complete circle, itself meeting itself; so that, if the immensity of the Atlantic sea did not prevent it, we could sail from Iberia to India along one and the same parallel over the remainder of the circle." Eratosthenes even believed in the Hypernoteans, arguing that the South wind arises somewhere in Ethiopia and that the land south of there is inhabited.[127] Still, his map of Iberia appears to have been more accurate than those that preceded it, likely based on information from the wars of Rome and Carthage in that land.[128]

The Roman conquests of the second half of the third century BC opened up the West to Greek inquiry less than a century before Polybius, and he may have been right to claim geographic priority, although we have little of what he said about the West.[129] The far west of Iberia had come to be known as Lusitania and was a very pleasant and fertile clime, on land and sea,[130] where oak trees rooted in the shallows of the sea dropped acorns on which tuna fed like sea pigs.[131] The Lusitanian Celts were gentle and civil (*hemeros* and *politikos*)[132] – at least before Rome embarked upon their conquest. The Spanish soil at New Carthage provided a wealth of silver.[133] The land of Gaul was fertile and strange. Between the Pyrenees Mountains and the city of Narbo, the fluvial plain was full of fish, which burrowed after the roots of a succulent plant;[134] up in the Alps was a deer with a boarlike neck and mane and a goatlike beard.[135] The gold in Aquileia lay right below the plow.[136] The Alps were not perhaps the fabled Rhipaeans, but they were astonishingly tall, had few passes, and were so extensive that they included lakes.[137] The people of this strange land, the Celts, were volatile and disorderly, because, being nomads similar to the Scythians, they carried all they owned with them, and they lacked the civilized arts, preferring war and drink, and acting under the compulsion of *thumos*.[138]

In the same era as Polybius, Greeks turned to astrology as the synthesis of their science; the world was again a unity, bound together by chains of sympathy extending even into heaven. One of the earliest of these astrological authors, an exact contemporary of Polybius, whose work travels under the names of two Egyptians, Nechepso and Petosiris, predicted regional fortunes based on eclipses and comets (e.g., there will be war in Mesopotamia, or there will be unrest in Asia Minor). His West was Italy, Tyrrhenia, Hispaniae (plural), and Germania, each of which he mentioned once or twice only, omitting Gallia entirely.[139] The later astrologer Ptolemy, relying on Hellenistic astrologers, followed the old Ionian outline: the South was inhabited by Ethiopians, dark and hot, while the North was occupied by Scythians, white, cold, and wet. Best was the middle zone, whose people were moderately colored and most civilized; among such civil folk, those of the East were more sunny, masculine, vigorous, and honest, while the Westerners were more lunar, feminine, secretive, and soft.[140] Ptolemy proceeded to describe Europe as governed by the stars of Zeus and Ares and the triangle of signs Ram, Lion, and Archer. Therefore, the people there were independent, freedom-loving, warlike, industrious, leader-like, pure, and magnanimous, and, coupled with such manliness, had a preference for sex with men.[141] Among those Westerners, Ptolemy says that the Spaniards and Tuscans were more independent, simple, and pure, while the folk of Britain, Gaul, and Germany were more fierce, wild, and bestial, both in contrast to the Italians, who were better leaders, benevolent, and cooperative (*Tetrabiblos* 2.3); one may suspect a pro-Roman source.

When Julius Caesar was an infant, Artemidorus of Ephesus mapped the world from west to east.[142] He told of the wild and wonderful Spanish coast, where the sun set much larger and very fast, as if off the flat edge of the earth,[143] and where the women sported curious headgear – veils draped over iron frames set on their shoulders.[144] At century's end, noble Iberia was to Strabo still the land of natural Western wealth, whose folk were wise and relied upon the written law.[145]

Diodorus of Sicily and Strabo of Amaseia both preserved further Celtic tales, tall enough to come from Posidonius,[146] and later, in his annual field dispatches, Caesar embedded some of those reports as his own.[147] Writers continued to conform their accounts to one or both of the images of barbarians used since the time of Herodotus and Democritus: the noble primitive or the subhuman savage.[148] For example, in northern Celtic climes it was so cold that the rivers froze and the winds a mere 20 kilometers up the Rhone blew hard enough to push stones, but the soil was still rich in gold.[149] The Celts themselves were both noble and debased. Their bravest man ate best, as was his hero's right,[150] and their wise men made peace and prevented wars,[151] but in the farther, colder, poorer North they fed on human flesh (mounting trophy heads) and washed it down with beer.[152] In wartime, they fought as if in the gymnasium, naked save for sword and shield.[153] Some even practiced divination from human sacrifice,[154] never a Greek custom, at least not since Agamemnon offered up Iphigenia. The Celtic priests often conducted their human sacrifices by imprisoning the victims in wicker cages and burning the ensemble[155] (Bonfante, Chapter 1, this volume, Fig. 1.1).

By the mid-first century, however, the Celtic culture, while curious, seemed neither primitive nor senseless: like the Pythagoreans, the Celts believed in transmigration;[156] like Plato, they were literate but believed that oral learning was superior to the written word;[157] like pious Romans, they honored dedicated spoils scrupulously.[158] There were indeed curiosities, with their oddly cut clothes, riding breeches and buckled-on cloaks colored with bright rectangles;[159] or the customs that allowed widows and widowers to inherit equally;[160] or that funerals involved a potlatch, cremating all that the deceased held dear.[161] Strabo described these Celts as "madly fond of war, high-spirited, and quick to battle," and he claimed that "always those who live towards the north and towards the ocean … make the best warriors"; he found them honest, if rather childishly vain and boastful.[162] Their land he knew well enough to describe its generous supply of navigable rivers, rendering the whole accessible to trade.[163]

At the time of Caesar's dispatches, it was the remote northern Germani who were the wild uncivil people. They worshipped but three gods – Sun, Moon, and Fire – and their lives were devoted to hunting and war; they dressed only in animal skins, and few of those; they fed upon milk and cheese and meat, and had no settled abode, in order to prevent the influx of greed and luxury.[164] In the endless northern woods of the Hercynian forest dwelt the fabled unicorn, not to mention elk, whose unbending legs the animal rested when it leaned against a tree at night; these they hunted by undercutting favored trees, thus bringing down tree and elk at bedtime.[165] That tall tale antedates Aristotle, who doubted an account, probably by Ctesias, that *elephants* could not bend their legs.[166] Agatharchides revived the rumor, adding that the Ethiopians exploited this to hunt elephants;[167] how Caesar came to apply it to German elk we may never know.

Conclusions: "West" Is Good to Think With

But Caesar marks the limit of Greek geography, and he won the West for Roman laws, so I turn now to an assessment of Greek views of the far West. All peoples seem to have a concept of themselves in contrast to outsiders.[168] "Barbarian" is thus a common cultural idiom, as in the Egyptian *p_dt* ("bow folk") or *ḥ3st* ("hill folk"),[169] Assyrian *nakru*,[170] Hebrew *goyim*, Latin *gentes*, Arabic *ᶜajam*, Chinese *ssu-i*,[171] or Japanese *gaijin*. However, lacking extensive direct experience of the peoples and lands of Western Europe, Greeks continued to perceive them in almost mythic terms, in contrast to their more developed and nuanced images of Eastern outsiders, such as Egyptians, Persians, and the rest.

From the start, Greeks painted the West in rosy colors, as fertile, rich, and filled with marvelous and noble inhabitants (though some were bestial). As Jonathan Swift knew, that which is remote appears beautiful and fine, and to the Greeks, the remote southern Ethiopians, wise eastern Gymnosophists, and fabled northern Hyperboreans were all noble happy folk. That myth endured longer in the West, because the area remained longer obscure. A portrait is a likeness but it also expresses opinions about that which is portrayed, thus becoming something of a *self*-portrait. We know that about Greek biography and history, and it is just as true of their geography. What do the Greeks reveal about themselves when writing on the West? Their Westerners were nothing so simple as "the Other"; they were multiple others, each hinting at some Greek desire or dread:

- The subhuman, incestuous cannibals correspond to the dread of passion unleashed – as seen also in various myths and tragedies.
- The disordered, impolitic braves correspond to the dread of *stasis* ("civil unrest") – as seen also in histories of Greek wars.
- The admirable, pure primitives correspond to the desire for the lost simplicity of the fabled golden age.
- The natural humans nursing at the bounty of nature's breast correspond to the desire for an easy life free of toil.

Greek geographers sought to see what was out there, but they also always saw what they themselves desired – or dreaded. Here we may leave our

Greeks, and their Celts and Ligurians and Ethiopians, in the haze of the same setting sun that colors our perceptions of outsiders.

Notes

1. Throughout, when citing fragments, I also give the source(s) of the fragment to clarify possible bias. The Byzantine excerpts of Polybius and Diodorus of Sicily are tagged as "(Byz.)," while the complex tradition of the fragments of Agatharchides is best seen in Burstein 1989. I am indebted to Nancy de Grummond, Denise Demetriou, Julie Laskaris, and Dagmar A. Riedel for critical readings and suggestions. I am most indebted to Larissa Bonfante for inviting me to give the talk upon which this chapter is based and for her unfailing kindness.
2. Cf. Hallpike 1979 and Hawke 2008.
3. Lloyd 1979, 226–267, esp. 234, 258, 264; he is building upon Vernant 1957/1965/1983.
4. Riesenberg 1976.
5. Janowski 2007.
6. Wiesehöfer 2007.
7. Six **Persian** histories: Dionysius of Miletus (ca. 445 BC; *FGrHist* 687), Hellanicus of Lesbos (ca. 425 BC; *FGrHist* 608, 687a), Ctesias of Cnidus (ca. 400 BC; *FGrHist* 688), Heracleides of Cyme (ca. 350 BC; *FGrHist* 689), Dion (ca. 345 BC; *FGrHist* 690), and Hermesianax of Colophon (ca. 300 BC; *FGrHist* 691). Three **Ethiopian** histories: Charon of Lampsacus (ca. 400 BC; *FGrHist* 687b), Dalion (ca. 300 BC; *FGrHist* 666), and Bion of Soloi (ca. 280 BC; *FGrHist* 668). **Egyptian** history: Manethon (ca. 280 BC; *FGrHist* 609). **Babylonian** history: Berossus (ca. 280 BC; *FGrHist* 680). Aristotle's lost *Constitution of the Carthaginians* was not a history of Carthage, although his *Constitution of Massalia* did include the foundation legend: fr. 549 Rose = Athenaeus, *Deipnosophists* 13 (576ab).
8. Champion 1985; Bichler 2000, 57–58, 98–99; Wells 2001, 107. The literature on Greek views of barbarians is immense; see, for example, Hall 1989 and de Romilly 1993.
9. Tyrtaeus, fr. 1 Gentili-Prato = *POxy* 2824 + Strabo 8.4.10 and fr. 8 Gentili-Prato = Stobaeus, *Anthology* 4.9.16. Later examples include Pindar, *Pythian* 1.62–65 and 5.69–76; Herodotus 5.43 and 8.144; Thucydides 1.95, 2.29, 3.86, and 6.44.3; Megasthenes, *FGrHist* 715 F 4.38–39 = Diodorus of Sicily 2.38–39; Isocrates, *Archidamos* 8–9, 16–33; and Polybius, book 9, fr. 2.1–2 (Byz.) criticizing the practice. On Tyrtaeus's appropriation of the Spartan past, cf. Malkin 1994, 15–45 = 1999, 29–64 and Gerber 1999, 39; on the appropriation of the Greek past among the colonies of South Italy and Sicily, see Malkin 1998, 178–257; on ancient Celtic appropriation of the Greek mythic past, see Rankin 1987, 80–82; in general, see the discussion by Bickermann 1952. Such appropriation is comparable to modern appropriations of archaeology by nationalists: for twentieth-century parallels, especially in Ireland, Nazi Germany, France, Poland, Israel, and India, see Jones 1997, 1–39 and 128–144; Kristiansen 1993 discusses the Danish appropriations of archaeology.
10. Eratosthenes, book 1, fr. B.9 Berger = Roller F154 (book 3) = Strabo 17.1.19.
11. Polybius 3.58–59 attributes greater geographical access and data to the conquests of Alexander in the East and the Romans in the West.
12. Keyser 1993.

13. Elysian fields: *Odyssey* 4.563–568; island: *Odyssey* 5. Cf. Müller 1972, 53–59.
14. See Müller 1972, 59–66; West 1985, 84–85, 127–130, 169–171 arguing that the poem was probably later than Hesiod. The fragments of *The Catalogue of Women* are edited by Merkelbach and West in Solmsen et al. 1990: frr. 151–157 cover the North, East, and South, mentioning Ethiopians, Libyans, Scythians, Pygmies, Hyperboreans, and the "Catoudaei" (cave dwellers, i.e., Troglodytes?). Only fr. 150 = *POxy* 1358 mentions anything in the West: Eridanus and its amber, Aetna and the Laestrygonians; the editors plausibly restore "Atlas," which, like the Pillars of Heracles, is in the extreme West by definition, if not discovery.
15. Stesichorus, fr. 7 Page = Strabo 3.2.11 places Tartessus in the far West; Anacreon, fr. 361 Page = Strabo 3.2.14 describes the king of Tartessus as very aged; Herodotus 1.163 calls Tartessus a city, located in the far West and still ruled by a very aged king (cf. 4.152); and Strabo 3.1.6 attributes versified laws written in the local script to the natives (probably following Polybius or an even earlier source). Archaeology confirms a literate pre-Phoenician trading culture (no actual city has been found): Chamorro 1987; Harrison 1988, 53–68; Aa. Vv. 1995; Villar and Beltrán 1997; Ruiz and Molinos 1998, 248–268; and Pérez 2001, 289–301.
16. Harrison 1988, 41–50; Negbi 1992; Aa. Vv. 1994; Aubet 2001; Bierling and Gitin 2001.
17. By about 650–600 BC, Phocaean colonists had founded Massalia; other Greek sites west of Sicily seem to be later than, or founded from, Massalia: Harrison 1988, 69–79; Hodge 1998.
18. Mimnermus, *Nanno* fr. 10 Gentili-Prato = Strabo 1.2.40 and fr. 5 Gentili-Prato = Athenaeus, *Deipnosophists* 11 (470a), on which see Allen 1993, 94–99.
19. His *periplus* is preserved in Rufus Festus Avienius, *Ora Maritima* 94–107, 154–157, 172–177, 182–194, 226–230, etc.; see Cunliffe 2001, 44–47; Keyser in *EANS* 535. Cf. also the merchant Midacritus in Pliny 7.197, otherwise unknown.
20. Roller 2006, 1–21; Gehrke 2007.
21. Pliny 2.169; Rufus Festus Avienius, *Ora Maritima* 117–129, 380–389, 402–415; Cunliffe 2001, 42–44.
22. Pindar, *Nemean* 4.70 (Europe), *Olympian* 7.18 (Asia), and *Pythian* 9.8 (Libya); cf. Herodotus 4.45.
23. Pindar, *Isthmian* 4.11–13, *Nemean* 3.21, 4.69–70, and *Olympian* 3.43–44: on which see Hubbard 1985, 11–27; Romm 1992, 17–18; Willcock 1995, 75; in Euripides, *Hippolytus* 744–745, the way is barred by the "old man of the sea"; cf. Barrett 1964, 303–304.
24. Sophocles, *TrGF* 956 = Strabo 7.3.1.
25. Erytheia (or Erythreia) in the far West: Hesiod, *Theogony* 289–294, 982–983; Pherecydes of Athens, *FGrHist* 3 F 18 = Strabo 3.5.4; Herodotus 4.8.2; Ephorus, *FGrHist* 70 F 129 = Pausanias of Damascus (known as "pseudo-Scymnus"), *Periplus* 152–169. See Marcotte 2000, 52–55, on Pausanias's treatment of far Western peoples and 160–163 on Erytheia and environs; cf. Dueck in *EANS* 630–631.
26. Otto 1975; Kurth 1980.
27. Heimpel 1986; Horowitz 1998, 330–334.
28. Janowski 2007.
29. Lloyd 1966, 40, 47, citing anthropological studies of Indonesia, of the Megwe, and of the Nuer; Arrighetti 1966; Austin 1973, 228–238; 1975, 90–102; Ballabriga

1986, 60–62, 77, 108–117; cf. also 147–156, 175–255; Ballabriga 1998, 7–10, 221–222, qualifying without rejecting his earlier work by attributing certain geographical items in Homeric epic to actual geographical discoveries of the seventh and sixth centuries BC, leading to a hypothesis of large-scale interpolations in the Homeric corpus during those centuries; and Nakassis 2004.

30. Pindar, *Pythian* 4.4–5, 74–75, *Paians* fr. 54 Maehler = Strabo 9.3.6 + Pausanias 10.16.3.

31. Epperlein 1971. The earliest attested use of "Hesperia" as a proper name is in Ennius, *Annales* fr. 20 Sk. = Macrobius 6.1.11; cf. also Dionysius of Halicarnassus, *Roman Antiquities* 1.35.3, citing no one, and 1.49.2 quoting Agathyllos.

32. Anaximander, fr. 12 A 6 DK = Eratosthenes, book 1, fr. B.5 Berger = Roller F12 = Strabo 1.1.11, and Hecataeus, *FGrHist* 1 T 12 = F 36a = Agathemerus 1.1 + Herodotus 4.36; see Müller 1972, 94–101; Dilke 1985, 56–57; Cunliffe 2008, 3–6.

33. Moret 2006 studies the tradition of Iberian toponymy from Hecataeus through its later development through Polybius, remarking upon its poverty and heterogeneity; on Hecataeus, see Kaplan in *EANS* 361.

34. Herodotus 2.23, 4.8, 4.36, and 4.45. Herodotus sought to base his world-picture upon travelers' reports, 4.42–44, rather than on the map of Anaximander; see Dilke 1985, 21–24, 57–59; Romm 1992, 32–41.

35. Herodotus 3.106: symmetry; 2.33, 49: Nile and Danube; 4.36: Hyperboreans and Hypernoteans. See Müller 1972, 101–131, and Hartog 1988, 14–19, on symmetries in Herodotus's world-picture.

36. *Airs, Waters, Places* 3–6, 12, 16, 23; cf. Müller 1972, 137–144; Jouanna 1996, 54–64; Laskaris in *EANS* 406. Similar is *Regimen* 2.37–38 (6.528–534 L.).

37. Euctemon in Rufus Festus Avienius, *Ora Maritima* 350; cf. pseudo-Scylax, *Periplus* 1 and 112; Plato, *Timaeus* 25d, *Critias* 108e–109a; and Aristotle, *Meteorology* 2.1 (354 a22–24).

38. Ctesias, *Indika, FGrHist* 688 F 45.12 and 45.18 = Photius, *Library* 72 (45b and 46a).

39. According to Pausanias of Damascus, *Periplus* 188–195, who listed his sources as Ephorus and more recent authors, *Periplus* 109–127; see also Rufus Festus Avienius, *Ora Maritima* 88–89. Marcotte 2000, 164–166, rejects Höschel's emendation to *boreios* and retains the crux *baria*; the pillar is clearly distinct from the Western ones and lies among the Celts along the Ocean. Marcotte suggests *briareos*, as in Aristotle, fr. 678 Rose = Aelian, *Historical Miscellany* 5.3, and in Plutarch, *Failure of Oracles* 18 (419e–420a), an allegedly old name for the Pillars of Heracles. See also Bianchetti 1990, who distinguishes the later references in Rufus Festus Avienius from that in Pausanias; and Kaplan in *EANS* 286–287.

40. Ephorus, *FGrHist* 70 F 172 = Pliny 6.199.

41. See Strabo 3.5.5 and Pliny 6.49 – not cited as Ephorus, but evidently a pre-Alexandrian source; cf. Diodorus of Sicily 17.9.5; Arrian, *Anabasis* 5.29.1; Plutarch, *Alexander* 62.4; and Q. Curtius Rufus 9.3.19.

42. Wiesehöfer 2007.

43. Pseudo-Scylax, *Periplus* 2–4 on Iberia and Gaul; 5 and 8–19 on Italy; cf. Kaplan in *EANS* 746.

44. Cf. Müller 1972, 145–147.

45. Eudoxus, *Geography*, book 6, fr. 66 Gisinger = Stephanus of Byzantium, s.v. "Agathe."

46. Atlantis: *Timaeus* 24e–25a and *Critias* 108e–109a; our globe: *Phaedo* 108–109 and *Timaeus* 40c. Romm 1992, 124–128, argues that both geographies are

mythic, while Guthrie 1975, 361–363, and Rowe 1993, 265–290, stress that the geography in the *Phaedo* is a myth. Presumably Plato wrote "ants or frogs" to emphasize both human ignorance and human insignificance.

47. See Strabo 4.5.5; cf. Müller 1972, 253–256. On Pytheas see Cunliffe 2001 and 2008, 6–8; and Roller 2006, 57–91.
48. Pytheas, F2, F5 Roseman = Strabo 1.4.2, 2.4.1; and T23 Roseman = Pliny 4.104. Cf. Rankin 1987, 56, on the Celtic name "Kron-" for the dead or frozen sea of the North, according to Philemon (in Pliny 4.95) and Plutarch, *Face in the Moon* 26 (941a).
49. Pytheas, F8 Roseman = Geminus, *Introduction* 6.9; T18a Roseman = Strabo 2.5.7 + Pliny 2.186–7; and T27 Roseman = Cleomedes 1.4.
50. Pytheas, T19 Roseman = Pliny 2.217; and T26 Roseman = Aëtios 3.17.3.
51. Herodotus 2.11 on Eastern tides; cf. 7.198 on tides in the Malic gulf.
52. Timaeus, *FGrHist* 566 F 164.22.3 = Diodorus of Sicily 5.22.3.
53. Amber: Pytheas, T25 Roseman = Pliny 37.35; Timaeus *FGrHist* 566 F 164.23 = Diodorus of Sicily 5.23: see Jacoby ad loc., pp. 593–594, and Geffcken 1892, 161–162. Timaeus *FGrHist* 566 F 75a = Pliny 4.94 + 37.35 mentioned the island.
54. Eratosthenes, book 3, fr. B.126 Berger (Roller omits) = Strabo 2.4.2; Timaeus, *FGrHist* 566 F 75b = Pliny 37.36.
55. Polybius, book 34, fr. 5.1–6.10 = Strabo 2.4.1–2, and book 34, fr. 10.6 = Strabo 4.2.1.
56. Aristotle, *Meteorology* 1.13 (350 b1–10) on the West and (351 a16–18) on the two great rivers, the second of which was probably the Po; see, respectively, Strohm 1970, 160 and 162.
57. Ligurian quakes: Aristotle, *Meteorology* 2.8 (368 b30–33); see Strohm 1970, 199, comparing Posidonius, fr. 229 EK = Strabo 4.1.7.
58. See Aristotle, *History of Animals* 7(8).28 (606 b2–5) and *Generation of Animals* 2.8 (748 a22–26).
59. Only five items: (1) *On Winds* 44: Lokroi; (2) *History of Plants* 3.17: Tyrrhenia and Lipari; (3) *History of Plants* 4.5.6: Adriatic ("they say"); (4) *History of Plants* 5.8: Latium and "they say" Corsica; (5) *History of Plants* 8.4 Akragas and Sicily.
60. Keyser 2001; Keyser in *EANS* 246.
61. Hesiod, *Works and Days* 527, and *Catalogue of Women* fr. 150.15 = Strabo 7.3.7. Remote northerners may also be Hyperboreans, as in Pindar, *Pythian* 10.27–44.
62. *Odyssey* 1.22–24, 5.282–287; Aeschylus, *Prometheus Unbound*, *TrGF* 192 = Strabo 1.2.27.
63. Herodotus 7.69–70. On western Ethiopians, see Lonis 1981, analyzing the representation as a three-stage development: mythological, anthropological, and then political. The "western" Ethiopians of Diodorus of Sicily 3.2–11 are those south of Egypt; cf. Desanges 1993.
64. Ephorus, book 4, *FGrHist* 70 F 30 = Pausanias of Damascus, *Periplus* 167–182 + Strabo 1.2.28 + Cosmas Indicopleustes, 2, p. 148; Ephorus, F 128 = Strabo 1.2.26; and Ephorus, F 131 = Pausanias of Damascus, *Periplus* 183–187 + Strabo 4.4.6. Cf. Müller 1972, 224–228, on Ephorus; see Rankin 1987, 1–14, 34–41, 45–56; Dobesch 1995, 25–39; and Bichler 2000, 73–77, on early Greek views of western Celts; and see Wells 2001, 74–83, on Greek perceptions of Celts.
65. Tribes to the north and west: *Iliad* 13.5–6, on which see Janko 1992, 42–43, and Romm 1992, 49–54; sunset Ethiopians: *Iliad* 1.423 and *Odyssey* 1.23–24.
66. Pindar, *Pythian* 10.27–44. Aeschylus spoke of the just "Gabioi" and of the law-abiding, mare-milking Scythians in *Prometheus Unbound* (*TrGF* 196 = Stephanus of Byzantium, s.v. "Abioi" and 198 = Strabo 7.3.7). See Romm 1992, 60–67.

67. Herodotus 1.71 and 9.122; on the latter, see Flower and Marincola 2002, 311–314. On noble Ethiopians, see Herodotus 3.21-23; cf. Romm 1992, 55-58.
68. *Airs, Waters, Places*, 12–24. Cf. Romm 1992, 67-77, citing also the Arismaspians from Herodotus 4.16 and Ctesias, *FGrHist* 688 F 45h = Aelian, *History of Animals* 4.27.
69. Ephorus, *FGrHist* 70 F 42 = Strabo 7.3.9; cf. Romm 1992, 45-49.
70. Plato, *Republic* 4 (435e), although in the *Politicus* 262de he denied the propriety of the dichotomy between Greek and barbarian. In *Laws* 1 (637d-e) he referred to drunken, bellicose peoples such as Scythians, Celts, Iberians, and Thracians. The Celts and Iberians were first brought to Greece by Dionysius in 368/367 BC: Xenophon, *Hellenica* 7.1.20 and Diodorus of Sicily 15.70. On the *Republic* passage, see Adam 1902, ad loc., and Müller 1972, 185-194; on the views of Plato and Aristotle about Celts, see Rankin 1987, 54-55.
71. Aristotle, *Politics* 7.6 (1327 b18-29). See Stewart 1892, 289; Newman 1902, 363-366; and Müller 1972, 197-208, esp. 203-204.
72. Celts take up arms against the sea: Aristotle, *Nicomachean Ethics*. 3.7 (1115 b24-28); cf. Aristotle, *Eudemean Ethics* 3.1 (1229 b25-30). European barbarians, unlike Asians, are illiterate: Androtion, *FGrHist* 324 F 54a = Aelian, *Historical Miscellany* 8.6. Kelts act by *thumos*, not by reasoning: Polybius 2.35.2-3. On the Androtion fragment, see Harding 1994, 73, 180-182; on Celts attacking the waters, see Rankin 1987, 56-59, comparing *Iliad* 21, Aeschylus, *Persae* 744-751, and Herodotus 7.33-35.
73. Lived only for war: *Politics* 7.2 (1324 b5-12); inured to cold: *Politics* 7.15 (1336 a3-18).
74. Tin to Massalia: Pytheas, T23 Roseman = Pliny 4.104. Timaeus, *FGrHist* 566 F 74 = Pliny 4.104 and F 164.21-22 = Diodorus of Sicily 5.21-22 offered a similar story, on which see Geffcken 1892, 159-160. Timaeus, F164.21.3-4 repeats Pytheas, T1a Roseman (= Strabo 1.4.3), and I assign Timaeus F164.21.5-6 (Diodorus of Sicily 5.21.5-6) to Pytheas as well.
75. Theopompus, *FGrHist* 115 F 75c = Aelian, *Historical Miscellany* 3.18; see also Theopompus, *Philippika* book 8, F 62 = Athenaeus, *Deipnosophists* 12 (526d). Cf. Müller 1972, 223-224.
76. Cole 1967/1990.
77. See Plato, *Laws* 3 (676a-683a), on which see Müller 1972, 189-191; Polybius, book 6, fr. 5.5-9 (Byz.), on which see Walbank 1957, 1.650-653; Lucretius 5.932-1457; and Diodorus of Sicily 1.8 - all traced to Democritus by Cole 1967/1990, 60-130.
78. Lucretius 5.937-952, to which compare Hesiod, *Works and Days*, 117-118. See Bailey 1947/1998, 1472-1474; Fowler and Fowler in Melville et al. 1997, 257-259; and Schrijvers 1999, 88-90, contrasting the view of Dicaearchus, *Bios Hellados* fr. 49 Wehrli = Porphyry, *Abstinence* 4.2, that early life was hard.
79. Lucretius 5.1014-1027, on which see Bailey 1947/1998, 1483-1484; Fowler and Fowler in Melville et al. 1997, 257-259; and Schrijvers 1999, 102-107.
80. Lucretius 5.1416-1435, on which see Bailey 1947/1998, 1539-1541.
81. Herodotus 4.110-117, on which see Cole 1967/1990, 143-145.
82. Megasthenes, *FGrHist* 715 F 12.2-4 = Arrian, *Indika* 7.2-4. See Müller 1972, 245-252, esp. 250-251; Dognini in *EANS* 537. The Fish-eaters in Herodotus 3.21-23 serve as spies to mediate an exemplum (the Ethiopians), not as exempla themselves.

83. Nearchus, *FGrHist* 133 F 1.29.9–16 = Arrian, *Indika* 29.9–16; cf. Strabo 15.2.2, 13; Diodorus of Sicily 17.105.3–5; and Q. Curtius Rufus 9.10.8–10. The Oritans are in F 1.24.9 = Arrian, *Indika* 24.9. See Müller 1972, 236–240; Kaplan in *EANS* 568–569.

84. Agatharchides, *On the Red Sea*, book 5, frr. 32–36; see fr. 31 for their nakedness and their community of women and children; for their naturally happy state, see frr. 38 and 49. Cf. Müller 1972, 281–290; Burstein 1989, 68–89; and Burstein in *EANS* 40–41.

85. Strabo 4.5.4, possibly from Pytheas, though Roseman omits. On cannibalism among barbarians, see, e.g., Herodotus 1.216.2–3, 3.38, 3.99, 4.26, 4.106; Ephorus, book 4, *FGrHist* 70 F 42 = Strabo 7.3.9; Aristotle, *Nicomachean Ethics* 7.5 (1148 b19–24); and Diodorus of Sicily 5.32.3–6. Cf. Hall 1989, 27, 105; Bichler 2000, 48–49; and Bianchetti 2002.

86. Pytheas, F7 Roseman = Strabo 4.5.5; cf. also Diodorus of Sicily 5.26.

87. Ephorus, book 4, *FGrHist* 70 F 42 = Strabo 7.3.9, in contrast to the cannibals.

88. Ptolemy, *FGrHist* 138 F 2 = Strabo 7.3.8 = Arrian, *Anabasis* 1.4.6–8; cf. Hammond 1993, 194. Rankin 1987, 59–60, and 1995, 24, suggests an apotropaic prayer, but I wonder if it could be an *adunaton* in an oath.

89. Dionysius of Halicarnassus, *Roman Antiquities* 1.6.1, preserves four testimonia from the third century BC: Antigonos of Carystos, *FGrHist* 816 T 1; Hieronymus of Cardia, *FGrHist* 154 F 13; Silenus, *FGrHist* 175 T 4; and Timaeus, *FGrHist* 566 T 9c. Moreover, Dionysius of Halicarnassus, *Roman Antiquities* 1.72.1–5, preserves several fifth- or fourth-century notes: Damastes of Sigeum, *FGrHist* 5 F 3; Hellanicus of Lesbos, *FGrHist* 4 F 84; Aristotle, *Barbarian Customs*, fr. 609 Rose (*FGrHist* 840 F 13a); Callias of Syracuse, *FGrHist* 564 F 5; and one author of about 195 BC masquerading as an early author: Hegesianax of Alexandria Troas ("Cephalon of Gergis"), *FGrHist* 45 F 9. Theopompus, *FGrHist* 115 F 317 = Pliny 3.57 is another fourth-century note.

90. Hesiod, *Theogony* 1011–1016, which West 1966, 433–436, suggests may date to the late sixth century, but Malkin 1998, 180–183, argues for an eighth-century date. On Etruscan appropriation of the Greek hero Odysseus, see Malkin 1998, 156–177.

91. Heracleides of Pontos, fr. 102 Wehrli = Plutarch, *Camillus* 22.2–4; cf. also Heracleides fr. 103 Wehrli = Seruius, *Commentary on the Aeneid* 1.273. Perhaps cf. also the legend of the Hyperborean foundation of Delphi in Alcaeus of Mytilene, fr. 307c Page = Himerius, *Oration* 48.10–11 and in Herodotus 4.33–35.

92. Cf. Hoffmann 1934, 104–128.

93. Cf. Grant 1980, 68–81; Gras 1985, 583–651. For Persian luxury, cf. Aeschylus, *Persians* 249–252; Herodotus 1.133 and 9.82; Thucydides 1.130; and Xenophon, *Agesilaus* 9.3. On Herodotus 9.82 see Flower and Marincola 2002, 251–253. Cf. also Briant 1989/2002.

94. Pelasgians were or became "Tyrsenoi" and had lived on Lemnos, according to four fifth-century authors: Aeschylus, *Suppliants* 250–270; Sophocles, *Inachos*, *TrGF* 270 = Dionysius of Halicarnassus, *Roman Antiquities* 1.25.2; Thucydides 4.109; and in two works of Hellanicus of Lesbos, the *Phoronis*, *FGrHist* 4 F 4 = Dionysius of Halicarnassus, *Roman Antiquities* 1.28.3, and 4 F 92 = Stephanus of Byzantium, s.v. "Metaon," and the *Founding of Chios*, *FGrHist* 4 F 71 = *Scholia to the Odyssey* 8.294 + *Scholia to Apollonius of Rhodes* 1.608. These authors were followed by Anticleides of Athens, *FGrHist* 140 F 21 = Strabo 5.2.4, and by Dionysius of

Halicarnassus, *Roman Antiquities* 1.26-29. Herodotus 1.57, 6.137-140, however, distinguished the Pelasgians from the Tyrrhenians. Greeks found Pelasgians in many places (Sourvinou-Inwood 2003), and some Pelasgians were described as apparently speaking Greek – although so were the Trojans.

95. Seafarers and naval warriors: Herodotus 1.165-167; Pindar, *Pythian* 1.71-75; Thucydides 6.88.6, 6.103.2, 7.57.11; and Diodorus of Sicily 20.61.6-7. Cf. Richardson 1964, 75-78.

96. Gras 1985, 681-694; Strabo 5.2.3 mentions the treasury of the Etruscan city Agylla (Caere) at Delphi.

97. Critias, fr. 88 B 2.4-5 DK = Athenaeus, *Deipnosophists* 1 (28b) + 15 (700c); Theopompus, *History* book 43, *FGrHist* 115 F 204 = Athenaeus, *Deipnosophists* 12 (517d-518b); Alcimos, *FGrHist* 560 F 3 = Athenaeus, *Deipnosophists* 11 (518b); Timaeus, book 1, *FGrHist* 566 F 1 = Athenaeus, *Deipnosophists* 4 (153d) + 12 (517d); Posidonius, *History* book 2, fr. 53 EK = Athenaeus, *Deipnosophists* 4 (153d); and Dionysius of Halicarnassus, *Roman Antiquities* 9.16.8. As Nancy de Grummond has pointed out to me, although these six citations range from the late fifth century through the mid-first, because five are from Athenaeus, we may be receiving a biased image; cf. Liébert 2006.

98. Stoning: Herodotus 1.167; cf. Herodotus 5.38 and Plato, *Laws* 9 (873ac). Torture: Aristotle, *Protrepticus*, fr. 60 Rose = Iamblichus, *Protrepticus* 8 + Vergil, *Aeneid* 8.478-488. See Gras 1985, 425-472.

99. *Homeric Hymn to Dionysus* 6-15; Philochorus of Athens, *FGrHist* 328 F 100 = *Scholia to Lucian "Voyage Downwards"* 25; *Syll.* 1225 (dated to about 280 BC); Diodorus of Sicily 5.9.4-5, 11.88.4-5; Strabo 5.2.2, 6.2.10; and Pausanias 10.11.3-4, 10.16.7. See Giuffrida Ientile 1983; Gras 1985, 514-529.

100. Briquel 1993.

101. Herodotus 1.94; cf. also Pausanias of Damascus, *Periplus* 220-221, and Strabo 5.2.1-2; see Briquel 1991.

102. Herodotus 1.7-22, 25-29, and already in Xenophanes fr. 21 B 3 DK = Athenaeus, *Deipnosophists* 12 (526a); note the tale of Solon's reaction to Croesus's wealth, Herodotus 1.30-33. Cf. Bichler 2000, 215-218.

103. Polybius, book 34, fr. 5.1-6.10 = Strabo 2.4.1-2; cf. Marcotte 2006. On the voyage of Polybius, see Roller 2006, 92-104.

104. Aelian, *History of Animals* 13.15: Iberian rabbits (*konikloi*); 13.16: tuna fishing with hooks, not nets, among the Celts, Massaliotes, and Ligurians; 15.8: British freshwater pearl oysters; 15.25: Celtic horses foddered on fish.

105. Diyllos, *FGrHist* 73, but omitted by Jacoby: Diodorus of Sicily 17.113.2; cf. Arrian, *Anabasis* 7.15.4 and Justin 12.13.1-2; and see Hammond 1983, 74; id. 1993, 298-299. Diyllos takes no account of Xenophon, *Hellenica* 7.1.20 (cited in note 70).

106. Callimachus, *Hymn to Delos* 171-187, with the scholion; Polybius 2.5.4, 2.7.6-10, 5.78.1-5; Pausanias 1.7.2; and see Rankin 1987, 100-101; 1995, 25-26.

107. Sicilian geography: Timaeus in pseudo-Aristotle, *Marvelous Things* 132-136, *FGrHist* 566 F 38 = Diodorus of Sicily 5.6.1, F 89-90 = Diodorus of Sicily 4.22-23, and F 164.2-12 (cf. 41, 90) = Diodorus of Sicily 5.2-12. Probably also Diodorus of Sicily 4.76-79, 4.83-85, and 11.89. See Geffcken 1892, 103-28; Müller 1972, 256-260; and Dueck 811-812 in *EANS*; on the pseudo-Aristotle passages, see Flashar 1972, 41, 137-140.

108. Illyria and Italy: pseudo-Aristotle, *Marvelous Things* 80-81, 93-95, 97, 102, 106-110. See Flashar 1972, 41, 107-108, 113-117, 121-127 (sections 80-81, 102,

and 106-110 definitely Timaeus, sections 93-95 and 97 perhaps Timaeus); Geffcken 1892, 129-50; *FGrHist* 566 omits.

109. Sardo and Cyrnos: pseudo-Aristotle, *Marvelous Things* 100 – see Flashar 1972, 41, 117-119 ("im Kern" Timaeus); Timaeus, book 2, *FGrHist* 566 F 3 = Polybius, book 12, fr. 3.7-8 (Byz.), and F 164.13-15 = Diodorus of Sicily 5.13-5; probably also Diodorus of Sicily 4.29-30, 81-82; see Geffcken 1892, 164-71.

110. Lifestyle of the Kyrnians: Timaeus, *FGrHist* 566 F 164.14 = Diodorus of Sicily 5.14.

111. Animals on Kyrnos: Polybius, book 12, fr. 3.9-4.4 (Byz.), denying Timaeus's claim of many wild animals and validating his own account of trumpet-summoned herds with the parallel of Italian swineherds likewise employing trumpets, book 12, fr. 4.5-12 (Byz.): see Walbank 1967, 2.322-323. Cf. also Varro, *Farming* 2.4.20.

112. Free Sardinians: Timaeus, *FGrHist* 566 F 164.15 = Diodorus of Sicily 5.15.

113. See pseudo-Aristotle, *Marvelous Things* 91 – see Flashar 1972, 41, 112-113 (perhaps Timaeus), and Geffcken 1892, 151; *FGrHist* 566 omits. Cf. also Diodorus of Sicily 4.20.2-3; Varro, *Farming* 2.10.9 (of Illyria); Posidonius, fr. 269 EK = Strabo 3.4.17.

114. Naked folk: Timaeus covered the "Gymnasiai" (naked) isles, *FGrHist* 566 F 65-66 = Strabo 14.2.10 + *Scholia to Lykophron "Alexandra"* 633, and recorded their inhabitants' nudity, F 164.17.1 = Diodorus of Sicily 5.17.1.

115. Timaeus, *FGrHist* 566 F 164.17.3-18.1 = Diodorus of Sicily 5.17.3-5.18.1.

116. Heracles's highway: pseudo-Aristotle, *Marvelous Things* 85 – see Flashar 1972, 41, 110 (perhaps Timaeus); *FGrHist* 566 omits; cf. Rankin 1987, 53-54.

117. See Lucretius 5.1241-1261; pseudo-Aristotle, *Marvelous Things* 87 – see Flashar 1972, 41, 110-111 (perhaps Timaeus); *FGrHist* 566 omits; Posidonius, fr. 239 EK = Strabo 3.2.9, cf. Diodorus of Sicily 5.35.3; perhaps cf. Democritus, *On Fire and Things in Fire*; see Cole 1967/1990, 57.

118. Silver anchors: pseudo-Aristotle, *Marvelous Things* 135 – see Flashar 1972, 41, 139 (definitely Timaeus); cf. Diodorus of Sicily 5.35-36; *FGrHist* 566 omits.

119. Blessed isle: pseudo-Aristotle, *Marvelous Things* 84 – see Flashar 1972, 41, 109-110 (definitely Timaeus), and Timaeus, *FGrHist* 566 F 164.19-20 = Diodorus of Sicily 5.19-20. Cf. Keyser 1993, 155-156.

120. Eratosthenes, book 3, fr. B.116 Berger = Roller F151 = Strabo 5.2.6. Cf. Müller 1972, 277-281, and Jones in *EANS* 297-300, on Eratosthenes in general. Corsica is visible from the coast of southern Tuscany.

121. Eratosthenes, book 3, fr. B.118 Berger = Roller F150 = Caesar, *Gallic War* 6.24. See text discussion on pages 51-52 for more on Caesar, *Gallic War* 6.

122. Eratosthenes, book 3, fr. B.122 Berger = Roller F153 = Strabo 3.2.11; cf. also Strabo 1.4.5.

123. Eratosthenes, book 3, fr. B.123 Berger = Roller F133 = Strabo 2.4.4; and book 3, fr. B.124 Berger (Roller omits) = Strabo 4.4.1.

124. Eratosthenes, book 3, fr. B.127 Berger (Roller omits) = Diodorus of Sicily 5.21.

125. Eratosthenes, book 2, fr. A.8 Berger = Roller F16 = Strabo 1.3.13.

126. Eratosthenes, book 2, fr. A.6 Berger = Roller F33 = Strabo 1.4.6; cf. Aristotle, *On the Heaven* 2.14 (298 a9-15) and *Meteorology* 2.5 (362 b28-30).

127. Eratosthenes, book 1, fr. B.21 Berger = Roller F20 = Strabo 1.3.22.

128. Prontera 2006.

129. Cf. Müller 1972, 295-306; Rankin 1987, 72-75; and Dueck in *EANS* 680-681. Polybius's general view was that Celts were found from Narbo to the Pyrenees, beyond which was Iberia, inhabited by many kinds of barbarians: 3.37.9.

130. Polybius, book 34, fr. 8b = Athenaeus, *Deipnosophists* 8 (330c); cf. Walbank 1979, 3.601–602.
131. Polybius, book 34, fr. 8a = Athenaeus, *Deipnosophists* 7 (302e) + Strabo 3.2.7; although Theophrastus, *History of Plants* 4.6.9, also has sea-rooted oak, it was likely a marine plant such as *Sargassum vulgare*, C.Agardh: cf. Walbank 1979, 3.599–600.
132. Polybius, book 34, fr. 9.3 = Strabo 3.2.15.
133. Polybius, book 34, fr. 9.8–11 = Strabo 3.2.10: cf. Walbank 1979, 3.605–607.
134. Polybius, book 34, fr. 10.1–4 = Athenaeus, *Deipnosophists* 8 (332a); cf. Strabo 4.1.6. The same marvel is recorded in three other passages: First, Aristotle, *History of Animals* 6.15 (569 a10–b16), which is not localized; second, Theophrastus, *On Fish*, fr. 363.3 FHSG = Athenaeus, *Deipnosophists* 8 (331cd) + pseudo-Aristotle, *Marvelous Things* 73, of Rhegion in Sicily (emended to Tios by Flashar) and of Heracleia Pontica; third, Eudoxus, book 3, fr. 77 Gisinger = Strabo 12.3.42 + pseudo-Aristotle, *Marvelous Things* 74 of Paphlagonia. On the Polybius fragment, see Walbank 1979, 3.610–611. On the Theophrastus fragment, see Sharples 1995, 87–88. On the passages from pseudo-Aristotle, see Flashar 1972, 41, 103–104, referring the citation in Strabo 12 to Eudoxus of Rhodes (about 240 BC), who was probably following Theophrastus.
135. Polybius, book 34, fr. 10.8–9 = Strabo 4.6.10: cf. Walbank 1979, 3.612, citing Pausanias 5.12.1, and 9.21.3 describing the method of hunting the elk as surrounding an area and then walking inward. I wonder if the *tarandos*, described as dwelling among the Scythians, having the size of a cow and the head of a deer, may be relevant: Theophrastus, *Creatures That Change Color*, fr. 365 FHSG = Photius, *Library* 278 (p. 525ab) + pseudo-Aristotle, *Marvelous Things* 30, on which see Flashar 1972, 40, 82, and Sharples 1995, 90–92.
136. Polybius, book 34, fr. 10.10–14 = Strabo 4.6.12: cf. Walbank 1979, 3.612–613; Diodorus of Sicily 5.27.1–2 of Gaul; Strabo 4.1.13 of the Tectosages, 4.2.1 of the Tarbelli on the Aquitanian coast.
137. Polybius, book 34, fr. 10.15–21 = Strabo 4.6.12: cf. Walbank 1957, 1.174–175 and 1979, 3.613–615 citing Polybius 2.14.6, 2.15.8–10, 3.39.9 on the Alps, the earliest extant reference to the Alps as such. Mountains are proven large by containing lakes in Aristotle, *Meteorology* 1.13 (350 a33–35), of the Caucasus.
138. Volatile: Polybius 2.7 and 2.17.1–7. Bellicose: Polybius 2.22, books 9, fr. 24.4 (Byz.), 18, fr. 41.7 (Byz.), and 22, fr. 21 (Byz.) + *Souda* O–639, s.v. "Ortiagon"; cf. Caesar, *Gallic War* 3.10.3 and 3.19.6. Fickle: Polybius 3.70.4 and 3.78.2. Simple folk: Polybius 2.17.8–12. Prone to drinking and fighting: Polybius 2.19.2–4 and book 11, fr. 3.1 (Byz.); cf. Diodorus of Sicily, book 23, fr. 21 (Byz.). Violators of festivals, like Scythians: Polybius, book 9, fr. 34.11 (Byz.). Driven by *thumos*, Polybius 2.35.2–3. See Eckstein 1995, 119–125; Rankin 1995, 28.
139. Nechepso-Petosiris on eclipses: fr. 6 Riess = Hephaestion 1.21; on comets: fr. 9 Riess = Joannes Laurentius "Lydus," *On Divination* 11–15, fr. 10 Riess = Hephaestion 1.24, and fr. 11 Riess = "Seruius Auctus," *Commentary on the Aeneid* 10.272. For the date of the work, see Fournet 2000; and Rochberg in *EANS* 637–638.
140. Ptolemy, *Tetrabiblos* 2.2. For pale, wet Scythians, cf. Diodorus of Sicily 5.28.1 and Galen, *Mixtures* 2.5 (1.616–618 K.), 2.6 (1.627–628 K.).
141. Earlier, Aristotle, *Politics* 2.6 (1269 b23–31), Diodorus of Sicily 5.32.7, and Strabo 4.4.6 also recorded the Celtic predilection for homosexuality. For claims that homosexuality was the more manly sort of love, see Plato, *Symposium* 178c–79b

(Phaidros's speech), 181bd (Pausanias's speech), 191e-192b (Aristophanes's speech), 208c-210b (Diotima's speech); Xenophon, *Symposium* 8.32-38; Ephorus, *FGrHist* 70 F149 = Strabo 10.4.21 (Crete); and Plutarch, *Pelopidas* 18-19.

142. Cf. Müller 1972, 291-292; Dueck in *EANS* 165.

143. Strabo 3.1.4-5; cf. Gallazzi and Kramer 1998; but note that Micunco 2006 and Canfora 2006 cast doubt on the authenticity of many aspects of this papyrus; the further debate has spawned an immense literature.

144. Strabo 3.4.17; cf. the mantilla headdress of modern Spain.

145. Compare note 15 on Tartessus; written laws in Strabo 3.1.6, 3.2.4-8 and cited as a sign of civilization by Gorgias, *Palamedes* 30 (fr. 82 B11a.30 DK); Euripides, *Suppliants* 430-437; Isocrates, *Panegyricus* 32-40; and *Syll.* 704.E.11-22 (dated to 117 BC). Written laws are epigraphically attested in Greece by about 650 BC: Gagarin 1986, 81-97; Garner 1987, 136-140 dates the use of law as a sign of civilization to the early fourth century BC.

146. On Posidonius as ethnographer, see Müller 1972, 310-347; Rankin 1987, 75-80; Dobesch 1995, 59-110; and Lehoux in *EANS* 691-692.

147. On Caesar as ethnographer, see Müller 1980, 67-79; Lund 1996; and Siebenborn 1998.

148. Rankin 1995, 26-27, suggesting the influence of rhetorical *topoi*.

149. Frozen rivers: Diodorus of Sicily 5.25.2-5. Wind pushing stones: Posidonius, fr. 229 EK = Strabo 4.1.7; cf. Diodorus of Sicily 5.26.1. Gallic gold: Posidonius, fr. 273 EK = Strabo 4.1.13.

150. Champion's portion: Diodorus of Sicily 5.28.4, to which cf. Posidonius, fr. 275 EK = Eustathius, *Commentary on the Odyssey* 8.475 and fr. 68 EK = Athenaeus, *Deipnosophists* 4 (154ac). See Rankin 1987, 60-62, comparing *Iliad* 9.208.

151. Wise men: Diodorus of Sicily 5.31.5; cf. Strabo 4.4.4. See Rankin 1987, 69-70.

152. See Diodorus of Sicily 5.32.3-6 (cannibalism), 5.29.4-5 (trophy heads), and 5.26.2-3 (beer). On cannibalism, see note 85. On trophy heads see esp. de Grummond, Chapter 10, in this volume; on Celtic trophy heads, cf. also Polybius 2.28.10, 3.67.3, Diodorus of Sicily 14.115.5, and Posidonius, *History*, book 23, fr. 274 EK = Strabo 4.4.5; on Scythian trophy heads see Herodotus 4.64, 103, and Sophocles, *Oinomaus*, TrGF 432 = Athenaeus, *Deipnosophists* 9 (410c). See Reinach 1913; Hartog 1988, 157-160; and Green 2001, 93-110, emphasizing the ritual nature of such trophies. On Western beer, cf. also Polybius, book 34, fr. 10.14-15 = Athenaeus, *Deipnosophists* 1 (16c) and Posidonius, fr. 67 EK = Athenaeus, *Deipnosophists* 4 (151e-152f).

153. Fighting naked: Polybius 2.28.8, 2.29.7, 2.30.2-3, and 3.114.4; Diodorus of Sicily 5.29.2 and 5.30.3. On the first Polybius passage, cf. Walbank 1957, 1.205; on the *topos*, see Rankin 1987, 68-69.

154. Divinatory human sacrifice: Strabo 3.3.6, 4.4.5, and 7.2.3; Diodorus of Sicily 5.31. Propitiatory human sacrifice was also alleged of barbarians by Herodotus, 4.62, 4.103, 7.114, and 7.197; by Isocrates, *Bousiris* 5, 36-37 (of Egyptians); and by Strabo 3.3.7. Propitiatory human sacrifice was alleged of Carthaginians in pseudo-Plato, *Minos* 315 BC, and in two fragments of Theophrastus (*On Piety* fr. 584a FHSG = Porphyry, *Abstinence* 2.27.2 and *On Etruscans* fr. 586 FHSG = *Scholia to Pindar "Pythian"* 2.2), as well as later by Diodorus of Sicily 20.14.4-6 and Plutarch, *Superstition* 13 (171b-d). It is found throughout Roman sources and is apparently confirmed by archaeology: Green 2001, 75-76, 153-154. Cf. Burkert 1985, 59-60, 65-66, 82-84, 149-152; Hall 1989, 146-148; Hughes 1991, 71-138; Burkert 1996, 53-55, 75-77, 108-110; and Bichler 2000, 54-56.

155. Wicker cages: Caesar, *Gallic War* 6.16.4–5; cf. Strabo 4.4.5 and perhaps Diodorus of Sicily 5.32.6.
156. Caesar, *Gallic War* 6.14.5. Strabo 4.4.4 simply records the belief in metempsychosis, while Diodorus of Sicily 5.28.6 and Timagenes of Alexandria, *FGrHist* 88 F 2.8 = Ammianus Marcellinus 15.9.8, attribute it to Pythagorean influence. On Timagenes and this fragment see Müller 1972, 292–294.
157. Caesar, *Gallic War* 6.14.3–4; cf. 1.29. Plato preferred the living word: *Phaedrus* 274c–275e.
158. Honoring dedications: Caesar, *Gallic War* 6.17.4–5; cf. Diodorus of Sicily 5.27.4.
159. Clothes: Diodorus of Sicily 5.30.1; cf. Strabo 4.4.3.
160. Caesar, *Gallic War* 6.19.1–2; Celtiberian daughters inherited according to Strabo 3.4.18. Contrast Greek law: MacDowell 1978, 92–108; Gagarin 1986, 67–69, 94–95.
161. Caesar, *Gallic War* 6.19.4–5, to which contrast Greek law: MacDowell 1978, 109; Gagarin 1986, 67. Some funerary potlatches involved human sacrifice: *Iliad* 23 and Herodotus 4.72–73; and cf. Hughes 1991, 49–70.
162. Spirited Celts: Strabo 4.4.2; boastful Celts: Strabo 4.4.5 and Diodorus of Sicily 5.31.1.
163. Strabo 4.1.2 and 4.1.14.
164. Caesar, *Gallic War* 6.21–22, to which compare Tacitus, *Germania* 7–27.
165. Fabled forest: *Gallic War* 6.25; unicorn: *Gallic War* 6.26; elks with unbending legs: *Gallic War* 6.27. The unicorn is from Ctesias, *FGrHist* 688 F 45q = Photius, *Library* 72 (p. 48b) + Aelian, *History of Animals* 4.52, to which compare Aristotle, *Parts of Animals* 3.2 (663 a18–23) and *History of Animals* 2.1 (499 b15–20). Henke 1998 argues that *Gallic War* 6.25–28 is a late antique interpolation.
166. Aristotle, *History of Animals* 2.1 (498 a3–13) and *Progression of Animals* 9 (709 a8–10). Although Aristotle did not attribute the tale of elephants' unbending legs to anyone, Ctesias is Aristotle's most likely source of tall tales about elephants: cf. Ctesias, *FGrHist* 688 F 48b = Aristotle, *Generation of Animals* 2.2 (736 a2–5), claiming that dried elephant semen is as hard as amber. On Greek knowledge of elephants, see Scullard 1974, 32–60.
167. Agatharchides, fr. 56 = Diodorus of Sicily 3.27.1–4 + Strabo 16.4.10. See Burstein 1989, 98–99.
168. See Hartog 1988, 212–216, 258–259 and Wells 2001, 30–31; for modern parallels, see Diamond 1992, 217–221, 228–231, 276–309.
169. Hannig 1995, 301, 584–585; 2000, 109 s.v. "Ausländer" and 131 s.v. "Barbar."
170. The adjectival form is *nakru*, and noun forms are *nakaru* and *nakiru*: see Reiner et al. 1980, 189–195.
171. Watson 1989, xxvi: *ssu* means "four," and traditionally there were four of these "foreigner" tribes.

Bibliography

Abbreviations:
AJA = *American Journal of Archaeology*
DK = Diels and Kranz
EANS = Keyser and Irby-Massie
EK = Edelstein and Kidd
FGrHist = Jacoby

FHSG = Fortenbaugh et al.
POxy = Grenfell et al.
Syll. = Dittenberger and von Gaertringen
TrGF = Snell et al.

Various authors. 1994. *Cartago, Gadir, Ebusus y la Influencia Púnica en los Territorios Hispanos.* Ibiza. = *Trabajos del Museo Arqueológico de Iberia* 33.

Various authors. 1995. *Tartessos: 25 Años después.* Jerez de la Frontera. = *Biblioteca de Urbanismo y Cultura* 14.

Adam, James. 1902. *The Republic of Plato*, vol. 1. Cambridge.

Allen, Archibald. 1993. *The Fragments of Mimnermus.* Stuttgart.

Andreotti, Gonzalo Cruz, Patrick le Roux, and Pierre Moret, eds. 2006. *La Invención de una Geografía de la Península Ibérica*, vol. 1, *La Época Republicana.* Málaga and Madrid.

Arrighetti, Gr. 1966. "Cosmologia Mitica di Omero e Esiodo." *Studi italiani di filologia classica* 15:1-60.

Aubet, Maria Eugenia. 2001. *The Phoenicians and the West: politics, colonies and trade.* 2nd ed. Cambridge.

Austin, Norman. 1973. "The One and the Many in the Homeric Cosmos." *Arion* 1:219-274.

     1975. *Archery at the Dark of the Moon.* Berkeley, CA.

Bailey, Cyril. 1947/1998. *Titi Lucreti Cari De Rerum Natura*, vol. 3. Oxford.

Ballabriga, Alain. 1986. *Le Soleil et le Tartare.* Paris.

     1998. *Fictions d'Homère.* Paris.

Barrett, W. S. 1964. *Euripides Hippolytos.* Oxford.

Berger, Hugo. 1880. *Die geographischen Fragmente des Eratosthenes.* Leipzig.

Bianchetti, S. 1990. "Avieno, *Ora mar.* 80 ss.: le colonne d'Eracle e il vento del nord." *Sileno* 16: 241-246.

     2002. "Cannibali in Irlanda? Letture Straboniane." *Ancient Society* 32:295-314.

Bichler, Reinhold. 2000. *Herodots Welt.* Berlin.

Bickermann, E. J. 1952. "Origines Gentium." *Classical Philology* 47:65-81.

Bierling, Marilyn J., and Seymour Gitin, eds. 2001. *The Phoenicians in Spain: An Archaeological Review of the Eighth–Sixth Centuries B.C.E.* Winona Lake, IN.

Briant, P. 1989/2002. "Histoire et idéologie: les Grecs et la 'décadence perse'." In *Mélanges P. Lévêque*, vol. 2 (Besançon), ed. M.-M. Mactoux and E. Geny, 33-47, translated by Antonia Nevill as "History and Ideology: The Greeks and 'Persian Decadence'. In *Greeks and Barbarians*, ed. Thos. Harrison. New York and London.

Briquel, Dominique. 1991. *L'origine lydienne des Etrusques: Histoire de la doctrine dans l'antiquité.* Rome.

     1993. *Les Tyrrhènes, peuple des tours: Denys d'Halicarnasse et l'autochtonie des Etrusques.* Rome.

Burkert, Walter. 1985. *Greek Religion*, translated by John Raffan. Cambridge, MA.
     1996. *Creation of the Sacred.* Cambridge, MA.

Burstein, Stanley M. 1989. *Agatharchides of Cnidus: On the Erythraean Sea.* London.

Canfora, L. 2006. "Postilla Testuale Sul Nuovo Artemidoro." *Quaderni di Storia* 64:45–60.

Chamorro, Javier G. 1987. "Survey of Archaeological Research on Tartessos." *AJA* 91:197–232.

Champion, Timothy C. 1985. "Written Sources and the Study of the European Iron Age." In Champion and Megaw 1985, 9–22.

Champion, Timothy C., and J. V. S. Megaw, eds. 1985. *Settlement and Society: Aspects of West European Prehistory in the First Millennium B.C.* Leicester.

Cole, Thomas. 1967/1990. *Democritus and the Sources of Greek Anthropology.* Chapel Hill, NC, and Chico, CA.

Cunliffe, Barry. 2001. *The Extraordinary Voyage of Pytheas the Greek.* London.
———. 2008. *Europe Between the Oceans 9000 BC–AD 1000.* New Haven and London.

De Romilly, Jacqueline. 1993. "Les Barbares dans la pensée de la Grèce classique." *Phoenix* 47: 283–292.

Derow, Peter, and Robert Parker, eds. 2003. *Herodotus and His World.* Oxford.

Desanges, Jehan. 1993. "Diodore de Sicile et les Éthiopiens d'Occident." *Comptes-rendus des séances de l'Académie des Inscriptions et Belles-Lettres* 137 (2): 525–541.

Diamond, Jared. 1992. *The Third Chimpanzee.* New York.

Diels, Hermann, and Walther Kranz. 1996. *Die Fragmente der Vorsokratiker*, 6th ed., 3 vols. Berlin. Originally published in 1951.

Dilke, O. A. W. 1985. *Greek and Roman Maps.* London.

Dittenberger, Wilhelm, and Fr. H. von Gaertringen. 1915–1924. *Sylloge inscriptionum graecarum*, 3rd ed., 4 vols. Leipzig.

Dobesch, Gerhard. 1995. *Das europäische «Barbaricum» und die Zone der Mediterrankultur.* Vienna.

Eckstein, A. M. 1995. *Moral Vision in the Histories of Polybius.* Berkeley, CA.

Edelstein, L., and I. G. Kidd. 1989–1999. *Posidonius*, 3 vols. = *Cambridge Classical Texts and Commentaries*, vols. 13, 14, 36. Cambridge.

Epperlein, S. 1971. "Zur Bedeutungsgeschichte von 'Europa,' 'Hesperia,' und 'occidentalis' in der Antike und im frühen Mittelalter." *Philologus* 115: 81–92.

Finney, B. R. 1976. *Pacific Navigation and Voyaging* = Polynesian Society Memoir 39. Wellington, New Zealand.

Flashar, Hellmut. 1972. *Aristoteles Werke in deutscher Übersetzungen*, vol. 18.2, *Mirabilia.* Berlin.

Flower, M. A., and John Marincola. 2002. *Herodotus: Histories, Book IX.* Cambridge.

Fortenbaugh, W. W., P. M. Huby, Robert W. Sharples, and Dimitri Gutas. 1992, 1995–2006. *Theophrastus of Eresus: Sources for His Life, Writings, Thought and Influence*, 2 vols = *Philosophia Antiqua* 54; *Commentary*, vols. 2, 3.1, 4, 5, 8 (of nine projected) = *Philosophia Antiqua* 103, 79, 81, 64, 97 (respectively). Leiden.

Fortenbaugh, W. W., and Eckart Schütrumpf, eds. 2001. *Dicaearchus of Messana: Text, Translation, and Discussion.* New Brunswick, NJ, and London.

Fournet, Jean-Luc. 2000. "Un fragment de Néchepso." In Melaerts 2000, 61–71, plate 7.

Gagarin, Michael. 1986. *Early Greek Law*. Berkeley, CA.

Gallazzi, C., and B. Kramer. 1998. "Artemidor im Zeichensaal: Eine Papyrusrolle mit Text, Landkarte und Skizzenbüchern aus späthellenistischer Zeit." *Archiv für Papyrusforschung* 44:189–208.

Garner, Richard. 1987. *Law and Society in Classical Athens*. New York.

Geffcken, Johannes. 1892. *Timaios' Geographie des Westens = Philologische Untersuchungen* 13. Berlin.

Gehrke, H.-J. 2007. "Die Raumwahrnehmung im archaïschen Griechenland." In Rathmann 2007, 17–30.

Gentili, Bruno, and Carlo Prato. 1988. *Poetarum Elegiacorum Testimonia et Fragmenta*, 2nd ed. Leipzig.

Gerber, D. E. 1999. *Greek Elegiac Poetry*. Cambridge, MA.

Gisinger, Friedrich. 1921. *Die Erdbeschreibung des Eudoxos von Knidos*. Leipzig.

Giuffrida Ientile, Margherita. 1983. *La pirateria tirrenica: momenti e fortuna*. Rome.

Grant, Michael. 1980. *The Etruscans*. London.

Gras, Michel. 1985. *Trafics tyrrhéniens archaïques*. Rome.

Green, Monica J., ed. 1995. *The Celtic World*. London.

    2001. *Dying for the Gods: Human Sacrifice in Iron Age and Roman Europe*. Stroud, England.

Grenfell, Bernard P., Arthur S. Hunt, et al.. 1898ff. *The Oxyrhynchus papyri*, 67 vols. to date. London.

Guthrie, W. K. C. 1975. *A History of Greek Philosophy*, vol. 4. Cambridge.

Hall, Edith. 1989. *Inventing the Barbarian*. Oxford.

Hallpike, C. R. 1979. *The Foundations of Primitive Thought*, Oxford.

Hammond, N. G. L. 1983. *Three Historians of Alexander*. Cambridge.

    1993. *Sources for Alexander the Great*. Cambridge.

Hannig, Rainer. 1995, 2000. *Großes Handwörterbuch Ägyptisch-Deutsch; Großes Handwörterbuch Deutsch-Ägyptisch*. Mainz am Rhein.

Harding, Philip. 1994. *Androtion and the Atthis*. Oxford.

Harrison, R. J. 1988. *Spain at the Dawn of History: Iberians, Phoenicians and Greeks*. London.

Hartog, François. 1988. *The Mirror of Herodotus*, translated by Janet Lloyd. Berkeley, CA.

Hawke, Jason. 2008. "Number and Numeracy in Early Greek Literature," *Syllecta Classica* 19:1–76.

Heimpel, W. 1986. "The Sun at Night and the Doors of Heaven in Babylonian Texts." *Journal of Cuneiform Studies* 38:127–151.

Helck, Wolfgang, and Eberhard Otto, eds. 1973–1986. *Lexicon der Ägyptologie*, 6 vols. Wiesbaden.

Henke, Rainer. 1998. "Jägerlatein in Caesars *Bellum Gallicum* (6, 25–28): Original oder Fälschung?" *Gymnasium* 105:117–142.

Hodge, A. Trevor. 1998. *Ancient Greek France*. London.

Hoffmann, W. 1934. *Rom und die griechische Welt im 4. Jahrhundert = Philologus* S.27. Leipzig.

Horowitz, Wayne. 1998. *Mesopotamian Cosmic Geography*. Winona Lake, IN.

Hubbard, T. K. 1985. *The Pindaric Mind: A Study of Logical Structure in Early Greek Poetry*. Leiden.

Hughes, Dennis D. 1991. *Human Sacrifice in Ancient Greece*. London.

Jacoby, Felix. 1923–1958. *Die fragmente der griechischen historiker*. Berlin.

Janko, Richard. 1992. *The Iliad: A Commentary*, vol. 4. Cambridge.

Janowski, Bernd. 2007. "Vom natürlich zum symbolisch Raum. Aspekte der Raumwahrnehmung im Alten Testament." In Rathmann 2007, 51-64.

Jones, Siân. 1997. *The Archaeology of Ethnicity*. London.

Jouanna, Jacques. 1996. *Hippocrate: Airs, Eaux, Lieux*. Paris.

Keyser, Paul T. 1993. "From Myth to Map: The Blessed Isles in the First Century B.C." *The Ancient World* 24:149-168.

    2001. "The Geographical Work of Dikaiarchos." In Fortenbaugh and Schütrumpf 2001, 353-372.

Keyser, Paul T., and Georgia L. Irby-Massie. 2008. *Encyclopedia of Ancient Natural Scientists: The Greek Tradition and Its Many Heirs*. New York and London.

Kristiansen, Kristian. 1993. "'The Strength of the Past and Its Great Might': An Essay on the Use of the Past." *Journal of European Archaeology* 1:3-32.

Kurth, D. 1980. "Manu." In Helck and Otto 1973-1986, vol. 3, 1185-1186.

Liébert, Yves. 2006. *Regards sur la truphè étrusque*. Limoges.

Lloyd, G. E. R. 1966. *Polarity and Analogy*. Cambridge.

    1979. *Magic, Reason, and Experience*. Cambridge.

Lonis, Raoul. 1981. "Les trois approches de l'Éthiopien par l'opinion gréco-romaine." *Ktèma* 6:69-87.

Lund, Allan A. 1996. "Caesar als Ethnograph." *Der altsprachliche Unterricht* 39 (2): 12-23.

MacDowell, D. M. 1978. *The Law in Classical Athens*. London.

Malkin, Irad. 1998. *The Returns of Odysseus: Colonization and Ethnicity*. Berkeley, CA.

    1994/1999. *Myth and Territory in the Spartan Mediterranean*. Cambridge, 1994 = *La Méditerranée spartiate: mythe et territoire*, translated by Odile Meslier. Paris, 1999.

Marcotte, Didier. 2000. *Géographes Grecs*, vol. 1: *Ps.-Scymnos: Circuit de la Terre*. Paris.

    2006. "De l'Ibérie à la Celtique: Géographie et Chronographie du Monde occidental avant Polybe." In Andreotti et al. 2006, 31-38.

Melaerts, Henri, ed. 2000. *Papyri in Honorem Johannis Bingen Octogenarii*. Leuven.

Melville, Ronald, Don Fowler, and Peta Fowler. 1997. *Lucretius: On the Nature of the Universe*. Oxford.

Micunco, St. 2006. "Figure di animali: il verso del papiro di Artemidoro." *Quaderni di Storia* 64:5-43.

Moret, Pierre. 2006. "La formation d'une toponymie et d'une ethnonymie grecques de l'Ibérie: étapes et acteurs." In Andreotti et al. 2006, 39-76.

Müller, Klaus E. 1972, 1980. *Geschichte der antiken Ethnographie und ethnologischen Theoriebildung*. 2 vols. Wiesbaden.

Nakassis, Dimitri. 2004. "Gemination at the Horizons: East and West in the Mythical Geography of Archaic Greek Epic." *Transactions of the American Philological Association* 134:215–233.

Negbi, Ora. 1992. "Early Phoenician Presence in the Mediterranean Islands: A Reappraisal." *AJA* 96:599–615.

Newman, W. L. 1902. *The Politics of Aristotle*, vol. 3. Oxford.

Otto, Eberhard. 1975. "Bachu." In Helck and Otto 1973–1986, vol. 1, 594.

Page, D. L. 1962. *Poetae Melici Graeci*. Oxford.

Pérez, Sebastián Celestino. 2001. *Estelas de guerrero y estelas diademadas: La precolonización y formación del mundo Tartésico*. Barcelona.

Prontera, Francesco. 2006. "La penisola iberica nella cartografia ellenistica." In Andreotti et al. 2006, 15–29.

Rankin, David. 1987. *Celts and the Classical World*. London.

   1995. "The Celts through Classical Eyes." In Green 1995, 21–33.

Rathmann, Michael, ed. 2007. *Wahrnehmung und Erfahrung geographischer Räume in der Antike*. Mainz am Rhein.

Reinach, Adolphe. 1913. "Les Têtes coupées et les trophées en Gaule." *Revue Celtique* 34: 38–60.

Reiner, Erica, et al., eds. 1980. *The Assyrian Dictionary*, vol. 11. Chicago.

Richardson, Emeline H. 1964. *The Etruscans: Their Art and Civilization*. Reprint 1976. Chicago.

Riesenberg, S. H. 1976. "The Organization of Navigational Knowledge on Puluwat." In Finney 1976, 91–128.

Riess, Ernst. 1893. *Nechepsonis et Petosiridis Fragmenta Magica* = *Philologus S. 6*, Bonn, 325–394.

Roller, Duane W. 2006. *Through the Pillars of Herakles: Greco-Roman Exploration of the Atlantic*. London and New York.

   2010. *Eratosthenes' Geography: Fragments Collected and Translated, with Commentary and Additional Material*. Princeton, NJ, and Oxford.

Romm, James. 1992. *The Edges of the Earth in Greek Thought*. Princeton, NJ.

Rose, Valentine. 1886. *Aristotelis qui ferebantur librorum fragmenta*, 3rd ed. Leipzig.

Roseman, C. H. 1994. *Pytheas of Massalia: On the Ocean*. Chicago.

Rowe, C. J. 1993. *Plato: Phaedo*. Cambridge.

Ruiz, Arturo, and Manuel Molinos. 1998. *The Archaeology of the Iberians*, translated by Mary Turton. Cambridge.

Schrijvers, P. H. 1999. *Lucrèce et les sciences de la vie*. Leiden.

Scullard, H. H. 1974. *The Elephant in the Greek and Roman World*. Ithaca, NY.

Sharples, Robert W. 1995. *Theophrastus of Eresus: Sources for His Life, Writings, Thought and Influence: Commentary on Sources on Biology*. Leiden.

Siebenborn, Elmar. 1998. "Barbaren, Naturvölker, edle Wilde." *Der altsprachliche Unterricht* 41 (4–5): 18–31.

Snell, Bruno, Richard Kannicht, and Stefan Radt. 1986. *Tragicorum graecorum fragmenta*, 4 vols. Göttingen.

Solmsen, Friedrich, R. Merkelbach, and M. L. West. 1990. *Hesiodi Theogonia; Opera et dies; Scutum; fragmenta selecta*, 3rd ed. Oxford.

Sourvinou-Inwood, Christiane. 2003. "Herodotos (and Others) on Pelasgians: Some Perceptions of Ethnicity." In Derow and Parker 2003, 103–144.

Stewart, J. A. 1892. *Notes on the Nicomachean Ethics of Aristotle*. Oxford.

Strohm, Hans. 1970. *Aristoteles: Meteorologie, Über die Welt*. Berlin.

Thomson, James Oliver. 1948. *History of Ancient Geography*. Cambridge. Reprint 1965. New York.

Vernant, J.-P. 1957/1965/1983. "Du mythe à la raison: La formation de la pensée positive dans la Grèce archaïque." *Annales: Économies, Sociétés, Civilisations* 12:183–206, reprinted in *Mythe et Pensée chez les Grecs: Études de psychologie historique*, Paris, 285–314, translated as *Myth and Thought among the Greeks*, London, 343–374 ("The Formation of Positivist Thought in Archaic Greece"), French reprint (1985), 373–402.

Villar, Francisco, and Francisco Beltrán. 1997. *Pueblos, Lenguas y Escrituras en la Hispania Prerromana. Salamanca. = Acta Salamanticensia: Estudios filológicos* 273.

Walbank, F. W. 1957/1967/1979. *Historical Commentary on Polybius*, 3 vols. Oxford.

Watson, Burton. 1989. *Tso Chuan: Selections from China's Oldest Narrative History*. New York.

Wehrli, Fritz. 1967/1969. *Die Schule des Aristoteles: Texte und Kommentare*, 2nd ed., vol. 1, *Dikaiarchos*; vol. 7, *Herakleides Pontikos*. Basel.

Wells, Peter S. 2001. *Beyond Celts, Germans and Scythians: Archaeology and Identity in Iron Age Europe*. London.

West, M. L. 1966. *Hesiod: Theogony*. Oxford.

    1985. *The Hesiodic Catalogue of Women*. Oxford.

Wiesehöfer, J. 2007. "Ein König erschließt und imaginiert sein Imperium: Persische Reichsordnung und persisiche Reichsbilder zur Zeit Dareios' I (522–486 v. Chr.)." In Rathmann 2007, 31–40.

Willcock, M. M. 1995. *Pindar Victory Odes*. Cambridge.

CHAPTER THREE

THE FUNERAL OF SCYTHIAN KINGS: THE HISTORICAL REALITY AND THE DESCRIPTION OF HERODOTUS (4.71–72)

Askold I. Ivantchik

Herodotus gives a detailed description of the funeral of Scythian kings (4.71–72). A systematic comparison of this description with the results of excavations of Scythian burial mounds in the northern Black Sea region – mostly royal or aristocratic tumuli – confirms the reliability of Herodotus's description. The source Herodotus was using possessed a detailed knowledge of Scythian burial customs and was acquainted with Iranian ideology; he was probably a Hellenized Scythian. The conclusion, that Herodotus's ethnographic descriptions can be considered as a reliable source for Scythian culture and society, does not leave much space for speculations about the invention by Herodotus of a Scythian as a model of the "Other." The "Mirror of Herodotus" reflects a historical reality.

The *Scythicos logos* that occupies the largest part of book IV of Herodotus's work is probably the best-known ethnographic description in Greek literature. It has often attracted scholarly attention but still remains under discussion. Among the different approaches to the analysis of the *Scythicos logos*, two basic kinds can be distinguished. The scholars attached to the first one consider the whole of Herodotus's writing, and the *Scythicos logos* in particular, above all as a literary work. They are interested in problems like the structure of the work, the character of Herodotus's narrative, the images of the Greeks and "Others," and similar questions. We can conventionally call this approach "philological." The scholars of the second group consider Herodotus first of all as a historical source, which allows us to reconstruct different features of the history and the culture of the Scythians and other peoples of the Black Sea region. This approach can be defined as "historical."

The two approaches are, of course, absolutely legitimate and potentially fruitful. The problem is only that they almost never meet. The scholars who belong to one field ignore not only the concrete research carried out in the other, but even the very problems that are important for this second field. Thus it is not surprising that the results reached in the frame of philological and historical approaches are often incompatible and contradict each other.

Scholars of the historical group usually use Herodotus's accounts as an objective testimony and base their conclusions largely on these accounts. The problem of the reliability and the objectivity of this evidence is not even raised; its trustworthiness seems evident and is taken for granted. Such a treatment of Herodotus's text is especially characteristic of archaeologists, and Scythian history is primarily studied by archaeologists, because the Scythians did not have writing and are known to us mainly through archaeological data. Such a naive perception of Herodotus's account and such unlimited faith in its reliability are possible only if one ignores completely the philological research on this subject not only of the last decades, but also of the last century and a half.

Nothing can be more remote from this approach than that which is standard in modern philological works on Herodotus. The authors of this group are usually not interested in the possibility of using Herodotus's work as a historical source, or generally in its relations with reality. If the problem of the reliability of the ethnographic descriptions of Herodotus is raised at all, the answer is usually negative. In this respect the book of Detlev Fehling devoted to the sources, or more exactly to the references to the sources by Herodotus, is very characteristic.[1] The author considers all of these references to be fictitious and explains away most of Herodotus's ethnographic descriptions as literary *topoi* of his own time. Thus, these descriptions have nothing to do with any historical reality, and the whole of Herodotus's work concerns not historians, but exclusively historians of literature.

The same can be said about the well-known book of François Hartog, *The Mirror of Herodotus*, which strongly influenced the study of Herodotus, in America especially after the publication of its English translation in 1988.[2] It can probably be considered an extreme example of the philological approach to the *Scythicos logos* and to the Greek ethnography in general. Hartog, following the traditions of the "Paris school" of Louis Gernet and Jean-Pierre Vernant, explains many of Herodotus's descriptions in terms of structuralist oppositions like "culture–nature," "marriage–war," "center–periphery," and so on. He declares that the Scythians of book IV are a functional analogue of the Athenian *epheboi* and that their customs are only the expression of their "ephebic" or "antihoplitic" nature. To formulate Hartog's conclusions in traditional rather than structuralist terms, one could say that Herodotus's description of the Scythians is to be explained solely by the peculiarity of his perception and by the character of his own culture, that is, Greek culture. The Scythians in his description are nothing more than a mirror image of the Greeks.

This crucial idea appears in the very title of Hartog's book. The problem of the historical reliability of Herodotus's work is not raised, but the reason for its absence is quite different than in the case of archaeological publications. Hartog simply ignores the very possibility that Herodotus's descriptions could reflect some historical reality. William Pritchett has devoted a whole book to a severe criticism of this approach. He deals first of all with the works by Fehling and Hartog, which he ranges, perhaps not very felicitously, under the rubric "The Liar School."[3] For if Fehling blames Herodotus for the conscious falsification (in particular for the creation of false source references), Hartog is simply not interested in this question: Herodotus's relations with reality are totally out of his field of vision.

It seems to me that for an appropriate comprehension of Herodotus's ethnographic descriptions, it is necessary to combine the two approaches. His *Histories* are, of course, a literary work and should be regarded as such. But at the same time, we cannot ignore the fact that the main aim of the author, at least as declared in his own words, was the description of reality: in this particular case, a description of the Scythians. It is clear that distortions of reality are unavoidable in any ethnographic description, but the problem is to know whether these distortions were intentional or not. Unintentional distortions can be related, for example, to an incomplete understanding of a foreign culture, which was moreover accessible to the author only through mediators, since he did not speak the local languages. The reason for intentional distortions could be the use of the reality the author describes for the confirmation of some general views not connected directly with this reality – for example, theories about the relations of cultivated and barbarian peoples, liberty and slavery, and so on. But it is necessary to analyze Herodotus's text before drawing any conclusions about the relations of fiction and reality in his descriptions, and no *a priori* decision is here admissible.

In my opinion, the central problem for both philological and historical approaches is that of the character and composition of Herodotus's sources and of his treatment of these sources. For historical research, the answer to this question implies a resolution of the problem of the reliability of Herodotus. If Herodotus based his account on personal impressions and information received from eyewitnesses, and tried to transmit this information exactly, his work can be considered a good historical source. But if Herodotus's sources were unreliable from the start, and if he consciously distorted them or compensated for the lack of real information with his imagination, the situation is very different.

The problem of the sources is no less important for the philological approach. If the historian used reliable sources and transmitted them accurately, the "Mirror of Herodotus" reflects not the Greeks, but real historical Scythians, and reasoning about the "invention of the Other" and similar subjects largely loses its raison d'être. If, on the other hand, historical reality is considerably distorted in Herodotus's work or irrelevant, the explanation for his ethnographic descriptions may be found primarily in the realm of the Greek imagination or in the personal literary method of the author.

A universal method of verifying a witness's account is to compare it with independent evidence. This method, which is completely applicable to Herodotus's ethnographic descriptions, can be carried out within the framework of classical literature even if Herodotus's description is much longer and richer than other comparable Greek texts. Many of these reports cannot, however, be considered completely independent. Classical authors share a common approach in their descriptions of other peoples, including the Scythians, and they were often guided by common stereotypes, a fact that can explain the similarity of their descriptions. Then, too, when we are speaking about the authors who wrote after Herodotus, his direct influence cannot be excluded.

Evidence from the traditions of other Iranian-speaking peoples can, however, be considered a wholly independent source of information about Scythian society. The Scythians and their eastern neighbors, the Sauromatians, spoke languages belonging to the Iranian group, more precisely east Iranian languages. An offspring of Sarmatian dialects, Ossetic, is still spoken in the mountains of the Central Caucasus.[4] In the fifth century BC, when Herodotus compiled his description of the Scythians, Iranian peoples were very close to each other in terms of language and to some extent culture. Iranian linguistic unity still existed in the second half of the second millennium BC, when the ancestors of all Iranian peoples shared a common culture. The division between Indo-Aryan and Iranian languages had taken place at least 500 years earlier, but the similarity in the description of the society and religion of Indo-Aryans and Iranians in the sacred books of the two peoples, the *Vedas* and the *Avesta*, is striking. We may therefore assume that the similarity between the ancient Iranian societies in the fifth century BC was no less important. This situation allows us to use the data from other Iranian traditions for verification of Herodotus's reports about the Scythians. This evidence is, of course, indirect and cannot replace direct witnesses, but its value consists in its independence.

Finally, archaeological data can play a very important role in the verification of Herodotus's evidence. During the past two centuries, about 3,000 Scythian tombs were excavated in the northern Black Sea region. These intensive excavations give us direct access to Scythian culture. Though the nature of the archaeological data does not always allow for a direct comparison with Herodotus's text, because the majority of the facts he describes leave no material traces, such a direct comparison turns out to be possible in some cases. I propose to discuss such a case.

This is the detailed description of the funeral of Scythian kings in chapters 71 and 72 of book IV, a description that almost seems to have been written specifically for the purpose of a comparison with the results of archaeological excavations. Indeed, Scythian culture is known to us primarily through the excavation of burial mounds, and information about the burial customs of the Scythians is abundant. Surprisingly, no systematic comparison of Herodotus's description with the archaeological data has yet been made.[5] Of course, archaeologists often use Herodotus's description, but they usually pick out from his text single details in order to interpret concrete elements of funeral rites discovered in excavated tumuli.[6] The opposite procedure, namely the task of verifying Herodotus's text with the help of archaeological data, does not come into their minds. As far as the scholars of the philological group are concerned, archaeological material usually remains simply unknown to them.

Before making such a comparison, it should be noted that this investigation faces a series of difficulties. In the first place, Herodotus does not describe an actual burial of a particular king, but gives a kind of general rule for a royal funeral ritual, so that even if his narrative carefully reflects actual Scythian customs, one should not expect that his description would conform exactly to the picture emerging from each individual excavated tumulus. There are always some deviations in the course of the application of a general rule, so we should analyze as many archaeological monuments as possible in order to reduce the influence of incidental deviations.

The second problem concerns the difficulty of identifying the royal burials among the 3,000 or so tombs excavated in the northern Black Sea area. Herodotus says that the ritual of the royal funeral he describes was different from that of the funeral of other Scythians. Thus, we should compare his description specifically with the royal and not with the common tumuli. Fortunately, the problem of the hierarchy of Scythian burial monuments has been well studied, especially by Russian and Ukrainian archaeologists, who proposed criteria that allow us to distinguish several hierarchical groups among these monuments and to single out the highest one, which we can recognize as the royal burials. These criteria include the height or volume of the burial mound, the number of human and horse burials accompanying the central burial, the use of gold in horse harnesses, and the richness of the funeral equipment. These indicators correlate with each other.[7] Despite divergences in some of the details, scholars generally agree that the highest hierarchical group among the Scythian tumuli of the fourth century BC includes the tumuli of Solokha,[8] Alexandropol,[9] Chertomlÿk,[10] and Oguz[11] (Map 3.1). Some scholars also consider the tumuli of Kozel[12] and Bol'shaya Tsymbalka to be royal tumuli.[13] The tumulus of Nechaeva Mogila (ca. 15 meters high), the only Scythian burial mound of this dimension that has never been excavated, probably also belongs to this group. These tumuli have heights of between

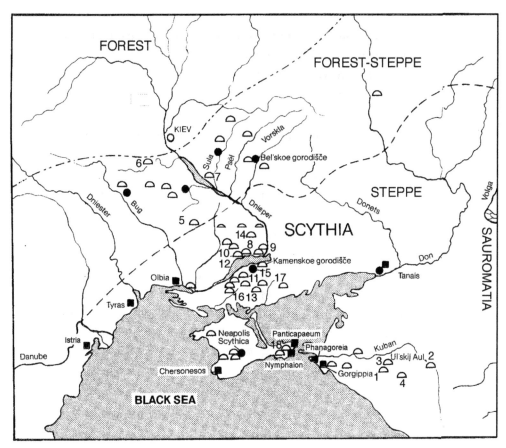

Map 3.1. Distribution map with the location of the richest royal Scythian tumuli. Seventh–sixth centuries BC. *North Caucasus*: **1**. Kelermes 1/V, 2/V, 3/S, 4/S; **2**. Krasnoe Znamya 1; **3**. Ul'skie; **4**. Kostromskoy. *Forest steppe*: **5**. Litoy (Melgunov); **6**. Perepyatikha; **7**. Starshaya Mogila. Fifth century BC. *Steppe*: **8**. Zavadskaya Mogila 1; **9**. Novogrigorievka 5; **10**. Raskopana Mogila; **11**. Velika Znamenka 1. Fourth century BC. *Steppe*: **12**. Chertomlÿk; **13**. Oguz; **14**. Alexandropol; **15**. Solokha; **16**. Kozel; **17**. Bol'shaya Tsÿmbalka; **18**. Kul-Oba. (After Rolle 1989, fig. 1).

14 meters (Kozel) and 21 meters (Chertomlÿk, Oguz). The number of accompanying human burials varies between three and eleven, and those of horse burials between four and sixteen; some horses have a harness with gold elements; and finally, the funeral equipment is very rich and includes numerous gold objects. The identification of the tumuli of the highest group as royal burials can be considered as well established. However, the boundary between this group and the next one, which includes so-called aristocratic tumuli, is rather conventional, and certain "aristocratic" tumuli are very close to the royal ones (for example, Tolstaya Mogila,[14] Kul-Oba,[15] Zheltokamenka,[16] Melitopol'skiy,[17] etc.).

Some scholars consider the tumuli of both groups to be royal burials, thus bringing their number to forty.

In addition, we have to bear in mind the ambiguity of the very notion of king, *basileus*. In the text we are examining it designates the supreme sovereign of the Scythians, but in other contexts βασιλεῖς means simply members of the nobility. In reality, several kings probably existed in Scythia at the same time. Their number, as well as the presence or absence of a supreme ruler, recognized by all of the "kings" or by a large majority of them, could vary from one period to another. These variations could also be reflected in the funeral rites.

The same criteria allow us to single out royal burials of the earlier period, the second half of the seventh and the beginning of the sixth centuries BC. These are burial mounds 1/V, 2/V, 3/S, and 4/S of the Kelermes necropolis[18] and 1 of the necropolis Krasnoe Znamya[19] in the north Caucasus,[20] as well as Litoy,[21] Perepyatikha,[22] and Starshaya Mogila[23] in the forest steppe of the Dnieper region. The royal burials of this period are very different from those of the fourth century (for which see the later discussion), and their tumuli are much lower.

The third difficulty refers to the chronology. Herodotus's description apparently dates to the mid-fifth century BC, but we do not know any undoubtedly royal tumuli from this period. The largest and richest tumuli interpreted as kings' burials date from between the beginning of the fourth and the beginning of the third centuries BC. Another group of "royal" tumuli dates from between the middle of the seventh and the middle of the sixth centuries BC. For the period of one and a half centuries that lies between these two groups, we do not know of any burials comparable in richness to the kings' tumuli mentioned previously, while the description of Herodotus belongs to this very period.

Nevertheless, some relatively rich burials of the fifth century BC have also been excavated (Zavadskaya mogila 1, Novogrigor'evka, Raskopana mogila, Bol'shaya Znamenka 1). Thus, we have to consider not only the group of undoubtedly royal burials of the seventh and sixth centuries and those of fourth century, but also the more modest tumuli of the fifth century BC. We cannot exclude that the people called kings by Herodotus were buried in these last-mentioned tumuli. In any case, no large tumuli comparable to the burial mounds of the fourth century were constructed in Scythia in the fifth century; otherwise, they would have been known to us. On the other hand, the Scythians did have kings in this period, and they must have been buried somewhere.

A further problem is related to the state of preservation of the richest Scythian tumuli, the majority of which were partly or completely plundered in antiquity. The robbers destroyed many details of the burials that could have been very important for this study; even the remains of buried persons were often destroyed. In addition, the majority of the large tumuli were excavated in the nineteenth or early twentieth centuries, when the methods of excavation were not satisfactory from the modern point of view, so that excavators lost information that could have been saved and completed the destruction of Scythian burials started by the robbers. Some of the richest tumuli – Kelermes, Chertomlÿk, Oguz – were re-excavated in the last decades, partly improving the situation, but others have been never re-excavated.

The situation thus does not seem very promising for a comparison of Herodotus's description with the archaeological data. But the result has exceeded any expectation. I divided Herodotus's text into separate reports, seventeen in all (see the following paragraph), and tried to find confirmation or refutation for each report in excavated Scythian burials. I based this comparative study on the tumuli of the two first hierarchical groups, that is, royal and aristocratic burials, but also considered common burials. All of the analyzed monuments I divided into three chronological groups: seventh to sixth, fifth, and fourth centuries BC, corresponding to the conventional divisions of Scythian culture. The results of the comparison are presented in Table 3.1.

(71) The tombs of the kings are in the land of the Gerrhoi, at the last point where the Borysthenes is still navigable (1). Here whenever their king has died, they dig a big quadrangular pit in the ground (3); when they make it ready, they take up the corpse – the body is covered with wax, the belly is ripped up and cleansed, filled with chopped galingale, incense, celery-seed, and anise, and sewn up again (4) – and carry him on a wagon to another tribe. These, when they receive the brought corpse, do the same as do the royal Scythians: they cut off a part of their ears, shear around their hair, cut round their arms, scratch their foreheads and noses, pierce their left hands with arrows (5). Thence they carry the king's body on the wagon to another of the tribes that they rule, and those to whom they have come before follow them. When they, carrying the corpse, make the round of everybody, they are in the land of the

Table 3.1. *Herodotus's Text and Archaeological Data*

Herodotus's Description	Archaeological Data		
	Seventh–Sixth Centuries	Fifth Century	Fourth Century
1. Tombs are in the area of the last point where the Borysthenes is still navigable	–	+	+
2. Kings' tombs are on the periphery	+	–	–
3. Big quadrangular pit in the ground	+	+	–
4. Body is embalmed[a]	?	?	?
5. Self-mutilation as an expression of mourning	?	?	+
6. The body is laid on a couch without any coffin	+	+/–	–
7. Planting of spears on both sides of the body	+	+	+
8. Pit with wooden roof covered by mats	+	+	–
9. A king's concubine is buried with him	+	+	+
10. King's retainers are buried with him	+/?	?	+
11. Horses are buried with the king	+	+	+
12. Horses and king are buried in the same grave	+	+/–	+/–
13. "First fruits" of everything	+	+	+
14. Gold bowls	+	+	+
15. No silver or bronze	+/–	–	–
16. Big burial mound	+	+	+
17. Guard of dead riders around the tumulus	?	?	+

[a] Confirmed by the excavations of the tumuli with "frozen tombs" belonging to the Pazÿrÿk culture (Altai).

Gerrhoi, who occupy the most distant region of all tribes under their rule (**2**), and at the place where the tombs are. Then, having laid out the corpse in the tomb on a couch (*or* mattress) (**6**) and planted spears on both sides of the body (**7**), they place above (the grave) the beams and then cover them over with mats (**8**); in the free room which is left in the tomb they bury, after strangling them, one of the (king's) concubines (**9**), and his cupbearer, carver, equerry, attendant, messenger (**10**), horses (**11, 12**), first-fruits of all else (**13**) and golden bowls (**14**) (they use neither silver or bronze [**15**]). Having done this they all heap up a great barrow, striving and seeking to make it as great as possible (**16**). (72) With the completion of a year they make again the following. They take the most suitable of the rest of the attendants (they are native-born Scythians, for only those serve him whom the king himself orders to do so, and there are no servants bought by money), they strangle fifty of these attendants and fifty finest horses, and having removed their entrails and cleansed, fill them with chaff and sew them up. Then they attach half of a wheel, which is turned upside down, to two posts, and the other half of a wheel to another pair (of posts), and they plant many of these in that way, and then driving thick stakes lengthways through the horses' bodies to their neck, they set them on the wheels so that the wheel in front supports the horse's shoulders and the wheel behind props up the belly near the hindquarters, and the legs on both sides hang down freely. Putting bridles and bits in the horses' mouths, they stretch (the bridles) to the front and bind them to pegs. They mount each one of the fifty strangled youths on the horse, mounting them in this way: they drive an upright stake through each body, running up the spine to the neck, and fix the end of this stake projecting below in a hole made in the other stake, that which passes through the horse (**17**). So having set such horsemen in a circle about the tomb they leave. (Herodotus 4.71–72. See the Greek text in the Appendix.)

Table 3.1 shows that the majority of details mentioned by Herodotus are confirmed by archaeological data. Some elements of his description reflect customs that are well attested to by excavations, with dozens of examples, and that had existed during the whole period of the development of Scythian culture. These are the planting of spears on both sides of the body (7), burying the king's concubine and horses with him (9, 11), putting into the tomb a variety of objects (13), including golden bowls (14), and constructing burial mounds the dimensions of which depend on the status of the buried person (16).

The spears planted in the ground (element 7) were found in several Scythian burials of different periods. Two iron spearheads planted in the ground in the southern part of the tomb were found in one of the royal burials of the Kelermes necropolis (4/S).[24] The same custom is repeatedly attested in both the steppe and the forest steppe in the fifth and fourth centuries BC (Balabanÿ-6; group of Solokha, tumulus 1 (24); Nikopol'skoe pole, tumulus 2, burial 17, etc.).[25] Thus, this custom was a stable element of the funeral rite, characteristic of the whole period of the existence of Scythian culture.

The burial of a woman, the wife or concubine, accompanying the main burial (element 9) is known in Scythia since the seventh century BC. This custom was not connected exclusively with the royal tombs: about 7 to 8 percent of Scythian burials are burials of couples. They are very rare in the steppe region in the seventh to sixth centuries BC[26] and are found only in the Crimea, but they are more common in the forest steppe, where the tombs are much richer,[27] and in the north Caucasus,[28] including the royal burial in the tumulus 3/S of Kelermes (in other tumuli of Kelermes, the burials were completely destroyed by the robbers).[29] The situation does not change in the fifth century: only 6 tombs out of 150 known in the steppe region are burials of couples,[30] but they are well attested in the forest steppe. On the other hand, burials of couples are well known in the fourth century BC in the Scythian tombs of the steppe region, where a woman's burial always accompanies the royal and aristocratic burials.

The horse burials (element 11) in the Scythian tombs are very well attested. One of the reasons is the fact that they are usually located on the periphery of the tomb, so they were less likely to have been destroyed by the robbers. Horse skeletons were found in the majority of Scythian burials of the seventh to fifth centuries BC in the north Caucasus. Their number depends on the status of the buried person and on the richness of the tomb: the tombs of simple warriors usually contain one skeleton, those of the upper level several dozen.[31] Numerous horses were found in the royal tombs of Kelermes: twenty-four in tumulus 1/V, twenty-one in tumulus 3/S, sixteen in tumulus 2/V, and seven in the partly excavated tumulus 4/S; the original number was not less than fourteen.[32] Twenty-two skeletons of horses were found in the Kostromskoy tumulus, which is slightly later than the tumuli of Kelermes, but it is not clear whether it was a burial mound or a sanctuary.[33] The horse burials were, on the contrary, not typical even of the richest tumuli of the forest steppe in this period: they are symbolically replaced by the harness (twenty sets in the Shumeyko tumulus, sixteen in Starshaya Mogila, fourteen in tumulus 2 near Aksyutintsy̆, and so on).[34] Horse burials are unknown in the seventh and sixth centuries in the steppe region but are well attested in the fifth century BC.[35] They are also well attested in the rich burials of the fourth century BC, with forty-eight cases. But their number, even in the richest burials, is smaller than in the royal burials of the seventh century in the north Caucasus: the maximum number for the fourth century BC, sixteen, is attested in the Alexandropol tumulus.[36]

The remark that the Scythians used to put into the tomb different objects (element 13) is very general, and we do not need to cite specific examples in order to confirm its reliability. The funeral equipment of Scythian burials, not only of the royal and aristocratic burials but also of common burials, is indeed very diverse and includes the most varied types of objects, from ceramics and objects of everyday life to weapons and cultic objects. Suffice it to say that the majority of our information about Scythian culture comes from the burial monuments.

As for the burial mounds (element 16), I mentioned previously that there is a direct correlation between the richness of the burial, the status of the buried person, and the dimensions of the burial mound. The dimensions of the tumulus, considered to be one of the most reliable indicators of the social status of the buried person, are used to identify the royal tombs. This correlation is characteristic for all periods of Scythian culture, although the height of the biggest tumuli can vary considerably, from one period to another and from one region to another. One of the largest tumuli of archaic Scythia is Perepyatikha in the forest steppe, which was 11 meters high; only four other tumuli on the right bank of Dnieper are higher than 7 meters.[37] The highest tumulus of the left-bank forest steppe, Starshaya Mogila, was 20 meters high.[38] The royal tumuli of the same period in the north Caucasus were lower: the height of the Kelermes tumuli varies between 2.25 and 7.10 meters;[39] that of tumulus 1 of Krasnoe Znamya was between 10 and 13 meters.[40] The royal tumuli of the fourth century were the largest. The height of tumuli Oguz, Chertomlŷk, and Alexandropol is 21 to 22 meters, that of Solokha is 18 meters, Bolshaya Tsŷmbalka is 15 meters high, and Kozel is 14 meters high.[41] Thus, this remark of Herodotus is also fully confirmed by the archaeological data.

Some details in Herodotus's description are more specific and testify to the fact that he represents only one of several funeral traditions that coexisted in Scythia. The funeral construction described by Herodotus, a large quadrangular pit with a wooden roof covered by mats (elements 3, 8), is the most widespread type of Scythian burial monuments of the seventh through the fifth centuries BC (about 70 percent). Aside from appearing in a large number of common burials, this type of construction was used in the royal tombs of Kelermes's necropolis in the seventh century BC[42] (Fig. 3.1), as well as in some rich burials of the fifth century BC – for example, in the tumulus Zavadskaya Mogila 1,[43] in the tumuli near

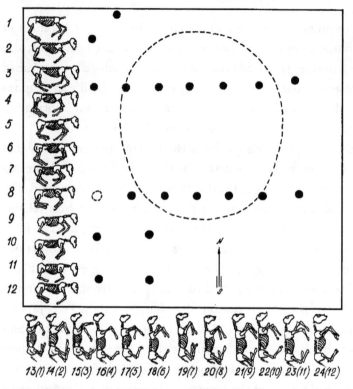

3.1. Tomb in tumulus 1/V of Kelermes. In the center: the counter of the pit dug by the robbers. Seventh century BC. (Schematic drawing by Nikolay Veselovskiy 1904. After Galanina 1997, 54, fig. 16).

Novogrigor'evka,[44] in Kulakovskiy's tumulus, in Zolotoy (Crimea),[45] and elsewhere. At the same time, there always existed other funeral customs in Scythia, some of which were also used in the rich tumuli – for example, burials in wooden or stone tombs constructed on the ground before erecting the burial mound (Krasnoe Znamya, Kostromskoy, Ul'skiy, Litoy, and so on). It is important to note that Herodotus does not report a series of separate details belonging to different funeral customs coexisting in Scythia; instead, he provides a consistent description of one of these customs. That the details he describes did indeed form a coherent system is proved by excavations.

Later, in the fourth century BC, all of the kings were buried in constructions of a completely different type, consisting of a vertical descent that archaeologists call an "entrance well," and a short horizontal corridor below, opening into a cave-like burial chamber (Fig. 3.2). Sometimes there are several chambers of this type, forming a complex structure

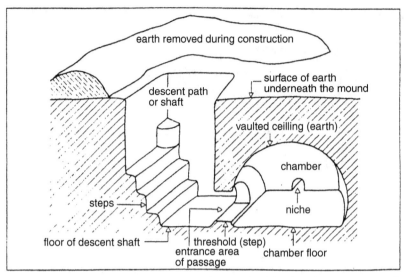

earth removed during construction

descent path
or shaft

surface of earth
underneath the mound

vaulted ceilling (earth)

chamber

steps

niche

floor of descent shaft

threshold (step)
entrance area
of passage

chamber floor

3.2. Diagram of Scythian "catacomb" tomb typical of the fourth century BC. (After Rolle 1989).

(Chertomlÿk, Solokha, and others [Fig. 3.3]).[46] This kind of burial is typical of the fourth century BC (around 65 percent of Scythian tombs, including all of the aristocratic and royal burials),[47] but it began to be used in Herodotus's time. His source, however, does not mention this apparently new custom, which became dominant in the fourth century BC, preferring to describe the more traditional one – the burial in a pit, typical of the rich burials of the seventh and fifth centuries BC.

The same can be said about the custom of laying the body out in a grave on a mattress or a couch (στιβάς), without any coffin or sarcophagus (element 6). It is typical of the Scythians of the seventh to fifth centuries BC,[48] including the royal tumuli of Kelermes and the aristocratic burials of Krasnoe Znamya, but it started to be gradually supplanted in Herodotus's time by the use of sarcophagi, probably under Greek influence, especially in the upper layers of society.[49] Sarcophagi were especially widespread in the rich burials of this period in the Crimea, where Greek influence was stronger. In the fourth century BC, sarcophagi, often imported from Greek colonies, were widely used in royal and aristocratic burials, for example in Chertomlÿk, Oguz, Gaymanova Mogila, Melitopol'skiy, and Kul-Oba,[50] and inhumations without any coffin or sarcophagus are found mostly in common burials. Thus, Herodotus's source prefers tradition to innovation in this instance as well: he describes an archaic custom that was going out of fashion in his

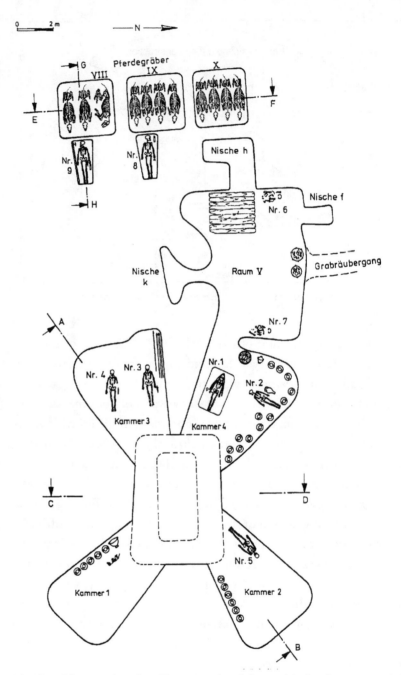

3.3. Plan of the central tomb and horses' tombs of Chertomlÿk, fourth century BC. (After Rolle et al. 1998, fig. 25a.)

time and completely disappeared later, but his description reflects a real Scythian practice.

The same is true for the burial of a king and his horses in the same grave (element 12). This was the situation in the earliest royal tumuli excavated in the necropolis of Kelermes. The horses in these burials are usually divided in two equal groups; the first one was placed in the western part of the bottom of the grave, the second one on its southern edge, on the especially prepared sloping surface[51] (Fig. 3.1). In the fourth century BC the horses in the aristocratic burials were usually buried in separate graves under the same tumulus, though the ancient custom did not disappear completely. The first custom is attested in thirty-one and the second in sixteen cases, including the royal Alexandropol tumulus. The separate horses' graves also appear in Herodotus's time (for example, Zavadskaya Mogila 1), but in this case, as in the others just mentioned, his source prefers the more archaic tradition.

One of the details, namely the burial of some of the king's retainers together with him (element 10), by contrast, can be confirmed primarily by materials of the fourth century BC. All the royal tumuli of this later period contained between three and eleven accompanying burials. These burials are missing in only two of the forty largest tumuli of this period (higher than 4 meters), and these two tumuli (Tomakovskaya Bliznitsa and Dort-Oba 1) are the lowest of the group.[52] The largest tumuli contained the highest number of accompanying burials. The central grave of Chertomlÿk contained the burial of a king and seven accompanying persons, including that of a woman of high social rank, probably the queen, and at least two burials of warriors of high rank. Four more burials were located outside the central grave: those of two equerries or grooms accompanying the horses' burial, the grave of a cupbearer surrounded by numerous amphorae, and another grave, of a warrior with a spear (Fig. 3.3).[53] Thus, the king buried in Chertomlÿk was accompanied by at least eleven persons. The "specialization" of four of them can be established: his wife or a concubine, two equerries, and the cupbearer. The burials in other royal tumuli had been largely destroyed by tomb robbers, but they also contained numerous accompanying burials; Alexandropol contained at least four persons, Oguz at least seven, and Solokha at least four.

The evidence for this custom in the earlier period, especially for the Kelermes tumuli, is very meager, because these graves have been so heavily destroyed by tomb robbers (only separate bones of the buried persons are preserved) that they neither confirm nor refute Herodotus's description. In 1984 N. A. Okhon'ko excavated an aristocratic Scythian tumulus of the same period in the territory of Stavropol that contained a burial of several persons, but this important monument is still unpublished. One of the rare examples testifying to the existence of this custom in an earlier period is the tumulus Perepyatikha of the seventh century BC, in the forest steppe, where at least fourteen burials accompanying the central one were found.[54] The custom is probably also attested in other archaic tumuli of the forest steppe, in tumulus 100 near Sinyavka, with three accompanying burials, and in tumulus 499 near the village of Turia, with the mixed bones of at least ten persons, but they were heavily destroyed by tomb robbers.[55] These data allow us to extrapolate the archaeological evidence of the fourth century to Herodotus's time. Thus, Herodotus's statements are also confirmed by the archaeological materials in this case. The specificity of the funeral equipment even allows us in some cases to identify some retainers mentioned by him, namely an equerry and a cupbearer.

Some elements of Herodotus's description would not be expected to be proved by the archaeological data. Yet two of them, self-mutilation as an expression of mourning (element 5) and the setting up of a guard of dead riders around the tumulus (element 17), have been unexpectedly confirmed by the new excavations of the burial mound Chertomlÿk in the 1980s. In the filling of the entrance well of the northern grave have been found numerous animal bones, which represent the remains of a funeral feast. Among these bones were six phalanxes of human fingers belonging to three or four different persons. The excavators convincingly suggested that the Scythians not only inflicted upon themselves the mutilations mentioned by Herodotus, but also cut off their fingers to express their mourning,[56] an explanation confirmed by the fact that traces of cuts were identified on two of the phalanxes.

Comparable exaggerated expressions of mourning are well known in other Iranian traditions and probably represent a common Iranian heritage, whose importance is confirmed by the fact that Zoroastrianism found it necessary to condemn them explicitly. They survived, however, in some Iranian traditions.[57] Herodotus's evidence can be compared with the description of mourning rituals in a Manichean Sogdian text, which mentions the sacrifice of a horse, the shedding of blood, scratching of faces, cutting and mutilation of ears, crying, pulling out of hair, and tearing of clothes.[58]

Close analogies for this text can be found in paintings from Central Asia. There is, first of all, a wall painting from the Sogdian city Piandzhikent, on the central part of the south wall of the main hall of building II (Plate III), which dates to the seventh century AD.[59] It represents people mourning for a crowned person, who is depicted in the upper part of the painting; the scene is probably an illustration of the legend of Geshtinanna-Persephone.[60] There are two groups of mourners, differing in the color of their skin. They are pulling their hair and beating their chests; the cuts made by their daggers are visible on their faces and bodies. One detail is especially important: they are cutting or cutting off their ears.

A similar scene can be found in a Buddhist painting in cave 158 (19bis according to Pelliot) of the Tun-huang region (Xinjiang, in the northwestern part of Kansu province), dating between AD 781 and 841 (the period of the "Tibetan occupation"). It represents mourning for Shakyamuni. The painter tried to depict representatives, usually kings, of all known peoples. Two figures among them are especially interesting: one is cutting his chest with two knives, and the second is cutting off his ear. Their clothes identify them as inhabitants of Hotan and Turfan (Fig. 3.4).[61] Similar images are also known in Turfan itself, for example a scene of mourning for Buddha in one of the caves in Ming-Öi y Qyzyl (3. *Anlage*, cave 5, ca. AD 700) that represents a group of men and women.[62] The men beat themselves and cut their faces with knives; the women pull out their hair and tear their clothes (Fig. 3.5).

Descriptions of such customs are also given in written sources. Two texts of al-Ṭabarī are especially worth mentioning. Speaking about the events of AD 728/729, he describes mourning for a chief from Transoxiana: "His Turks cut off their ears, becoming the worst of those with bowed heads, weeping."[63] Ten years later (AD 738/739) Arabs killed a Turgesh leader in Transoxiana Kūrṣūl. His mourning is described in a similar way: "They cut their ears and tore the skin on their faces and began weeping over him."[64] The heritage of the Iranian nomads played

3.4. Mutilation of mourners. Wall painting in Cave 158 of Tun-huang, eighth or ninth century AD. (After Akiyama and Matsubara 1969, plate 65.)

a very important role in the culture of the Turkic nomads, especially in pre-Islamic Central Asia, so the fact that al-Ṭabarī is speaking here not about the Iranians but about the Turks is not disturbing. The custom of cutting off the ears as an expression of mourning is also mentioned by Nikolaos of Damas (*FGrHist* 90 F 119). According to him, the closest "friends" of the Taurian kings were buried with him, but in case of the death of his friend, the king himself cut off his ear or part of it, according to the importance of the friend. These actions can be explained in

3.5. Mutilation of mourners. Wall painting in Cave 5 (*3. Anlage*) in Ming-Öi y Qyzyl, AD 700. (After von le Coq and Waldschmitt 1928, 81, plate 15.)

connection with the well-known Ossetic ritual of consecrating a horse to the deceased (*Bæx fældisyn*).[65] During this ritual, the ear of a horse was cut on the tomb; after that, the horse was considered to belong to the dead. The symbolic dedication of the horse no doubt replaced a sacrifice that is well attested among ancient Iranian-speaking nomads. Thus, it can be supposed that the cutting off of ears symbolically replaced a suicide committed in order to follow the dead king. These texts, and the iconographic materials, represent an indirect confirmation of the evidence of Herodotus.

The existence of the guard composed of dead riders (element 17) was equally confirmed by the excavations of the burial mound of Chertomlÿk. The excavators carefully studied four sections of its perimeter (their length was 40, 11.5, 22, and 19 meters), where the supporting wall that surrounded the tumulus in antiquity was well preserved. On the outside of this wall they found several areas of concentration of horses' bones, situated at a roughly equal distance from each other, mixed with elements of harnesses and separate human bones. Five persons were also identified – three youths, one man between thirty-five and fifty-five years old, and one man between thirty and fifty-nine.[66] These bones were not buried but simply lay on the ancient surface. It is difficult to find an explanation for these finds other than that they were the remains of the guard of dead riders described by Herodotus.

Herodotus's report of the embalming of the king's body (element 4)[67] can be confirmed only by indirect evidence, because the bodies are not preserved in the natural conditions of the Black Sea region. This indirect evidence comes from the tumuli of the Pazÿrÿk culture in the mountains of Altai, in the eastern part of the Eurasian steppes. The tumuli date from roughly the same period as Herodotus's text and belong to a culture very close to that of the Scythians. The formation of permafrost under these tumuli resulted in the freezing of everything that was inside; as a result, organic materials in these tumuli, including the bodies, are so well preserved that one can even see the tattoos on the skin of the buried persons. All of the excavated bodies, not only in royal but also in common graves, were embalmed. Their cavities had been opened, the internal organs removed and replaced by a compound of different plants and resins, and they had been sewed up again. The composition of this compound varies from one necropolis to other, and the bodies were sometimes covered by wax mixed with resin and oil.[68] The custom of embalming dead bodies attested in Altai coincides therefore with the description of Herodotus. These monuments date between the mid-fifth and the end of the fourth centuries BC, that is, in Herodotus's time. This is indirect evidence, however, because Pazÿrÿk culture belongs not to the Scythians, but to a different people, albeit a kindred one.

The location of the kings' burials of his time is also correctly indicated by Herodotus (element 1). The problem of the localization of the Gerrhoi and Gerrhos (cf. Hdt. 4.53) has often been discussed in scholarly literature.[69] The most convincing interpretation is the simplest one: that the point where Borysthenes becomes no longer navigable should be identified as the rapids of the Dnieper, which used to make all navigation impossible for a stretch of about 75 kilometers. Boris Mozolevskiy, who argued convincingly in favor of the hypothesis of the location of Gerrhos in this region, remarked that twelve of the sixteen richest Scythian tumuli of the fourth century are indeed situated

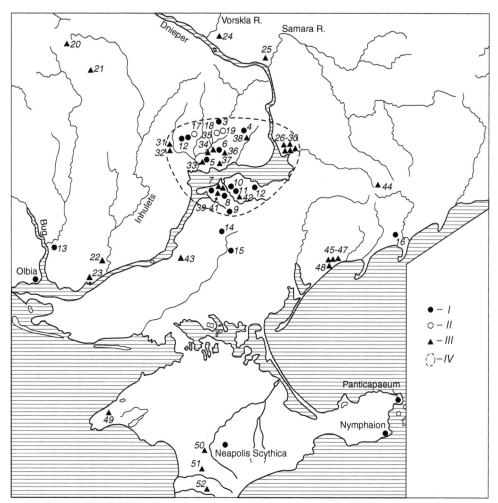

Map 3.2. Distribution of "royal" and "aristocratic" tumuli in the steppe region. I – Excavated tumuli of the fourth century BC. II – Tumuli of the fourth century BC not yet excavated. III – tumuli of the seventh to fifth centuries BC; IV – Region of concentration of the richest tumuli of the fifth and fourth centuries BC (Gerrhos). (After Terenozhkin and Mozolevskiy 1988, fig. 161).

inside the circle with a radius of 45 kilometers from a center just below the rapids, while two of the remaining four tumuli are located slightly farther off, to the south of this region.[70] As for the fifth century BC, six of the nine largest Scythian tumuli, not counting the tumuli of the Kerch peninsula, are located in the same region (Map 3.2). At the same time, not a single rich tumulus of the seventh and sixth centuries is known in this area. Thus, this point of Herodotus's description is confirmed by archaeological data: the richest tumuli of the fifth and fourth centuries BC are indeed concentrated in the region adjacent to the rapids of the Dnieper.

Two elements of Herodotus's description contradict the archaeological data. The first is the statement that the kings' tombs are situated in the territory of the most remote people under Scythian rule (element 2). This statement also contradicts the location given previously, because the rapids of the Dnieper are not on the periphery of the Scythian territory. But this indication conforms to the situation that existed in the previous period: the royal tombs of the seventh and sixth centuries BC are indeed situated on the periphery of Scythia – in the northern Caucasus, like the tumuli of Kelermes, or in the forest steppe. The concentration of the richest Scythian tumuli in the first region is even the basis for the opinion, shared by many Scythologists, that the main center of the Scythian culture was located in this period not in the north Pontic steppes, but in the north Caucasus. But rich burials, some of them close to those of the Kuban region, are also attested on the opposite, northwestern periphery of the Scythian area, in the Dnieper region. This is, for example, true of the Litoy tumulus, which contained objects so similar to those found in the Kelermes necropolis that it is generally accepted that they were produced in the same workshop.[71]

Many rich tumuli were also excavated in the Sula region, in the territory of the Dnieper forest steppe. The monuments of these two regions, separated by hundreds of kilometers of the steppe, are culturally close to each other, although there are some local differences. In the steppe itself, Scythian monuments of this period are also known, but they are less numerous and much poorer. It seems to me natural to explain this situation in the following way. The north Pontic steppes were the principal Scythian territory during this period, as well as in the later period. But the Scythians buried their dead, especially those belonging to the elite, not in the Pontic steppe, but on the periphery of the territory they controlled: in the southeast, in the Kuban region, and in the northwest, in the Dnieper region. Thus, Herodotus's account reflects two different realities. He correctly indicates the location of the royal necropolis of the fifth and fourth centuries BC in the region of the rapids of the Dnieper. At the same time, his indication that it was situated on the periphery corresponds not to the situation of his own time, but to an earlier period, that is, to the seventh and sixth centuries BC. One could suppose that Herodotus himself included this element in his description, but its accordance with the reality of the seventh and sixth centuries suggests another solution. I think it can be connected with the devotion of his source to the archaic tradition, which I have already noted in other cases. Thus, both statements go back to the Scythians, but they reflect two traditions: a "conservative" one and a "modernist" one.

The second element contradicting the archaeological data is the statement that the kings use only golden, not silver or bronze objects, or silver or bronze bowls (element 15). The only bowls found in Kelermes are indeed golden, but the later tumuli also contain silver and bronze bowls. This divergence can, however, be explained in the context of the Old Iranian ideology of royalty.

In the ideology of the Scythians and other Old Iranians, the specific charisma of kingship, called $x^v ar\partial nah$-, or $farnah$-, played a very important role.[72] The possession of this charisma was a necessary condition for obtaining and preserving kingship. The $farnah$- was not only an abstract notion, but also had a material form. It was associated with gold, in particular with gold insignia of royalty. Gold was perceived as a royal metal, one of the incarnations of royalty. In this context, the statement that a real king must use only gold appears in a different light. Thus, we can suppose that Herodotus's notice reflects a conception of ideal kingship characteristic of the Scythians. This ideal conception could hardly have been fully applied in the everyday life of Scythian kings, who undoubtedly also used other metals.

It is particularly important to note that this remark concerns bowls, as well as the very fact that Herodotus singles out bowls among other funeral equipment. The Scythians considered a golden bowl as one of the most important symbols of kingship, which symbolizes its priestly aspect. In both versions of the Scythian legend about the origin of the Scythians related by Herodotus at the beginning of his book 4 (5–10), a golden bowl is one of the sacred objects taking possession of which means also obtaining kingship. An analysis of these legends[73] shows that they represent versions of the Old Iranian legend about the $farnah$- and that the golden objects mentioned by Herodotus were considered an incarnation of this charisma.

The special marking out of bowls, and the emphasis on the require-ment that they should be gold, precisely reflect the Scythian notions of kingship, and its symbolism, even if they are not completely confirmed by archaeological data. Golden bowls are indeed often found in royal tumuli. Two golden bowls, one inside the other, were found in tumulus 1/S of Kelermes,[74] while other royal and aristocratic tumuli often con-tain wooden bowls covered by gold-ornamented plates, which represent cheaper substitutes for golden bowls. They are especially characteristic of the steppe tombs of the fifth century BC.[75] Gold- or silver-gilded bowls are often also found in the rich tombs of the fourth century BC.[76]

The data previously discussed allow us to form an idea of the source that Herodotus was using in the passage under consideration. Its author possessed detailed knowledge of Scythian burial customs. He also had an opinion concerning which ritual, out of the several used by the Scythians, befitted kings' funerals, and he was well acquainted with Iranian ideology, which is attested by his emphasis on the presence of bowls and the importance of gold. While speaking about the king's funeral, he chose to relate the most traditional and even archaic burial customs, which were already becoming extinct in his time. He did not report a series of separate details belonging to different funeral customs coexisting in Scythia, but instead provided a consistent description of one of these customs: the details of his description form a coherent system, attested by excavations. This ritual comes closest to the ritual used in the Kelermes tumuli of the seventh century BC, while the royal tombs of the fourth century, by contrast, show many deviations from this burial practice. One could suppose that this source was much older than Herodotus and was known to him through some intermediary. This hypothesis, however, contradicts the fact that the source also contained up-to-date information about the localization of the royal tombs that did not conform to the reality of the previous period. But even in this case its author, as a real adherent of tradition, could not resist the temp-tation to indicate where the kings' burials *must* have been located: on the periphery, even though this was no longer the case.

The best way to explain the deep knowledge of the Scythian culture that is characteristic of Herodotus's source is to suppose that its author himself belonged to this culture. It therefore seems to me very proba-ble that Herodotus received his information from a Hellenized Scythian and that he transmitted the information of his source accurately. Earlier, I reached the same conclusion by the analysis of a very different text from the beginning of book 4, which contains the two legends about the origin of the Scythians. This analysis was based on a different method, namely, on a comparison with the mythological traditions of other Iranian peoples, but the result was the same.[77]

Needless to say, this conclusion does not leave much space for the speculations about the mirror of Herodotus or about his "invention" of a Scythian as a model of the "Other." We should look for an explanation of the Scythian customs Herodotus described, including the burial customs, not in Greek culture but in Scythian reality, and more generally in the context of Iranian culture.

Appendix[78]

(71) Ταφαὶ δὲ τῶν βασιλέων ἐν Γέρροισί εἰσι, ἐς ὃ ὁ Βορυσθένης ἐστὶ προσπλωτός. Ἐνθαῦτα, ἐπεάν σφι ἀποθάνῃ ὁ βασιλεύς, ὄρυγμα γῆς μέγα ὀρύσσουσι τετράγωνον, ἕτοιμον δὲ τοῦτο ποιήσαντες ἀναλαμβάνουσι τὸν νεκρόν, κατακεκηρωμένον μὲν τὸ σῶμα, τὴν δὲ νηδὺν ἀνασχισθεῖσαν καὶ καθαρθεῖσαν, πλήν κυπέρου κεκομμένου καὶ θυμιήματος καὶ σελίνου σπέρματος καὶ ἀννήσου, συνερραμμένην (συνεραμμένην A, συρρεραμμένην B, συρρεραμένην C, συνερραμένην V, συνεραμμένην M) ὀπίσω, καὶ (om. ABCTM) κομίζουσι ἐν ἁμάξῃ ἐς ἄλλο ἔθνος. (2) Οἳ δὲ ἂν παραδέξωνται κομισθέντα τὸν νεκρόν, ποιεῦσι (ποιέουσι MDRSV) τά περ οἱ βασιλήιοι Σκύθαι· τοῦ ὠτὸς ἀποτάμνονται, τρίχας περικείρονται, βραχίονας περιτάμνονται (τρίχας … περιτάμνονται om. ABCT), μέτωπον καὶ ῥῖνα καταμύσσονται, διὰ τῆς (τῆς τε MPDRSV) ἀριστερῆς χειρὸς ὀϊστοὺς διαβυνέονται. (3) Ἐνθεῦτεν δὲ κομίζουσι ἐν τῇ ἁμάξῃ τοῦ βασιλέος (τοῦ βασιλέως D, om. C) τὸν νέκυν ἐς ἄλλο ἔθνος τῶν ἄρχουσι· οἱ δέ σφι ἕπονται ἐς τοὺς πρότερον ἦλθον. Ἐπεὰν δὲ πάντας περιέλθωσι τὸν νεκρὸν (νέκυν ABCT) κομίζοντες, ἐν Γέρροισι (ἔν τε τοῖσι DRSV, ἔν τε Γέρροισι coni. Stein) ἔσχατα κατοικημένοισί εἰσι τῶν ἐθνέων τῶν ἄρχουσι καὶ ἐν τῇσι ταφῇσι. (4) Καὶ (om. DRSV) ἔπειτα, ἐπεάν θέωσι τὸν νέκυν ἐν τῇσι θήκῃσι ἐπὶ στιβάδος, παραπήξαντες αἰχμὰς ἔνθεν καὶ ἔνθεν τοῦ νεκροῦ ξύλα ὑπερτείνουσι καὶ ἔπειτα ῥιψὶ (ῥίψει ABCPD) καταστεγάζουσι, ἐν δὲ τῇ λοιπῇ εὐρυχωρίῃ τῆς θήκης τῶν παλλακέων (παλακέων CMRSV)

τε μίαν ἀποπνίξαντες θάπτουσι καὶ τὸν οἰνοχόον καὶ μάγειρον καὶ
ἱπποκόμον καὶ διήκονον καὶ ἀγγελιηφόρον καὶ ἵππους καὶ τῶν ἄλλων
ἁπάντων (πάντων ABCT) ἀπαρχὰς καὶ φιάλας χρυσέας· ἀργύρῳ
δὲ οὐδὲν οὐδὲ χαλκῷ χρέωνται· ταῦτα δὲ ποιήσαντες χοῦσι πάντες
χῶμα μέγα (om. DRSV), ἁμιλλώμενοι (ἁμιλλεώμενοι DRSV) καὶ
προθυμεόμενοι ὡς μέγιστον ποιῆσαι. (72) Ἐνιαυτοῦ δὲ περιφερομένου
αὖτις ποιεῦσι τοιόνδε· λαβόντες τῶν λοιπῶν θεραπόντων τοὺς
ἐπιτηδεοτάτους (ἐπιτηδειοτάτους ABT, ἐπιτηδεωτάτους CMP) (οἱ
δέ εἰσι Σκύθαι ἐγγενέες· οὗτοι γὰρ θεραπεύουσι (γὰρ δὴ θεραπεύουσι
DSV) τοὺς ἂν αὐτὸς ὁ βασιλεὺς κελεύσῃ, ἀργυρώνητοι δὲ οὐκ εἰσί
σφι θεράποντες), (2) τούτων ὦν τῶν διηκόνων ἐπεὰν ἀποπνίξωσι
πεντήκοντα καὶ ἵππους τοὺς καλλιστεύοντας (καλλίστους
ABCTMP) πεντήκοντα, ἐξελόντες αὐτῶν τὴν κοιλίην καὶ καθήραντες
(καθάραντες AB) ἐμπιπλᾶσι ἀχύρων καὶ συρράπτουσι. (3) Ἀψῖδος δὲ
ἥμισυ ἐπὶ δύο ξύλα στήσαντες ὕπτιον καὶ τὸ ἕτερον ἥμισυ τῆς ἀψῖδος
ἐπ᾽ (om. ABCT) ἕτερα δύο, καταπήξαντες τρόπῳ τοιούτῳ πολλὰ
ταῦτα, ἔπειτα τῶν ἵππων κατὰ μήκεα (καὶ τὰ μήκεα AB, καταμήκεα
CMP) ξύλα παχέα διελάσαντες μέχρι τῶν τραχήλων (τραχίλων
D) ἀναβιβάζουσι (ἀναβιβάζονται ABCT) αὐτοὺς ἐπὶ τὰς ἀψῖδας·
(4) τῶν δὲ αἱ μὲν πρότεραι ἀψῖδες ὑπέχουσι (ὑπερέχουσι ABCT) τοὺς
ὤμους τῶν ἵππων, αἱ δὲ ὄπισθε παρὰ τοὺς μηροὺς τὰς γαστέρας
ὑπολαμβάνουσι, σκέλεα δὲ ἀμφότερα κατακρέμανται (κατακρέμαται
ABCTMP) μετέωρα. Χαλινοὺς δὲ καὶ στόμια ἐμβαλόντες ἐς (om.
DRSV) τοὺς ἵππους κατατείνουσι ἐς τὸ πρόσθε αὐτῶν καὶ ἔπειτα ἐκ
πασσάλων δέουσι. (5) Τῶν δὲ δὴ νεηνίσκων τῶν ἀποπεπνιγμένων
τῶν πεντήκοντα ἕνα ἕκαστον ἀναβιβάζουσι ἐπὶ τὸν ἵππον (ἐπ᾽ ἵππον
PDRSV, ἐπ᾽ ἵππων M), ὧδε ἀναβιβάζοντες· ἐπεὰν νεκροῦ ἑκάστου
παρὰ τὴν ἄκανθαν ξύλον ὀρθὸν διελάσωσι μέχρι τοῦ τραχήλου
(τραχίλου D), κάτωθεν δὲ ὑπερέχει τοῦ ξύλου τούτου τὸ ἐς τόρμον
πηγνῦσι (πηγνύουσι ABCTMP) τοῦ ἑτέρου ξύλου τοῦ (om. ABCT)
διὰ τοῦ ἵππου. Ἐπιστήσαντες (σπείσαντες DRSV) δὲ κύκλῳ τὸ σῆμα
ἱππέας τοιούτους ἀπελαύνουσι.

Notes

1. Fehling 1989 (rev. ed.; originally published 1971 in German).
2. Hartog 1988 (original French edition 1980, subsequent editions 1991, 2001).
   The chapter devoted to the description of the funeral of the Scythian kings here

under discussion was also published as Hartog 1982, 143–154. For the necessity to complete the analysis of Herodotus's text conducted by F. Hartog on the basis of "internal criticism" by the confrontation with external data see Buxton 1994, 77. Many scholars who wrote after Hartog adopted his interpretation; see, for example, Malkin 1998, 19; cf. Cartledge 1993.

3. Pritchett 1993.
4. It was demonstrated in the works by V.F. Miller, see especially Miller 1881–1887.
5. Rubinson (1975, 16–20) raises this problem but limits herself to some general remarks. Also, the author directly compares Herodotus's description with the data from Pazÿrÿk tumuli, which is wrong from a methodological point of view, because these monuments did not belong to the Scythians described by Herodotus. The article by Thordarson (1988, 539–547) also contains only general remarks. The article by Lincoln (1987, 267–285) is no less superficial, although the author mentions some concrete Scythian tumuli (his only source of information about them is the book by Rolle 1979) and criticizes directly the approach of Hartog; but Lincoln is acquainted only with one of his articles and seems not to know the book, while it is in the latter that Hartog presents the bulk of this argument. All of these authors remark that Herodotus's description is on the whole confirmed by the excavations, but this statement remains a simple declaration, which is not corroborated by concrete data. Cf. also Bichler 2000, 85, whose only source of information about the Scythian funeral rite is also Rolle 1979. Basing his remarks on this limited and incomplete information, which is partly outdated, he states that Herodotus's description is not confirmed by archaeological data.
6. The best work on the Scythian funeral rites is Ol'khovskiy 1991. This book is based on the material of 1857 Scythian burials excavated in the steppes of the north Pontic region, but it does not include the burials from the north Caucasus and the forest steppe. For a comparison of archaeological data with Herodotus's descriptions from the archaeological point of view, see Ol'khovskiy 1978.
7. Mozolevskiy 1979, 148–157; Rolle 1979, 33–155; Terenozhkin and Mozolevskiy 1988, 150–158, 248–249; Boltrik and Fialko 1994, 49–52; Galanina 1994, 76–81; Alekseev 1996, 102–104; Rolle et al. 1998, Bd. I, 179–181, cf. Mozolevskiy and Polin 2005, 287–294, 299–300.
8. Mantsevich 1987.
9. *Drevnosti gerodotovoy Skifii*. I. 1866, 1–28; Lazarevskiy 1895, 24–46; Il'inskaya and Terenozhkin 1983, 136–138.
10. Rolle et al. 1998.
11. Fialko 1994; Boltrik and Fialko, in press.
12. Il'inskaya and Terenozhkin 1983, 149–150.
13. Il'inskaya and Terenozhkin, 1983, 149.
14. Mozolevskiy 1979.
15. Grach 2001, 5–43, with references.
16. Mozolevskiy 1982, 179–222.
17. Terenozhkin and Mozolevskiy 1988.
18. Galanina 1997.
19. Petrenko 2006.
20. The rich tumuli of the Ul'skie group (Ivantchik and Leskov in press, with references on previous publications) and the Kostromskoy (Razmennÿy) tumulus

(Ol'khovskiy 1995), which were often considered to be royal burials, are probably not burial mounds, but sanctuaries.

21. Pridik 1911; Tunkina 2007.
22. Skorÿy 1990, 1991.
23. Il'inskaya 1968, 24–26; Il'inskaya and Terenozhkin 1983, 316.
24. Galanina 1997, 40–41.
25. Ol'khovskiy 1978, 96–97, with references; Bessonova 1984, 20–21; Ol'khovskiy 1991, 110.
26. Ol'khovskiy 1991, 57, 66–67, 81.
27. Il'inskaya 1968, 83–86, 196–199; Il'inskaya 1975, 89.
28. Makhortÿkh, 1991, 38.
29. Galanina 1997, 70–71.
30. Ol'khovskiy 1991, 66–67, 81.
31. Cf. Makhortÿkh 1991, 41.
32. Galanina 1997, 70–71.
33. Ol'khovskiy 1995, 85–98.
34. Il'inskaya 1968, 83, 86, 103; Il'inskaya 1975, 108–112.
35. Ol'khovskiy 1991, 73, 77, 92.
36. Rolle 1979, 96–102; Ol'khovskiy 1991, 117, 126.
37. Skorÿy 1990, 106.
38. Il'inskaya 1968, 24.
39. Galanina 1997, 32–67.
40. Petrenko 2006, 18.
41. Terenozhkin and Mozolevskiy 1988, 248–249.
42. Galanina 1997, 68–71, 78–81.
43. Mozolevskiy 1980, 86–112.
44. Samokvasov 1908, 121–123; Il'inskaya and Terenozhkin 1983, 97.
45. *OAK* 1890, 4–6; *OAK* 1895, 17–18; Il'inskaya and Terenozhkin 1983, 109–110.
46. For a selection of the material concerning the rich "catacomb" tombs of the fourth century BC, see Rolle 1979.
47. Rolle 1979, 158; Ol'khovskiy 1991, 26–40, 66, 94–95.
48. Ol'khovskiy 1991, 58, 82.
49. Ol'khovskiy 1991, 67–68, 88.
50. Ol'khovskiy 1991, 104–106, 140.
51. Galanina 1997, 70–71.
52. Terenozhkin and Mozolevskiy 1988, 168. Despite the opinion of Mozolevskiy, tumulus Deev contained an accompanying burial of a warrior.
53. Rolle et al. 1998, I, 70–100.
54. Skorÿy 1990, 1991.
55. Kovpanenko 1981, 13–14, 51–52, 91.
56. Rolle et al. 1998, I, 102; III, 117–118.
57. Widengren 1965, 36–37, 133–134, 241, 318–319, 325, 340; Briant 1991, 1–3.
58. M 549: Henning 1944, 142–144; cf. Widengren 1965, 325.
59. See Yakubovskiy and D'yakonov 1954, plates XIX–XXIII, for a commentary see Belenitskiy 1954, 33–34, 76–82; D'yakonov 1954, 111–112; cf. von Gabain 1979, 51, 127–128.
60. Grenet and Marshak 1998, 5–18.
61. Pelliot 1914–1924, plates 94 and 95; Akiyama and Matsubara 1969, 221, plate 65.

62. Grünwedel 1912, 179-180, fig. 415; von Le Coq and Waldschmitt 1928, 81, Taf. 15. Cf. the similar representation of this scene (but without knives) in the neighboring cave *A mit Kamin*.
63. II, 1520 Goeje, trans. Blankinship 1989, 57.
64. II, 1691 Goeje, trans. Hillenbrand 1989, 27-28.
65. Thordarson 1989, 27-28.
66. Rolle et al. 1998, I, 48-59, 67-69; III, 105-108, 117.
67. Cf. a detailed commentary to this evidence of Herodotus in Kamenetskiy 1995, 68-76.
68. Rudenko 1953, 43; Rudenko 1960, 329-334; Polos'mak 1996, 163-165; Polos'mak 2000, 120-124; Polos'mak 2001, 238-255.
69. See the summary of different interpretations in Dovatur et al. 1982, 307-309; Terenozhkin and Mozolevskiy 1988, 179-194; Mozolevskiy and Polin 2005, 17-20. Cf. also Belozor 1987, 18.
70. Terenozhkin and Mozolevskiy 1988, 188, fig. 161.
71. About the swords from Kelermes and Melgunov (Litoy), see especially Chernenko 1980, 7-30; Metdepenninghen 1997, 109-136.
72. See Gnoli 1999, with references ; cf. Ivantchik 1999, 169-189.
73. Ivantchik 1999, 141-192; Ivantchik 2001a, 207-220; Ivantchik 2001b, 324-350, with references.
74. Galanina 1997, 147-148, 225-226.
75. Ol'khovskiy 1991, 72, 89. About these bowls, see Mantsevich, 1966.
76. Rolle 1979, I, 131-134; Ol'khovskiy 1991, 115.
77. Ivantchik 1999, 169-189; Ivantchik 2001a, 207-220; Ivantchik 2001b, 324-350.
78. The text and the *variae lectiones* according to edition: Herodoti *Historiae*, ed. H. B. Rosén, vol. I, Leipzig, 1987. *Sigla*: A - Laurentianus plut. LXX 3 (saec. IX--X), B - Romanus Angelicus graecus 83 (saec. XI--XII), C - Laurentianus Conv. Suppr. gr. 207 (saec. XI), D - Vaticanus gr. 2369 (saec. XI), M - Mutinensis Estensis 221 (saec. XVI), P - Parisinus gr. 1633 (saec. XIV), R - Vaticanus gr. 123 (saec. XIV), S - Cantabrigensis Sancroftianus coll. Emmanuelis gr. 30 (saec. XIV-XV), T - Laurentianus plut. LXX 6 (a. 1318), V - Vindobonensi phil. gr. 85 (saec. XIV).

Bibliography

Akiyama, T., and S. Matsubara. 1969. *Arts of China*. II. *Buddhist Cave Temples: New Researches*. Tokyo and Palo Alto, CA.

Alekseev, A. Yu. 1996. "Skifskie tsari i 'tsarskie' kurganÿ V-IV vv. do n.é. (Scythian Kings and 'Royal' Tumuli of the 5th-4th Centuries BC)." *Vestnik drevney istorii (Journal of Ancient History)* No. 3:102-108. (In Russian.)

Belenitskiy, A. M. 1954. "Voprosÿ ideologii i kul'tury Sogda (po materialam pyandzhikentskikh khramov) (Problems of the Ideology and Culture of Sogd (According to Materials of Piandzhikent Temples)." In Yakubovskiy and D'yakonov 1954, 25-83. (In Russian.)

Belozor, V. P. 1987. "O sushchnosti skifskogo Gerrosa (About the Scythian Gerrhos)." In *Kimmeriytsÿ i skifÿ: Tezisÿ dokladov Vsesoyuznogo seminara, posvyashchennogo pamyati A.I. Terenozhkina (Cimmerians and Scythians: Abstracts of the Talks at the All-Union Seminar Dedicated to the Memory of A. I. Terinozhkin)*. I., 18. Kirovograd. (In Russian.)

Bessonova, S. S. 1984. "O kul'te oruzhiya u skifov (About the Cult of Arms among Scythians)." In *Vooruzhenie skifov i sarmatov (Armor of the Scythians and Sarmatians)*, ed. E. V. Chernenko, 3–21. Kiev. (In Russian.)

Bichler, R. 2000. *Herodots Welt. Der Aufbau der Historie am Bild der fremden Länder und Völker, ihrer Zivilisation und ihrer Geschichte.* Berlin.

Blankinship, Kh. Ya., trans. 1989. *The History of al-Ṭabarī*, vol. XXV, *The End of Expansion.* New York.

Boltrik, Yu. V. and E. E. Fialko. 1994. "Kurganÿ tsarey Skifii vtoroy polovinÿ IV v. do n.é. Poisk istoricheskikh realiy (Burials of the Scythian Kings of the Second Half of the Fourth Century BC: In Search of Historical Realities)." In *Elitnÿe kurganÿ stepey Evrazii v skifo-sarmatskuyu épokhu (Elite Tumuli of the Eurasian Steppes during the Scytho-Sarmatian Period)*, ed. A. Yu. Alekseev, N. A. Bokovenko, L. S. Marsadolov, and V. A. Semenov, 49–52. St. Petersburg. (In Russian.)

In press. *Kurgan Oguz. Mogila odnogo iz poslednikh tsarey Skifii (The Oguz Tumulus: Burial of One of the Last Kings of Scythia)*. Moscow. (In Russian.)

Briant, P. 1991. "Le roi est mort: vive le roi! Remarques sur les rites et rituels de succession chez les Achéménides." In *La religion iranienne à l'époque achéménide*, ed. J. Kellens (*Iranica Antiqua*, Suppl. 5), 1–11. Ghent.

Buxton, R. 1994. *Imaginary Greece: The Context of Mythology.* Cambridge.

Cartledge, P. 1993. *The Greeks: A Portrait of Self and Others.* Oxford and New York.

Chernenko, E. V. 1980. "Drevneyshie skifskie paradnÿe mechi (Mel'gunov i Kelermes) (The Most Ancient Scythian Parade Swords [Melgunov and Kelermes])." In *Skifiya i Kavkaz (Scythia and Caucasus)*, ed. A. I. Terenozhkin, V. A. Il'inskaya, B. N. Mozolevskiy, and E. V. Chernenko, 7–30. Kiev. (In Russian.)

Dovatur, A. I., D. P. Kallistov, and I. A. Shishova. 1982. *Narodÿ nashey stranÿ v "Istorii" Gerodota. Tekstÿ, perevod, kommentariy (Peoples of Our Country in "Histories" of Herodotus: Texts, Translation, Comments).* Moscow. (In Russian.)

Drevnosti gerodotovoy Skifii (Antiquities of the Scythia of Herodotus). 1866. I. St. Petersburg. (In Russian.)

D'yakonov, M. M. 1954. "Rospisi Pyandzhikenta i zhivopis' Sredney Azii (Paintings of Piandzhikent and Art of Central Asia)." In Yakubovskiy and D'yakonov 1954, 83–158. (In Russian.)

Fehling, D. 1989. *Herodotus and His "Sources": Citation, Invention and Narrative Art*, rev. ed. (Originally published 1971 in German.) Leeds.

Fialko, E. E. 1994. "Pogrebal'nÿy kompleks kurgana Oguz (Funerary Complex from the Oguz Tumulus)." In *Drevnosti skifov (Antiquities of the Scythians)*, ed. E. V. Chernenko, V.Yu. Murzin, and S. A. Skorÿy, 122–144. Kiev. (In Russian.)

Galanina, L. K. 1994. "O kriteriyakh vÿdeleniya 'tsarskikh' kurganov ranneskif-skoy épokhi (About the Criteria Distinguishing the 'Royal' Barrows of the Early-Scythian Period)." In *Elitnÿe kurganÿ stepey Evrazii v skifo-sarmatskuyu épokhu (Elite Barrows of the Eurasian Steppes during the Scytho-Sarmatian Period)*, ed. A. Yu. Alekseev, N. A. Bokovenko, L. S. Marsadolov, and V. A. Semenov, 76–81. (In Russian.)

1997. *Die Kurgane von Kelermes: "Königsgräber" der frühskythischen Zeit (Steppenvölker Eurasiens 1)*. Moscow.

Gnoli, G. 1999. "Farr(ah)." In *Encyclopaedia Iranica*, vol. 9, fasc. 3, London and New York.

Grach, N. L. 2001. "Kul-Oba Studies." *Ancient Civilizations from Scythia to Siberia* 7:5–43.

Grenet, F. and B. Marshak 1998. "Le mythe de Nana dans l'art de la Sogdiane." *Arts Asiatiques* 53:5–18.

Grünwedel, A. 1912. *Altbuddhistische Kultstätten in Chinesisch-Turkistan: Bericht über archäologische Arbeiten von 1906 bis 1907 bei Kuča, Qarašahr und in der Oase Turfan*. Berlin.

Hartog, F. 1982. "La mort de l'Autre: les funérailles des rois scythes." In *La mort, les morts dans les sociétés anciennes*, ed. G. Gnoli and J.-P. Vernant, 143–154. Cambridge and Paris.

1988. *The Mirror of Herodotus*. Berkeley, CA. (Original French edition 1980; subsequent editions 1991 and 2001.)

Henning, W. B. 1944. "The Murder of the Magi." *JRAS*, 133–144.

Hillenbrand, C., trans. 1989. *The History of al-Ṭabarī*, vol. XXVI, *The Waning of the Umayyad Caliphate*. New York.

Il'inskaya, V. A. 1968. *Skify dneprovskogo lesostepnogo Levoberezh'ya (kurgany Posul'ya) (Scythians of the Forest-Steppe of Dniepr Left-Bank [Tumuli of Sula Region])*. Kiev. (In Russian.)

1975. *Ranneskifskie kurgany basseyna r. Tyasmin (VII–VI vv. do n.é.) (Early Scythian Tumuli Along the Tyiasmin River [7th–6th Centuries B.C.])*. Kiev. (In Russian.)

Il'inskaya, V. A., and A. I. Terenozhkin. 1983. *Skifiya VII–IV vv. do n.é (Scythia of the 7th–4th Centuries BC)*. Kiev. (In Russian.)

Ivantchik, A. I. 1999. "Une légende sur l'origine des Scythes (Hdt. 4.5-7) et le problème des sources du *Scythicos logos* d'Hérodote." *Revue des études grecques* 112:169–189.

2001a. "Eshche raz o 'grecheskoy' legende o proiskhozhdenii skifov (Herod. 4.8-10) (Once More about the 'Greek' Legend about the Origins of the Scythians)." In *Mif 7, Ἀποθέωσις, Na akad. Dmitriy Sergeevich Raevski*, 324–350. Sofia. (In Russian.)

2001b. "La légende 'grecque' sur l'origine des Scythes (Hérodote 4.8-10)." In *Origines gentium (Ausonius – Publications, Etudes 7)*, ed. V. Fromentin and S. Gotteland, 207–220. Bordeaux.

Ivantchik, A. I., and A. M. Leskov, eds. In press. *Ulskii Burial-Mounds: Cultic and Burial Ensemble of the Scythian Period in the Northern Caucasus*. Moscow, Berlin, and Bordeaux.

Kamenetskiy, I. S. 1995. "O bal'zamirovanii umershikh tsarey u skifov (About Embalming of the Dead Kings among Scythians)." *Istoriko-arkheologicheskiy al'manakh (Historico-Archaeological Almanac)* 1:68–76. Armavir and Moscow (In Russian.)

Kovpanenko, G. T. 1981. *Kurgany ranneskifskogo vremeni v basseyne r. Ros' (Tumuli of the Early Scythian Period Along the Ros' River)*. Kiev. (In Russian.)

Lazarevskiy, Ya. 1895. "Aleksandropol'skiy kurgan (Alexandropol Tumulus)." *Zapiski Rossiyskogo Arkheologicheskogo obshchestva* (*Notes of the Russian Archaeological Society*) 7:24–46. (In Russian.)

Lincoln, B. 1987. "On the Scythian Royal Burials." In *Proto-Indo-European: The Archaeology of a Linguistic Problem: Studies in Honor of Marija Gimbutas*, ed. S. N. Skomal and E. C. Polomé, 267–285. Washington, DC.

Makhortÿkh, S. V. 1991. *Skifÿ na Severnom Kavkaze* (*Scythians on the Northern Caucasus*). Kiev. (In Russian.)

Malkin, I. 1998. *The Returns of Odysseus: Colonization and Ethnicity*. Berkeley and Los Angeles, CA, and London.

Mantsevich, A. P. 1966. "Derevyannÿe sosudÿ skifskoy épokhi (Wooden Vessels of the Scythian Period)." *Arkheologicheskiy sbornik Gosudarstvennogo Érmitazha* (*Collection of Archaeological Essays of the State Hermitage*) 8:23–38. (In Russian.)

     1987. *The Solokha Kurgan*. Leningrad.

Metdepenninghen, C. 1997. "La relation entre l'art urartéen au temps du roi Rusa II et les épées-*akinakes* de Kelermès et de Melgounov." *Iranica Antiqua* 32:109–136.

Miller, V. F. 1881–1887. *Osetinskie étyudÿ* (*Ossetian Studies*), vols. I–III. Moscow. (In Russian.)

Mozolevskiy, B. M. 1979. *Tovsta Mogila*. Kiev. (In Ukrainian.)

     1980. "Skifskie kurganÿ v okrestnostyakh g. Ordzhonikidze na Dnepropetrovshchine (raskopki 1972–1975 gg) (Scythian Tumuli in the Vicinities of Ordzhonikidze in the Dnepropetrovsk Area [Excavations of 1972–1975])." In *Skifiya i Kavkaz* (*Scythia and Caucasus*), ed. A. I. Terenozhkin, V. A. Il'inskaya, B. N. Mozolevskiy, and E. V. Chernenko, 86–112. Kiev. (In Russian.)

     1982. "Skifskiy 'tsarskiy' kurgan Zheltokamenka (Zheltokamenka, a Scythian 'Royal' Tumulus)." In *Drevnosti stepnoy Skifii* (*Antiquities of the Steppe Scythia*), ed. A. I. Terenozhkin, B. N. Mozolevskiy, and E. V. Chernenko, 179–222. Kiev. (In Russian.)

Mozolevskiy, B. M., and S. V. Polin 2005. *Kurganÿ skifskogo Gerrosa IV v. do n.é.* (*Babina, Vodyana i Soboleva mogilÿ*) (*Tumuli of the Scythian Gerrhos of the Fourth Century* BC *[Babina, Vodyana and Soboleva Mogila]*). Kiev. (In Russian.)

Ol'khovskiy, V. S. 1978. "Ranneskifskie pogrebal'nÿe sooruzheniya po Gerodotu i arkheologicheskim dannÿm (Early Scythian Burial Structures According to Herodotus and Archaeological Data)." *Sovetskaya arkheologiya* (*Soviet Archaeology*), No. 4. (In Russian.)

     1991. *Pogrebal'no-pominal'naya obryadnost' naseleniya stepnoy Skifii* (*VII–III vv. do n.é.*) (*Burial and Wake Rites of the Population of the Steppe Scythia [7th–3rd Centuries* BC*]*). Moscow. (In Russian.)

     1995. "Pervÿy Razmennÿy kurgan u stanitsÿ Kostromskoy (First Razmennÿi Tumulus Near the Kostromskaia Village)." *Istoriko-arkheologicheskiy al'manakh* (*Historico-Archaeological Almanac*) 1:85–98. Armavir and Moscow. (In Russian.)

OAK= *Otchetÿ Imperatorskoy Arkheologicheskoy Komissii.* St. Petersburg.

Pelliot, P. 1914–1924. *Les grottes de Touen-houang.* Paris.

Petrenko, V. G. 2006. *Krasnoe Znamya: Aristocratic Necropolis of the Early Scythian Period in North Caucasus (Steppenvölker Eurasiens* 3). Moscow, Berlin, and Bordeaux.

Polos'mak, N. V. 1996. "Pogrebenie znatnoy pazÿrÿkskoy zhenshchinÿ (Burial of an Elite Pazyryk Woman)." *Vestnik drevney istorii (Journal of Ancient History)* No. 4:163–165. (In Russian.)

— 2000. "Mumifitsirovanie i bal'zamirovanie u pazÿrÿktsev (Mummifying and Embalming among the Pazyryk People)." In *Fenomen altayskikh mumiy (Phenomenon of the Altai mummies),* ed. A. P. Derevyanko and V. I. Molodin, 120–124. Novosibirsk. (In Russian.)

— 2001. *Vsadniki Ukoka (Horsemen of Ukok).* Novosibirsk. (In Russian.)

Pridik, E. M. 1911. *Mel'gunovskiy klad (The Melgunov Treasure) (Materialÿ po arkheologii Rossii [Materials on Archaeology of Russia]* 31). St. Petersburg. (In Russian.)

Pritchett, W. K. 1993. *The Liar School of Herodotos.* Amsterdam.

Rolle, R. 1979. *Totenkult der Skythen.* Teil I, 1. *Das Steppengebiet (Vorgeschichtliche Forschungen* 18, 1). Berlin and New York.

— 1989. *The World of the Scythians.* London and Berkeley, CA. Translation of Rolle 1980.

Rolle, R., V. Ju. Murzin, and A. Ju. Alekseev. 1998. *Königskurgan Certomlyk. Ein skythischer Grabhügel des 4. vorchristlichen Jahrhunderts.* Bd. I. Mainz.

Rubinson, K. S. 1975. "Herodotus and the Scythians." *Expedition* 17 (4): 16–20.

Rudenko, S. I. 1953. *Kul'tura naseleniya Gornogo Altaya v skifskoe vremya (Culture of the Population of the Mountain Altai during the Scythian Period).* Moscow. (In Russian.)

— 1960. *Kul'tura naseleniya Tsentral'nogo Altaya v skifskoe vremya (Culture of the Population of the Central Altai during the Scythian Period).* Moscow. (In Russian.)

Samokvasov, D. Ya. 1908. *Mogilÿ Russkoy zemli (Burials of Russia).* Moscow. (In Russian.)

Skorÿy, S. A. 1990. *Kurgan Perep'yatikha (Tumulus Perepyatikha).* Kiev. (In Ukrainian.)

— 1991. "Der Kurgan Perepjaticha." *Hamburger Beiträge zur Archäologie* 18:85–105.

Terenozhkin, A. I., and B. N. Mozolevskiy. 1988. *Melitopol'skiy kurgan (Tumulus Melitopolskiy).* Kiev. (In Russian.)

Thordarson, F. 1988. "The Scythian Funeral Customs: Some Notes on Herodotus 4:71–75." *Acta Iranica* 28 (2nd ser. 12) (*A Green Leaf: Papers in Honour of Professor Jes P. Asmussen*), 539–547.

— 1989. "Bæx fældisyn." In *Encyclopaedia Iranica,* III. 1989, 876–877. London and New York.

Tunkina, I. V. 2007. "Academician G. F. Miller and the Treasures from Litoi Kurgan." *Ancient Civilizations from Scythia to Siberia* 13:193–224.

von Gabain, A. 1979. *Einführung in die Zentralasienkunde.* Darmstadt.

von Le Coq, A., and E. Waldschmitt. 1928. *Die buddhistische Spätantike in Mittelasien*. Bd. VI. *Neue Bildwerke* II. Berlin.

Widengren, G. 1965. *Die Religionen Irans*. Stuttgart.

Yakubovskiy, A.Yu., and M. M. D'yakonov, eds. 1954. *Zhivopis' drevnego Pyandzhikenta* (*Painting of Ancient Piandzhikent*). Moscow. (In Russian.)

CHAPTER FOUR

THE SCYTHIANS: BETWEEN MOBILITY, TOMB ARCHITECTURE, AND EARLY URBAN STRUCTURES

Renate Rolle

In contrast to the funeral rituals of Scythian nobles and their beliefs about the next world, the question of their royal residences has seldom been treated as a central theme. Various ancient authors describe the nomadic Scythians as people living in oxen-tracked chariots. But this mobile home nomadism does not exclude a more or less mobile way of life, with stable quarters in winter and urban-like settlements. Recent research at the massive Scythian hill fortresses (gorodishche) of the Ukraine suggests that these localities were handcraft and trading places and centers of the economy as well as residences of the nomadic nobility. This is the case for the hill fortress of Bel'sk near Poltava, probably one of the centers of power of Scythian kings during the seventh and sixth centuries BC with their enormous caravans of chariots and livestock. It could be the ancient city of Gelonos described in ancient sources, with a mixed population of Greco-Scythian language.

The mobile life of the Scythian is echoed in the well-known journey of the Russian Czarina Catherine II to visit the Crimea (Fig. 4.1). She left for the south from St. Petersburg on January 18, 1787, with subzero temperatures and amid enormous snowdrifts. For her and her entourage of fourteen, wooden wagons were fitted with golden runners. The special royal coaches were designed like miniature houses, in which a person could easily walk upright. They contained upholstered seats, beds, benches, tables, and carpets along with every other imaginable comfort. At all four sides of the wagons, light passed through three

4.1. The sledge of Czarina Catherine II during her visit to the Crimea in 1787. (After Neumann-Hoditz 1988, 104. Drawing from 1787.)

windows. Each wagon was pulled by eight to ten horses, which were switched at every station. The escort and servants followed the trekking party in 124 wagons more simply outfitted; livestock and other supplies were transported on 40 sleighs. The journey led via Moscow to Kiev, where the wagons arrived on February 9. Here seven luxurious galleys and numerous dinghies were waiting to escort the empress along the Dnieper to the Crimea. The journey of the wagons took place with legendary speed; nonetheless, three weeks were needed to travel 400 miles due to nearly daily luxurious stops for either parties or banquets. Holding court, performing political work, conversing with foreign diplomats and ambassadors, communicating by courier service and post and all such business took place during this time from the mobile residence of the czarina. The whole journey was a demonstration of political power, undertaken by the elderly czarina on the occasion of the twenty-fifth anniversary of her ascension to the throne. The journey and its details are treated frequently in literature. It is little known, however, that Catherine II not only traveled through the territory of ancient Scythia, but also that she lived the same kind of life as a Scythian ruler would have done.

History of the Area

The archaeology of the Scythians, or Scythology, combines elements of prehistory, classical archaeology, and Near Eastern archaeology. Including both archaeological and historical elements and combining their sources and methods, Scythology explores the origins, structural development, and cultural history of both European and Asian Scythians (Sacae). Eastern European archaeology poses specific methodological problems and yields certain excavation results that can be linked with written traditions of the Near East. Likewise, prehistoric conditions of the Pontic-Caspian steppes, which must be viewed in close cultural context with the East Eurasian steppe region (Kazakhstan, Altai, Tuva), can be linked with a larger transcontinental network of relations.

The land of the Scythians, described in Book 4 of Herodotus's *Histories*, comprised a square area of 20 days' journey on a side (approximately 700 kilometers), stretching from the coast of the Pontic Sea to the south, the River Danube to the west, and the River Don to the east. At certain times, however, it extended much farther west and southeast, right into the Dobrudzha and the Caucasus. The northern boundary cannot be definitively established and is the subject of discussion to the present day.

Two principal opinions have been formulated concerning this northern boundary of the Scythian territory. One limits it to the grassland steppes of the northern Pontic area. The other, which is nowadays more widely accepted, places large parts of the northern zone of wooded steppes within the Scythian realm. Any attempt to reconstruct the ancient landscape as it may have been in Scythian times remains very difficult, however. Over the past centuries, massive anthropogenic interference has devastated the fragile natural ecosystem of the former steppes. This pattern of destruction is particularly notable in the Dnieper region (the River Borysthenes of antiquity), which used to form the central axis, as it were, of the Scythian territory. Also, it has not been possible so far to establish precisely how the climate changed during the Scythian period or how the steppes, the forest steppes, and the surrounding woodlands originated and developed. Thus, it is not yet possible to make definite statements about conditions in the first millennium BC. To the south, there lay the legendary woodland of Hylaia (Herod. IV, 9, 18, 19, 76), remnants of which lasted into medieval times.

Due to natural conditions, specifically the rich black soil and plentiful water, the region has been a rather cool but favorable grassland, perfectly suited as pastureland for nomadic cattle herders and horse breeders. Well-founded studies of the Scythian economy and the Scythian use of resources, however, are scarce.

During the first millennium BC, from Mongolia in the east to the Carpathians in the west, there evolved economic systems with a strong nomadic element. As a consequence, a characteristic material culture (*Sachkultur*) evolved, which comprised certain "index items" (*Leitformen*) that show a striking similarity across a vast area. It is assumed that several related populations using some ancient Indo-Iranian language were the bearers of this Scytho-Siberian type. In the northern border areas, these people are said to have been in contact with proto-Slavic peoples west of the Borysthenes.

Given our present state of knowledge, it is most likely that mounted warriors first appeared in Eastern Europe during the second quarter of the second millennium BC: there are some rare archaeological finds from the so-called Sabatinovka culture that support this conclusion. It is further hypothesized that a considerable increase in nomadic populations with an emphasis on horse breeding took place in the North Pontic region at the turn of the tenth to ninth century BC. It is likely, however, that this tradition of mobile life reaches back even further in time. There is proof of the development of four-wheeled covered wagons during the Bronze Age period, which would have provided one major prerequisite for the wagon nomadism of Early Iron Age times.

Together with the Cimmerians, the Scythians lead the line of mounted-warrior peoples known to us by name (Chernogorovka and Novocherkassk find levels). The Cimmerians, who date from the ninth to the seventh century BC, have long been a mystery and still pose a major problem for research today. Archaeological identification of the Cimmerians with pre-Scythian finds proves difficult. From the late eighth century BC on, the Cimmerians undertook raids across the Caucasus, posing a serious threat to the Near East, and from approximately the last third of the seventh century BC on, the Scythians followed the Cimmerians, obviously joining forces with other peoples and often barely distinguishable from the Cimmerians.

This period of raids into the Near East lasted for about one and a half centuries, some being little more than raids for booty, others attempts at extensive acquisition of land. In those days of political tension in the ancient Orient, the Scythians had an important political and military role to play. During the second half of the seventh century BC, the Scythians allegedly held supremacy in the Near East for twenty-eight years. Writing after the fact, Herodotus tells of dramatic incidents at the beginning and end of this reign.

Certain archaeological finds of arrowheads, bridle bits, and other horse gear, as well as items decorated in the typical Scythian animal-art style, point to Scythian participation in the destruction of the kingdom of Urartu at the end of the seventh century and the beginning of the sixth century BC. Some of these finds occur even in characteristic layers of destruction found at the citadels of Urartu towns (such as Karmir-Blur, Argištiḥinili, Erebuni, Çavustepe, Bastam, Toprakkale or Kef Kalesi, etc.; see also Rolle 1977). A summary revision of these finds still has to be made. Even so, some of the material can be connected to north–south movements from the Near Eastern Trans-Caucasian toward the south at the same times as the end of this development in the archaeological finds of the North Pontic region. The successful military raids into the Near East opened a land bridge across the Caucasus for cultural influences from the south, resulting in a development of the characteristic Scythian culture in contact with, and as a reaction to, the urban civilizations of the Near East – Assyria, Media, Urartu, and perhaps even Egypt.

The origins and the status of cultural development of the Scythians are subject to extensive discussions. Since the excavation of the Kurgan of Arzhan (Kurgan 1) at Tuva and the definition of the ninth- to seventh-century level of Arzhan-Chernogorovka, we can assume that a certain continuity existed and that there were close links between various nomadic cultures right into the eastern portion of Central Asia, links that conceivably suggest a larger transcontinental network of relations.

During the time of the military campaigns into the Near East, the Kuban region and wide parts of the northern Caucasus apparently formed the home country of the Scythian tribes and the base for their raids, according to the evidence provided by both burials and single finds. Around the middle of the sixth century BC, the center of power shifted toward the grassland and woodland steppes along the lower Dnieper in the course of a huge westward movement. Presumably there were several reasons that set off this migration: apart from the excellent grazing grounds to be found in that area, there was the direct contact with the Greek colonial cities that had by then been founded along the north coast of the Pontic Sea, as well as the possibility of controlling the major trade routes connecting the coastal area with the farming regions of the woodland steppes.

Written Sources

Herodotus, Pseudo-Hippocrates, Lucian, and others have recorded a multifaceted image of the Scythians and their more or less closely related neighboring tribes. Archaeologists have often commented on Herodotus's book 4, the "Book of the Scythians." In modern specialist literature the positive identification of the fluvial systems described by Herodotus, and in particular the exact location of the various Scythian tribes and neighboring peoples, are subjects of heated discussion. On some points there is great diversity of opinion, especially about all rivers to the east of the Borysthenes and in particular the River Gerrhos, which marks the burial grounds of the Scythian kings. It is also Herodotus who reports on the genealogy of the Scythian kings: among them Idanthyrsos, and Ataias, the latter known from other sources as an opponent of Philip II of Macedonia in the fourth century BC, seem to have been particularly outstanding personalities. However, archaeologists have not yet succeeded in identifying any historically known persons within the group of "royal graves."

Attempts have been made by archaeologists to find scenes that derive from Scythian mythology, as related in Greek literary sources, on toreutic works of art in the Greco-Scythian style. None of the images on this metalwork, however, can be easily connected with the ancient texts without making far-fetched assumptions concerning persons and actions. Much basic research has been done on the Scythians' snake-footed goddess, on their Herakles, and on their pantheon of the gods, as well as on their religious rites and beliefs. The written sources of the Persian-Scythian conflict, in which Darius I, king of the Persians during the Achaemenid period, undertook a campaign against the Scythians of the North Pontic area, have also been scrutinized by Scythologists in order to better assess the validity of such sources dealing with military campaigns.

Archaeological Evidence

Scythological historical research has seen several significant changes of approach over time. The first phase began with the opening of the Litoj-Kurgan, situated on a tributary of the River Ingul, by Mel'gunov in 1763. This mound may have contained a royal grave dating from the turn of the seventh to the sixth century BC. In 1831, Paul Dubrux excavated the Kul' Oba Kurgan near Pantikapaion; this was followed by a number of further excavations, some of which yielded spectacular results. This phase of almost exclusive concentration on the burials of the upper strata of society lasted into the time of World War I.

The Soviet period ushered in a phase in which research was mainly and emphatically focused on the remains of the common people. At this time, the first extensive settlement excavations were begun. The result was a new material basis that formed the starting point for today's structuring of the cultural groups of the Scythian period (Map 4.1). Due to ideological biases in the interpretation of the finds, the general political situation during Soviet times, and a considerable lack of communication of knowledge, however, there ensued a certain isolation of Scythological research. Under these difficult circumstances, the work of scientists like Franz Hančar was all the more important. Hančar was the first archaeologist who clearly defined the importance of the Scythians as a central field of research in Eurasia. He also made available to scientists in the West a study of the historical and political background of prior research and gave an objective assessment of the state of research.

Apart from one rescue excavation at the Melitopol' Kurgan, the systematic excavation of huge burial mounds did not take place again before 1969, when bulldozers and other heavy equipment were used. In the years after 1969, extensive exploratory excavations under the charge of the Kiev Archaeological Institute of the Soviet Academy of Sciences

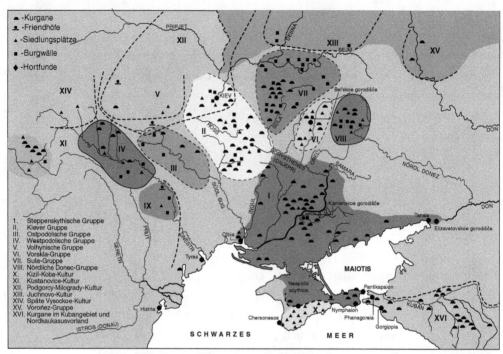

Map 4.1. Archaeological groups during the Scythian period. Geographical areas of grass-land, woodland steppes, and settlements. (From *Skytho-Sarmatische und antike Archäologie* 1986, 62–63, with Supplement. Drawing R. Rolle.)

were carried out. The aim was to investigate thoroughly the kurgans of the Scythian elite, which had hitherto been neglected, setting them within the wider scheme of an interdisciplinary research program in order to be able to fit in old finds with the new results.

The Chertomlyk, Oguz, and large Ryzhanovka kurgans proved to be of particular interest. It was impossible for archaeologists in Soviet times to obtain aerial photographs for the documentation and cartography of remaining kurgans and it still is difficult today within the CIS States, so only rough estimates can be given. In any case, there must have been an enormous number and a high density of graves. Often thousands of barrows formed a huge necropolis. Clusters of mounds of a monocultural structure and others of a multicultural structure can be distinguished. These necropolises, with earthen or wooden platforms specifically erected for ritual sacrifices and other landmarks, formed whole burial complexes.

Apparently, the shape of the kurgan was chosen to fit in with the surrounding landscape, and the site of the mound was carefully selected

4.2. Kurgan Nechaeva Mogila. Highest extant burial mound in the North Pontic area. (Photo R. Rolle.)

to mark its ritual significance (Fig. 4.2). The master builders of the royal tombs erected kurgans with extremely steep silhouettes, sometimes reaching the height of a modern seven-story building, with a base of more than 100 meters in diameter (Plate IV). Modern excavations not only look at the artifacts from the burials but also pay attention to the whole burial mound. So, the kurgan itself became an important research object and some of the technical details of the tomb architecture became visible.

The raising of a mound was an organized communal activity, with a clear concept of earthen architecture. The main elements of this architecture were cut sods of grass, turf, and mud, which were shaped by beating and patting. Soil analyses have shown that these earthen building materials must have been of particularly rich grassland from estuary flats, so they can also be seen as an important burial gift to the deceased, like a pasture for all eternity. Stone circles or low walls around the base made the burial mounds stand out against the surrounding grassland steppe. On top of the burial mounds stood large human (male) stone sculptures (Figs. 4.3, 4.5). The first survey of these sculptures resulted in more than 100 finds.

With thorough planning and effective organization, the construction of such a kurgan could be carried out within a fairly short time. The

4.3. *Kamennaja Baba* ("Old Stone Wife" in Russian, though Scythian stone statues were male). Originally situated on top of a kurgan. Museum of the Archaeological Institute of the National Academy of Science, Kiev. (Photo R. Rolle.)

grounds around the perimeter of the mound had stones set up, and these stone circles provided room for later sacrificial offerings. Repeatedly, remains of horses and human skeletons were found surrounding the base of the mound. These are now referred to in the literature by the German term *Totenreiter*. Remnants of these so-called death riders have been documented, but the only example in situ was discovered by Renate Rolle and V. Ju. Murzin in 1985 at the Chertomlyk Kurgan[1] (Fig. 4.4).

The inner construction of the kurgans can be found on different levels – sometimes above the original soil surface, sometimes right on

4.4. *Totenreiter*. Reconstruction of the death riders according to Herodotus's description of royal Scythian tomb ritual. Scythian Exhibition at De Nieuwe Kerk, Amsterdam, 1994. (Helms Museum, Hamburg. Courtesy Ralf Busch. Photo Jürgen Rieger.)

the surface, and sometimes deep below (Fig. 4.5). The types vary in accordance with the geography of the two major geographical zones. Wooden-chambered tombs are the characteristic types of grave architecture of the woodland steppe. Chest and chamber tombs are common; also known are forms of mortuary houses. Insulation layers, textile linings, and furnishings created a comfortable interior. On the steppe, catacomb graves represent the typical grave architecture. Their origin and the beliefs that connect them with the hereafter are still unknown. The most outstanding feature of the catacomb graves is their "architecture in the negative" created by the excavation work in the subsoil.

In the graves of the social elite the shafts can reach down 16 meters below the original soil surface. At that level, passages spread out sideways in all directions, reaching a length of 10 to 20 meters. The burial chambers could form complicated systems of caves with main and side rooms, niches for domestic tasks, and treasure pits (*tajniki*) for the most precious grave goods (Fig. 4.6). Here the embalmed corpses of the deceased were deposited.

Herodotus (4.71) described the custom of killing chosen servants and attendants within the grave, which can also be documented through the archaeological record (Fig. 4.7) (see Chapter 3 in this volume). The

4.5. Kurgan with tomb of Scythian warrior. Village of Pervomaievka. (Reeder 2001, fig. 1. Drawing by Korniienko. Archaeological Institute, Academy of Sciences, Kiev.)

persons killed during the funeral in order to serve their lord or lady beyond death can often be identified by certain attributes in their dress, and by the weapons and tools associated with them that showed both their social status and the jobs appointed for them in the hereafter. The offerings of horses, sometimes along with their grooms and weapons, as well as other weapons, parts of wagons, carpets, and textiles of various kinds, household items, foodstuffs, and other objects are all documented, although grave robbers have penetrated most of the mounds. Large quantities of wine were stored, sometimes in sealed amphorae, and valuable items made from precious metals were hidden in treasure pits. The interior of the graves therefore apparently reflects the expectations of the hereafter. In this instance, the royal tombs reflect in a very special way the deceased's former lifestyle and the nearly boundless willingness of the whole people to work and make sacrifices to fulfill the mortuary rituals.

Rescued from the underground burial chambers, the gold and silver artifacts with figure representations are a source of particular fascination

4.6. Corner with domestic vessels in the Kurgan Gajmanova Mogila. Excavations of V. Bidzilja, 1969. (Photo G. Kovpanenko. Archaeological Institute, Academy of Sciences, Kiev.)

because of the dynamism of the animal ornamentation and the so-called Greco-Scythian art style. These images allow us to look at the Scythians' complicated imaginary world and their cultural and historical milieu, as well as their lifestyle and their human–animal relationships. The origin of the Scythian-Siberian animal style was the subject of much controversy in the past, with varying degrees of influence assigned to Greece, the Near East, Central Asia (especially toward Altai and Tuva – for example, Arzhan, Kurgan 2), and China. New archaeological finds show amazing, hitherto unknown aspects of the style, which is now reappraised differently within the culture provinces of Eurasia.

The Greco-Scythian style of these precious metal artifacts reflects the material culture of those in power, because it was for them that this style was invented. It was restricted to the upper social classes. To the present day, it remains an unsolved mystery who the master craftsmen and creators of this style were and where they worked. Certainly the precision of the portrayals suggests a geographical and intellectual closeness between the artist and his subject.

Scythian archaeology has elaborated a much-needed corrective to the ancient sources. The focal point at the beginning for the culture

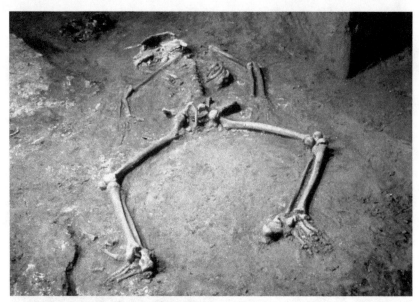

4.7. Skeleton of a kitchen maid or wet nurse killed during funeral rites in Kurgan Tolstaja Mogila (side grave). Excavation B. Mozolevskij, 1971 (Photo R. Rolle.)

were the elements of the so-called *triade*,[2] the homogeneous weapons, horse harnesses, and animal style presented in the archaeological material. Numerous studies of the arms and armor of the Scythian warrior have been of major significance; they have verified, for example, that the Scythian army was backed by riders with several varieties of armor, showing a noticeable inventiveness in technical design (Plate V).

Knowledge from archaeology about the social status of women and the importance of children in Scythian society shows a more complex picture than is found in the written sources. The significance of the wagon as a major aspect of the lives of women was made visible by the archaeological record. Furthermore, all of the legends about Amazons find their visible archaeological reflection within the grave goods. Female warriors' graves were found that contained a large number of weapons, both offensive and defensive, including body armor. Aspects of Amazons' way of life, like the injuries they were most likely to suffer, as well as their way of death – the women buried together with their toddlers, the lack of concentrated burial groups, the existence of familiar burial complexes, and so on – all of these can in fact be reconstructed through archaeology.

Data from settlement archaeology have revealed urban-like settlement patterns, with extensive production areas, as well as a clarification

4.8. Terra-cotta model of a Scythian wagon. From Kerch, Crimea. (Rolle et al. 1991, 89.)

of social structures. While the burial customs of the Scythian social elite and the related beliefs of the hereafter are confirmed by archaeological evidence, questions about their accompanying *Fürstensitze*, or princely residences, have seldom been taken as a central theme. Various authors of antiquity described the nomadic Scythians as people living on ox-drawn wagons (Fig. 4.8). These wagons served as the favored living spaces of women and children as well as for the elderly and sick.

This mobile home nomadism does not exclude permanent quarters in winter in urban-like settlements. It is best to think of the Scythians as living a more or less mobile way of life, this being one benefit derived from their living in mobile architecture. Herodotus (4, 46) explicitly attributes to the Scythians the invention of taking their homes with them, for their homes rested on wagons. The advantage of this way of life was the fact that no one marching against them could escape them, while on the other hand, no one was able to seize the Scythians unless they allowed themselves to be found.

Mobile home nomadism as a way of life has major consequences not only for settlement structure but also for the way of thinking about the population. "We don't have any cities," states the Scythian high king Idanthyrsos to his Persian wartime enemy in the Classical records before adding, "that are worth fighting for." This is an important and wrongly underestimated additional remark, which is often left out in discussions about Scythians and whether they had permanent settlement structures.

The wagon also comes into play in the ceremonial last royal *Totenumfahrt*, a procession around the country with the corpse of the deceased king, which reflects everyday life. During the *Totenumfahrt*, the king is brought one last time before his subjects, just as he had appeared

Tilt cart.

Tent upon cart.

Jurta folded up.

fold up. felt.

Tent lifted down off cart. white felt.

Cart for carrying Jurta.

Kundure Tartars c. 1790, Pallas. Travels in Southern Provinces of Russia. I p.li

4.9. Meeting between P. S. Pallas and thousands of Kundure-Tartars with their "mobile homes." (Pallas 1771–1776, reprint 1967, 549.)

among them when he was alive, when he surveyed his royal property during a pasture tour.[3]

Pindar, Aeschylus, Pseudo-Hippocrates, and others have described the Scythians as a people living on oxen-drawn chariots. A certain part of the population walked on foot during movement from one pasture ground to another, while the warriors were usually on horseback. The wagons are repeatedly mentioned as the domicile of women and children, who would save themselves and their belongings independently during crises, as described in an episode of the Persian campaign against the Scythians.[4]

Pseudo-Hippocrates, who strongly criticizes the disadvantages of this "settled" way of life on horseback or on wagons, drawing attention to the negative health effects on boys and women, gives a short description of the construction and interior furnishing of the typical Scythian wagon. Each is covered with felt and furnished like a house inside, with two or even three rooms, and drawn by two or three pair of oxen.[5] A caravan of Scythian wagons permitted a permanent nomadism, moving on a fixed axis around the pasture grounds with their vital springs. The average speed, 5 to 8 kilometers per day, corresponded to the speed of grazing cattle.

The Scythians were by no means the only people living this mobile home nomadism. A similar lifestyle is recorded for the Sarmatians, Huns, Khazars, Petchenegae, Polovci, and Mongolians. Modern ethnographic research, however, no longer knows of any equivalent to this

4.10. Reconstruction of a so-called Genghis Khan yurt shown at Expo, Hanover, 2001. (Photo K. Schietzel.)

type of nomadism. Peter Simon Pallas, a German traveler in the name of science in the eighteenth century AD, seems to be one of the last observers of such a style of life. He tells about his encounter on the lower Volga, on June 8, 1773, with the "Kundure" Tartars (*kundurofskische Tataren*, or *Mankatten*), who came from the region of the Kuban River and had about 1,000 mobile yurts with them (Fig. 4.9).[6]

These yurts were not taken to pieces, but instead placed on huge two-wheeled wagons, where they stretched out beyond the wheels. Tall wagon-yurts, like the reconstruction of a Genghis Khan yurt presented at the Expo in Hanover, Germany, in 2001, were characteristic of Mongolians and their towns, either on pasture tours or at their residences (Fig. 4.10).

There are parallels with the great treks during periods of colonization of North America, Australia, and South Africa: these modern events reveal certain limited aspects of mobile home nomadism, such as transportation, defensive strategies, and the style of life during a trek. From the life of herdsmen in Spain and Hungary we know of pasture-wagons, which were used by a single person. In contrast, the way of life of the Sinti, the Roma, and the Tinkers in Ireland of recent times gives a good example of constant living on wagons. But this development is a fairly recent one, from only about the last 100 years; it stems from the time when five variants of horse-drawn caravans were invented in Great Britain. An echo of this kind of nomadic life is connected with the picture of *Fahrendes Volk* or gypsies, generally with negative and pejorative connotations.

Other comparisons may be relevant for obtaining an idea of the life of the Scythian nobility. In this context, there are many reports about historical nomadic people that provide information about the lifestyle of the social elite. Apart from the colorful outline of luxurious wagons, the camps may hold the greatest interest. The removable superstructure of the wagons allowed fast setup of a complete room or a building complex that could fulfill a variety of functions. Noble families, especially the women, owned a wide range of wagons. Sources from the Middle Ages confirm the size of such camps. The combination of thousands of wagons, yurts, and tents could create the impression of cities in the eyes of a foreign visitor. On short notice, these cities on wheels could be taken down and refashioned as mobile units. It is exactly this high-class way of mobile life that was taken on by Potemkin for Czarina Catherine II's famous journey described at the beginning of this chapter.

Recent research at the Scythian massive hill fortresses (gorodishche) of the Ukraine and parts of southern Russia suggests that these localities could have been centers of handicraft production and of trade as well as of commercial activities or residences of the nomadic nobility. Good examples are Elizavetovskoe at the Don Delta and the Kamenskoe Gorodishche near Kamenka at the lower Dnieper. Such an interpretation is also possible for the hill fortress of Bel'sk near Poltava on the Vorskla River. This could be the ancient city of Gelonos, described in classical literature as having a mixed population who spoke a Greco-Scythian language. According to the archaeological record, Bel'sk was probably one of the centers of power of the Scythian kings during the seventh and sixth centuries BC. Bel'sk is located near the southern boundary of the geographical woodland steppe zone, which is notable in particular toward the east, where there are larger areas of dense woodlands. Situated on a plateau with steep flanks up to 60 meters high, the ramparts, with a total length of more than 34 kilometers, enclose an inner area in the shape of an irregular triangle, about 4,000 hectares

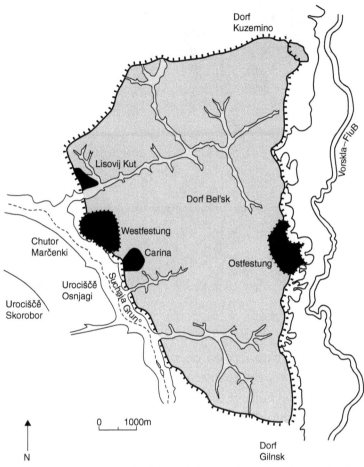

4.11. Fortification system of Bel'sk. (Bol'shoe Bel'skoe gorodishche. After Šramko 1987, 27, with new results; Rolle et al. 1991.)

in size (Fig. 4.11). Two separate fortifications of roughly the same size, including 72 and 65 hectares, respectively, and enclosed by impressive ramparts, jut out from the main structure to the east and west as types of outpost citadels (Fig. 4.12).

Excavations have been conducted jointly at Bel'sk since 1992 by a team of German and Ukrainian archaeologists[7] from the Archaeological Institute of the National Academy of Sciences of Ukraine at Kiev and the Archaeological Institute of Hamburg University.[8] For some years now, the project has also been assisted by the geophysicists Burkhart Ullrich and Henning Zöllner, of Eastern Atlas Berlin, as well as by their Ukrainian colleagues of the Institute of Geophysics, National Academy of Science, directed by M. Orljuk.

4.12. Aerial photograph of the western part of the western fortification of Bel'sk. (Photo L. Spree, ZDF. G. Graichen, ZDF.)

Our investigations have focused on two major points: the complicated interior structures and the necropolis of kurgans to the west of the complex. There are no large urban structures from the Bronze Age; these first appear within the context of Scythian culture, probably as a reaction to the influence of the Near East.

Up to now, we have explored two fairly large settlements within the rampart system. A third one has been found within the village of Bel'sk. Situated outside the citadels but within the rampart system, it was inhabited by the craftsmen who created the artifacts that form the most recognizable remnants of Scythian material culture.

The Gorodishche of Bel'sk forms an extremely large fortification system and belongs to a completely new type of urban-like or proto-urban settlements, hitherto unknown. The structure of the fortification system dates to the first half of the seventh century BC, with some single finds even dating back to the second half of the eighth century BC. This impressive system of fortifications and ramparts was therefore already in existence as a center of power and representation at a time when ancient Greek colonies in the coastal region were insignificant, and above all unfortified settlements (Fig. 4.13). Bel'sk was the destination

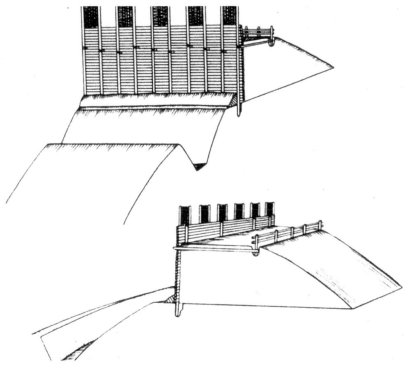

4.13. Detail of a wooden wall, plastered white on the outside, surrounding the fortification system of Bel'sk. Reconstructed from white fragments from the eastern section of the wall. (After Šramko 1987, 27.)

of Greek traders with a rich supply of goods, as can be seen from the archaeological record. The most interesting questions are how it was possible to concentrate such a massive work output and who was behind it.

The common opinion, which has been contradicted by the finds, was that the geographical situation of Bel'sk would not be expected to have a structure of this kind. A place like this ought not to have existed there. Taking into consideration the location of the site in relation to other centers of civilization at that time, and including the sea and land routes developed at that time, it becomes obvious that Bel'sk was a kind of "town at the edge of the world" (Map 4.2).[9] Nevertheless, Bel'sk was a place of intensive trade.

Such a huge structure, as magnificent and complex as this one, can only have been realized under the central direction and protection of Scythian kings. Here lived a population in a nomadic or seminomadic way, together with resident inhabitants. The necropolis of Bel'sk shows

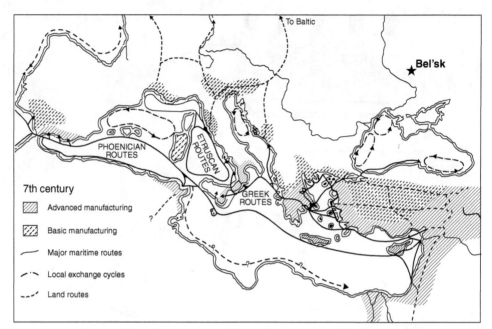

Map 4.2. Map of trade routes of the Mediterranean and Black Sea, seventh century BC. The star shows the position of Bel'sk in the so-called periphery. (Sherratt and Sherratt 1992, 373.)

a concentration of the graves of Scythian nobles, from which a detailed reconstruction of their armament was made for a special exhibition, "Scythian Warriors and Amazons" (Plate VI).

Whether we consider yurts, tents, or various types of wagons as the mobile homes of the Scythians, setting them up and arranging them in an organized manner must have required a great deal of space. In addition, during the winter months there had to be sufficient pasture ground for the herds. Considering these space requirements, structures of a size like that of Bel'sk, which I have described here, are not surprising.

Our recent research at this massive Scythian hill fortress, or goro-dishche, in the Ukraine suggests that the site could have served as the center for crafts and trading as well as for the residence of the nomadic nobility. Such an interpretation of the hill fortress of Bel'sk near Poltava could also be suggested for the city of Gelonos described in ancient sources: Gelonos was probably one of the centers of power of the Scythian kings during the seventh and sixth centuries BC, with its tremendous caravans of chariots and livestock as well as armored warriors on horseback.

The End of Scythian Culture

Around or just after 330 BC, classical Scythian culture suddenly broke off. The reasons for this are still mysterious and in dispute. Discussions about possible causes focus on either politico-military or climatic-ecological crises. One of the decisive factors may have been the advance of the militarily successful Sarmatians from the east, gradually forcing the Scythians back to the southern coastal regions and on to the Crimean peninsula. During the third and second centuries, a new Scythian realm was established in the Crimea, with its new capital at Neapolis Scythica on the Petersfelsen near Simferopol replacing an older center.

Members of the royal family traced here under Skiloros and his son Palakos were entombed in a magnificent mausoleum by the city wall, near the gates. They maintained many classical Scythian funerary rituals, and their architecture incorporated palatial structures into the extensive fortifications. They maintained the lifestyle of the ruling classes to the end, moving at their ease between palace, tent or yurt, and caravan.

Notes

1. See Rolle et al. 1997, I, 51. See Chapter 3 in this volume.
2. A technical term, from *triada*, used by Grakov 1978 to refer to the three typical elements of Scythian culture – weapons, horse harness, and animal style.
3. See also the Thracian "Royal Round," Chapter 5 in this volume.
4. Herodotus 4.121.
5. Pseudo-Hippocrates, *de aere, aquis, locis*, chap. 18.
6. Pallas 1771–1776, reprint 1967, 549. See commentary by Minns 1913, 52.
7. From 1958 on, a team of archaeologists from Charkov University investigated the site under the direction of Boris Šramko.
8. The German National Science Funding Corporation (Deutsche Forschungsgemeinschaft = DFG) has been supporting our research, which was originally directed by Vjacheslav Murzin, since 2003 by Evgenij Chernenko, and since 2005 by Sergej Machortych and the author.
9. Map, Sherratt and Sherratt 1992, 373.

Bibliography

Skytho-Sarmatische und antike Archäologie. 1986. In *Archaeologija Ukrainskoj* SSR, Bd. 2. Kiev.

Aruz, J., A. Alekseev, and E. Korolkova. 2000. *The Golden Deer of Eurasia: Scythian and Sarmatian Treasures from the Russian Steppes*. Catalogue, Metropolitan Museum of Art, New York.

Bonn 1997. *Das Gold der Skythen und Griechen: Aus der archäologischen Schatzkammer der Eremitage in St. Petersburg*. Bd. I. Katalog Kunst- und Ausstellungshalle der Bundesrepublik Deutschland. Bonn.

Černenko, E. V. 1984. *Skifo-persidskaja vojna* (*The Scythian Persian War*). Kiev. (In Russian.)

2006. *Die Schutzwaffen der Skythen. Prähistorische Bronzefunde* (*PBF*). Abt. III, Bd. 2. Stuttgart.

Chochorowski, J., J. Rydzewski, and S. Skoryj, S. 1999. *Wielki kurhan Ryzanowski* (*The Large Kurgan Ryzanowski*). Catalogue, Archäologisches Museum Cracow. (In Polish.)

Derevjanko, A. P., and V.I. Molodin, eds. 2000. *Phenomenon of the Altai Mummies*. Novosibirsk. (In Russian with English summary.)

Galanina, L. 1997. *Die Kurgane von Kelermes: Königsgräber der frühskythischen Zeit. Steppenvölker Eurasiens*, Bd. I. Moscow.

Galanina, L., N. Grach, H.-J. Kellner, and G. Kossack. 1987. *Skythika: Vorträge zur Entstehung des skytho-iranischen Tierstils*. Bayer. Akademie der Wissenschaft, Phil.-Hist. Klasse, Abh. N. F. 98.

Grakov, B. N. 1978. *Die Skythen*. Berlin.

Hančar, F. 1950. "*Die Skythen als Forschungsproblem.*" *Reinecke Festschrift*, ed. G. Behrens, 67–83. Mainz.

Kiev 1986. *Skifo-sarmatskaja i antičnaja archeologija* (*Scythian-Sarmatian and Ancient Archaeology*), vol. 2. In *Archeologija Ukrainskoj SSR* (*Archaeology of Ukraine SSR*). 3 vols. Kiev. (In Russian.)

Kossack, G. 1987. "Von den Anfängen des skytho-iranischen Tierstils." In Galanina et al. 1987, 24–86.

Menghin, W., H. Parzinger, A. Nagler, and M. Nawroth. 2007. *Im Zeichen des goldenen Greifen: Königsgräber der Skythen*. Exhibition Catalogue, Munich, Berlin, London, and New York.

Minns, E. H. 1913. *Scythians and Greeks*. Cambridge.

Moscow 1989. *Stepi evropejskoj časti SSSR v skifo-sarmatskoe vremja* (*The Steppe of the European Area of the USSR in the Scythian-Sarmatian Period*). Moscow. (In Russian.)

1992. *Stepnaja polosa Aziatskoj časti SSSR v skifo-sarmatskoe vremja.* (*The Steppe of the Asian Area of the USSR in the Scythian-Sarmatian Period*). Moscow. (In Russian.)

Mozolevskii, B., and S. Polin. 2005. *Kurgans of Scythian Gerros of the Fourth Century B.C.* Kiev.

Neumann-Hoditz, R. 1988. *Katharina die Große*. Hamburg.

Niemeyer, H. G., and R. Rolle, eds. 1991. *Beiträge zur Archäologie im nördlichen Schwarz-Meerraum. Hamburger Beiträge zur Archäologie* 18. Mainz 1996.

Pallas, P. S. 1771–1776. *Reise durch verschiedene Provinzen des Russischen Reichs*. Reprint Graz 1967.

Parzinger, H. 2004. *Die Skythen*. Munich.

Petrenko, V. G. 2006. *Krasnoznamenskii Burial-Ground: Early Scythian Elite Burial-Mounds in the Northern Caucasus. Steppenvölker Eurasiens*, vol. III. Berlin, Bordeaux, and Moscow.

Reeder, Ellen D. 1999. *Scythian Gold*. New York.

Rolle, R. 1973. "Skythen – Reitervolk am Schwarzen Meer." *Westermanns Monatshefte* 22–33.

1977. *Urartu und die Reiternomaden*. Munich.

1979. *Totenkult der Skythen. Teil I: Das Steppengebiet. Vorgeschichtliche Forschungen* Bd. 18, 1–2. Berlin and New York.

1989. *The World of the Scythians*. London and Berkeley, CA. (Translation of Rolle 1980).

Rolle, R., M. Müller-Wille, and K. Schietzel, eds. 1991. *Gold der Steppe: Archäologie der Ukraine*. Catalogue, Archäologisches Landesmuseum Schleswig.

Scythian Exhibition at De Nieuwe Kerk. 1994. Amsterdam.

Rolle, R., V. J. Murzin, and A. A. Alekseev. 1997. *Königskurgan Čertomlyk: Ein skythischer Grabhügel des 4. vorchristlichen Jahrhunderts. Hamburger Forschungen zur Archäologie* Bd. 1 (I–III). Hamburg.

Rolle, R., V. Ju Murzin, and B. A. Šramko. 1991. "Das Burgwallsystem von Bel'sk (Ukraine). Eine frühe stadtartige Anlage im skythischen Landesinnern." *Hamburger Beiträge zur Archäologie* 18:57–84.

Schiltz, V. 1994. *Die Skythen und andere Steppenvölker. 8. Jahrhundert v. Chr. bis 1. Jahrhundert n. Chr.* Munich.

2001. *L'Or des amazons: Peuples nomades entre Asie et Europe*. Catalogue, Musée Cernuschi. Paris.

Sherratt, S., and A. Sherratt. 1992. "The Growth of Mediterranean Economy in the Early First Millennium BC." *World Archaeology* 24 (3): 361–378.

Šramko (Shramko), Boris Andreevich. 1987. *Bel'skoe gorodisce skifskoj epochi (gorod Gelon). (Belsk Fortified Settlement of the Scythian Epoch [Gelon Town])*. Kiev. (In Russian.)

CHAPTER FIVE

PHILOMELE'S TONGUE: READING THE PICTORIAL TEXT OF THRACIAN MYTHOLOGY

Ivan Marazov

The ancient region of Thrace covers modern northwestern Bulgaria, Romania, Moldova, European Turkey, the northern Aegean coast, and eastern Serbia. Northwestern Thrace, a region of the northern Balkans, was inhabited by tribal communities composed of Thracians, Illyrians, and Celts who played important roles in the history and culture of southeastern Europe during the first millennium BC. The most powerful tribal community that emerged in the fifth century BC was known as the Triballi, a Thracian people described in Herodotus (4.49) and other ancient sources. In Aristophanes's comedy The Birds, *for example, a Triballian is introduced as a barbarian par excellence. The Triballi did not have writing, so we know their myths, customs, and rites from Greek, Roman, and Byzantine authors, as well as from the imagery. These images were not merely illustrations of transmitted myths; they constituted an autonomous language of myth that has to be interpreted in the context of Thracian society, in particular its royal ideology.*

Pictorial Language of Myth in Ancient Thrace

Can we really use the term "art" for objects created by and for barbarians? In the case of the Thracians, neither the artists nor their patrons viewed these works from an aesthetic point of view: first and foremost were their functions within the system of the royal ideology, and their designation of who was powerful and must be ensured of continuing power. The images on these objects are not mere decoration. They are full of meaning, but a scholar attempting to decipher their meaning must elicit their essential principles and restore a dialogue with antiquity.

In order to do this, one must try to understand the thought processes of the Thracians. This is not easy. The ancient sources are varied and unequal, as is true for the rest of the barbarian world. Written sources are from non-Thracian cultures and must thus be subjected to critical reinterpretation;[1] they are also unsystematic and fragmentary, which renders them even less reliable. The only local sources from Thrace are pictorial texts. Though these are often treated as illustrations of oral or written texts, we do not find that the myths depicted in Thracian art are consistent with known myths that reflect an oral tradition. It is difficult, for example, to recognize any known Thracian deities in the images that have survived. Pictorial texts are not so much illustrations as parallel translations of myths into another form. The scholar must thus find a means of interpreting this kind of original source.

A metaphor can shed light on the procedure for encoding and read-ing a text written in an artificial secondary language.[2] In the myth of the Thracian king Tereus, his wife, Prokne, and her sister, Philomele,[3] the barbarian king is in love with his wife's sister; he abducts her, rapes her, and cuts off her tongue so that she cannot tell his wife of his crime. Philomele is banished to a cave, but she weaves a cloth and asks Tereus to take it to Prokne.

Later authors explained that Philomele wove the story into the cloth with either images or some kind of writing – although barbarians were known to have been illiterate. From a mythical-ritual point of view, how-ever, there was no need to weave or write anything into the cloth. The very fact that a maiden had finished weaving a cloth indicated that she was no longer a virgin. Although deprived of natural language, Philomele used another language to convey her message, and it was clearly deciphered. There is no more semiotic ancient myth than this one, because every action was correctly and accurately deciphered, just like a written text. In studying the archaic art of the European barbarians, our task is to reveal the rules for deciphering the texts written into them. For modern schol-ars, Philomele's message is complicated but not impossible to decipher.

Comparisons with Indo-European mythology[4] can help us explain relationships between figures when written evidence is missing. One example is a series of appliqués from the Letnitsa treasure, in which severed equine and human heads are depicted behind a horseman[5] (Figs. 10.13–10.14). These might be explained with reference to the Thracian practice of ritual sacrifices, along the lines of those of the Indian Ashvamedha and Purushamedha.[6]

Comparisons with contemporary Greek artistic models in terms of content clearly show differences in world outlook, rather than similarities or convergences that could be interpreted as Greek influence. During the fourth century BC, Thracians and Greeks lived as neighbors, exchanged gifts and ideas, intermarried, traded, and fought, but they lived in different worlds. While the Greeks were listening to Plato's dialogues of Socrates, who said that Homer should be expelled from the schools and beaten with sticks, the songs of Orpheus were the only trustworthy source of knowledge for the Thracians. The code of conduct professed by Thracian kings is similar to the system of aristocratic values defining the ideal of *arete* among Homer's heroes.[7] The founder of the Odrysian kingdom, Teres, claimed that when he was not at war, he began to resemble the grooms of his horses.[8]

In the Classical period, the Greeks no longer understood many of the Thracian customs, including their proverbial cruelty, which was sometimes manifested in the form of human sacrifice, or their insane aspiration to prove their manliness in combat. But they could simply have compared them, not with the behavioral norms of fifth-century BC Athenians, but with the ideals of warrior valor among Homer's heroes. This chasm between the Greek and barbarian worldviews is often equally difficult to grasp by modern researchers. If we wish to understand the Thracian worldview, we must be able to identify with their archaic model of behavior – a system of heroic values that they shared with an earlier, epic stage of Greek culture.

In the nonliterary society of the Thracians, art became the principal language for recording mythological ideas. We do not know what gods Herodotus had in mind when he named the members of the Thracian pantheon Ares, Dionysos, and Artemis (Herodotus 4.7). The Thracian character of a deity is much clearer in the only preserved iconographic image – albeit in a Greek interpretation – of a Thracian divinity, the Bithynian goddess Bendis[9] (Fig. 5.1). She has the features that match her description in the written sources. But it is not possible to identify her with certainty in the numerous images of female deities in Thracian

5.1. Votive relief of Bendis from Athens (Piraeus), 424 BC. London, British Museum. (Marazov 1996, 269, fig. 169.)

art. Similarly, Greek sources often mention the names and the deeds of Orpheus and Zalmoxis, but there is not even a trace of their images in the local pictorial texts.

This drastic discrepancy between written and iconographic data[10] is characteristic of Thrace and creates additional difficulties in identifying images of indisputable mythological character. Clearly, however, the function of art did not require the identifiable depiction of such deities and heroes. The images on the objects were not intended to be placed in temples. They were not connected with the cult of the deity they represented and therefore did not need features identifying the specific deity, that is, a fixed sign system. For the royal ideology, it was not important for the deity to be identified by means of attributes. In that communication system it was necessary to present only the attributes that characterized the deity or the hero in terms of his or her function or status.

Art as a Language of Myth

The role of pictorial texts as the language of myth and the laws of mytho-poetic thinking has been the object of research by many theoreticians of religion, beginning with Ernest Cassirer (1955). In order to identify the underlying myth system, we must interpret the available data as a comprehensive and functioning semantic system. Mythological thinking is systematic: it defines the entire world outlook of archaic people, seeking a precedent for every contemporary event. Time, in this way of thinking, is cyclical and recurring; the myth itself is unhistorical.[11] The fact that mythological thinking is deeply conservative determines the traditional character of the images and motifs that appear in the art.

Usually we expect a scene to provide a narrative, but in the art of the Thracians, narrative – even reduced to the simplest causal sequence in the development of the plot – is very rare. Instead of narration, the Thracian artist organized mythological information in a cumulative code.[12] The figures are not engaged in interrelationships, but are merely juxtaposed. This makes possible far greater semantic productivity of the image structure than does the action of a plot. The movement is without linear sequence; it does not reveal psychological states but rather marks the action. It is most often reduced to a gesture, a static rendering that creates an effect of rite and ceremony. In the visible myth, the Thracian images lack unity of place and time, as well as features that identify the environment. The pictorial text is structured on the basis of the application, combination, and permanent change of different mythological codes: spatial, by attribute – object, animal, and so on.

Cult Signs or Language of the Narrative

Nor did each sign have a fixed meaning, with the kinds of attributes inherent in a concrete Greek deity, for example, as signs of the cult presence of that deity in every context. The clearest example is that of the allusions to wine and to the travel companions of Dionysos, which are regularly taken as signs of a Dionysiac symbolism. This bias has influenced the interpretation of the images on the jug from Borovo,[13] which have been read as the marriage of Dionysos and Ariadne, although they differ in many ways from Greek iconography. Instead, what is represented is the precedent of the sacred marriage, the *hierogamy*, as in the mysteries of the Kabeiroi. The abundance of wine, the Sileni, and the Maenads are also found in numerous scenes on the vases in the Theban Kabeiroon. It could hardly have been a reference to Dionysos or even to a "syncretism" – always a convenient term if one is unable to read a pictorial text clearly. The Dionysiac symbolism is here a system of signs, a language used to render information taken from another cult or another myth.

5.2. Caryatids from the Sveshtari Tomb, first half of the third century BC. (Marazov 1998, 35, fig. 1.)

Floral ornaments are usually interpreted as symbols of a fertility cult, though it is not clear how a palmette could function as a sign of fertility. Rather than applying fixed meanings to vegetal symbolism, it is more productive to examine them in the contexts in which they appear. In the hands of the goddess from a Rogozen jug (no. 157), for example, these vegetal signs could refer to her matronal position, a status confirmed by her clothes and hairstyle.[14] In a scene on a belt from Lovets, on the other hand, the three lotus blossoms placed between the two boars could be a reductive image of the world tree, whose roots the boar is trying to undermine – a symbol of the destruction of life.[15] The presence of floral signs in the figures of the caryatids from the tomb in Sveshtari (Fig. 5.2) could signify a new birth; the meaning that these ritual images initially carried was of special significance for the semantic program of a tomb.[16]

The pictorial text is the only way for the fixation of the myth accessible to the nonliterate Thracians. It is specific, but it is repeatable, and provides a relatively accurate reproduction of the imprinted mythologem. Because it was constructed from traditional formulae and clichés, this text is easily identifiable.

It is quite a different matter to know whether all Thracians understood the entire depth of the mythical content, or whether it was accessible only to the level to which everyone was admitted during initiation into the doctrine.[17] Such a distinction in perception is in principle inherent in Thracian pictorial texts. Since every sign is polysemantic, it is perfectly possible that its meanings were deliberately restricted on the basis of social criteria. Thus, unlike the Greek practice of complete openness, the Odrysian royal court made the secrets of the mysteries of the Kabeiroi accessible only to the aristocratic elite. It is likely that Kotys himself initiated his guests – the dynasts from the northern regions of Thrace – into these sacral and closed rites. As a sign of this initiation, one Getic king took away with him the set of the Kabeiroi, which is known today as the Borovo Treasure (Plate VII).

Art as the Language of the Royal Ideology

The process of state formation in Thrace took place at an uneven rate. During the last phase of the Bronze Age settlements developed rather intensively; they then abated, to develop again, creating relatively stable kingdoms, in the middle of the fifth century BC.[18] At that time, Thracian art changed entirely in materials, range of objects, iconographic repertoire, and stylistic character.[19] The direct and close connection between art and the political situation proves that art was now entirely subordinated to new interests. Rather than serving the sphere of the myth and the cult exclusively, it focused predominantly on the royal ideology.

There was not, however, a sharp differentiation between these two spheres; they were isomorphous, being isofunctional as a system for communication. Simply stated, there occurred an inner shift in the emphasis of the verbal and the figural narrative. Only images and mythical situations that appeared to be most suitable for motivating or enhancing power were selected from the infinite wealth of the myth. For one thing, the local iconography of the Thracians was dominated by female deities; the supreme male deities of the Indo-Europeans – notably the god of storms – were seemingly irrelevant to the Thracian artist.[20]

In addition to the goddess, the figure of the hero is accorded a prominent place in the art of the Thracians. The iconography is focused on him and reflects the technology of royal choice: trials, consecration, investiture, and marriage. Trials in Thracian art are coded most often as the hunting of real or fantastic predators.[21] The boar is the principal antagonist: it personifies chaos, destruction, and death and becomes the hunter's chief prey.

The ideological plan includes the deity's battle with the dragon, as on the appliqués from Letnitsa (Plate VIIIA), Homina Mogila, and Stancheshti, and the golden helmet from Baicheni.[22] Like the boar, this fantastic creature is simultaneously associated with different cosmic zones, different elements, and different animals. In Thrace it is often depicted with a boar's head; sometimes it has three heads and sometimes three bodies. Other features are also related to its clear identification with chaos.

The victorious hero combines the functions of the first man and the first king, the progenitor of both the people and the dynasty.[23] By defeating the forces of chaos, he introduces order into the world. His victory is a means of subordinating that order to the laws of hierarchy. In an aristocratic society, as Thracian society undoubtedly was, genealogy was extremely important. The Thracian kings worshiped their god Hermes separately from the simple people, swore by his name, and claimed descent from him (Fig. 5.3). Kotys I was also the son of Apollo; in this way, he presented himself as an earthly Orpheus. On the other hand, the name of that dynast is a derivative from the name of the Thracian goddess Kotys or Kotyto,[24] which again makes him a descendant of the gods.

The hero was obliged periodically to prove his dignity and his right to the throne. Hence the agonic principle[25] features prominently in the iconography: the race is a way to prove the favorable attitude of the deity, because it was believed that the deity chose the victor; see the jug from the Mogilanska Mogila tumulus (Fig. 5.4), the phiale from the Bashova Mogila tumulus, and the chariots from the Kazanluk tomb or from the tomb in Muglizh.

5.3. Silver coin of the Derronae Thracian tribe, first half of the fifth century BC.

5.4. Golden jug from the Mogilanska Mogila tumulus, second half of the fourth century BC.

The aim of the trial or *agon* was to restore the order of the world, which was perceived as a hierarchy. The victor stands at the top, thus expressing social status with a spatial code. The hero-king is always depicted in Thracian iconography in an elevated position. He is a rider: the actual mounting of his horse secures his elevated position, while his servant

5.5. Cheek piece from a gold helmet from Baicheni, Romania, second half of the fourth century BC. (Marazov 1998, 61, fig. 16.)

runs after him. By mounting the horse, he is symbolically enthroned. The seated posture also suggests an equilibrium between the vertical and the horizontal: it is the most stable position, marking a high, accomplished status. Gods or heroes are usually seated (Fig. 5.5), whereas mortals stand beside them or kneel below them. Sitting on a throne may be a visual and actional variant of the proto-Slavic verbal formula, *sideti – gliadeti*, "sit and look,"[26] signifying the exercise of the control that underlies all power.

The defeated person in the *agon* is in a lower position. This lower position is evident in an appliqué from Letnitsa, in the rendering of the wolf slain by the hero-horseman. It has fallen on its back and its legs are raised, so that it is also depicted in an upside-down and thus helpless position. Maybe this is an example of visual etymology; an exact parallel can be found in the restored Indo-European poetic formula: "May the enemy fall at your feet."[27]

The *agon*, a contest in manhood, is characteristic of the mythical biography of the dynast, whose principal episodes, hunting and combat, are presented in the frescoes in their tombs.[28] The total absence of warrior themes in the metalwork of the Thracians is surprising in light of the special significance attached to the agonic principle in royal ideology, especially given the proverbial militancy of that ancient people. This anomaly can probably be explained by noting that armed combat is a field for manifesting the personal qualities of the already accomplished dynast, whereas the iconography in Thracian metalwork focuses more on the process of initiation and consecration of that dynast, in which the choice of the deity is essential.

The art of the Thracians has preserved a local image of the Thracian Ares. Known as *Kandaon*, or "dog-strangler,"[29] the war god is presented by means of a peculiar iconography – as a winged half-centaur, with equine hind legs and tail, carrying a strangled wolf on his shoulders. This association between the war deity and the dog-wolf is inherent in Indo-European mythology[30] (Fig. 5.6), in which the two are either identified or opposed. The killing or taming of the monstrous dog is one of the initiation rites of the military hero – the Greek Heracles, the Germanic Odin, the Thracian Lykourgos, and the Irish Cuchulain. This is also the central theme of the initiation ideology: the young warriors are a "pack": they behave like dogs or are incarnated in canine creatures. In Thracian bronze work the hero is also usually accompanied by a dog during hunting. The centaur-like nature of the Thracian Ares should not surprise us, because the mythical centaurs are a reflection of the members of the male initiation alliances, the *Maennerbund*.[31]

Although he is not depicted in combat with a human adversary, the Thracian horseman is indisputably rendered as a warrior through the code of dress. He always wears body armor, and sometimes also a helmet and greaves. He is usually armed with a spear, which is used both in hunting and in battle. In tomb paintings, he is followed by a servant or armor-bearer.

A fundamental feature of the Indo-European military hero is his anger, his lupine fury.[32] This is true of the Thracian kings. We learn from Greek written sources about the absence of restraint in their behavior. They

5.6. Bronze matrix from Gorno Avlanovo, second half of the fourth century BC. (Marazov 1998, 36, fig. 2.)

rapidly change their mood, and since they bear no social responsibility, they can kill with impunity even people in their immediate environment. In the images in profile on the plaques, Letnitsa, the mouth of the hero-horseman, is always open, as if in an angry cry like that of Lykourgus, which made even the god Dionysos tremble (*Iliad* 6, 130–140).

The warrior qualities of the Thracian hero can also be coded in other indirect ways. Since hair is easily manipulated without affecting the structure of the body, it becomes a convenient classifier for marking a new status[33] (Fig. 5.7). Indo-Europeans mark the warrior function with a special hairstyle: see the ancient Persian (Iranian) term used for young warriors, *gaešu*, "braided hair." In some scenes from Thracian metalwork, hunting warriors are also depicted with curled hair; the perfection of the curls is represented on the greaves. A number of ancient authors speak about the Thracians as *akromoi*, "with hair piled on top of their head" (Homer, *Iliad* 4.520–530; Plutarch, *Thes.* 5) and explain this fashion as related to their military character. The iconography has also preserved this hairstyle in two appliqués from the Letnitsa Treasure (Fig. 5.7; Chapter 8, Bonfante, this volume, Plate XXI).

Gold objects of the fifth-fourth centuries BC, widely attested in finds from Thrace, reflected social distinctions. The precious metal itself is very strongly charged with mythological meanings.[34] According to Thracian

5.7. Silver appliqué from the Letnitsa Treasure. Detail. Second half of the fourth century BC. (Marazov 1998, 164, Cat. 93.)

legend, gold came to mortals from the other world to mark the position of the chosen individual with its brilliance and with its immortality. The Greeks accused the barbarians of adorning themselves with gold, like women – a scornful comparison within the Greek obscene vocabulary. However, when we imagine the appearance of the Thracian dynast wearing shiny armor, a gold or silver helmet (Plate VIIIB), gold pectoral, gold belt, and a silver greave with gilt inlay, carrying a divinely decorated shield and riding a horse with precious appliqués, we understand why the Thracians referred to their nobility as *zibythides*, that is, "brilliant, shining."[35]

During the Classical period, the status of the gold material was no longer sufficient to enhance social position. Objects and their functions connected with the king became defined with growing clarity: they included articles of adornment, protective armor, sets of tableware, and horse-trappings.[36] These objects usually accompanied the deceased dynast in his burial, because they were perceived as political insignia and helped the king restore his rank in the next life. The diversity of object forms, which reflects the high degree of specialization of these objects, especially of the vessels, suggests their ritual function. The amphora rhyton from the Panagyurishte Treasure was probably used in fraternization rites, and also as a vase related to the mysteries in the cult of the

5.8. Silver phiale from the Rogozen Treasure with an inscription: *Kotyos ek Beou*, second half of the fourth century BC. (Marazov 1998, 185, Cat. 122.)

Kabeiroi, as evidenced both by the Theban theme on its sides and by the figures of the child Heracles and of the adult Silenus on its base.

The object groups play a role in the functioning of the ritual system of the royal ideology. We find the same objects and signs both in artistic images and in burials and excavated treasures. In the mythological sphere of royal ideology, the group of particular objects is transformed into an attribute code that is informative about the designation of the royal rank; therefore – as in the epic tradition – it became the principal language of art as well. The language of objects is of special significance for the social characterization of the participating figures, as in the tomb from Alexandrovo.[37] Already in the Chalcolithic Age, according to finds from the Varna necropolis, the ruler was perceived through an aggregate of object-social signs and insignia that constituted the political body of the king. After his physical death, his symbolic body could be reconstructed from that aggregate.

The insignia marking the man chosen by the goddess to be the legitimate king cover the three ideological functions of the Indo-European dynast.[38] The cup or phiale (Fig. 5.8), jug, and rhyton constitute the first functional sign: with it, people performed libations in honor of the gods and fraternization toasts. The bow and the spear belong to the sign system of the warrior function.[39] Wealth – horses, like those of Rhesus, the legendary king of the Edones – marks the third function.[40] Investiture scenes regularly emphasize the action of holding the insignia – cup, bow, eagle, spear, reins, and so on. Thus, the actional code reflects the semiotic charge of the verb in the royal ideology: the dynast *holds* the rule – hence the etymology of the word *derzhava*, "state," in Slavonic languages.[41]

The king assumes the quality of a deity because he is successful and powerful. The possession of wealth as the main feature of social characterization is emphasized by the use of the possessive dative in the sacral formulae written on the vessels. To have means to rule. The toponym following the preposition "from" (*ex*) is clearly identified with the object itself in their common quality of property of the dynast: KOTYOS EG BEOU, that is "*Kotyos eks Beou,*" "of Kotys, from [the city of] Beos" (Fig. 5.8).

The epic hero and the historical king are viewed as the synthesis of the three functions.[42] A good example is the description of Sitalkes, one of the greatest Thracian dynasts. He is said to have inherited his kingdom as a small land but, through his own valor and mind, increased his power manifold, because he ruled over his subjects *fairly* (first function – author's emphasis), he was a *brave* and *experienced general* in battle (second function – author's emphasis), and in addition, he worked very hard *to increase his revenues* (third function – author's emphasis) (Diodorus 12.50).

Inscriptions are found only on vessels, because they are the main mythical insignia of the first, priestly function. Therefore, in Apollo's set from Rogozen, the king of the Odrysae, Kotys I, is presented as *pais*, that is, as mysterial son, servant, or slave of the deity Apollo.[43] However, as this was also the way to designate the youths serving the older participants in the symposium, it also means that Kotys performed the function of cup-bearer in the cult of that god. We can compare the Erotes from the Borovo jug-rhyton, who act as *paides* of the Kabeiroi[44] (Plate IX).

In view of the significance of gold in the royal ideology, it is not surprising that both Greek written sources and Thracian iconography contained references to the myth of the golden ram. According to one version, the ram was born from the union of Poseidon to the Thracian princess Bysaltis; according to another, it was the progeny of Hermes and Rhene. The myth of the Golden Fleece dates back to the Mycenaean age; ever since, the possession of the skin of the golden ram was indissolubly linked with the notion of the legitimacy of power.[45] This animal appears repeatedly in Thracian iconography. A repeated image is that of the *kriobolion*, or ram sacrifice: on the cheek pieces of the gold helmet from Kotsofeneshti (Fig. 5.10 and Plate XI),[46] the warrior is pressing the animal with his knee while it falls under his weight, its legs folded under its body in a familiar sacrificial posture.[47]

Royal Ritual Practices: Investiture by Gold and Fire

In the symbolism of the rite, gold is related to the sun and to fire. The sanctuary of Dionysos in Thrace – which, incidentally, Bulgarian archae-ologists and amateurs seem to discover every year, at different places in the Rhodope Mountains – was famous for its royal oracles.[48] A high flame flaring from the wine poured over the burning altar was considered a good omen for the man performing the libation to be chosen king.[49] This ritual is the inverse of the Scythian myth of the royal insignia that fell from the sky amid flames. In that story, the action is directed down-ward, and the fire has to die down before the legitimate king – the one chosen by the goddess of the hearth, Tabiti – is allowed to come close to the objects of power (Herodotus 4.5).

The place and role of the royal feast[50] in the ideology of the Thracians are significant, hence the large proportion of drinking equipment and plates present in the art of the Thracians – about 240 precious phialae, 40 rhytons, and 90 jugs, in addition to other types of vessels. The inves-titure is like the preparation for a feast, when the goddess offers a cup to the hero as insignia with which he can communicate with the world of the gods (Fig. 5.9). The heroic apotheosis is then presented as partic-ipation in a feast, with the hero seated on a throne holding a phiale in one hand and and a rhyton in the other, as shown on the golden helmet from Baicheni.

The royal wedding is another episode in the investiture. Since it is the goddess who usually chooses the dynast, communion with her takes the form of marriage. At the end of the series of trials, the hero marries the captive he has rescued from the dragon. This trial and the event that follows are mandatory steps along his road to power, because in the archaic way of thinking, the princess personified the territory of the kingdom in the other world. A dynast began his journey with mar-riage: this is reflected in two versions in the frescoes from the tombs in Kazanlak (Plate X) and Sveshtari. Since marriage is a classifier of the social norm, it is also a good visual code by which a dynast's legitimacy is recognized.

The royal round is another ritual act that was mandatory for many of the archaic dynasts, in both antiquity and the Middle Ages.[51] In addi-tion to the ancient written sources that specifically attest to this rite for

5.9. Gold ring from Brezovo, second half of the fourth century BC. (Marazov 1994b, 180, Cat. 110.)

Thracian kings, inscribed vessels also suggest that it was familiar in the royal palace of the Odrysae. The toponyms in the votive formulae indicate the periodic visits that Kotys I paid to several major settlements in the southeastern part of Thrace: Geistai, Argiskes, Beos, Sauthabas, and Apros. The king's round seems to have included mostly sacral centers of the kingdom: the sanctuary of the Kabeiroi, or the Great Gods, was apparently in the city of Beos, while that of Apollo was in Argiskes. We may assume that in Thrace there were itineraries of the *via sacra* type. Herodotus (7.115) speaks of the journey of the Persian dynast Darius in an itinerary that crossed the eastern part of Thrace, and that the Thracians continued to worship as sacred.[52]

Thracian iconography of the fifth and fourth centuries BC is therefore connected with themes of the royal ideology. The increased role of objects and the diversity of object forms in the ritual system of royal ideology explain the growing need for a richer iconographic fund of images, ornaments, and pictorial and epigraphic texts relating to kingship, making their function more concrete. An example of this are the eyes on gold and silver Thracian helmets, which reflect the possession of sacral, closed, hermetic, doctrinal knowledge (Plates VIIIB and XI) and present the dynast as an *epoptes* who has gained insight into doctrinal secrets that are inaccessible to the remaining members of society. Since the helmet marks the uppermost point in the anthropomorphized cosmos, the head, it metaphorically marks the king as the "head" of society.[53] The peaked helmet, or *pilos*, worn by the hero from

5.10. Sacrifice of the Golden Ram (*kriobolion*). Cheek piece of a gold helmet from Kotsofeneshti, Romania, second half of the fourth century BC. (Marazov 1998, 67, fig. 27.)

the *kriobolion* on the cheek pieces of the gold helmet from Kotsofeneshti (Fig. 5.10 and Plate XI) was a distinctive sign of the noble Thracians, who were referred to as *pilophoroi* or *pileati* on account of it.[54] It is clear that the depiction of this theme on an attribute of power is also connected with royal ideology.

The role of shamanism among the Thracians is also something revealed by the decoration of Thracian helmets.[55] The hat is an important

5.11. Hybrid eight-legged animal. Silver goblet from Agighiol, Romania, second half of the fourth century BC. (Marazov 1998, 65, 69, figs. 24, 28.)

element in the shamanic costume. In many shamanic traditions the hat is crowned with the figure of a bird or bird feathers,[56] like those included in the iconography of the Thracian helmets. In finds from Agighiol and the Iron Gates, furthermore, helmets have been found together with silver goblets, whose biconical shape can be traced back to Iranian prototypes from the end of the second millennium BC.[57] The presence of a fantastic animal in the repertoire of their decoration suggests a shamanic interpretation. This key figure in the animal repertoire of their decoration is an eight-legged animal, a hybrid with the hooves of a horse, the muzzle of a he-goat, and a stag's enormous antlers, whose tips pass into the heads of birds of prey (Fig. 5.11). In many traditions, the animal on which the shaman is riding has eight legs, for example Slepnir, the horse of the Germanic god-shaman Odin. Feathers are also often included in the rendering of various animals.

In contrast to, but also along with this variety of representations and the variety of their meanings, the depth of the myth communicated through the iconography is relatively limited. We cannot expect to be able to arrive at a reconstruction of a specific variant of the myth, such as the name of a particular mythical figure, or the exact place where an action takes place. The iconography does not give names, but only designates certain structures. In the myth, concrete information, such as the names of the heroes and the motivation of their actions, constitutes the most superficial and the least stable layer of the mythical content. While these elements are susceptible to change and innovation, the structure preserves the most profound and most constant meanings of myth. (An oral myth, too, always exists throughout a generation of variants.) The relatively undefined character of Thracian iconography offers a broader range of interpretative possibilities and allows for different types of updating of the pictorial myth, corresponding to the different degrees of initiation.

Iconography and Style in Thracian Art

Most of the material in the burials and treasures from Thrace is dated to the fourth century BC. The evolution of the iconography and style of Thracian art is difficult to trace, because the art is conservative in principle and operates with a limited iconographic and stylistic repertoire. Monuments of Thracian art often feature similar or even identical images and scenes, not only because they are by the same artist, but also because they translate the same notions into pictorial language. In these cases the iconography functions like a literary retelling of the myths, or the epic poems of those ancient societies with a developed literary tradition – Egyptians, Sumerians, and Hittites. The fixing of the myth, whether in word or in stone, restricts its variability. The recorded variant becomes the only model that all of the other narratives must take into account, and the fixed myth no longer corresponds to the continually evolving myth, which by its nature is continually updated with new variants and versions.

In Thrace there was no need for the existence of similar models within the iconographic tradition, because the priestly function did not have a developed theology. We should consider Thracian iconography more as the result of common notions among the different Thracian tribes than as an attempt to create and endorse patterns fixing these notions. It is not a record of the myth. The function of the art of the Thracians is still far from being like that of the frescoes, sculpture, icons, and books of the Middle Ages, which constituted the Bible of the illiterate. The principles for building the epic narrative provide better analogies for its figurative language, for the key mythological images in Thracian iconography are the goddess and the hero, and its key themes include the status of the female deity and her relations with the hero. Broadly speaking, this constitutes the whole of the iconographic content of Thracian art.

In this context, it is difficult to separate the categories of iconography and style, because the style has meaning. The frontal posture characteristic of Thracian art emphasizes the figure's importance. Depicted *en face*, the protagonist is excluded from the general line of the narrative and exists in other dimensions.[58] It is not by accident that within a scene in which images are shown in profile, the head of the predator is always depicted *en face* (jug No. 155 from Rogozen).

Symmetry is also a way of expressing the duality of a certain image (jug Nos. 157 and 155 from Rogozen) (Fig. 5.12). A central motif dividing two symmetrical images highlights the agonic character of the scene (a jug from Vratsa), while a repetitive rhythm gives the composition a more ceremonial, ritual character (frescoes from Sveshtari and Kazanlak).

Gilding, one of the most characteristic techniques in Thracian metalwork, is a way to mark the magical, sacred nature of an image, because everything made of gold was believed to come from the other world. The semantics of color has special importance in painting. In the hunting scenes in frescoes from the central burial chamber of the newly discovered tomb in Alexandrovo, the horses of the hunters are of different colors: white, red, gray, and gold. In my opinion, these colors reflect the Indo-European tripartite ideology: white as the color of the priests, red of the warriors, and black of the third function;[59] but parallels are also seen in the color symbolism of fairy tales. The horseman riding the golden horse probably represents the hero-progenitor who lives in the world beyond (Fig. 5.13 and Plate XII), into whose image the deceased dynast has to merge in order to be transformed into an *anthropodaimon*.

We must not confuse the roles of the iconography and what it means. Often ostensibly different scenes, such as those of hunting, have an

5.12. Winged divinity holding animals, flanked by winged creatures. Silver jug from the Rogozen Treasure, second half of the fourth century BC. (Marazov 1998, 152, Cat. 80.)

identical content. There is no fixed iconography. Different meanings occur through changes in the context, as for example by involving the concrete sign in various types of structural interactions with other signs. Consequently, apparently close iconographic themes might in fact have a very different content.

Formulaic Language in the Animal Style

The art of Eurasia was, from the first millennium BC, characterized by a common phenomenon: the total domination of the so-called animal style[60] (Plate XIII). Hundreds of weapons and metal appliqués are

5.13. Hero on a golden horse from frescoes on the dome of the central chamber of the Alexandrovo Tomb, first half of the fourth century BC. (Photo Marazov.)

decorated with animal figures belonging to different species and shown in different positions. Until recently, this was believed to reflect a lower degree of religious conscience, which ruled out the existence of anthropomorphic notions about deities. But it should not be assumed that these beasts simply coded the totemic notions of the ancient tribes inhabiting the vast territory from present-day Austria to China; could they all have derived their origin from a tiger, wolf, stag, or horse? Instead of seeking an explanation in unknown beliefs or in the existence of a zoomorphic pantheon, we can see in this animal repertoire an image vocabulary of a mythological language and code. This was why this style was preserved long after human images gained prominence in art. The animal figures and their postures or movements are signs of another reality that lies beyond them, and the grammar of these images in itself produces meaning.

Let us take the motif of the curled-up wolf[51] (Fig. 5.14). The wolf has a place in the military initiation through which young boys have to pass in order to become full-fledged men – adult warriors. Through various associations, the warrior is identified with the wolf.[62] Why is the animal in these monuments curled up? Predators have this habit, but only when they are asleep; at other times, the eye of the beast is usually wide open. A different explanation could be that the circle formed by the curled-up

5.14. Wolf on a gold pectoral from Bashova Moghila, second half of the fifth century BC. (Marazov 1998, 196, Cat. 136.)

figure is a sign of a completed cycle; in terms of time, space, or status, it is a sign of periodicity. Perhaps these appliqués were initiation gifts, bearing metaphors related to the boys' initiations, which were given to them after they had been initiated.

Young warriors in Iran received a belt that encircles the body, that is, it closes the circle.[63] Belts often have symbolic meaning. The Germanic myth about the cosmic wolf Fenrir narrates how the gods decided to tie the monster so as to postpone the day of the global catastrophe, when it was to devour the world. For the Indo-Europeans, the defeated adversary or criminal had to be tied.[64] The curled-up wolf could be an image of the magic force of the warrior, or of his god, through which he would be able to tie up or paralyze his enemy.

Human figures entered the basic visual code of the local craftsman only in the fourth century BC. But why did anthropomorphic images appear so late? The Thracians were already familiar with the anthropocentric art of the Greeks in the early fifth century BC. Why did they wait so long to yield to the temptation? Clearly, internal prerequisites were more important than any aspiration toward something foreign or exotic. Around the beginning of the fourth century BC, the dynamism of the processes of state formation in Thrace was intensified. Kingdoms multiplied rapidly, especially to the north of the Haemus Mountain, and local dynasts felt the need to legitimize their authority through the image language of art. The synchronicity of anthropomorphism and the use of inscriptions reflect the isofunctionality of the epigraphic and pictorial code of myth. We have seen that art in Thrace is connected with and dependent on social and political processes. The thin social base of art and its dependence on the royal courts of the dynasts are characteristic features of this type of artistic production. Around the middle of the third century BC this art disappeared, because the land was occupied by Celts who founded their kingdom there.

The local style developed mainly in northern Thrace; the dynasts to the south of the Haemus Mountain relied mainly on imports from Greek workshops. The territories of the Odrysian kingdom were the richest in Greek objects, a fact that is connected with its development and expansion in the late fifth and the fourth centuries BC.[65] Such exotic objects tend to be rare occurrences in finds from the northern principalities.

The problem of the workshops remains open for lack of sufficient material, but it would seem that the unity of the local style was due to a relatively rapid exchange between different workshops resulting from the custom of exchanging gifts and from sharing matrices, some of which were used by several artists; good examples are those from Gorno Avlanovo (see Fig. 5.6) and Koubrat.

In an archaic society, the place and the role of the artist were similar to those of the priest: both were familiar with the sacred history of myth and of royal ideology. They rendered it in different languages, but it performed identical functions. To what extent, however, was the artist himself involved in the inner circle of the initiated, and how was this social order structured? In order to answer this question, we must examine the social status of the Thracian artist and see whether he still possessed the high position of the goldsmith from the Varna Chalcolithic necropolis or if he had the status of a mere craftsman, a status close to that of the slave.

His art addressed a strictly defined group and would have been comprehensible only to the initiated – the aristocrats who had access to the mysteries. But what freedom in formulating the iconography did he possess? The artist was in the position of the singer, of the *aedes*, or bard, who had the knowledge and the formulae, the equivalent of the artist's matrices. The treasure from Rogozen offers an interesting example: on a phiale we encounter the Thracian name *Disloias* in combination with the verb *epoiese*, "made." To whom did this name belong – the artist or the person who commissioned the vessel? The etymology of the theophoric name, which is equivalent to the Slavic *Bogoslav*, "glorifying God" or "glorified by God," suggests a noble origin. Moreover, the phiale on which the name is inscribed is among the least representative vessels from Thrace, so we cannot assume any creative pride on the part of the craftsman. The name of an ordinary artist could hardly appear side by side with the name of one of the greatest Odrysian dynasts – Kotys. I therefore propose to see this name, rather than that of the artist, as the name of the magistrate who ordered the vase as a gift or a sign of subordination for the king who was visiting his city.

Several silver vessels from the Bashova Moghila tumulus feature yet a different inscription: *Da-da-le-me*. I am inclined to seek its meaning in the Greek etymology of the precious object – compare the Slavic iz-*delie* – and not, as has been suggested, in the sacral formula of the type "Goddess, Earth, protect me."[66] This interpretation offers yet another proof of the role of luxury objects in the ideology of the Thracian kings, and seems to take us back to the legendary Mycenaean world in which the mythical artist Daedalus created objects as signs for designating their dynast Minos as king.[67]

The Archaic Artist and Singer of Tales

The numerous finds from Thracian burials and treasures reveal the work of many ancient artist-goldsmiths. It is not enough to say that these products are *daedala*, beautiful and exquisite. It would be interesting to find out more about the process of their creation – not just the technology used by the artist, but also the creation of forms, the choice of a theme or image, and its subsequent transformation into a figure or scene.

Every archaic image has a sacred element to its character. The barbarian artist, like a priest or a singer – *aedes*, rhapsode – was the guardian of the sacral tradition. Just as during the feasts in the royal court the *aedes* sang epic poems,[68] the artist came to the dynast's palace to forge these poems in gold and silver. Pictorial texts can be seen as a completely autonomous, albeit parallel, language, just as important as the other mythological languages, both verbal and actional. Reading the images is like interpreting the content of the myth or the epic song; it requires prior knowledge not only about the concrete narrative, but also about the essence of the myth. This knowledge does not require any specialized training on the part of the spectator: in an archaic society, learning the mythology and the epic tradition occurred naturally and acquired greater depth during the different phases of the human life cycle. For archaic peoples, such knowledge seemed natural, almost instinctive: "I have no idea why this is so, but I know that it is so."

The essence, the function, and the communicative fabric of the three languages – myth, epic, and art – are structurally similar: the archaic artist was guided by similar mythopoietic principles and mechanisms. In recent years, studies of folklore have not only confirmed but also expanded and deepened conclusions concerning the character and structure of the epic tradition,[69] which can be applied in the study of the pictorial tradition of archaic peoples.

What they have in common is their formulaic language. The language of formulas is one of the mechanisms through which the epic narrative is built. The formula is formed from a noun that plays the role of agent, accompanied by its characteristic adjective (epithet): for example, "green forest," "first love," "young and wild," "sparkling wine," "cherry-black eyes," "sweet voice." A series of Thracian vessels bear inscriptions using the same kind of formula, for example, KOTYOS EG BEOV "*Kotyos ek Beo*," "[of, belonging to] Kotys, [given] by [the city of] Beos" (see Fig. 5.8). If the formula is enlarged by adding a verb, an actional text is obtained: "and he rode a black horse," "lifted the spear menacingly," "pierced the heart," and so on.

Absence of Logical Motivation

In both the epic tradition and the myth, certain actions of the protagonists seem absolutely unjustified by the inner logic of the narrative itself. Motivation is among the least stable elements of the mythological narrative. The same mythical structure, the action, or quality, is often differently motivated, because the real reason for one action or another is outside the actual narrative and must be sought in the behavioral norms of the respective society, in the scale of values that it has created and adheres to.

Why is the Amazon[70] breastless or with only one breast? Later Greek narratives explain this mythical characterization of the maiden-warrior in practical terms: the Amazon cut off her right breast because it interfered with her ability to shoot her bow. The mythological reason, however, lies in the social nature of the image. Since she does not pass through the female initiation and cannot perform the function of the woman in archaic society, the heroic maiden is pushed toward the male pole: she abandons all female occupations (spinning, weaving, etc.) and takes up activities that are characteristic of men (war, battle). Though biologically a woman, she finds her realization in the actional sphere of the man.[71] The breast serves for breast-feeding babies: the Amazon, a heroic maiden, does not need it because she will never raise children. The myth does not explain; it merely codifies a social norm in an artistic image. A mythological narrative often appears to be incoherent, as if logical elements are missing. In the pictorial text of the myth, the motivation of the action is missing for the same reason: it is not the action itself that is important, but its meaning. And the meaning is most often outside the narrative.

As we have seen, the style of barbarian art is based mainly on rhythms of repetition, as in music, or more precisely as in the singing epic tradition. Symmetry is not only a stylistic means; it produces meaning. It is like the echo that reflects the voice, like a mirror reflection of a motif through which suggestion is heightened. The doubling of the image is not an aim in itself, nor is its decorative effect. On jug No. 155 from the Rogozen Treasure, the figure of a goddess riding on a lioness appears on both sides of the central motif typical of the animal style (Fig. 5.15 and Plate XIV). Through repetition, the artist codes the actual dual nature of this image, which combines matronal and virginal features. As a form of repetition, symmetry is also a means of introducing rhythm in the structure of the image. Because symmetrical compositions are presented on pictorial fields that are closed, they stabilize the scene in terms of both composition and meaning. The semantic accent falls on the central motif around which the composition develops. This proves to be most often the most intensively charged with meaning, with referent significance with respect to the symmetrical figures. This is the case in the jug from Rogozen, where the lion attacking the doe is an animal metaphor

5.15. Two goddesses riding on lionesses. Drawing. Silver jug from the Rogozen Treasure, second half of the fourth century BC. (Marazov 1996, 58.)

of the hero chasing the maiden. He catches her, which also explains the duality in the image of the goddess: only at the moment of marriage can the woman combine the two statuses.

Sometimes the central motif is a more modest sign than the images flanking it. On the jug from Rogozen it is semiotically weaker, because it belongs to the lower order of the animal repertoire. In the gold jug from Vratsa the two chariots meet in front of an enormous palmette, which represents an even lower classification – plants. But the central motif probably also possesses a more intensive semantic charge as the referent goal of the race, that is, a peculiar image metaphor of the world tree. In ancient Near Eastern art, divine or semidivine creatures, demons, are placed near such a tree of life, though they too have a lower semantic and informational activity than the central motif.

A linear frieze ordering of the figures also carries a meaning. The repeated movements of figures walking one after the other create the rhythm of the folk song, which is based on repetition of both text and melody. In contrast to a symmetrical order, the choreography of such images presupposes an open composition. The addition of more images from the same or a similar order attributes to it a greater duration; it is like an endless open chain-dance, performed to the rhythm of a monotonous melody. There is no clash or comparison here; the competitive agonic element is missing. The frieze composition, characteristic of Near Eastern-type ceremonial themes, has a greater potential for marking quality in terms of solemnity, as for a religious procession or parade. It therefore features prominently in works connected with the ideology of royal power. The monotonous repetition finds analogies in the actional code of a ritual, as well as in its music.[72]

When the Thracians appeared in the art of antiquity, it was dominated by two artistic languages, Persian and Greek. The attraction of Thracian artists to the Iranian tradition is only natural, because it was ideologically closer to the royal patrons in Thrace.[73] Indeed, the itinerary followed by Darius was considered to be sacred there. By the fifth century BC, however, the art market had been taken over by Greeks.

In a Scythian environment, Greek artists were attempting to render local myths using the Greek artistic language; but among the Thracians, Greek works of art did not carry purely Greek mythological information. Any reinterpretation therefore needs to start at the level of the myth rather than at the level of adaptation to the local mythological tradition. How familiar with Greek mythology were the Thracians? Some believe that they were already Hellenized in the fourth century BC. To know a culture, however, you must speak its language in order to understand its secondary modeling systems. We know that even the kings of the Thracians did not speak Greek: they communicated with the Greeks through interpreters. The inscriptions on the Thracian vases, which include numerous spelling mistakes, suggest that the artists too knew the Greek language only slightly.

The phiale with Auge and Heracles from the Rogozen Treasure (Fig. 5.16 and Plate XV) shows the role of the attribute code in understanding the profound mythical significance of the scene. The local owner of this ancient metalwork, Didykaimos, was hardly sufficiently familiar with Greek mythology to understand the content of the violent scene, nor did the inscriptions directly naming the figures in the scene help him. The Greek artist, however, offered him other codes, ritual and object, for reading the scene. Auge is depicted with one sandal, as a *monosandalos*[74] – a detail that is absent in the Greek myth and in other images of this theme. Unlike many modern scholars, the Thracians understood the meaning of this asymmetry: Auge is depicted at a moment of transition – she is no longer a maiden, but she is not yet a wife either. This is a moment of violence, which the military hero normally exercises over the woman from the first ideological function.

The iconography of Greek vase painting from Thrace suggests the same selective attitude. The most frequently occurring themes are from the Dionysiac mythical and ritual circle: the ancient Greeks were convinced that Dionysos came to them from Thrace. The Thracian burial of Bashova Moghila yielded the red-figured hydria where, for the first time,

5.16. Silver phiale from the Rogozen Treasure, second half of the fourth century BC. (Marazov 1998, 176, Cat. 107.)

the Samothracian deities are identified with the Kabeiroi.[75] On the vessels from the Panagyurishte and Borovo treasures, Greek artistic means have been used to present mythical precedents from the mysterial ideology of the Kabeiroi, which had become a part of the royal doctrine for the Odrysae. The reason for the portrayal of so many images of Heracles in Thracian metalwork is that he provided the iconographic model of a hero to all ancient peoples who did not have a pictorial tradition of their own (Fig. 5.17).

Clearly, the Thracians did not accept Greek influences passively. The activity of Thracian clients was manifested in their choice of images, scenes, and motifs from Greek iconography. They might choose iconographic themes connected with a common cult doctrine – Apollo, Dionysos, and the Kabeiroi, or the reinterpretation of an iconographic theme or image – Heracles, Auge and Heracles, Heracles and the Amazon. Or they might make a selection that involved reinterpreting the functions of the object with the addition of new texts, as in phiale No. 42 from Rogozen.

Certain images from Thracian iconography are sometimes too hastily identified through comparisons with the Greek or Near Eastern tradition (for example, jug No. 158 from Rogozen). Because the iconography

5.17. Heracles and the Nemean Lion. Silver appliqué from Dolna Koznitsa, second half of the fourth century BC. (Marazov 1998, 107, Cat. 20.)

is not perceived as a system, partial comparisons are made with single attributes or features. The fact that the Thracians resorted to partial borrowings does not mean that they preserved the mythological meaning of the model, however. Most often the iconography was borrowed, like the script in which other texts were written – for instance, the inscriptions from rocks near Kyolmen or on the gold ring from Ezero. All this constitutes the system of *interpretatio thracica*.

The Persian Tradition and the Thracians

The Thracian kings naturally preferred everything that was connected with Persian culture. The Achaemenid monarch was a model from which the penetration of iconographic themes occurred along with their stylistic details. The motif of the lion and a number of fantastic animals came from Near Eastern iconography, as did the depiction of the human figure – head and feet in profile and frontal torso. Sometimes stylistic details followed the iconographic model as well as the object form itself, in the case of armor, or tableware such as the goblets, rhytons, amphora-rhytons, and phialae.

A Thracian-Scythian cultural *koine* is not a modern construction; it existed in reality. Finds from Scythia, Homina Moghila, Ogouz, and other locations have an indisputable Thracian character. In recent years, furthermore, a number of objects have been found in Thrace decorated with elements of the Scythian animal style, dating from the late sixth and the fifth centuries BC, and thus created at a time when the transition between the Early Iron Age and the Late Iron Age was not yet completed in Thrace. Thracian art was not yet in a position to respond to the new requirements of the royal ideology, but it responded to the Scythian artistic production that flourished at that time. In the second half of the fourth century BC, however, the motivation of power through the products and the images of art had attained a higher stage, the configuration of the interaction changed, and the Thracians became suppliers of ideas and of a more developed artistic tradition in which the human image had already developed.

The language of Philomele can start to speak, provided that its statements are not examined separately, but within the larger text of Thracian culture. In the rules of this culture, both the narrative and the cumulative texts attain the same effect, translating ideas that reflect and designate the values and norms of behavior inherent in the entire cultural community. As we have seen, the iconography of art reflects not the historical reality as a whole, nor life as a whole, but only those segments that are appropriate as classifiers of specific ideas. Stylistic details and the epigraphic evidence allow for a relatively accurate dating of the objects of barbarian art. But any attempt to date the myth according to its appearance in a certain artifact would be incorrect.[76] There is no stratigraphy of the pictorial sources from which we can trace and develop a chronology of the myth in art, for change in the mythological language, or the transition to another code, do not necessarily mean a radical change of the mythological material itself.

I shall cite only one example. During the late Hellenistic period, the iconography of Thracian art was reduced to two principal images: the goddess and the hero-horseman. A serious change occurred in the style as well. Yet behind these changes lay the same ideological reality that had produced other images during the preceding period. The image of the Thracian hero-horseman was associated to a much greater extent with the cult during the Roman period, but though it no longer served the royal ideology, its iconography preserved the essential features of the equestrian hero-king from the fourth century BC. This iconography was preserved as a sign system, even as another, older level in its semantics – the mythological and cult level – was updated. The fact that in many votive reliefs from Roman Thrace the horseman is referred to as *kyrios*, "master," suggests that it represented a transition of the terminology from the royal ideology to religion.

In the Roman period, the image of the *heros* perpetuated the mythical genealogy of the hero and first king from the period of the flourishing of Thracian culture. So, too, with similar mythopoietic mechanisms, there reappeared in Bulgarian folklore images of the medieval kings – guardians of the people who had turned into legends during the centuries of Ottoman domination. Like the legendary Thracian dynast Rhesus, they had remained isolated in the rocks until the day came for them to go out and to free their enslaved people.

Appendix: New Finds of Thracian Art in Bulgaria

New discoveries made in recent years in the territory of ancient Thrace have enriched the picture of Thracian art with many new objects and iconographic motifs.

Excavations of tumuli at Chernozem, near Plovdiv (2000–2003), uncovered a rare specimen of Greek metalwork of the second half of the fifth century BC, a silver kylix with a scene of Bellerophon killing the Chimaera (Fig. 5.18).[77] This hero appears to have been well known to the Thracian aristocracy, because his battle with the monster appears on a pitcher from the Rogozen Treasure and the murals from the Ostrusha tomb. Obviously, the Thracians interpreted the Greek myth in terms of their own ideology, recognizing in Bellerophon and his deed their cultural hero. The gold pectoral found in the same grave (Fig. 5.19)[78] attests to another source of inspiration aside from that of the Greek myth and the Greek origin of the mask of Medusa stamped in the middle of the plaque. The shape and iconography of the object, as well as the style of the animal figures surrounding the Gorgoneion, suggest that they were modeled on Eastern patterns. Items of this type have usually

5.18. Bellerophon killing the Chimaera. Kylix from Chernozem. Second half of the fifth century BC.

been described as "pectorals," but it is now obvious that at least some of them might have had another function.

The Svetitsa tumulus was excavated in 2004; a gold mask was the most interesting find[79] (Fig. 5.20). The red-figured Greek pottery included in the grave goods date the find to the end of the fifth century BC. The bearded wide face seems to possess individual features, but it is more probable that it depicted the typified features of the hero. This is confirmed by another gold mask, several decades later, from the excavations of the Dalakova Moghila tumulus of the first half of the fourth century BC, in which we see a rather summary image.[80] A third gold mask, acquired by the Vassil Bojkov Collection,[81] shows an intermediate stage in the development of the type: the face, rendered

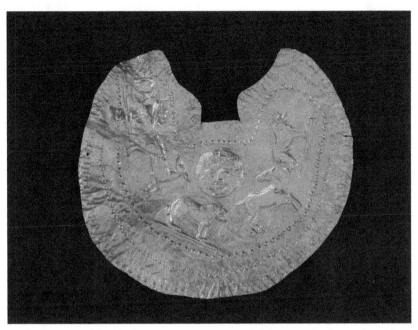

5.19. Gold pectoral with the Gorgoneion surrounded by animals, from Chernozem. Second half of the fifth century BC.

5.20. Gold mask from the Svetitsa tumulus mound. End of the fifth century BC.

5.21. Priam reaching for the altar of Zeus Herkeios. Detail, rhyton from the Dalakova Mogila tumulus. First half of the fourth century BC.

as a summary and stylized volume, is reminiscent of the Greek pictorial formula for a barbarian. It is surrounded by a flat band decorated with ornaments characteristic of the late sixth or first half of the fifth century BC, and the forehead is crowned with a ribbon of the type worn by the Thracian aristocrats *tarabosteis*.[82] Close analogies are found in gold masks recently discovered near Pella, which were worn under bronze helmets. The same collection also includes a gold "half-mask" with an opening cut out for the nose in the upper part and plastically rendered lips below it.[83]

The burial in Malomirovo-Zlatinitsa, dating back to the second half of the fourth century BC, is another important grave find in recent years.[84] In addition to the ornamentation of horse-trappings and phialae, which are characteristic of Thrace, the burial yielded two gilt silver rhytons with a short horn and a stag's head terminals. A lion and a griffin are attacking a bull on the horn of the first rhyton (Plate XVI). The horn of the second one features a boar hunt: two *ephebi* assisted by dogs are assaulting the enormous animal on both sides with a spear and a *labrys*. In this way, the main theme of the royal trial – the "boar hunt" – has now appeared in a new find from a Thracian tumulus (see Plate XII).

5.22 Andromache with *labrys*. Detail, rhyton from the Dalakova Mogila mound. First half of the fourth century BC.

The two silver rhytons from the Dalakova Mogila tumulus were also made by a Greek silversmith.[85] One of them has a long horn and ends with the protome of a centaur holding up a stone in his right hand. The other rhyton has a short horn ending with a ram's head (Figs. 5.21, 5.22). A scene from the *Iliupersis* is depicted in low relief: urged by Odysseus, Neoptolemos kills Priam with a sword near the altar of Zeus Herkeios (Fig. 5.21), in spite of Polyxena's protest and the *labrys* raised for protection in Andromache's hands (Fig. 5.22).[86] This scene proves the importance of the Trojan epic cycle for the royal ideology of the Thracians. If the theme was an emblematic manifestation of *hybris* for

5.23. Thracian women killing Orpheus. Silver kantharos from the Vassil Bojkov Collection. Last quarter of the fifth century BC.

the Greeks in the first half of the fourth century BC, for the Thracians it probably coded the behavior of the victor. This is also what the victorious ruler did in the iconography of Eastern art: he killed all the previous generations of the dynasty of the kingdom he had conquered.[87]

The number of rhytons found in the lands of the ancient Thracians has grown substantially in the last several years. Eight silver rhytons are kept in the Vassil Bojkov Collection. Particularly interesting are the specimen with a ram's head and the one with the protome of a he-goat (last quarter of the fifth century BC).[88] The long horn of the first rhyton is decorated with the myth of Melanippe and her twins, rarely illustrated. The second one, made at the same time, presents a mythological scene dealing with a Thracian subject, the killing of Orpheus by the Thracian women. On a silver kantharos in the same collection, this scene takes place before two herms that probably marked the entrance to the sanctuary of the Samothracian gods[89] (Figs. 5.23, 5.24a–c). The Thracian singer is also to be seen in the musician playing the lyre to a Thracian in ecstasy on a kylix from the same collection[90] (Fig. 5.25). Five rhytons end

5.24a. Thracian women killing Orpheus. Details of a kantharos from the Vassil Bojkov Collection. Last quarter of the fifth century BC.

5.24b. Thracian women killing Orpheus. Details of a kantharos from the Vassil Bojkov Collection. Last quarter of the fifth century BC.

5.24c. Thracian women killing Orpheus. Details of a kantharos from the Vassil Bojkov Collection. Last quarter of the fifth century BC.

5.25. Orpheus playing a lyre to a Thracian reclining on a *kline*. Kylix from the Vassil Bojkov Collection. Last quarter of the fifth century BC.

with the protome of a running stag (Plate XVII), one with the protome of a horse, and another one with a lion's head.

A silver greave with the image of a goddess on the knee and with scenes depicted in relief on the body was also discovered in Malomirovo (Plate XVIII and Fig. 5.26a–b). A centaur is offering a hare (Fig. 5.26a) to a horseman who holds a large rhyton in his hand (Fig. 5.26b). The race of centaurs is well represented in Thracian iconography. But this is the first time we see this fantastic creature characterized as Chiron, the teacher and tutor of young heroes during the period of their initiation. Below him is a well-known emblem: an eagle holding a hare in his talons. A goddess, seated on a throne, holds a phiale and a distaff in her hands, with a female servant standing behind her (Fig. 5.26b). The pictorial text unites two main themes of the royal ideology of the Thracians: the investiture, and the marriage of the hero who has undergone his value trial. Two more bronze greaves with the image of Athena were discovered in the Golyama Kosmatka tumulus near Kazanlak. They were probably an Athenian gift to the Odrysian ruler Seuthes III (331–300 BC), because they were found together with a bronze Chalcidian-type helmet with the image of the same goddess and the inscription *SEUTHOY* on the forehead, as well as silver phialae and an oinochoe with the same formula[91] (Fig. 5.27). A third greave of the same type is in the Vassil Bojkov Collection.

5.26a. Scene on the side of a greave from the Malomirovo-Zlatinitsa tumulus mound. Detail. Left: centaur holding a hare; below, eagle holding a hare in its talons.

Grave goods preserved in the third monolithic chamber of the tomb in the Golyama Kosmatka tumulus consist of weapons (Plate XIX), a gold wreath, and vessels. The marble doors (Fig. 5.28) of the vaulted chamber closed from within, which is evidence that ritual practices were performed there before the construction below the tumulus became a tomb. The black image of Medusa is seen on the left wing of the door, and on the right wing is the red image of Apollo/Helios. The ruler probably descended to the chthonian kingdom that is symbolized by the left wing of the door, Medusa and the vaulted chamber; then, after some

5.26b. Scene on the side of a greave from the Malomirovo-Zlatinitsa tumulus mound. Detail. Right: horseman holding a rhyton; below, seated goddess and female servant.

time, he climbed through the right wing of the door to the light of the solar god, so as to be reborn. We can compare the Indo-European mythological formula of birth as "seeing the light."[92] A similar ritual has been described by Herodotus in connection with the Getic deity Zalmoxis (Herodotus 4.85). When the ruler became familiar with the road to the world beyond, he was ritually prepared for his immortality. In front of the dromos leading to the tomb was found a large bronze head with the portrait features of Seuthes III (Fig. 5.29).

5.27. Inscription on the forehead of a bronze helmet from the Golyama Kosmatka tumulus mound: *seuthou* ("of Seuthes"). Detail. Second half of the fourth century BC.

5.28. Doors with the heads of Medusa and Apollo/Helios, from the Golyama Kosmatka tumulus mound. Second half of the fourth century BC.

5.29. Bronze head of the Odrysian king Seuthes III, from the Golyama Kosmatka tumulus mound. Second half of the fourth century BC.

Horse-trappings from the Vassil Bojkov Collection include two cheek pieces, each with a winged figure in flight (Figs. 5.30, 5.31). On one of the cheek pieces, the figure holds two small animals by the neck; on the other, a spear and a shield (or an arrow and a tambourine). So far, the image of a winged centaur was the only winged creature known in Thracian iconography. These two flying figures probably presented a twin structure similar to the twin sons of the Thracian north wind Boreas.[93]

New additions to museums and private collections raise the issue of the increasing number of imported Greek objects in Thrace in the last quarter of the fifth century BC. That was the time of the Peloponnesian Wars, when the Athenians needed a secure rear guard and when they

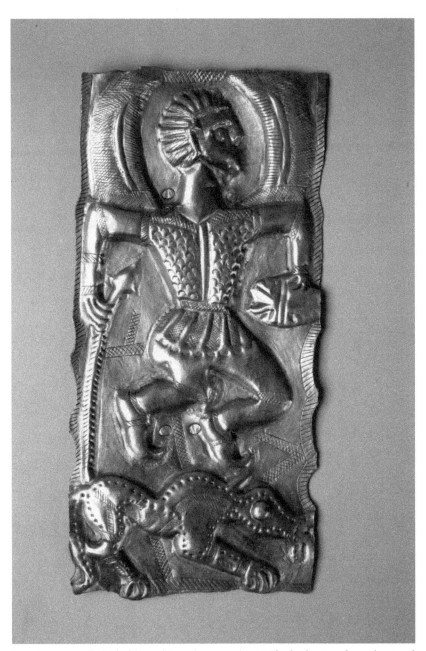

5.30. Figure in flight holding objects (weapons?). Detail, cheek piece from the Vassil Bojkov Collection. Fourth century BC.

5.31. Figure in flight holding small animals. Detail, cheek piece from the Vassil Bojkov Collection. Fourth century BC.

needed the military assistance of their northern neighbors. Most of the Greek phialae, jugs, kylixes, kantharoi, and rhytons found in the course of both regular and illegal archaeological excavations should probably be viewed as precious gifts of Athenian diplomats seeking to establish diplomatic relations with the Thracian rulers.[94] Sometimes even the figures decorating them could be interpreted in this light. For example, in Greek mythology, the twins that Melanippe bore to Poseidon were believed to have been the legendary founders of cities along the Thracian coast of the Propontis; and the entire ancient world was convinced of the Thracian origin of Orpheus. On the other hand, the emergence of so many scenes of a mythological nature in Thrace proves the growing role of the epic tradition in the Thracian royal court owing to the development of the royal ideology in the young states. Such a construct allows us to view the issue of these foreign influences from a new angle. They did not result from a process of intensified Hellenization: rather, they filled the need for a pictorial language that would translate their epic legends into visual images.

Notes

1. Hartog 1980.
2. Raevsky 1985; Bradley 1990; Sourvinou-Inwood 1991; Tilley 1991, 1999.
3. Marazov 1995.
4. Puhvel 1987; Dumézil 1992; Sergent 1995; Miller 1999.
5. Marazov 1980.
6. Hubbel 1928; Koppers 1936; Puhvel 1955; Nagy 1990.
7. Nagy 1979.
8. Plutarch, *Reg. et imper. apopth.* 174C.
9. Simms 1988; Montepaone 1990; Marazov 1994a, 48–73.
10. Goody 1986.
11. Raevsky 1994.
12. Marazov 1987.
13. Marazov 1986; Daumas 1998.
14. Marazov 1996, 180–191.
15. Marazov 1996,160–179.
16. Marazov 1983.
17. Cf. Fol 1986.
18. Fol 1972.
19. Venedikov and Gerassimov 1974.
20. In this respect, the role of Hermes as a royal deity, suggested by Herodotus, is quite indicative. Apollo and Dionysos, however, were also cast in this role in Thrace.
21. On the mythical significance of hunting see Fontenrose 1981; Vidal-Naquet 1986; Schnapp 1997; Barringer 2000.

22. Propp 1946; Berciu 1974; Watkins 1995; Johansen 1996.
23. Christensen 1912–1934; Campbell 1968.
24. Detschev 1976.
25. Brelich 1969, 1978.
26. Katičic 1990.
27. Watkins 1995.
28. Kazanlak and Alexandrovo: see Kitov 2001.
29. Lycophr. *Cass.* 937; Ivanov 1975.
30. Przyluski 1940; Schlerath 1954; Jacobson 1966; Buxton 1987; McCone 1987; Ivantchic 1988; Sergent 1992.
31. Wikander 1938; Nagy 1985.
32. Henry 1982; Dumézil 1985; Lincoln 1991.
33. Leach 1958; Hallpike 1969; Firth 1973; Hara 1986; Eilberg-Schwartz and Doniger 1995; Hiltebeitel and Miller 1998; Miller 1998b.
34. Marazov 1994b.
35. Detschev 1976, s.v. Compare Old Persian *xvarna*: Duchesne-Guillemin 1979; Gnoli 1990.
36. Dubuisson 1978b, 1986.
37. Kitov 2001.
38. Connor 1988.
39. Blaive 1991.
40. Puhvel 1970.
41. Nylander 1979.
42. Mac Cana 1955, 1956; Gurney 1960; Widengren 1960; Hocart 1969; Dubuisson 1978a; Root 1979; Choksy 1988; Ahn 1992; Cannadine and Price 1992; Herbert 1992; Miller 1998a, 1999.
43. Marazov 1996, 258–261.
44. Hemberg 1950; Cole 1984.
45. Orgogozo 1949, 1950.
46. Marazov 1981.
47. Cf. Raevsky 1985; for the nature of sacrifice see Burkert 1983; Malamoud 1989; Lincoln 1991.
48. Sueton. *Vitae Caes. Aug.* 3–4; Aristot. *De mirab. auscult.* 29–24; Marazov 1994a, 98.
49. This happened to Alexander the Great and to Octavius, the father of Augustus.
50. Murray 1990; Milano 1994; Murray and Tecuşan 1995.
51. Gourevich 1972; Ardzinba 1982.
52. Asheri 1996. The itinerary passed through places highly significant for their nature or culture.
53. Lincoln 1986; Roux 1995; Torelli 1997.
54. Iordanes *Getica* 39–41; Abaev 1984.
55. Gignoux 1981; Bogdanov 1991; Marazov 1992, 309–339.
56. Eliade 1974.
57. Negahban 1970; Marazov 1996, 220–242.
58. Frontisi-Ducroux 1991.
59. Gerschel 1966.
60. Leach 1964; Rostovtseff 1973; Raevsky 1985; Perevodchikova 1986; Bunker 1997.
61. Marazov 2002.
62. Marazov 1991.
63. Widengren 1970; Bennett 1997.

64. Gerstein 1974; Jacoby 1974; Weitenberg 1991.
65. The "Valley of the Kings," the Panagyurishte Treasure, etc.
66. Cf. Georgiev 1977, s.v.
67. Morris 1992 with discussion of the significance of the term *daidalos*.
68. Parry 1930, 73-147; Lord 1981, 1991; Padgett 1995.
69. Propp 1946; Dundes 1980; Foley 1991.
70. DuBois 1982; Tyrrell 1984.
71. Vernant 1985.
72. Bayburin 1993.
73. Vénedikov and Gerassimov 1974.
74. Déonna 1940; Brelich 1955/1957; Mac Cana 1973; Ginzburg 1992, 213-267.
75. Marazov 2001.
76. Detienne 1977.
77. Kisyov 2005, 45-48.
78. Kisyov 2005, 45-48.
79. Kitov 2005.
80. Kitov 2007.
81. Marazov 2009a, n. 48.
82. Abaev 1984.
83. Marazov 2009a.
84. Agre 2006.
85. Kitov 2008.
86. Marazov 2009b.
87. Bahrani 2008.
88. Marazov 2009a, Nos. 17, 25.
89. Marazov 2009a, n. 31.
90. Marazov 2009a, n. 29.
91. Kitov 2005.
92. Nagy 1990.
93. Marazov 2009a, n. 66.
94. Marazov 2009a, 2009b.

Bibliography

Abaev, V. I. 1984. "Frakiiskiy sotsial`nyy termin tarabosteis (The Thracian Social Term *tarabostei*.")." In *Etnogenesis narodov Balkanskogo poluostrova i severnogo prichernogomoria, (Ethnogenesis of Peoples from Balkans and Northern Black Sea Coast)*, 18-20. Moscow. (In Russian.)

Afshar, M. Z. 1988. "The Immortal Hound: The Genesis and Transformation of a Symbol in Indo-Iranian Traditions." Ph.D. dissertation, Harvard University.

Agre, D. 2006. "La tomba del sovrano a Malomirovo-Zlatinita." In *Tesori della Bulgaria. Catalogo*, 68-75. Rome.

Ahn, G. 1992. *Religiose Herrscherlegitimation im achamenidischen Iran*. Leiden, Louvain.

Ardzinba, V. G. 1982. *Ritualy I mify drevney Anatolii (Rites and Myths of Ancient Anatolia)*. Moscow. (In Russian.)

Asheri, D. 1996. "L'ideale monarchico di Dario: Erodoto III 80-82." E DNb Kent. *AASA* NS 3:99-106.

Bahrani, Z. 2008. *Rituals of War: The Body and Violence in Mesopotamia*. New York.

Barringer, J. 2000. *The Hunt in Ancient Greece*. Baltimore.

Bayburin, A. K. 1993. *Ritual v traditsionnoy kul'ture (Ritual in Archaic Culture)*. St. Petersburg. (In Russian.)

Bennett, M. J. 1997. *Belted Heroes and Bound Women: The Myth of the Homeric Warrior King*. Lanham, MD.

Berciu, D. 1974. *Contribution à l'étude de l'art thraco-gète*. Bucharest.

Blaive, F. 1991. "La fonction arbitrate du combat singulier dans le monde indo-européen d'Homère a Grégoire de Tours." *Ollodagos* 3.2:109–127.

Bogdanov, B. 1991. *Orphey i drevnata mitologiia na Balkanite (Orpheus and the Ancient Mythology of the Balkans)*. Sofia. (In Bulgarian.)

Bradley, R. 1990. *The Passage of Arms: An Archaeological Analysis of Prehistoric Hoards and Votive Deposits*. Cambridge.

Brelich, A. 1955/1957. "Les monosandales." *La Nouvelle Klio* 7.9:469–84.

⎯⎯. 1969. *Paides e Parthenoi. Incunabula Graeca* 36. Rome.

⎯⎯. 1978. *Gli eroi greci*. Rome.

Bunker, E. 1997. *Ancient Bronzes of the Eastern Eurasian Steppe from the Arthur M. Sackler Collections*. New York.

Burkert, W. 1983. *Homo Necans*. Berkeley and Los Angeles, CA.

Buxton, R. G. A. 1987. "Wolves and Werewolves in Greek Thought." In *Interpretations of Greek Mythology*, ed. J. Bremer, 60–79. London.

Campbell, J. 1968. *The Hero with a Thousand Faces*. Bollingen Series XVII. Princeton, NJ.

Cannadine, D, and S. Price, eds. 1992. *Rituals of Royalty: Power and Ceremonial in Traditional Societies*. Cambridge.

Cassirer, E. 1955. *The Philosophy of Symbolic Forms*. New Haven, CT.

Choksy, J. 1988. "Sacral Kingship in Sasanian Iran." *Bulletin of the Asia Institute* NS 2:35–52.

Christensen, A. 1912–1934. *Les légendes du premier homme et premier roi en Iran*. 2 vols. Stockholm.

Cole, S. G. 1984. *Theoi Megaloi: The Cult of the Great Gods at Samothrace*. Leiden.

Connor, P. 1988. "The Cup and the Sword." *Archäologischer Anzeiger* 41–53.

Daumas, M. 1998. *Cabiriaca: Recherches sur l'iconographie du culte des Cabires*. Paris.

Déonna, W. 1940. "Les Monosandaloi." *REA* 42:111–130.

Detienne, M. 1977. *Dionysos mis à mort*. Paris.

Detschev, D. 1976. *Die thrakischen Sprachreste*. 2 Aufl. Vienna.

Dubois, P. 1982. *Centaurs and Amazons*. Ann Arbor, MI.

Dubuisson, D. 1978a. "Le roi Indo-Européen et la synthèse des trois fonctions." *Annales* 33.1:21–34. Paris.

⎯⎯. 1978b. "L'équipement de l'inauguration royale de l'Inde védique et en Irlande." *RHR*.189.2:154–164.

⎯⎯. 1986. *La légende royale dans l'Inde ancienne: Rāma et Rāmāyana*. Paris.

Duchesne-Guillemin, J. 1979. "La Royauté iranienne et le xvarnah." *Iranica* 10:375–386.

Dumézil, G. 1985. *Heur et malheur du guerrier*. Paris.

1992. *Mythes et dieux des Indo-Européens*. Paris.

Dundes, A. 1980. *Interpreting Folklore*. Bloomington, IN.

Eilberg-Schwartz, H., and W. Doniger. 1995. *Off with Her Head*. Berkeley, CA.

Eliade, M. 1974. *Shamanism: Archaic Techniques of Ecstasy*. Princeton, NJ.

Firth, R. 1973. "Hair as a Private Asset and Public Symbol." In *Symbols, Public and Private*, ed. R. Firth, 262–298. Ithaca, NY.

Fol, A. 1972. *Polititseska istoriia na Trakite (Political History of Ancient Thrace)*. Sofia. (In Bulgarian.)

1986. *Trakiiskiat orfizum (Thracian Orphism)*. Sofia. (In Bulgarian.)

Foley, J. M. 1991. *Immanent Art: From Structure to Meaning in Traditional Oral Epic*. Bloomington, IN.

Fontenrose, J. 1981. "Orion: The Myth of the Hunter and Huntress." *Classical Studies*, Vol. 23. Berkeley, CA.

Frontisi-Ducroux, F. 1991. *Le dieu-masque: Une figure de Dionysos d'Athènes*. Paris and Rome.

Georgiev, V. 1977. *Trakite i tehnijat ezik (Thracians and Their Language)*. Sofia. (In Bulgarian.)

Gerschel, L. 1966. "Couleur et teinture chez divers peuples indo-européens." *Annales ESC*, 21:608–631. Paris.

Gerstein, M. 1974. "Germanic Warg: The Outlaw as Werewolf." In *Myth in Indo-European Antiquity*, ed. G. J. Larson, 131–156. Berkeley, CA.

Gignoux, P. 1981. "Les voyages chamaniques dans le monde iranien." *AL* 21:244–265.

Ginzburg, L. 1992. *Le sabbat des sorcières*. Paris.

Gnoli, G. 1990. "On Old-Persian Farnah-." *Iranica Varia. Papers in Honor of E. Yarshater*. Acta Iranica 30 (16): 83–92. Leiden.

Goody, J. 1986. *The Logic of Writing and the Organization of Society*. Cambridge.

Gourevich, A. 1972. *Kategorii srednevekovoy kul`tury (Categories of Medieval Culture)*. Moscow. (In Russian.)

Gurney, O. K. 1960. "Hittite Kingship." In *Myth, Ritual and Kingship*, ed. S. H. Hook, 105–121. Oxford.

Hallpike, C. R. 1969. "Social Hair." *Man* NS. 4.2: 256–264.

Hara, M. 1986. "The Holding of the Hair" (*Keśa-srahana*). *Acta Orientalia* 47:67–92.

Hartog, F. 1988. *The Mirror of Herodotus*. Berkeley, CA. (English translation of *Le miroir d'Hérodote*, 1980. Paris.)

Hemberg, B. 1950. *Die Kabiren*. Uppsala.

Henry, P. L. 1982. "Furor Heroicus." *Zeitschrift für celtische Philologie* 39:235–242.

Herbert, M. 1992. "Goddess and King: The Sacred Marriage in Early Ireland." In *Women and Sovereignty*, ed. L. Fredenburg. *Cosmos* 7: 264–275. Edinburgh.

Hiltebeitel, A., and B. D. Miller, eds. 1998. *Hair: Its Power and Meaning in Asian Cultures*. Albany, NY.

Hocart, A. M. 1969. *Kingship*. Oxford.

Hubbel, H. 1928. *"Horse Sacrifice in Antiquity."* YCS 1:181–192.

Ivanov, V. V. 1977. "Drevnebalkanskiy I obshcheindoevropeyskiy tekst mifa o geroe-ubiytse Psa I ego evraziyskie parelleli (Ancient Balkan and Common

Indo-European Text of the Myth about the Hero Wolf Killer and Its Euro-Asian Parallels)". In *Slavyanskoe I balkanskoe yazykoznanie (Slavic and Balkan Linguistics)*, ed. V. N. Toporov, 181–213. Moscow. (In Russian.)

Ivantchic [Ivantchik], A. I. 1988. "Voiny Psy:.*Mujskie soyuzy I sifskie vtorjenia v Perednyu Aziyu*. ("Warriors-Dogs: *Maennerbunde* and Skythian Invasions in Asia Minor)." *Sovietskaia Etnografiia Soviet Ethnography*) 5:38–48. (In Russian.)

Jacobson, R. 1966. "Sobaka – Kalin-tsar." In *Selected Writings*, ed. R. Jacobson, vol. 4, 16–18. The Hague and Paris.

Jacoby, M. 1974. *Wargus, vargr "Verbrecher," "Wolf." Eine sprach- und rechtsgeschichtliche Untersuchung*. Uppsala.

Johansen, B. 1996. "The Transformative Dragon: The Construction of Social Identity and Use of Metaphors during the Nordic Iron Age." *Current Swedish Archaeology* 4:83–102.

Katičič, R. 1990. "Weiters zur Rekonstruktion der Texte eines urslavischen Fruchtbarkeitsritus" (2). *WSIJ* 36:61–93.

Kisyov, K. 2005. *Thrace and Greece in Ancient Times: Classical Age Tumuli in the Municipality of Kaloyanovo*. Plovdiv.

Kitov, G. 2001. "A Newly Found Thracian Tomb with Frescoes." *Archaeologica Bulgarica*, 2:15–29.

2005. *The Valley of Thracian Kings*. Varna.

2007. "Dolinata na trakiyskite tsare v Slivensko (Predvaritelno saobshtenie) (The Valley of Thracian Kings in Sliven Region)." *Bulletin of the Museums of Southeastern Bulgaria (Buletin na muzeite ot yuoiztocna Bulgaria)* 13:44–57. (In Bulgarian.)

2008. "Dalakova mofhila ("Dalakova Moghila Mound)." In *Problemi I izsledvaniya na trakiyskata kultura (Problems and Investigations of the Thracian Culture)*,Vol. III, 138–163. Kazanlak. (In Bulgarian).

Kitov, G., and N. Theodossiev. 2003. "I colori dei Traci." *Archeo* 19:34–47.

Koppers, W. 1936. "Pferdeopfer und Pferdekult dei den Indogermanen." *Wiener Beitrage zur Kulturgeschichte und Linguistik* 4:279–411.

Leach, E. 1958. "Magical Hair." *Man* 88:147–168.

1964. "Anthropological Aspects of Language: Animal Categories and Verbal Abuse." In *New Directions in the Study of Language*, ed. E. Lenneberg, 23–63. Cambridge, MA.

Lincoln, B. 1986. *Myth, Cosmos, and Society*. Cambridge, MA.

1991. *Death, War, and Sacrifice*. Chicago.

Lord, A. 1981. *The Singer of Tales*. Cambridge, MA.

1991. *Epic Singer and Oral Tradition*. Ithaca, NY.

Mac Cana, P. 1955. "Aspects of the Theme of King and Goddess in Irish Literature." *EC* 7.1: 76–114.

1956. "Aspects of the Theme of King and Goddess in Irish Literature." *EC* 8:59–65.

1973. "The Topos of the Single Sandal in Irish Tradition." *Celtica* 10: 160–166.

Malamoud, Ch. 1989. *Cuire le monde: Rites et pensée dans l'Inde ancienne*. Paris.

Marazov, I. 1980. "Sledy na Ashvamedha i Purushmedha v Trakitiskykh rituali" ("Traces of Ashvamedha and Purushmedha in Thracian Rituals"). *Izkustvo (Art)*, 8:7–17. (In Bulgarian.)

——— 1981. "Sacrifice of a Ram on the Thracian Helmet from Cotsofeneshti." *Pulpudeva* 3:81–101.

——— 1983. "A New Discovered Thracian Tomb Near Sveshtari, Bulgaria." *Bulletin of the Ancient Orient Museum* 5:65–82. Tokyo.

——— 1986. "Kanichkata-riton ot Borovskoto sukrovishte (A Pitcher-Rhyton from the Borovo Treasure and the Cult of the Cabiri)." *Izkustvo (Art)* 5:46–52. (In Bulgarian.)

——— 1987. "*Interpretatio Thracica*, or the Deciphering of Thracian Art." In *Gold of the Thracian Horsemen*, ed. V. Schiltz, 48–61. Montreal.

——— 1991. "A Structural Iconographic Analysis of the Gundestrup Cauldron." In *Thracian Tales on the Gundestrup Cauldron*, ed. F. Kaul, I. Marazov, Jan Best, and Nanny de Vries, 43–75. Amsterdam.

——— 1992. *Mit, ritual i izkustvo u Trakite (Myth, Ritual, and Art among the Thracians)*. Sofia. (In Bulgarian.)

——— 1994a. *Mitologia na Trakite (Thracian Mythology)*. Sofia. (In Bulgarian.)

——— 1994b. *Mitologia na zlatoto (Mythology of Gold)*. Sofia. (In Bulgarian.)

——— 1995. "Philomele the Weaver and Bendis the Spinner." In *Studia in Honorem Georgii Mihailov.*, ed. A. Fol and B. Bogdanov, 307–317. Sofia.

——— 1996. *The Rogozen Treasure*. Sofia.

——— 1998. *Ancient Gold: The Wealth of the Thracians*. New York.

——— 2001. "Une nymphe Cabirique de l'Egéide du Nord." *Orpheus* 10:1–47.

——— 2002. "The 'Coiled-up' Carnivore: Visual Etymology of the Motif." *Silk Road Art and Archaeology* 8:255–271.

——— ed. 2009a. *Saved Treasures from Ancient Thrace*. Sofia.

——— 2009b. "Riton s glava na oven ("Rhyton with a Ram's Head)." *Buletin na muzeite na iugoiztochna Bulgaria (Bulletin of the Museums of Southeastern Bulgaria)* 14:12–73. (In Bulgarian.)

McCone, K. R. 1987. "Hund, Wolf und Krieger bei den Indogermanen." In *Studien zum indogermanische Wortschatz*, ed. W. Meid, Innsbucker Beitrage zur Sprachwissenschaft 52:101–154.

Milano, L., ed. 1994. *Drinking in Ancient Societies*. Padua.

Miller, D. A. 1998a. "The King, the Hero, and the Gods: An Explanatory Note on the Functions and the Supernatural." In *Proceedings of the 9th Annual UCLA Indo-European Conference 1997*, ed. K. Jones-Bley, A. della Volpe, M. Dexter, and M. Huld. *JIES* Monograph 28:192–203.

——— 1998b. "On the Mythology of Indo-European Heroic Hair." *JIES* 26:41–60.

——— 1999. "Who Deals with the Gods? Kings and Other Intermediaries." In *Miscellanea Indo-Europea*, ed. E. Polomé. *JIES* Monograph 33:161–274.

Montepaone, C. 1990. "Bendis tracia ad Atene: l'integrazione del 'nuovo' attraverso forme dell'ideologia." *AASA* 12:103–117.

Morris, S. 1992. *Daidalos and the Origins of Greek Art*. Princeton, NJ.

Murray, O., ed. 1990. *Sympotica: Symposion on the Symposion*. Oxford.

Murray, O., and M. Tecušan, eds. 1995. *In Vino Veritas*. Rome.

Nagy, G. 1979. *The Best of the Achaeans: Concepts of the Hero in Archaic Greek Poetry*. Baltimore.

Nagy, J. F. 1985. *The Wisdom of the Outlaw: The Boyhood Deeds of Finn in Gaelic Tradition*. Berkeley, CA.

   1990. "Hierarchy, Heroes, and Heads: Indo-European Structures in Greek Myth." In *Approaches to Greek Myth*, ed. L. Edmunds, 199–239. Baltimore.

Negahban, E. O. 1970. "Metal Vessels from Marlik." *Prähistorische Bronzefunde*. Abt. II. Bd. 3.

Nylander, C. 1979. "Achaemenid Imperial Art." In *Power and Propaganda*, ed. T. Larsen, 322–360. Copenhagen.

Orgogozo, J. 1949. "Hermès des Achéens." *RHR* 1:11–30.

   1950. "Hermès des Achéens." *RHR* 2:139–179.

Padgett, J. M. 1995. "A Geometric Bard." In *The Ages of Homer: A Tribute to Emily Townsend Vermeule*, ed. J. Carter and S. Morris, 389–406. Austin, Texas.

Parry, M. 1930. "Studies in the Epic Technique of Oral Verse-Making. I. Homer and Homeric Style." *Harvard Studies in Classical Philology* 41:73–147.

Perevodchikova, E. 1986. *Iazik izobrazhennii zhivotnykh (The Language of Animal Images)*. Moscow. (In Russian.)

Petrescu-Dîmbovița, M. 1975. "Le trésor de Băiceni (dep. De Jassy)." *Dacia* 19:106–123.

Propp, V. 1946. *Historical Roots of the Fairy-Tale*. Leningrad.

Przyluski, J. 1940. "Les confréries des loups-garous dans les sociétés indo-européennes." *RHR* 121:137–145.

Puhvel, J. 1955. "Vedic *ashvamedha-* and Gaulish *IPOMIIDVOS*." *Language* 31:353–354.

   1970. "Aspects of Equine Functionality." In *Myth and Law among the Indo-Europeans*, ed. J. Puhvel, 159–172. Berkeley, CA.

   1987. *Comparative Mythology*. Baltimore.

Raevsky, D. 1985. *Model mira skifskoi kultury (World Model of the Skythian Culture)*. Moscow. (In Russian.)

   1994. *Skythian Mythology*. Sofia.

Root, M. C. 1979. *The King and Kingship in Achaemenid Art*. Leiden.

Rostovtseff, M. 1973. *The Animal Style in South Russia and China*. Princeton, NJ.

Roux, J.-P. 1995. *Le roi: Mythes et symboles*. Paris.

Schlerath, B. 1954. "Der Hund bei den Indo-Germanen." *Paideuma* 6.1:25–40.

Schmitt Pantel, P. 1992. *La cité au banquet*. Rome.

Schnapp, A. 1997. *Le chasseur et la cite: Chasse et érotique en Grèce ancienne*. Paris.

Sergent, B. 1992. "Celto-Hellenica III: Achille et Cuchulainn." *Ollodagos* 4.2:127–280.

   1995. *Les Indo-Européens*. Paris.

Simms, R. R. 1988. "The Cult of the Thracian Goddess Bendis in Athens and Attica." *The Ancient World* 18.3 and 18.4:59–76.

Sourvinou-Inwood, Ch. 1991. *"Reading" Greek Culture*. Oxford.

Tilley, C. 1991. *Material Culture and Text: The Art of Ambiguity*. London and New York.

1999. *Metaphor and Material Culture*. Oxford and Malden, MA.

Torelli, M. 1997. *Il rango, il rito e l'immagine*. Milan.

Tyrrell, W. B. 1984. *Amazons: A Study in Athenian Mythmaking*. Baltimore.

Venedikov, I., and T. Gerassimov. 1974. *Thracian Art*. London.

Vernant, J.-P. 1985. "Introduction." In *Problèmes de la guerre en Grèce ancienne*, ed. J.-P. Vernant, 9–30. Paris.

Vidal-Naquet, P. 1986. *The Black Hunter: Forms of Thought and Forms of Society in the Greek world*. Baltimore. (Translation of *Le chasseur noir*, 1983. Paris.)

Watkins, C. 1995. *How to Kill a Dragon: Aspects of Indo-European Poetics*. Oxford.

Weitenberg, J. 1991. "The Meaning of the Expression 'To Become a Wolf' in Hittite." In *Perspectives on Indo-European Language, Culture and Religion: Studies in Honor of E. Polomé*, vol.1. *JIES* Monograph 7:189–198.

Widengren, G. 1960. "La légende royale de l'Iran antique." In *Hommages à G. Dumézil*, 225–237. Collection Latomus 45. Brussels.

1970. "Le symbolisme de la ceinture." *Archaeologia Iranica: Miscellanea R. Ghirshman*, 133–155. Leiden.

Wikander, S. 1938. *Der Arische Männerbund*. Lund.

CHAPTER SIX

IN THE FABULOUS CELTIC TWILIGHT

Barry Cunliffe

The origin and indeed the meaning of the Celts have recently been much debated, with some scholars taking the extreme view that the term "Celt" is worthless and should be abandoned. This chapter examines the different meanings attached to the concept of Celts from Classical sources, linguistic studies, and archaeology, as well as the importance of the Atlantic coastal trading to the development of Celtic language and society.

The title of this chapter comes from an address given by J. R. R. Tolkien almost fifty years ago in Cardiff. Reflecting on the excesses of linguistic etymologies he said, "Celtic of any sort is ... a magic bag into which anything may be put, and out of which anything may come.... Anything is possible in the fabulous Celtic twilight, which is not so much a twilight of the gods as of the reason" (Tolkien 1963, 29, 30).

Tolkien's words, carefully divorced from their context, have been used by a number of writers in more recent years in the spirited debate that has raged over the validity of the term "Celtic."[1] The Celtic-deniers, if such I may unkindly call them, angered by a web of misconceptions surrounding the concept of "the Celts" and the sloppy misuse of the term by many groups, from nationalists to new-worlders, have argued that at best the word has very limited validity and at worst should be abandoned altogether. One has only to glance at popular outpourings on the subject to have much sympathy for this view, and yet belief in the Celts as a people is deeply embedded in the archaeological literature of the last 300 years. Moreover, Classical writers, conscious of the ethnopolitical groupings of their familiar Mediterranean – Greeks, Romans, and Phoenicians – considered the Celts, along with the Scythians and the Libyans, to be the principal peoples of the surrounding barbarian lands. Celts, then, are deserving of our consideration.

That there has been so much misuse of, and lack of clarity about, the concept of the Celts is largely due to the fact that for the last three centuries it has been locked into a straightjacket of circular argument. The circle began to be constructed at the end of the seventeenth century when antiquarians, studying the indigenous languages of the Atlantic fringe of Europe, chose to call them Celtic and went on to pose the question "When did the Celts arrive here?" It was well known at the time that the Classical writers had, rather vaguely, located the Celts in the west of Europe, but had more specifically described migrations of Celts pouring down from West-Central Europe to attack Mediterranean lands in the fourth and third centuries BC. The belief, therefore, took root that Celts had also migrated westward to Britain and Ireland, carrying the Celtic language with them. In the nineteenth century, a growing awareness of the material culture of prehistoric Europe led to the identification of a "Celtic" assemblage and of a "Celtic" art. The distribution of this was used to identify the extent and spread of Celtic culture, and the then-current belief that material culture was spread by migrating peoples was used to underpin the linguistic model.

By the early twentieth century, linguists could confidently assert that archaeology supported their long-established hypothesis, while archaeologists could claim that the linguistic model explained the archaeological distributions. The argument had become a self-generating circle of compossibilities. Embedded in the rigid hoop were a series of strands – a 300-year-old unchallenged linguistic hypothesis, a series of ethnic stereotypes created and embroidered by Classical writers, and a huge body of multivariate archaeological data requiring explanatory context. Added to this, content to bowl the hoop along, were a number of Atlantic-fringe communities seeking to define an identity for themselves to counter the growing power of modern nation-states – England, France, and Spain. It is, by any standards, an eclectic mix but by no means atypical for such a mélange to arise when questions of ethnicity are in debate.[2]

To deconstruct such a tangle of long-held beliefs is not my aim; rather, all I wish to do is to tease out some of the individual strands of evidence and to expose them to brief scrutiny, leaving aside the fascinating question of the re-creation of modern Celtic identities that has been thoroughly discussed elsewhere.[3] The three aspects of the Celtic question we shall examine are geography, language, and belief systems.

The Classical concept of the Celts, as one of the great peoples of the barbarian world, was neatly summed up by the fourth-century BC Greek historian Ephorus of Cymae. In his simple structuralist view, the world outside the Mediterranean center could be divided into the four quarters from which the cardinal winds blew: to the east were the Indians, to the south the Ethiopians, to the north the Scythians, and to the west the Celts.[4] Ephorus was, of course, generalizing, but was basing his simple scheme on the observations and writings of others going back over two centuries or more. The late sixth-century ethnographer Hecataeus of Miletus knew something of the Celts. Massalia (Marseilles), founded about 600 BC, lay in Ligurian territory near Celtica, while Narbon (near modern Narbonne), 120 miles to the west, was a Celtic city. A later writer, Herodotus, writing in the fifth century BC, believed that the Celts occupied territory west of the Pillars of Hercules (the Straits of Gibraltar) as far as the land of the Cynesii, who lived in the extreme southwest of Portugal. He also believed that the Danube rose in the land of the Celts, placing the source near the city of Pyrene (which is thought to be cognate with Pyrenees).[5] In this somewhat muddled geography he was evidently conceiving of the Celts as essentially a Western people. The reference to the Danube could have come from a view that the Celts extended to West-Central Europe, but it could equally be the result of a preconceived geographical model of the world.

Much of the information that Hecataeus and Herodotus made use of is likely to have come from merchants trading with the Greek cities of the Golfe de Lions – Massalia, Agathe (Agde), and Emporion (Ampurias), whose inhabitants would have had some firsthand knowledge of the natives of their hinterlands. Nor is it unlikely that Greek traders who visited the Phoenician port of Gadir (Cadiz) and the Tartessan port at modern Huelva, both on the Atlantic coast of Iberia, ventured even farther and brought back stories of the natives they encountered or were told about. At any event, what emerged by the fifth century BC was the belief that Celtic peoples inhabited a broad arc of Western Europe stretching from southwestern Iberia to the western Alps.

Knowledge of the barbarian West was greatly extended by the exploration of Pytheas of Massalia, whose journeys, some time around 320 BC, took him across Gaul to the Atlantic coast and then northward to circumnavigate Britain and possibly to venture even farther into the unknown. At an early stage in his journey he encountered the Armorican peninsula (modern Brittany), which he describes as a great peninsula extending westward into the Ocean, terminating in promontories beyond which was the island of *Ou[e]xisame* (probably Ushant). This westerly projection, he says, lay north of Iberia and was part of the land of the Celts (*Keltikê*).[6] The late third-century polymath Eratosthenes adds some further details about Iberia, commenting on the prominence of the Celts who lived there in his time.

By the first century BC, the westerly distribution of the Celts was widely known. Rome had been engaged in bitter battles against the Celtiberi – a powerful group of individually named tribes occupying much of the center of northern Iberia, while tribes called Celtici are recorded in the southwest. In Gaul, Julius Caesar is helpfully explicit in the opening paragraph of his *Gallic Wars*, telling us that at the time of his intervention Gaul could be divided into three broad zones: southwest of the Garonne were the Aquitani; north of the Seine and Marne was the territory of the Belgae; and in the vast area lying in between are "the people we call Gauls, though in their own language they are called Celts."[7]

The Classical sources, then, from the sixth to the first centuries are in broad agreement about the location of the Celtic homeland. They also imply that there was internal mobility and re-formation of the Celts. As early as the beginning of the sixth century BC, Polybius suggests that Celts from beyond the Alps had begun to move down into and settle in the Po Valley, but Livy suggests that the force of the migrating movement was not really underway until the end of the fifth century, when "a vast host, some mounted, some on foot" set out from eastern Gaul to colonize the Po Valley and from there to stage a long-drawn-out engagement in Italy south of the Apennines.[8] Instability in the period from about 400 to 200 BC was endemic and seems to have involved large numbers of people, drawn extensively from west and north of the Alps, in migratory movements and cycles of raiding extending into the Balkans (whence the famous raid on Delphi in AD 279), and soon after into Asia Minor. The disparate peoples involved in these upheavals were lumped together by Greek and Roman writers as Celts or Gauls. That some were indeed from Celtica we owe to Livy,[9] but it is highly likely that the eastward thrust involved people of very mixed origins emanating from the broad zone north of the Alps. The direct engagement of these disparate mobile northern groups and Mediterranean civilization created the classical stereotype of the Celt – the Celt as "Other" – the antithesis of the civilized human. Celts are "wild beasts," "war mad," excitable, easily dispirited, loud and boastful, unlike we, who are civilized, controlled, steadfast, and sober. Their womenfolk are viragos and promiscuous at that, not like our delicate, demure wives, and they have peculiar, almost laughable, habits: they go naked into battle, rub lime in their hair to make it stand out like a mane, and have long, drooping moustaches through which they slurp their wine … undiluted! And then they fall about drunk. As with all caricatures there are, of course, elements of truth in the picture, but to create a recognizable and distinctive image, the unusual and bizarre are emphasized. The Celtic stereotype – the Celt as "Other" – pervaded the contemporary Classical literature and was reinforced by monumental sculptures such as the famous composition from Pergamon depicting the Celts in defeat (Hannestad 1993). Every Roman schoolboy would have known what was meant by Celt.

By the end of the second century BC a rather different image begins to emerge, partly, one suspects, because of increasing interaction between the Greco-Roman world and the inhabitants of Gaul and Iberia along the long interface stretching from the Maritime Alps to the Algarve – an interaction bringing increasing trade beneficial to both. Instrumental in the creation of this new image was Posidonius of Apamea – a Stoic philosopher who appears to have traveled in the West at the end of the second century BC and wrote an account of the Celts in his great work, *Histories*, probably based on firsthand observations. *Histories* no longer survives, but sections of his Celtic ethnography are widely quoted by later writers, in particular Diodorus Siculus, Strabo, and Athenaeus. Piecing these scraps together, we get a somewhat different vision of the Celts; now it is the Celts as "noble savages" representing the values of an earlier age. They were simple, childlike in a boisterous sort of way, but "not of evil character." They were justly ruled by a sophisticated priesthood, the Druids, who were learned men. Brave and honorable, they showed courteous hospitality to strangers. To the Stoic Posidonius they were the children of a Golden Age unspoiled by the evils of civilization.[10] And so, the old stereotype of the Celt as "Other" began subtly to change. In less than 100 years, their successor lineages in Iberia and Gaul were well on the way to becoming productive citizens of the expanding Roman Empire.

There is, then, a consistency about the Classical concept of the Celts. They were thought to occupy much of the territory between the Atlantic and that of the tribes extending along the Mediterranean fringe – the Ligurians, Iberians, and others – while the mobile bands who poured into Italy, the Balkans, and Asia Minor, who made their presence felt for two centuries or so, shared a material culture and an elite system that allowed Mediterranean observers to characterize them as one people. But to what extent these mobile, disparate groups regarded themselves as Celts is impossible to say, nor can we assume that all, or even most, had familial links with the Celts of Gaul. As I will argue, it is not to be assumed that value systems and the associated material culture necessarily reflect ethnic identity.

A great deal of the confusion surrounding the Celtic question comes from the uncritical acceptance by archaeologists and others of the theories of linguists put forward about 300 years ago. One of the key figures in these early debates was Edward Lhuyd, who worked first as assistant keeper and then as keeper at the Ashmolean Museum in Oxford from 1691 until 1709.[11] The later years of his life were devoted to the production of an ambitious work, *Archaeologia Britannica*, which was to present an account of the peoples of the British Isles in what we would now call the "prehistoric period." Lhuyd spent years collecting material, involving formidable programs of fieldwork and eventually, in 1707, the first (and only) volume of *Archaeologia* appeared. It was subtitled *Glossography* and presented grammars and vocabularies of Irish, Breton, and Cornish. These languages, Lhuyd recognized, belonged to the same family as his own native Welsh and as Gaulish. In searching for a name for this group he came up with the idea of calling them "Celtic," largely, one suspects, because "British" and "Gaulish" were epithets already being used by the English and the French; besides, he needed a word that transcended national geographies. He could equally well have called the group "Gallo-British," "Atlantean," or "language group A" had he been so minded, but he chose "Celtic," and so the concept of the Celtic language was born.

Lhuyd's studies led him to distinguish between different forms of Celtic. Irish, he recognized, stood apart from Welsh, Cornish, and Breton: the difference needed historic explanation. And so, he began to sketch out an invasionist hypothesis that envisaged successive waves of Celtic speakers spreading outward from continental Europe.

It was an influential model that was given further coherence and wide dissemination by Sir John Rhŷs, professor of Celtic at Oxford University, in his book *Early Britain: Celtic Britain*, published in 1882. Here Rhŷs presented the developed hypothesis. There were two Celtic migrations, the first of Goidelic Celts speaking an early version of Celtic called "Q-Celtic." They came from Gaul and colonized the British Isles and Ireland. Later, the Brythonic Celts (speaking "P-Celtic") arrived in southern Britain, spreading throughout much of the country, but not to Ireland, where the Q-Celtic speakers remained. Although Rhŷs presented the developed theory with scholarly reserve, it was eagerly accepted as historical fact, not least by archaeologists who thereafter used the invasionist model to structure their mute data. It was not until the 1960s that serious doubts began to be expressed.[12]

In parallel with all this came the study of the early language groups of the Iberian peninsula and the realization that the Celtiberi in the center, and probably the Lusitanians of the west, also spoke an early form of Celtic. This too needed explanation. Archaeologists were eager to oblige and so developed another invasionist hypothesis, which gained credibility and was widely disseminated after the publication of Bosch-Gimpera's famous paper, "Two Celtic Waves in Spain," originally given as a lecture to the British Academy.[13]

I have sketched out this historical background because it is helpful to know where some of the preconceptions embedded in the literature come from and why questions like "When did the first Celts arrive in Ireland?" are sometimes still asked. If, however, we try to leave aside the baggage of the past and look as objectively as possible at the evidence, rather different explanatory models present themselves.

At one level of abstraction we can say that in the pre-Roman period, over a substantial area of Western Europe, people spoke a similar language that, for the sake of objectivity, we might refer to as "Atlantic European." Traces of Atlantic European are to be found in rare inscriptions and in place-name evidence in Gaul and Iberia, as well as in the

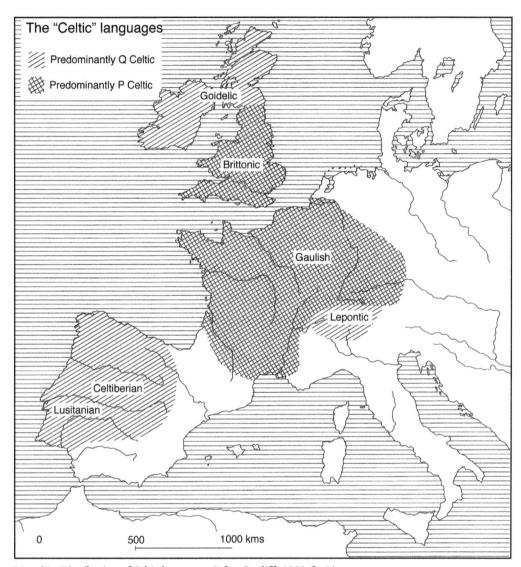

Map 6.1. Distribution of Celtic languages. (After Cunliffe 2003, fig.8.)

living languages (or recently living languages) of Brittany, Cornwall, Wales, the Isle of Man, Ireland, and Scotland (Map 6.1). Stated so baldly, the simplest explanation would be that Atlantic European was an indigenous language that may have evolved locally over a considerable period of time. There is no need at all to call up invasionist models involving marauding Celts to explain the observed facts. But what of nomenclature? If we were starting afresh now, we might indeed have chosen the phrase "Early Atlantic European" to describe the pre-Roman language group spoken widely (but not exclusively) in Iberia, Gaul, Britain, and Ireland before the Roman onslaught, referring, perhaps, to the living survivals as "Developed Atlantic European," but since they have been called Celtic for 300 years, we might as well continue to use the term; after all, there is a considerable degree of coincidence between the distribution of the "Celtic" languages and the Classical world's early conception of the Celts as a Western European people. However, if we choose to continue to describe the early Atlantic European languages as Celtic, we must rid the term of all the pseudohistorical clutter it has accumulated over the years so that a statement like "Irish is a Celtic language" should not automatically generate the question "When did the Celts arrive in Ireland?"

The acceptance of the possibility that the Celtic languages may have *developed* in Atlantic Europe raises a number of interesting questions and indeed helps to explain many of the problems inherent in the old invasionist hypotheses. Here we can only touch on some of them. The most pressing, and perhaps the most difficult, issue to arise is posed by the questions "Under what circumstances did the Celtic language group emerge?" and "By what time did it emerge?" There is broad agreement that Celtic was spoken at least as early as the sixth century BC.[14] Before that we can only speculate, but here archaeology may be of some help.

If we stand back from the huge body of data now available, it is possible to argue that the Atlantic seaways provided a broad corridor of communication from the Straits of Gibraltar to the Shetland Islands for several millennia before the emergence of the Roman Empire.[15] In all probability, the seaways first began to be exploited in the Mesolithic period, when coastal communities, developing the resources of the littoral zone, took to sea in pursuit of fish shoals,[16] thus extending their land-based hunting-gathering territories. Navigation skills, developed on land, could be adapted and extended to suit the maritime environment. The comparative ease with which journeys could be made by sea enabled more extensive territories to be worked, which in turn would have brought hitherto isolated communities into contact through overlapping networks of seasonal gathering. The growing complexity of these interactions would, in turn, have encouraged the exchange of goods and the dissemination of technologies, ideas, and beliefs over considerable distances. By the end of the fifth millennium BC, by which time knowledge of plant cultivation and animal husbandry had spread to the Atlantic zone, the maritime networks were a conduit through which ideologies were spreading. As vivid witness of this, one has only to look at the distribution of passage-graves, embodying beliefs and cosmologies as well as concepts of art and architecture, extending along the Atlantic seaways from southern Portugal to Orkney in the millennium and a half from about 4500 to 3000 BC. While no professional archaeologist today thinks in terms of "megalithic missionaries" or embraces diffusionist beliefs, most are in agreement that the remarkable phenomenon of the megalithic burial tradition rests heavily on the networks of exchange and communication that facilitated the spread of ideas. During this period, we can only suppose that language developed to the extent that ideas and beliefs could be widely communicated.

The exploitation of metals, principally gold, copper, and tin, after the middle of the third millennium BC introduced an entirely new dynamic. Until this time the Atlantic networks would have been largely self-contained, but the simple fact that the Atlantic region was a metal-rich producer zone, while the Mediterranean region was a comparatively metal-poor consumer zone, led to the development of new networks of exchange crossing the European peninsula by means of which commodities could flow. These networks tended to favor the major rivers. There is reasonable evidence to suggest that the movement of metal intensified with time and was at its height in what is conventionally the Late Bronze Age, roughly 1300–800 BC. It was during this period that the communities of the entire Atlantic façade seem to have embraced a common value system, manifest in the deposition of votive offerings in watery contexts, and an elite system involving similar weapon sets and feasting gear.[17] Social interaction must now have been intense. If one is looking for a single period when a distinctive language might have crystallized out from the lingua francas and creoles of *longue durée* trade and exchange, then the period 1300–800 BC is most likely it.[18] The level of communication and the complex concepts involved called for a developed language. Since this was the last period when all the Celtic-speaking parts of Atlantic Europe could be shown to be bound in networks of interaction, we might tentatively suggest that it was at this time that the earlier form of Celtic (which was formerly referred to as Q-Celtic) was spoken.

In the centuries to follow, the archaeological evidence suggests that there was some degree of fragmentation within the Atlantic system. In the South, the foundation of an active trading colony at Gadir (modern Cadiz) by the Phoenicians by about 800 BC and their rapid development of the sea lanes southward down the coast of Morocco and northward up the Iberian coast, probably as far as Galicia, brought the southern part of the network under the direct control of a Mediterranean-based elite. The Celtic-speaking communities of Iberia were no longer part of the broader Atlantic community, and their languages would have taken on a different trajectory of development.

In the North, the archaeological evidence suggests that after the seventh century BC, Ireland may have entered into a period of isolation, which lasted until the third or possibly even the second century. Why this was so is not immediately evident, but it might have resulted from the declining importance of copper as a commodity at the time when iron came more generally into use. At any event, increasing isolation may have led to divergence in language between Ireland and the rest of Britain and Gaul. I will argue later that active links were maintained between central and southern Britain and Gaul from the fifth century BC until the Roman conquest. It is hardly surprising, therefore, that the languages spoken on the two sides of the English Channel should have developed in parallel.

The preceding sketch is sufficient to show that the archaeological evidence is consistent with the view that the Celtic language group developed among the indigenous populations of Atlantic Europe essentially as a lingua franca facilitating trade and exchange, in much the same way as Swahili emerged among the maritime communities of East Africa. This relieves us of the necessity of explaining its spread by means of migration or some such mechanism or of having to define a distinctive Celtic material culture accompanying the language. That Classical writers, as far back as the sixth century BC, were identifying communities in central and western Iberia and in Gaul as Celts, even though there was considerable variation in material culture across this broad zone, might suggest that it was commonality of language that they were taking to be the prime ethnic indicator.

A convenient way to begin to approach the development of elite culture in West-Central Europe in the first millennium BC is to see the

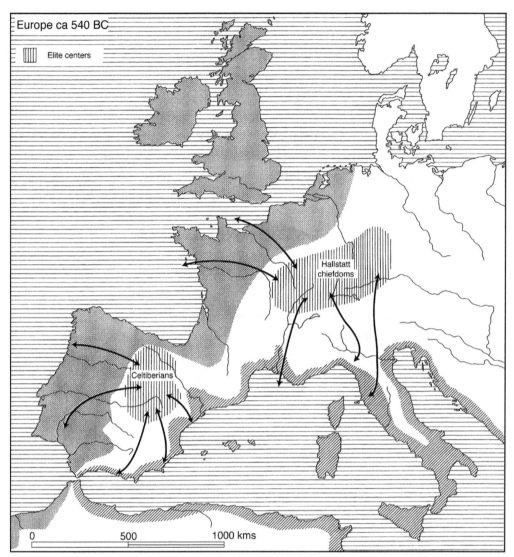

Map 6.2. Europe, about 540 BC, showing the emergence of elite centers between the Atlantic and Mediterranean zones. (After Cunliffe 2003, fig. 3).

peninsula in terms of its two maritime zones – the Mediterranean and the Atlantic – and to consider the effects of their interactions in the broad intervening inland territory that separates them. It is in this zone, particularly in the nodal regions where the major riverine routes converge, that cultures with distinctive elite systems emerge. Map 6.2 shows the situation toward the end of the sixth century. In West-Central Europe, within a broad zone stretching from Burgundy to southern Germany, the highly distinctive Late Hallstatt culture developed, characterized by very rich burials like the well-known examples found at Vix and Hochdorf and by adjacent "seats of nobility" – defended hilltop settlements such as Mont Lassois and Heuneburg, where concentrations of exotic goods indicate elite occupation.[19] It has been suggested that such sites reflect a prestige goods economy in which the paramounts and the tiers of the hierarchy below them maintained the stability of the social system by controlling the flow and distribution of rare commodities, among them exotic consumer durables made in the Mediterranean. Another way of characterizing the phenomenon is to see the Hallstatt chiefdoms as the beneficiaries of their geographical location, commanding, as they evidently did, the major routes between the Atlantic production zone, whence came a range of valuable raw materials, and the Mediterranean consumer zone. The Celtiberian elite, who emerge somewhat less spectacularly in north-central Iberia, occupy a similar intermediary position between the Atlantic and Mediterranean zones.

It is impossible, from the available archaeological evidence, to estimate the volume of the commodities passing through the exchange networks at this time or, for that matter, to model the exact processes of exchange. What we are seeing in the sixth century BC is really nothing more than a continuation of systems that date back many centuries but that now intensify, possibly as the result of increased Mediterranean demand. In such contexts, it would not be surprising if the trade language of the West – Celtic – became more widespread and more firmly established, possibly even becoming the language of the elite.

The Hallstatt prestige goods economy was comparatively short-lived – three generations at the most. Thereafter, some time around 480 BC, the focus of innovation shifted to the northern fringe of the zone, where, in four separate centers, new elites emerged in what is conventionally referred to as the "La Tène-A period." The largest and richest of these centered on the Rhine–Moselle confluence, with another, less extensive, group on the Marne Valley and lesser centers in the region of Bourges in the west and in Bohemia in the east (Map 6.3). These new fifth-century elites displayed their status in different ways to their Hallstatt predecessors. Grave goods proclaimed warrior status, the richest among the elites burying their dead with two-wheeled vehicles strongly reminiscent of war chariots. The accompanying luxury wine-drinking equipment seems mostly to have come from Etruria. So numerous were the

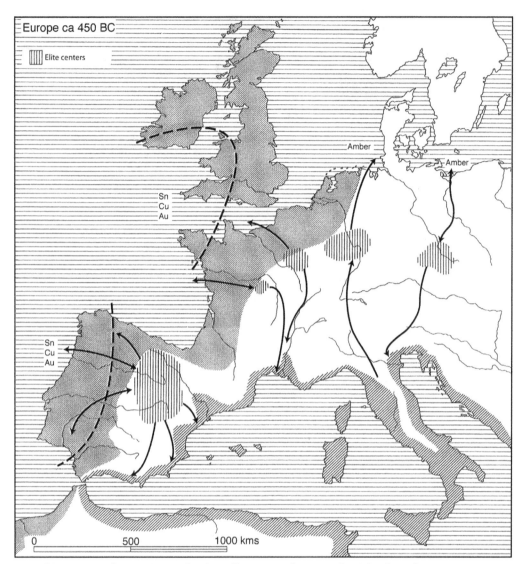

Map 6.3. Europe, about 450 BC, showing elite centers between the Atlantic and Mediterranean zones. Those in central west Europe belong to the La Tène culture that in Iberia represents the Celtiberian tribes. (After Cunliffe 2003, fig. 4.)

Etruscan beaked flagons, found particularly in the Moselle region, that it is tempting to suggest the establishment of a direct trading axis through the Alpine passes.

A glance at Map 6.4 is sufficient to emphasize the strategic location of the new elite centers, each commanding a riverine route to resources beyond – metals and salt to the west and amber and furs to the north. There may, however, have been another factor at work. It remains a distinct possibility

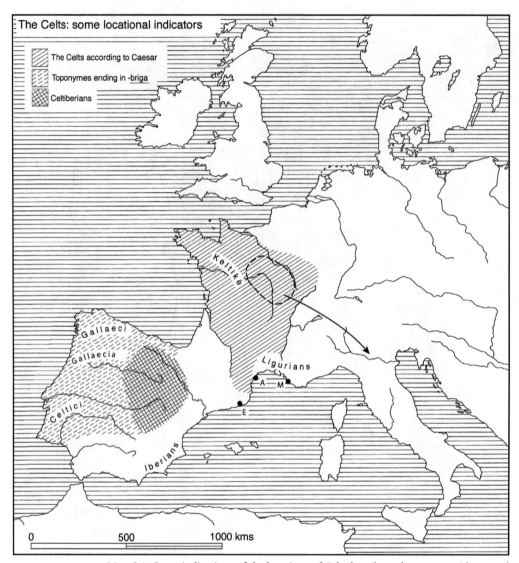

Map 6.4. Some indications of the locations of Celts based on place-name evidence and Classical sources. The arrow indicates possible migration of tribes 400 BC. M = Massalia; A = Agathe; E = Emporion. (Author's map.)

that northern slaves were a commodity in demand in the Mediterranean world. Could it be that the Early La Tène elites emerged in the peripheral zone where slave raiding was endemic? That weapons were a frequent accompaniment to the deceased might support the suggestion.

It was in the courts of the Early La Tène elite, especially those of the Marne-Moselle region, that craftsmen began to transform the motifs of the Mediterranean into a highly distinctive art style usually now referred to as "Early Celtic Art." This began essentially as an aristocratic art but soon became far more widely dispersed both socially and geographically. As some writers would have it, the art style became democratized.

The large-scale folk movements described by writers like Livy and Polybius, which reached their peak at the end of the fifth and the beginning of the fourth centuries BC, seem to have originated in this elite arc: the Classical writers certainly believed this to be the case, and there is some archaeological evidence to suggest social disruption in the core areas. Why major population movements took place at this time is not immediately apparent, but in all probability a combination of factors came into play. The inherent instability of a warrior aristocracy predicated on raiding, and uncertainty about the supply of prestige goods and population growth may together have caused the system to collapse; and once movement had begun, the momentum was difficult to stop. Populations from the northeast of Gaul, from the Moselle, and probably from Bohemia joined in with the massive series of folk movements to the south and east: these are the migrations that Classical writers ascribe to the Celts. Whatever the ethnic affiliation of these people, some, perhaps most, would have spoken Celtic. It was in this way that an elite material culture and the belief systems embedded within it became associated, in the writings of Classical observers and in the minds of many archaeologists, with the concept of the Celt.

By the end of the fourth century BC, then, the notion of the Celt had been further refined. Upon the broad brush strokes of geography and language has been laid a dab of finely textured material culture. However, by focusing too closely on it, we tend to lose sight of the broader picture. Elsewhere within the West European zone, in Iberia, the material culture of the elite was very different. The extent to which there might have been folk movements in the peninsula is unclear, but the Celtic and Gallic ethnonyms found in the south and west of Iberia might be thought to indicate some outward movement of small populations from the Celtiberian homeland. There is, however, no reliable chronology that can be ascribed to this movement.

The distinctive material culture of the Early La Tène period and its comparatively rapid spread throughout much of Middle Europe raise a fascinating series of questions that it is only possible to touch on here. Crucial to the debate must be the acceptance that the adoption of an artifact set outside its area of origin may result from a variety of processes. On the one hand, it could imply the actual movement of people, as presumably it does with the spread of La Tène cultural attributes into Transdanubia and Transylvania in the fourth century BC. But on the other hand, it may mean nothing more than the spread of objects through networks of exchange. La Tène–style items found in Poland and Denmark can most probably be explained in this way. In between these extremes we may be able to recognize a different process – the acceptance of elements of a belief or value system taking with it the physical attributes of that system in the form of material culture. It is this process that, I believe, we can discern across large parts of Western Europe, particularly in Gaul, Britain, and Ireland.

The clearest manifestation can be found in the acceptance of design systems – what we crudely label as Celtic art – within which are embedded levels of meaning. Much of this art, as I have said, originates in the fifth-century elite centers, where it must reflect a very complex system of values and beliefs. Within a comparatively short time we find it spreading throughout Gaul, to be embraced, interpreted, and reproduced in a variety of local contexts. In the southwest of France, in the Haute-Garonne and Cantal, a group of elaborately decorated gold torques, usually named after the find from Aurilliac, reflect what appears to be a local school of craft production reproducing a range of La Tène motifs but in a highly original way. The simplest interpretation of this group of finds is that it reflects local inventiveness responding to the stimulus of new ideas but interpreting them in an original manner for their own elites.

In Armorica (modern Brittany) a rather different interaction is detectable. Here it is the local potters who responded, taking up the complex motifs developed to ornament metalwork in the Marne region and transferring them to their bowls and jars in the form of curvilinear patterns tooled into the vessels' surfaces when the clay was leather hard. The famous vessels from Saint Pol-de-Léon (Finistère) and Blavet, Hénon (Côtes-d'Armor), illustrate this interaction particularly well. The parallels in design are with the beaked flagon from Besançon, the helmet from Berru (Marne), and the basin from Les Saulces-Champenoise (Ardennes). The implication is that the Armorican potters were embracing the art of the metalwork, copied, one supposes, from items imported into Brittany that have so far not appeared in the archaeological record. There are, however, a number of finds of bronze vessels dating to the late sixth and early fifth centuries BC in southern Armorica that clearly came, ultimately, from West-Central Europe and may well reflect an axis of exchange in operation along the valley of the Loire. In the Early La Tène period the same route may well have continued to function, augmented now by another that made use of the Seine and the English Channel to access the metal supplies of the Southwest.[20]

A third example is provided by the rapid adoption of La Tène art styles in Britain, and eventually in Ireland, to decorate sword scabbards, shields, and other elite metalwork. In the east of Britain a highly skilled craft school can be discerned, producing masterpieces like the shields from the River Witham and the Thames at Wandsworth and the pony cap and drinking-horn terminals from Torrs in Scotland. Here all the items of elite display, complete with the symbols that give them meaning, have been adopted by the local community.[21]

In these three examples – the gold torques from southwestern France, the pottery of Armorica, and the ornamented warrior gear from Britain – we are seeing the acceptance of the belief systems and values of the Early La Tène elites of the Marne-Moselle region by the more distant indigenous communities of Gaul, Britain, and Ireland. There is no compelling reason in any of the archaeological, historical, or linguistic evidence to call up invasion or migration to account for this. The existing networks of interaction pervading this Atlantic zone and linking it to the continental hinterland through the long-established riverine routes are sufficient to account for the phenomenon. By the time of the Roman conquest, much of the old Celtic-speaking population had embraced, in their different ways, many of the values of the La Tène elites who had emerged briefly in the fifth century BC along their inland fringe. Only the Iberian Peninsula, isolated to some extent by the Pyrenees and brought more closely into the ambit of Mediterranean culture, had in cultural development taken a different trajectory.

And so, who are the Celts? If there is anything to be learned from the debate about the Celts, so briefly outlined here, it is that, as with all questions of ethnicity, the issues are intriguingly complex. Perceptions change across time, and the many different observers, contemporary or modern, can have only a very partial view of the full picture. That said, if we separate the principal components of "Celticness" – contemporary perception of outsiders, language, and belief and value systems – and examine them against the *longue durée* of European development, the Celts take on a distinctly Atlantic aspect. They can be characterized as the indigenous peoples of Atlantic Europe closely related through millennia of cultural interaction, whose border elites briefly intruded into the Mediterranean sphere and whose successors today continue to occupy much the same territories as their distant ancestors.

Notes

1. Criticism of the way in which the concept of the Celts has been used has come from anthropologists (Chapman 1992) and from some archaeologists (Collis 1993, 1996; James 1999). Measured responses to these views, mainly from linguists (Sims-Williams 1998; Evans 1999; Koch 2001), have attempted to redress the balance of the debate.
2. I have laid out some of the background to these developments in more detail elsewhere. See Cunliffe 1997; 2003.
3. James 1999.
4. Ephorus wrote a *Universal History* in thirty books, none of which survive. His view of the barbarian world is quoted by Strabo (*Geog.* 1.2.28). For a full consideration of the earliest Greek sources on the Celts, see Freeman 1996.
5. Herodotus, *Hist.* 2.33; 4.49. The location of Pyrene has been discussed by Hind (1972), who argues that it is the early name of Emporion (Ampurias).
6. The text of Pytheas's work, *On the Ocean*, no longer survives but can be partially reconstructed from scraps quoted by other writers. The relevant texts have been brought together in Roseman 1994, and the journey has been considered against its archaeological background in Cunliffe 2001b.
7. Caesar, *De Bello Gallico* 1.1.
8. For a summary of these issues see Cunliffe 1997, 68–78. The historical background is dealt with in detail in Rankin 1987, 103–116, and the archaeological evidence is fully explored by Kruta and Manfredi 1999.
9. In *Hist.* 5.34 he states that at the time the Celts of Gaul were dominated by the Bituriges, and it was from here that the migration was instigated, but it involved people from a number of other tribes, among which he lists the Arverni, Senones, Aedui, Ambarri, Carnutes, and Aulerci. Too much geographical precision cannot be given, but if the tribal configuration had not changed too much between the time of the migration and the first century BC, when Caesar recorded the political geography of Gaul, then the migrants must have come from a wide territory in central Gaul extending from the middle of the Loire Valley to the valley of the Rhône, an area that lies wholly within Caesar's Celtic part of Gaul.
10. The Celtic ethnography of Posidonius has been helpfully brought together with all the relevant texts presented in full in Tierney 1960. Posidonius as a historian and geographer is considered in detail by Clarke (1999, 129–192), while Posidonius's soft primitivism is a theme thoroughly explored by Stuart Piggott in his classic treatment of the Druids (Piggott 1968).

11. Emery 1971 provides the most accessible account of the life and works of Lhuyd.
12. The last full statement of the invasion hypothesis was laid out in Hawkes 1959. It was challenged by Hodson (1960) in the first of a series of papers and later by Clark 1966, who sought to demolish invasionist models in general.
13. Bosch-Gimpera 1939. The question of the Celtiberian language is considered fully in Tovar 1961. A volume of papers edited by Almagro-Gorbea and Ruiz Zapatero (1993) offers detailed debates on the Celtic question in Iberia. Renales and Renero-Arribas (1999) give a background to nineteenth-century historiography, while Ruiz Zapatero (1995) critically considers nineteenth- and twentieth-century attitudes to the various interpretations of Celts in Spain.
14. Koch 1986, 1991.
15. This is a theme that I have developed in detail elsewhere (Cunliffe 2001a), and what follows is a brief summary of some of the issues there raised.
16. Clark 1977.
17. Cunliffe 2001a, 275–289.
18. Some of these issues are explored in Waddell and Conroy 1999.
19. Cunliffe 1997, 39–57.
20. For further details of these issues with full references see Cunliffe 1990 and 2000.
21. Objects of Celtic art found in Britain are frequently to be found in publications, but the most thorough discussion of the entire corpus is in Jope 2000.

Bibliography

Almagro-Gorbea, M., and G. Ruiz Zapatero, eds. 1993. *Los Celtas: Hispania y Europa.* Madrid.

Black, R., W. Gilles, and R. Ó Maolalaigh. 1999. *Celtic Connections: Proceedings of the Tenth International Congress of Celtic Studies. Volume One: Language, Literature, History and Culture.* East Linton, England.

Bosch-Gimpera, P. 1939. "Two Celtic Waves in Spain" (Rhys Lecture). *Proceedings of the British Academy* 26:25–148.

Chapman, M. 1992. *The Celts: The Construction of a Myth.* New York.

Clark, J. G. C. 1966. "The Invasion Hypothesis in British Archaeology." *Antiquity* 40:172–189.

1977. "The Economic Context of Dolmans and Passage Graves in Sweden." In *Ancient Europe and the Mediterranean*, ed. V. Markovic, 35–49. London.

Clarke, K. 1999. *Between Geography and History: Hellenistic Constructions of the Roman World.* Oxford.

Collis, J. R. 1993. "Los Celtas en Europa." In Almagro-Gorbea and Ruiz Zapatero, 1993, 63–76.

1996. "The Origin and Spread of the Celts." *Studia Celtica* 30:17–34.

Cunliffe, B. 1990. "Social and Economic Contacts between Western France and Britain in the Early and Middle La Tène Period." In *La Bretagne et l'Europe Préhistoriques. Mémoire en hommage à Pierre-Roland Giot. Revue Arch de l'Ouest,* Supplément 2:245–251.

1997. *The Ancient Celts.* Oxford.

2000. "Brittany and the Atlantic Rim in the Later First Millennium BC." *Oxford Journal of Archaeology* 19 (4): 367–386.

2001a. *Facing the Ocean: The Atlantic and Its Peoples*. Oxford.

2001b. *The Extraordinary Voyage of Pytheas the Greek*. London.

2003. *The Celts: A Very Short Introduction*. Oxford.

2008. *Europe between the Oceans: Themes and Variations: 9000 BC to AD 1000*. New Haven, CT, and London.

Emery, F. V. 1971. *Edward Lhuyd F.R.S. 1660–1709*. Cardiff, Wales.

Evans, D. E. 1999. "Linguistics and Celtic Ethnogenesis." In Black et al. 1999, 1–18.

Freeman, P. M. 1996. "The Earliest Greek Sources on the Celts." *Études Celtiques* 32:11–48.

Hannestad, L. 1993. "Greeks and Celts: The Creation of a Myth." In *Centre and Periphery in the Hellenistic World*, ed. P. Bilde, T. Engberg-Pedersen, L. Hannestad, J. Zahle, and K. Randsborg, 15–38. Aarhus.

Hawkes, C. F. C. 1959. "The ABC of the British Iron Age." *Antiquity* 33:170–182.

Hind, J. 1972. "Pyrene and the Date of the 'Massaliot Sailing Manual'." *Rivista Storica dell'antichità* 2:39–52.

Hodson, F. R. 1960. "Reflections on the ABC of the British Iron Age." *Antiquity* 34:138–140.

James, S. 1999. *The Atlantic Celts: Ancient People or Modern Invention?* London.

Jope, E. M. 2000. *Early Celtic Art in the British Isles*. Oxford.

Koch, J. T. 1986. "New Thoughts on Albion, Ierné and the Pretanic Isles." *Proceedings of the Harvard Celtic Colloquium* 16:1–28.

1991. "Érin, Alba and Letha: When Was a Language Ancestral to Gaelic First Spoken in Ireland?" *Emania* 9:17–27.

2001. "Celtoscepticism: Some Intellectual Sources and Ideological Implications." *Indo-European Studies Bulletin* 9 (2): 1–8.

2009. *Tartessian: Celtic in the South-West at the Dawn of History*. Aberystwyth.

Kruta, V., and V. M. Manfredi. 1999. *I Celti in Italia*. Milan.

Piggott, S. 1968. *The Druids*. London. (New York edition 1985.)

Rankin, H. D. 1987. *Celts and the Classical World*. London.

Renales, J., and V. M. Renero-Arribas. 1999. "Celtiberian Studies and Spanish Celtic Historiography in the Nineteenth Century." In Black et al. 1999, 108–125.

Roseman, C. H. 1994. *Pytheas of Massalia: On the Ocean*. London.

Ruiz Zapatero, G. 1995. "Celts and Iberians. Ideological Manipulation in Spanish Archaeology." In *The Identity of Ancient Europe*, ed. C. Gamble, S, Jones, and P. Graves, 179–195. London.

Sims-Williams, P. 1998. "Celtomania and Celtoscepticism." *Cambrian Medieval Celtic Studies* 36:1–35.

Tierney, J. J. 1960. "The Celtic Ethnography of Posidonius." *Proceedings of the Royal Irish Academy* 60C:189–275.

Tolkien, J. R. R. 1963. "On English and Welsh." In *Angles and Britons: O'Donnell Lectures*, ed. H. Lewis, 1–25. Cardiff.

Tovar, A. 1961. *The Ancient Languages of Spain and Portugal*. New York.

Waddell, J., and J. Conroy. 1999. "Celts and Others: Maritime Contacts and Linguistic Change." In *Archaeology and Language IV: Language Change and Cultural Transformation*, ed. R. Blench and M. Spriggs, 125–137. London.

CHAPTER SEVEN

THE ANCIENT GERMANS

Peter S. Wells

The focus of this chapter is on the relationship between the ways that the peoples of northern continental Europe represented themselves through their material culture – house forms, jewelry, ornamental metalwork, pottery, ritual structures – and the images that Roman commentators such as Caesar and Tacitus created. Did the Roman writers create their portrayals of the Germans principally from traditional Roman ideas about "barbarians" or were these characterizations based on real information about those societies? Three disciplinary approaches, historical, linguistic, and archaeological, generally disagree in the methods they use and the results they reach. An example of this is the sharp distinction that Caesar described between the Gauls west of the Rhine and the Germans east of it, which is not apparent in archaeology.

The question "Who were the ancient Germans?" is extremely complex. Historians, linguists, and archaeologists have very different answers, and practitioners within each discipline often have widely differing opinions. A useful overview of the issues is "Germanen, Germania, Germanische Altertumskunde" in *Reallexikon der germanischen Altertumskunde* (1998).[1] Here I briefly outline the main lines of thought in each of three disciplinary approaches, then turn to a discussion of the archaeology of the peoples whom we usually mean when we speak of ancient Germans (Map 7.1).

Map 7.1. Sites mentioned in the text. (Courtesy Ancient World Mapping Center, copyright 2010, www.unc.edu/awmc.)

The Ethnic Name and the Written Sources

The first description that survives from ancient texts of peoples called "Germans" (*Germani*) is in Julius Caesar's commentaries on the Gallic War (58–51 BC). (The Greek writer Posidonius may have described people he called Germans at a slightly earlier date, but his works do not survive.) In his account of his campaigns in Gaul, Caesar had occasion to mention Germans a number of times in different contexts, and Caesar's use of the name established its meaning for the Roman world.[2] Subsequent authors, such as Strabo and Tacitus, followed Caesar in his usage. Thus, all early applications of the name Germans go back to Caesar's initial characterization of those peoples.

Caesar's purpose in his commentaries was not to write about the Germans. Rather, it was to present to Roman readers an account of his campaigns against the Gallic groups who resisted Rome's armies. His remarks about Germans need to be understood in that context. Caesar refers to *Germani* throughout his commentary. He informs us that the *Germani*, who were comprised of different groups (usually translated today as "peoples" or "tribes"), lived, for the most part, east of the Rhine, whereas the Gauls, against whom Caesar was fighting, lived west of the Rhine. He makes this point about the cultural geography in the first part of the first book of his work and reiterates it several times later.

Caesar makes it clear that the peoples he called Germans were less civilized and lived in smaller communities than the Gauls; they had no urban centers comparable to the *oppida* of Gaul; and their economic systems and religious practices were less complex. For example, he writes, "The Germans differ much from [the Gauls]. They have no Druids to regulate divine worship…. They reckon among the gods those only whom they see and by whose offices they are openly assisted…. Their whole life is composed of hunting expeditions and military pursuits …" (6.21). And further, "For agriculture they have no zeal, and the greater part of their food consists of milk, cheese, and flesh … " (6.22).

Sometime later, Tacitus wrote a work, completed in AD 98, specifically about the peoples whom the Romans called Germans, titled *De Origine et Situ Germanorum*, generally referred to simply as the *Germania*. During the century and a half between Caesar's account and the descriptions of Tacitus, Rome had created its elaborate infrastructure in the three provinces of Gaul, conquered the region between the upper Danube and the Alps in what is now southern Bavaria, and added the territory between the upper Rhine and Danube rivers that is today Baden-Württemberg. Thus, the Roman world had impinged much more intensively on the groups east of the Rhine and had had considerable opportunity to become more familiar with the peoples whom Caesar had designated as Germans.

Tacitus's use of the name Germans is fundamentally the same as that of Caesar, but he goes into much more detail about what he supposed to be their origins and about individual groups. In a much-discussed passage he writes, "the name of 'Germany' is new and a recent application. The first tribes in fact to cross the Rhine and expel the Gauls ... bore the name Germans ... little by little the name – a tribal, not a national, name – prevailed, until the whole people were called by the artificial name of 'Germans' ..." (2). Tacitus goes on to portray the Germans in ways similar to those of Caesar – as physically robust and tough (4), living in a challenging environment, accustomed to simple ways of life (6, 17), morally virtuous (18–20), and maintaining customs uncorrupted by Roman commercial interests (5).

There exists a large critical literature about Caesar's and Tacitus's representations of the Germans.[3] Increasingly, researchers are approaching those texts as "literary artifacts," not as objective statements of fact, and interpreting them in terms of the backgrounds, assumptions, and purposes of the writers. Caesar's remarks about the Germans have been understood largely in the context of his political aims. His commentary on the Gallic War has been viewed as a text that he intended to use to gain support for his cause in Rome. Since rivers were frequently understood as ethnic or national boundaries in the ancient world, Caesar portrayed the Rhine as the boundary between Gauls and Germans and thus as a "natural" limit for his conquests. His representations of the Germans as very different from the Gauls may have been intended to reinforce the idea that since the Gauls were more like Romans, Roman armies could more easily conquer them, and Rome would benefit from the conquest. The Germans, beyond the Rhine, remained strange and foreign to the Roman sensibility.[4]

Rather than being considered an ethnography, as it had been by earlier generations of scholars, Tacitus's Germania is now largely viewed as a literary work, informing us more about the attitudes and values of Romans of Tacitus's time than about the Germans he was describing.[5] One set of views of Tacitus's work suggests that it was intended to chastise Roman readers for their easy and decadent lives, portraying their northern neighbors as vigorous, morally upright, and at one with nature.

Thus, both Caesar's and Tacitus's texts about the Germans are no longer accepted as straightforward descriptive accounts of the peoples east of the Rhine during the first century BC and the first century AD. What they provide most importantly to us are representations of Roman ideas about the peoples that inhabited the extensive and to a large extent still little-understood regions beyond the Rhine and the Danube.[6]

Accounts by later Roman writers follow the usage established by Caesar and Tacitus. The "tribal confederations," such as the Alamanni, Burgundians, Goths, Franks, Langobards, and Saxons, that appear in Roman written sources from the third century AD on are represented as direct descendants of the Germans described by Caesar and Tacitus and possessed of the same basic cultural characteristics.[7]

The name German, used in reference to the many peoples east of the Rhine at the time of Caesar and Tacitus and later during the Late Roman Period and the early Middle Ages, was thus a Roman creation. The actual origin of the name Germani is unclear; some believe it to have been of Gallic (Celtic) origin;[8] others trace it to a Latin background.[9] As far as we know, before and during the Roman Period (roughly 50 BC–AD 500), these peoples never referred to themselves with the overarching name Germans. It is even doubtful that they thought of themselves as belonging to a single entity.[10] It was not until 1,000 years after Caesar's use of the name that people in those regions began to think of themselves as members of a common group.

Language

Linguists know very little about the language group called Germanic before the middle of the Roman period, around AD 300. As preliterate peoples, the communities thought to have spoken such languages left no inscriptions from pre-Roman times. Linguists attempt to reconstruct the languages and their distributions on the basis of inscriptions of the Roman period, runes, and the personal, place, and especially deities' names recorded in Roman and later sources.[11] We do not know of any Roman who could understand the language spoken by the peoples whom Caesar and Tacitus called Germans, and Roman and Greek writers did not use language as a criterion for distinguishing Celts (Gauls) from Germans.[12] Thus, the written accounts by Roman and Greek authors are of very little help regarding linguistic issues. In the Rhineland, where numerous inscriptions from the Roman period have been recovered and studied, linguists recognize a complex mixture of elements that, in later times, would be attributed to both the Celtic and the Germanic languages.[13]

Some linguists hypothesize, through a study of rates of change in languages, that what are today considered Germanic languages first emerged from other Indo-European languages at the time of what is known as the "Germanic sound shift," sometime around the middle of the first millennium BC.[14] Others would push the date back to between 2500 and 1000 BC for the development of that language group.[15]

What may be the earliest inscription known in a Germanic language has been identified on a bronze helmet from a deposit of twenty-three helmets found at Ženjak (Negau) in Slovenia.[16] While dating the inscription presents numerous difficulties, it appears most likely that it dates to around 100 BC. In northern Europe, especially on Jutland and in surrounding areas, runic inscriptions during and after the Roman Period provide extensive linguistic evidence for understanding the Germanic languages developing at that time.[17] Among important early examples are an inscribed fibula bow from Meldorf in northern Germany,[18] dated to the first century AD, and an inscription from a deposit of weapons and ornaments at Vimose in Denmark, from about AD 160.

Archaeology

The archaeological evidence pertaining to the peoples whom Caesar and Tacitus called Germans is much more abundant than that for historical and linguistic reconstruction. But linking the archaeological evidence with the descriptions by Caesar and Tacitus, and with the linguistic information, presents complex problems. For well over a century, archaeologists have attempted to identify when Germans can first be recognized in the material evidence. The major problem with this endeavor is that the name and concept of Germans are based on texts. Matching historical information with archaeological evidence is often immensely difficult. The types of evidence examined and interpreted by the disciplines are very different, and it is unlikely that we shall ever achieve a match – a delineation of Germans that is satisfactory to archaeologists, historians, and linguists.

I cannot review the long and complex history of attempts to identify Germans archaeologically,[19] but rather will cite several significant recent studies of the question. In a wide-ranging interdisciplinary investigation, Hachmann, Kossack, and Kuhn[20] attempted to bring together all of the relevant information to examine the problem of defining Celts and Germans archaeologically and of identifying the boundary between them during the Late Iron Age and at the time of the arrival of the Roman armies. Through examination of specific categories of archaeological evidence, Peschel, Stöckli, and Rieckhoff[21] have tried to match particular sets of material culture with the peoples whom the Roman writers called Germans. The success of all such attempts has been limited, because they are based on the assumption that the groups whom Caesar named Germans possessed a material culture that was recognizably distinct from those of other peoples. Modern research on the theoretical issues involved, as well as on the archaeological data, suggests that this was not the case.[22]

Based on early Greek and Roman texts that call peoples of Iron Age Western Europe Celts (Gauls), on Caesar's assertions about Celts (Gauls) inhabiting the regions west of the Rhine, and on linguistic evidence that becomes available in inscriptions in southern France from the third century BC on, the Late Iron Age material culture designated as La Tène has been linked with the Celts.[23] East of the Rhine, and especially concentrated in northern Germany, southern Denmark, and Poland, the material culture known as "Jastorf" has been linked with Germans as early as the sixth century BC.[24] Pottery, ring jewelry, belt hooks, fibulae, and other metalwork associated with the Jastorf complex are distributed widely in northern regions of continental Europe. The principal problem with this approach is that it assumes that the concept Germans (which was a Roman, not an indigenous category, as noted earlier) had an ethnic or national reality that changed little over time. There is no evidence to suggest that the peoples who lived in the lands in which Jastorf-type material culture is found had any sense of group identity that might correspond to the Roman concept German.

Problems Integrating the Sources

In the brief introduction, I have tried to lay out the problems of understanding the idea of the ancient Germans from the perspectives of text-based history, linguistics, and archaeology. The central problem is that the term Germans does not name a discrete, clearly definable group of peoples who lived 2,000 years ago. The name, as it was, and is, applied to many tribal groups east of the Rhine, was a creation of Roman military officials and writers, outsiders who did not understand (and perhaps did not care to understand) the ways in which the peoples beyond the Rhine thought about themselves.[25] The linguistic approach is based on nineteenth-century linguistic categories that were created through the study of modern languages.[26] It is not clear whether these categories can even be applied to the linguistic situation 2,000 years ago.[27] The archaeological approach attempts to match patterns in the material evidence with assertions by the Roman writers. Many archaeologists assume that the entity that Roman writers called Germans was one of long standing by the time of the Roman arrival. Yet modern understanding of changes among peoples living in frontier zones,[28] such as those on the edge of the Roman Empire, leads to a very different approach that focuses on questions of cultural changes that such indigenous groups undergo rather than on any long-standing group identities.[29]

I turn first to the archaeology of the peoples east of the Rhine – the region in which Caesar and Tacitus tell us Germans lived – from the latter part of the prehistoric Iron Age through the Early Roman Period. I begin with a brief review of what the archaeology indicates about the society and economy of the peoples before the arrival of Caesar's troops in Gaul in 58 BC. Then I turn to the period during which Rome established its 500-year frontier on the Rhine. Since our concept of Germans is based on Roman writers' representations of them, it is important to consider these peoples in relation to their interactions with the Roman world across the Rhine frontier. By arbitrarily dividing the Early Roman Period into three phases, I emphasize the substantial changes that the peoples of northern Europe experienced during this period of regular and often intensive interaction.

Pre-Roman Iron Age (700–58 BC)

As in earlier times, most settlements were small during the pre-Roman Iron Age, on the scale of individual farmsteads or very small villages, with community populations usually under fifty persons. Houses typically were large, post-built structures, oriented east–west, with human habitation at one end and livestock housed at the other. They were built with sizable vertical posts sunk into the ground, wattle-and-daub walls, and roofs of thatched grasses. A well-excavated example is at Grøntoft in Denmark.[30] The predominant livestock was cattle; sheep, goats, and pigs were also kept for food, and horses and dogs were often raised as well.

Other buildings on settlements were workshops and storage sheds.[31] Pottery manufacture is well represented, as is the working of wood, leather, and textiles. Many, if not most, communities smelted and forged their own iron[32] and were thus able to maintain the supply of tools they required. For clothing, wool from the sheep and linen made from flax were used.[33]

Beyond the settlements were agricultural fields. Throughout much of the North European Plain, archaeologists have identified field systems consisting of rectangular fields bounded by banks, ditches, and hedges.[34] The construction of such fields suggests intensified strategies of agriculture involving the definition of private property, the practice of crop rotation, and the use of fertilizer. Emmer wheat, along with other wheat varieties, was a common crop; other cereals cultivated included barley, millet, and rye. Peas, lentils, and beans were also grown. Berries and fruits were gathered from the local environment, and hunting, especially of deer, supplemented the meat from the domestic animals.

There are many indications that in the latter part of the pre-Roman Iron Age, economy and society were becoming more complex and that communities were becoming increasingly integrated into larger political units. The settlement at Hodde in Jutland reflects the increased size of some communities by around 100 BC, as well as status differences represented in the character of houses and in the quality of manufactured products consumed, such as pottery.[35]

Trade with other regions is evident in imported goods. Bronze, commonly used for personal ornaments, such as fibulae, bracelets, and belt hooks, had to be imported, probably from mountainous regions to the south. Amber was obtained along the shores of the Baltic and North seas and was much favored for beads and pendants. From the large urban centers at the *oppida* to the south in the hilly upland regions of Central Europe, communities imported fine pottery, metal vessels, glass bracelets, coins, and other goods.[36] These foreign objects show that the communities of Northern Europe were in increasingly active contact, direct or indirect, with peoples in other parts of the Continent, and that they were producing surplus goods (perhaps leather, hides, preserved meat) to exchange for the items they desired.[37]

Supracommunity political organization is apparent in the construction of wooden trackways across marshy areas. For example, one excavated at Ockenhausen is 1.3 kilometers in length, built of some 13,000 oak planks fashioned from 3,000 trees.[38] The purpose of such trackways was to provide passage across wetlands. They are important in indicating that a political structure existed that enabled the coordination of labor drawn from several villages to create infrastructure for the common good.

Another indicator of supracommunity organization is the weapons find at Hjortspring on the island of Als in southern Denmark. Here a boat designed to carry twenty warriors was purposely sunk in a small pond, along with weapons to outfit a military force of eighty fully armed soldiers. The weapons include iron swords and spearheads, wooden shields, and the earliest chain mail known in Europe. This deposit, which dates to around 350 BC, is interpreted as the result of an offering of the weapons and vehicle of a defeated enemy.[39] Particularly significant is what the find tells us about organized warfare. Outfitting eighty warriors, and presumably four warships altogether, was a task far beyond the ability of any single community and can only have been accomplished by a much larger political structure that involved participants drawn from many settlements. The Hjortspring deposit is also important for what it tells us about the military background and experience of peoples in this part of Europe well before the arrival of the Roman armies on the Rhine.

Hjortspring is one of hundreds of ritual sites known in Northern Europe, where it was common practice to deposit offerings to deities in bodies of water, including rivers, lakes, and bogs.[40] Deposited objects range from simple ceramic vessels to the complex weapon sets such as that at Hjortspring. Ornate wagons, built of wood and adorned with bronze ornaments, are among the objects offered. Elaborate metal vessels form another category of offerings, including the ornate bronze cauldrons from the Danish sites of Brå and Rynkeby and the gilded silver cauldron from Gundestrup.[41]

As this very brief review suggests, the communities east of the Rhine were much more complex, and had considerably more developed economies and political systems, than Caesar's remarks suggest.

Early Roman Period: Conquest and Earliest Roman Phase (58 BC–AD 50)

As discussed previously, the early Germans, as the Romans described them and as we understand them today, were a creation of Roman writers, especially Caesar and Tacitus. As Timpe[42] has shown, Roman observers seem to have fixed their ideas about the character of the people they called Germans on the basis of Caesar's writings. The subsequent texts suggest that they did not appreciate the extent to which the peoples beyond the Rhine changed over time. The archaeological evidence, on the other hand, makes it clear that very substantial changes took place among the peoples east of the Rhine during the Roman Period, in part as a result of interactions with the Roman provinces across the Rhine and the Danube.

A significant change that took place around the middle of the first century BC was the more widespread tendency for settlements to be enclosed within a palisade rather than open to the outside. Whether the purpose of the palisades was more for defense or to draw boundaries between the village and the outside world, the effect was a more clearly structured physical landscape. A small settlement at Meppen in northern Germany[43] had both an enclosing palisade around the whole community and fences between individual houses.

Communities that focused on craft production became economically more significant in the landscape. At Daseburg in Nordrhein-Westfalen, situated 150 kilometers east of the Roman Rhine frontier, a small settlement with typical house-barn structures, granaries, and food-producing tools also had workshops and furnaces for working iron, bronze, and, surprisingly, silver and lead.[44] Fibulae are the products most in evidence, but other forms of ornaments and implements were manufactured here as well between AD 20 and 60. The processing of silver in a small farming settlement represents a major change from earlier patterns of craft production.

Two important changes are apparent in burial ritual in the lands east of the Rhine. One is the new practice of placing weapons in many men's graves from the middle of the final century BC.[45] In some cases, complete sets of weapons – sword, spear, and shield – are present; in others, partial sets. Sometimes the weapons are accompanied by spurs and by bronze vessels, often of Roman origin, as, for example, in a number of burials in the large cemetery at Harsefeld, near Hamburg.[46] Since burial practices reflect a society's most deeply held values and attitudes, this shift indicates a profound new attitude toward weapons and their roles in men's lives. One approach is to understand this change in terms of response to the wars raging in Gaul at the time between Caesar's army and the Gallic troops. Caesar made two forays across the Rhine, in 55 and 53 BC, and perhaps the new emphasis on weaponry in burial ritual indicates the communities' feelings of the need for greater military preparedness in the face of the threat of Roman aggression.

The spurs suggest another interpretation. In his commentaries, Caesar mentions that he employed German cavalry troops because of their skill on horseback. It is possible that some or all of the men buried with spurs as well as weapons were identified in their funerary ceremonies as auxiliaries who had served with Rome. The presence of ornate Roman bronze vessels in some of these burials might add support to this interpretation.[47]

Another change is the appearance of substantial numbers of graves that were exceptionally richly outfitted. Characteristic grave goods in these burials, which occur as far east as Poland, north into Norway, and south into the Czech Republic, are Roman bronze (and occasionally silver) vessels, drinking horns, gold and silver ornaments, and, in some cases, swords and other weapons.[48] Early in the first century AD, more graves east of the Rhine were outfitted with increasing quantities of Roman luxury goods. At Putensen, south of the Elbe River near Hamburg, archaeologists have excavated 988 graves. Most contained cremation burials with local handmade pots as urns, but in 7 cases, bronze vessels of Roman or Central European manufacture held the cremated remains. Many graves at Putensen contained iron weapons, including swords, spears, lances, and axes, as well as chain mail and shields.[49]

In Grave 150 at Putensen, the cremated remains of a thirty-year-old man were found in a bronze cauldron.[50] Weapons in the grave included a sword and scabbard, shield, lance-head, and knife. Horseback-riding equipment was represented by rein ornaments and three pairs of spurs. Two bronze casseroles of Roman origin were present, and with them were attachments from two locally made drinking horns. Other objects in the grave included six silver fibulae, a bronze fibula, an iron fibula, and a silver pin. This grave, more lavishly outfitted than most, is representative of a series of burials in this period that point to several interrelated themes that relate to changes during the period. The man's special social status is reflected in the silver ornaments, the drinking horns, and the bronze cauldron. His role as a warrior is marked by the set of weapons. His links to the Roman world are shown in his spurs and in the bronze casseroles.

Early Roman Period: Middle Phase (AD 50–200)

During the latter half of the first century and in the second century AD, substantial changes are apparent in settlement as well as in burial. The first century AD was a very prosperous time for the Roman Rhineland, and a variety of effects are apparent in the lands east of the river. Just beyond the frontier, many communities became very closely connected economically to towns on the west bank of the Rhine. At Westick near the Ruhr River, excavations reveal that vast amounts of Roman material culture were consumed.[51] About one-third of the pottery and one-third of the metal objects recovered at the settlement were of Roman origin. Farther from the frontier, quantities of Roman products were fewer, but objects of much higher value were used and deposited.

A settlement had been established in the second half of the first century BC at Feddersen Wierde, on the North Sea coast, north of the modern city of Bremerhaven.[52] The first phase of the settlement was similar to the typical settlements mentioned previously. The excavators interpret the evidence to indicate a community of five farmsteads, with long house-barn structures, and with a total stall capacity for livestock of ninety-eight animals, most of which, if not all, were cattle. These five structures of the initial settlement indicate families of equal status. Over time, the settlement grew in size, Roman imports increased in number, and stall capacity multiplied fivefold, to a peak of 443. Along with these changes, status differences within the community grew. Smaller house-barns contained as few as twelve stalls, while larger ones had as many as thirty. The greatest changes are apparent during the second century AD. One larger dwelling stood out from the rest of the settlement, and it was accompanied by a special workshop. Associated with this complex is a horse burial, suggestive of ritual linked to the higher status of the family that inhabited this house. Also during the second century AD, the quantities of Roman imports at the settlement increased. They include fine pottery, glass vessels, glass beads, fibulae, coins, basalt grindstones from the quarry site at Mayen on the middle Rhine, and such exotic luxuries as a fan with a carved ivory handle.[53]

Feddersen Wierde is interpreted as a community that specialized in producing livestock for trade with the Roman military and civil settlements along the lower and middle Rhine. The Roman army required large quantities of cattle for meat and for leather. An inscribed tablet found to the west of Feddersen Wierde, at Tolsum in the Netherlands, attests to a transaction in which Romans acquired cattle from native farmers.[54]

The evidence at Feddersen Wierde for increasing stall capacity, social differentiation, and commerce with the Roman world during the first and second centuries AD suggests major ways in which peoples east of the Rhine changed, largely in response to commercial opportunities offered by the Roman demand for goods.[55]

Early Roman Period: Late Phase (AD 200–300)

An outstanding development of the third and fourth centuries AD east of the Rhine is the emergence of major centers of political, economic, and religious activity in northern parts of the European Continent. The best studied is at Gudme on the island of Fyn in Denmark.[56] Excavations at the major cemetery at Gudme, in the locale of Møllegårdsmarken, recovered 130 Roman imports, including vessels of bronze, glass, and pottery. Roman objects from the Gudme settlement include over 500 silver coins, Roman silver tableware, a bronze helmet, and a near-life-size bronze statue.[57] These and other imports were brought to Gudme via the port at Lundeborg, 5 kilometers to the east on the coast. There, workshops have been excavated that processed a wide variety of materials including iron, bronze, silver, and gold. Gudme developed into a major regional political center, with the largest building known from Roman period northern Europe, 47 meters long and 10 meters wide.[58] Inside the remains of that structure archaeologists recovered silver and gold ornaments and coins. The complex of Gudme-Møllegårdsmarken-Lundeborg illustrates the emergence of political and economic centers east of the Rhine engaged in active commerce with the Roman world. The question of the causal role that interaction with the Roman world may have played in the formation of such centers is beyond the scope of this chapter.

In northern Germany, Denmark, and southern Sweden, weapon deposits similar in character to that at Hjortspring, but much larger in size, are numerous during the third and fourth centuries AD. About thirty such deposits have been studied to date. At Illerup in Denmark, excavation of 40 percent of the site has yielded about 100 swords, 1,000 spears and lances, and 300 shields, along with other weapons. In some cases, as at Nydam, ships were deposited. The fact that many of the weapons recovered from these deposits are of Roman manufacture is of interest, but the more important point here is what these deposits tell us about political organization. These deposits are the remains of huge offerings of weaponry from defeated enemies.[59] In the centuries since the period of Hjortspring, considerably larger political entities had developed, with bigger and more powerful armies. We know from textual and epigraphic sources that the Roman army on the frontier employed many auxiliaries from beyond the Rhine. The formation of these larger military forces in Northern Europe was surely related to such experience with the Roman army.

New Identities in the Late Roman Period

During the third century AD, we first encounter in Roman textual sources names of groupings east of the Rhine that were much larger than the tribes of Caesar's and Tacitus's times – names such as Alamanni, Burgundians, Franks, Goths, Langobards, and Saxons. These have been characterized by modern scholars as confederations of tribes, and in them researchers see a political development well beyond that of the groups with whom the Romans interacted earlier.[60] At the same time that the written sources describe these larger political entities, the archaeological evidence shows the gradual formation of a new style of ornament, known today as "Germanic art." The style is especially well represented in metalwork on fibulae, pendants, jewelry rings, and weapons.

The emergence of this new style of art can be understood in terms of the creation of new material signs of identity by peoples growing in political and military power, increasingly willing and able to challenge Rome. As Haseloff,[61] Roth,[62] and others have noted, the new style has multiple roots in the turbulent third, fourth, and fifth centuries AD. It developed east of the middle and lower Rhine, and one of the early centers of production became what is now Denmark. Three main sources have been identified for this new style.

One is local traditions of metalwork that go back to the Jastorf style of the prehistoric Iron Age. The ornamented objects of the Late Roman and Early Medieval periods can be understood as developments of the fibulae, ring jewelry, belt ornaments, and decorated weapons of the pre-Roman and Early Roman periods. Much of the iconography in the new style can be linked to ornaments of the late prehistoric Iron Age, as displayed on the cauldrons from Brå, Rynkeby, and Gundestrup.

The second principal source of elements in the new style is late Roman ornament. Animal and human heads from late Roman decorative metalwork served as models for some of the new designs. The technique known as "chip-carving," employed in much of the metal ornament in the new style, was borrowed from metalwork on late Roman military belts.[63]

The third main source was the decorative traditions of Southeast Europe, the lands west and north of the Black Sea associated at this time with the Goths. From that region derived the openwork gold technique and inlay with garnet, a new combination in temperate Europe.[64] Several recent studies[65] draw attention to evidence indicating strong links between Southeastern and Northern Europe during the late prehistoric Iron Age and the Early Roman period.

The new style, which reached its full development at the end of the fifth century AD, was adopted widely throughout Central and Northern Europe and, eventually, Western Europe as well, in late and post-Roman times. Now this style represented peoples who were no longer prehistoric, but were the well-documented historical Germanic peoples of the early Middle Ages.

In Caesar's time, the Romans can be said to have created the Germans, in the sense that the name German, used to designate diverse peoples beyond the Rhine, was a Roman invention. By the fifth century AD, the cultural descendants of those peoples were forging their own identities in larger and much more powerful political entities.[66] Their relation to the Roman world had changed greatly. But Roman ideas and texts also play important roles in the ways that we understand these later peoples.

Notes

1. *Reallexikon der germanischen Altertumskunde*, vol. 11 (1998), 181–438.
2. Lund 1998; Pohl 2000.
3. E.g., Walser 1956; Beck 1986; Dobesch 1989; Jankuhn and Timpe 1989; Timpe 1989, 1998; Trzaska-Richter 1991; Neumann and Seemann 1992; Flach 1995; Lund 1998, Welch and Powell 1998; Potter 1999; Pohl 2000; Grane 2003.
4. Timpe 1989.
5. Neumann and Seemann 1992; Mellor 1993; Woodman 1993; Wiegels 1995.
6. De Caro 1997.
7. Demandt 1993; Hedeager 1993; Wolfram 1997.
8. Wolfram 1997.
9. Untermann 1989; Pohl 2000.
10. Lund 1998.
11. Mallory 1989; Untermann 1989.
12. Untermann 1989, 219–220.
13. Meid 1986.
14. Schutz 1983, 312; Mallory 1989.
15. Todd 1992, 11.
16. Urban and Nedona 2002.
17. Antonsen 1986; Stoklund 1995, 1996, 2003.
18. Düwel and Gebühr 1981.
19. See Kühn 1976; Lund 1998; Künzl 2008.
20. Hachmann et al. 1962.
21. Peschel 1988; Stöckli 1993; Rieckhoff 1995.
22. Wells 1998. See Bonfante, Chapter 1, this volume.
23. Green 1995; Müller 2001.
24. Keiling 1989; Brandt 2001.
25. Lund 1998.
26. Untermann 1989.

27. Meid 1986.
28. E.g., Ferguson and Whitehead 1992; Hill 1996.
29. E.g., Ament 1984; Pohl 2000.
30. Jensen 1982, 205–207.
31. Seyer 1988.
32. Jöns 1999. See Bonfante, Chapter 8, on the possible etymology of the German word *erz*.
33. Hald 1980.
34. Müller-Wille 1973.
35. Hvass 1985.
36. E.g., Heege 1987; Grasselt et al. 2003.
37. See Chapters 1, 5, 6, and 7, in this volume, for trade in amber, bronze, and luxury items in exchange for raw materials, and influences from Italy.
38. Fansa and Schneider 1993.
39. Randsborg 1995; Kaul 2003.
40. Randsborg 1995; Bradley 1998; Ilkjaer 2003.
41. Wells 1994.
42. Timpe 1989, 1996a, 1996b.
43. Zoller 1977.
44. Günther 1990.
45. Schultze 1986.
46. Hässler 1977.
47. Wells 2001, 120–121.
48. Gebühr 1974.
49. Wegewitz 1972.
50. Roggenbuck 1983.
51. Schoppa 1970.
52. Schön 1999.
53. Erdrich 2001, 117–119.
54. Boeles 1951, 129–130 and plate 16.
55. Brather 2002.
56. Thomsen et al. 1993; Nielsen et al. 1994.
57. Michaelsen 1994.
58. Michaelsen and Sørensen 1993.
59. Randsborg 1995; Ilkjaer 2000, 2003; Jensen 2003; Jørgensen and Petersen 2003.
60. Demandt 1993; Wolfram 1997.
61. Haseloff 1981.
62. Roth 1986, 1998.
63. Roth 1986, 1998.
64. Arrhenius 1985.
65. E.g. Storgaard 1994; Kaul and Martens 1995.
66. Hedeager 1993, 2000.

Bibliography

Ament, H. 1984. "Der Rhein und die Ethnogenese der Germanen." *Praehistorische Zeitschrift* 59:37–47.

Antonsen, E. H. 1986. "Die ältesten Runeninschriften." In Beck 1986, 321–343.

Arrhenius, B. 1985. *Merovingian Garnet Jewellery: Emergence and Social Implications.* Stockholm.

Beck, H., ed. 1986. *Germanenprobleme in heutiger Sicht*. Berlin.

Boeles, P. 1951. *Friesland Tot de Elfde Eeuw* (*Frisia to the Eleventh Century*). S'Gravenhage. (The Hague). (In Dutch.)

Bradley, R. 1998. *The Passage of Arms: An Archaeological Analysis of Prehistoric Hoard and Votive Deposits*, 2nd ed. Oxford.

Brandt, J. 2001. *Jastorf und Latène*. Rahden.

Brather, M.-J. 2002. "Im Inneren Germaniens: Siedlung und Metallverarbeitung." In *Menschen-Zeiten-Räume: Archäologie in Deutschland*, ed. W. Menghin and D. Planck, 289-292. Stuttgart.

Caesar, J. 1986. *The Gallic War*. Trans. H. J. Edwards. Cambridge MA (Loeb Classical Library).

De Caro, S. 1997. "The Northern Barbarians as Seen by Rome." In *Roman Reflections in Scandinavia*, ed. E. Björklund, 25-29. Rome.

Demandt, A. 1993. "Die westgermanischen Stammesbünde." *Klio* 75:387-406.

Dobesch, G. 1989. "Caesar als Ethnograph." *Wiener Humanistische Blätter* 31:18-51.

Düwel, K., and M. Gebühr. 1981. "Die Fibel von Meldorf und die Anfänge der Runenschrift." *Zeitschrift für Deutsches Altertum und Deutsche Literatur* 110 (3): 159-175.

Erdrich, M. 2001. *Rom und die Barbaren: Das Verhältnis zwischen dem Imperium Romanum und den germanischen Stämmen vor seiner Nordwestgrenze von der späten Republik bis zum gallischen Sonderreich*. Mainz.

Fansa, M., and R. Schneider. 1993. "Die Bohlenwege bei Ockenhausen/ Oltmannsfehn, Gde. Uplengen, Ldkr. Leer." *Archäologische Mitteilungen aus Nordwestdeutschland* 16:23-43.

Ferguson, R. B., and N. L. Whitehead, eds. 1992. *War in the Tribal Zone: Expanding States and Indigenous Warfare*. Santa Fe, NM.

Flach, D. 1995. "Der taciteische Zugang zu der Welt der Germanen." In *Arminius und die Varusschlacht*, ed. R. Wiegels and W. Woesler, 143-166. Paderborn.

Gebühr, M. 1974. "Zur Definition älterkaiserzeitlicher Fürstengräber vom Lübsow-Typ." *Praehistorische Zeitschrift* 49:82-128.

Grane, T. 2003. "Roman Sources for the Geography and Ethnography of Germania." In Jørgensen et al. 2003, 126-147.

Grasselt, T., T. Völling, and W. Walther. 2003. "Nordbayern und Thüringen: Drehscheibe archäologischer Kulturentwicklung in einem Verkehrsraum." In *Menschen-Zeiten-Räume: Archäologie in Deutschland*, ed. W. Menghin and D. Planck, 232-235. Stuttgart.

Green, M., ed. 1995. *The Celtic World*. London.

Günther, K. 1990. *Siedlung und Werkstätten von Feinschmieden der älteren Römischen Kaiserzeit bei Warburg-Daseburg*. Münster.

Hachmann, R., G. Kossack, and H. Kuhn, eds. 1962. *Völker zwischen Germanen und Kelten*. Neumünster.

Hald, M. 1980. *Ancient Danish Textiles from Bogs and Burials: A Comparative Study of Costume and Iron Age Textiles*. Copenhagen.

Haseloff, G. 1981. *Die germanische Tierornamentik der Völkerwanderungszeit*. Berlin.

Hässler, H.-J. 1977. *Zur inneren Gliederung und Verbreitung der vorrömischen Eisenzeit im südlichen Niederelbegebiet.* Hildesheim.

Hedeager, L. 1993. "The Creation of Germanic Identity: A European Origin-Myth." In *Frontières d'empire: Nature et signification des frontières romaines,* ed. P. Brun, S. van der Leeuw, and C. R. Whittaker, 121–131. Nemours.

——— 2000. "Migration Period Europe: The Formation of a Political Mentality." In *Rituals of Power: From Late Antiquity to the Early Middle Ages,* ed. F. Theuws and J. L. Nelson, 15–57. Boston.

Heege, A. 1987. "Die Siedlung der vorrömischen Eisenzeit am 'Steinbühl' bei Nörten-Hardenberg, Ldkr. Northeim." *Nachrichten aus Niedersachsens Urgeschichte* 56:59–116.

Hill, J. D., ed. 1996. *History, Power, and Identity: Ethnogenesis in the Americas, 1492–1992.* Iowa City.

Hvass, S. 1985. *Hodde: Et vestjysk landsbysamfund fra aeldre jernalder.* Copenhagen.

Ilkjaer, J. 2000. *Illerup Ådal.* Moesgård.

——— 2003. "Danish War Booty Sacrifices." In Jørgensen et al. 2003, 44–65.

Jankuhn, H., and D. Timpe, eds., 1989. *Beiträge zum Verständnis der Germania des Tacitus,* part 1. Göttingen.

Jensen, J. 1982. *The Prehistory of Denmark.* London.

Jensen, X. P. 2003. "The Vimose Find." In Jørgensen et al. 2003, 224–239.

Jöns, H. 1999. "Iron Production in Northern Germany." In *Settlement and Landscape,* ed. C. Fabech and J. Ringtved, 249–260. Højbjerg.

Jørgensen, L., and P. V. Petersen. 2003. "Nydam Bog: New Finds and Observations." In Jørgensen et al. 2003, 258–285.

Jørgensen, L., B. Storgaard, and L. Gebauer, eds. 2003. *The Spoils of Victory: The North in the Shadow of the Roman Empire.* Copenhagen.

Kaul, F. 2003. "The Hjortspring Find: The Oldest of the Large Nordic War Booty Sacrifices." In Jørgensen et al. 2003, 212–223.

Kaul, F., and J. Martens. 1995. "Southeast European Influences in the Early Iron Age of Southern Scandinavia: Gundestrup and the Cimbri." *Acta Archaeologica* 66:111–161.

Keiling, H. 1989. "Jastorf und die Germanen." In *Archäologie in der Deutschen Demokratischen Republic,* vol. 1, ed. J. Herrmann, 147–155. Stuttgart.

Kühn, H. 1976. *Geschichte der Vorgeschichtsforschung.* Berlin.

Künzl, E. 2008. *Die Germanen.* Stuttgart.

Lund, A. A. 1998. *Die ersten Germanen: Ethnizität und Ethnogenese.* Heidelberg.

Mallory, J. R. 1989. *In Search of the Indo-Europeans.* London.

Meid, W. 1986. "Hans Kuhns 'Nordwestblock'-Hypothese: Zur Problematik der 'Völker zwischen Germanen und Kelten'." In Beck 1986, 183–212.

Mellor, R. 1993. *Tacitus.* New York.

Michaelsen, K. K. 1994. "Godt skrot: en romersk statue i Gudme." *Årbog for Svendborg & Omegns Museum 1994:* 8–15.

Michaelsen, K. K., and P.Ø. Sørensen. 1993. "En kongsgård fra jernalderen." *Årbog for Svendborg & Omegns Museum 1993:* 24–35.

Müller, R. 2001. "Latènekultur und Latènezeit." *Reallexikon der germanischen Altertumskunde* 18:118–124.

Müller-Wille, M. 1973. "Acker und Flurformen." *Reallexikon der germanischen Altertumskunde* 1:42–50.

Neumann, G., and H. Seemann, eds. 1992. *Beiträge zum Verständnis der Germania des Tacitus*, part 2. Göttingen.

Nielsen, P. O., K. Randsborg, and H. Thrane, eds. 1994. *The Archaeology of Gudme and Lundeborg*. Copenhagen.

Peschel, K. 1988. "Kelten und Germanen während der jüngeren vorrömischen Eisenzeit (2.-1. Jh.v.u.Z.)." In *Frühe Völker in Mitteleuropa*, ed. F. Horst and F. Schlette, 167–200. Berlin.

Pohl, W. 2000. *Die Germanen*. Munich.

Potter, D. S. 1999. *Literary Texts and the Roman Historian*. New York.

Randsborg, K. 1995. *Hjortspring*. Aarhus.

Reallexikon der germanischen Altertumskunde. Berlin, 1973–.

Rieckhoff, S. 1995. *Süddeutschland im Spannungsfeld von Kelten, Germanen und Römern*. Trier.

Roggenbuck, P. 1983. "Das Grab 150 von Putensen, Kr. Harburg." *Hammaburg* 6:133–141.

Roth, H. 1986. *Kunst und Handwerk im frühen Mittelalter*. Stuttgart.

——— 1998. "Germanische Kunst." *Reallexikon der germanischen Altertumskunde* 11:356–368.

Schön, M. D. 1999. *Feddersen Wierde, Fallward, Flögeln*. Bad Bederkesa.

Schoppa, H. 1970. "Funde aus der germanischen Siedlung Westick bei Kamen, Kreis Unna: Das römische Fundgut." In *Spätkaiserzeitliche Funde in Westfalen*, ed. H. Beck, 222–249. Münster.

Schultze, E. 1986. "Zur Verbreitung von Waffenbeigaben bei den germanischen Stämmen um den Beginn unserer Zeitrechnung." *Jahrbuch der Bodendenkmalpflege in Mecklenburg* 1986:93–117.

Schutz, H. 1983. *The Prehistory of Germanic Europe*. New Haven, CT.

Seyer, R. 1988. "Siedlungs- und Stammesgebiete in den Jahrzehnten um den Beginn unserer Zeitrechnung." In *Die Germanen*, ed. B. Krüger, 203–225. Berlin.

Stöckli, W. E. 1993. "Römer, Kelten und Germanen: Probleme von Kontinuität und Diskontinuität zur Zeit von Caesar und Augustus zwischen Hochrhein und Rheinmündung." *Bonner Jahrbücher* 193:121–140.

Stoklund, M. 1995. "Die Runen der römischen Kaiserzeit." In *Himlingøje-Seeland-Europa: Ein Gräberfeld der jüngeren römischen Kaiserzeit auf Seeland, seine Bedeutung und internationalen Beziehungen*, ed. U. L. Hansen, 317–346. Copenhagen.

——— 1996. "Runes." In *Roman Reflections in Scandinavia*, ed. E. Björklund, 112–114. Rome.

——— 2003. "The First Runes: The Literary Language of the Germani." In Jørgensen et al. 2003, 172–179.

Storgaard, B. 1994. "The Årslev Grave and Connections between Funen and the Continent at the End of the Later Roman Iron Age." In Nielsen et al. 1994, 160–168.

Tacitus. 1980. *Germania*. Trans. M. Hutton. Cambridge, MA (Loeb Classical Library).

Thomsen, P. O., B. Blaesild, N. Hardt, and K. K. Michaelsen. 1993. *Lundeborg: en handelsplads fra jernalderen.* Svendborg.

Timpe, D. 1989. "Entdeckungsgeschichte: Die Römer und der Norden." *Reallexikon der germanischen Altertumskunde* 7:337–347.

1996a. "*Memoria* und Geschichtsschreibung bei den Römern." In *Vergangenheit und Lebenswelt,* ed. H.-J. Gehrke and A. Möller, 277–299. Tübingen.

1996b. "Rom und die Barbaren des Nordens." In *Die Begegnung mit dem Fremden,* ed. M. Schuster, 34–50. Stuttgart.

1998. "Germanen: Historisch." *Reallexikon der germanischen Altertumskunde* 11:182–245.

Todd, M. 1992. *The Early Germans.* Oxford.

Trzaska-Richter, C. 1991. *Furor teutonicus: Das römische Germanenbild in Politik und Propaganda von den Anfängen bis zum 2. Jahrhundert n. Chr.* Trier.

Untermann, J. 1989. "Sprachvergleichung und Sprachidentität: Methodische Fragen im Zwischenfeld von Keltisch und Germanisch." In *Germanische Rest- und Trümmersprachen,* ed. H. Beck, 211–239. Berlin.

Urban, O. H., and R. Nedona. 2002. "Negauer Helm." *Reallexikon der germanischen Altertumskunde* 21:52–61.

Walser, G. 1956. *Caesar und die Germanen.* Wiesbaden.

Wegewitz, W. 1972. *Das langobardische Brandgräberfeld von Putensen, Kreis Harburg.* Hildesheim.

Welch, K., and A. Powell, eds. 1998. *Julius Caesar as Artful Reporter: The War Commentaries as Political Instruments.* London.

Wells, P. S. 1994. "Interactions between Denmark and Central Europe in the Late Prehistoric Iron Age." In Nielsen et al. 1994, 151–159.

1998. "Identity and Material Culture in the Later Prehistory of Central Europe." *Journal of Archaeological Research* 6:239–298.

2001. *Beyond Celts, Germans and Scythians: Archaeology and Identity in Iron Age Europe.* London.

Wiegels, R. 1995. "Zur deutenden Absicht von Tacitus: Germania." In *Aspekte römisch-germanischer Beziehungen in der frühen Kaiserzeit,* ed. G. Franzius, 155–175. Espelkamp.

Wolfram, H. 1997. *The Roman Empire and Its Germanic Peoples.* Trans. T. Dunlap. Berkeley, CA.

Woodman, A. J. 1993. *Tacitus and the Tacitean Tradition.* Princeton, NJ.

Zoller, D. 1977. "Eine Siedlung der vorrömischen Eisenzeit bei Meppen, Kr. Emsland." *Nachrichten aus Niedersachsens Urgeschichte* 46:233–239.

CHAPTER EIGHT

THE ETRUSCANS: MEDIATORS BETWEEN NORTHERN BARBARIANS AND CLASSICAL CIVILIZATION

Larissa Bonfante

The Etruscan cities developed in central Italy between the Tiber and the Arno rivers in the course of the Villanovan Iron Age, and their aristocratic society flourished from the Orientalizing period of the eighth and seventh centuries BC down to the end of the Hellenistic period, when they became Romans. They were highly literate, but their literature has almost completely disappeared: we know them principally from the richly furnished tombs they built for their noble ancestors. They expanded into the Po Valley to the north and into Campania in the south; in the sixth century, Etruscan kings ruled at Rome. They affected the course of the history of both Greeks and Romans, and sent innovations north to Europe by way of Italy, which acted as a funnel for ideas, customs, artistic motifs, and fashions from the south. But there were other reasons for the role the Etruscans played in mediating between the Mediterranean and their neighbors in Italy and beyond the Alps.

We know more about the thousand-year history of the Etruscan cities than about other peoples of Europe, because so much of their art and architecture has survived, and because Classical historians refer to events that concern the Etruscans as part of Greek and Roman history. These ancient historians made biased and erroneous assumptions about Etruscan life and culture, but even so, they reflect a number of the underlying realities relating to the Etruscans.

We cannot take seriously the information handed down by Herodotus, said to be in favor of an Eastern, Lydian origin, and by Dionysius of Halicarnassus, who states that the Etruscans were autochthonous, native to Italy. As noted some time ago by Elias Bickerman,[1] ancient historians had their own agenda, which was very different from that of modern scholars. In the end, Massimo Pallottino declared the problem of Etruscan origins to be a sterile question; he urged Etruscan scholars to abandon it and to turn their attention in the more productive direction of the formation of the culture.[2]

The following brief account of Etruscan civilization focuses on their role as mediators for Classical culture and their contacts with their northern neighbors, the barbarians of Europe.

Both literature and archaeology bear out the international role of the Etruscan cities and their place in the wider world of the Mediterranean and Europe. I will deal with the time of their early contacts and of their greatest impact in Europe, the Villanovan and Orientalizing periods.

Etruscan Culture

Etruscan craftsmen learned to exploit their rich mineral resources early on, in contact with the Hallstatt people of the north. They also learned much from their neighbors to the west. Not far from Populonia, the northern Etruscan city on the Tyrrhenian coast, lies the island of metal-rich Elba; beyond is Sardinia, where Phoenician and other artisans were creating sophisticated bronze figures by at least the eleventh century BC.[3] Etruscan ceramics, another specialty, were inspired by the color and decoration of their bronze wares. The city of Arezzo, which gave the name used in German for metal, *Erz*, was famous for its bronze statue of the Chimera, and its famous red mold-made "Arretine" ware of Augustan times imitated the decoration on metalwork, as did the Etruscans' black bucchero in the seventh and sixth centuries BC.

When the Greeks came to Italy around 800 BC they found there an Iron Age people, the Etruscans, who were well on their way to developing into an urban culture and had at least as much to give as to receive: the Greeks were attracted westward toward their mineral wealth, competed with them on the sea, and called them "pirates."[4]

There were many early contacts with the Greeks. The one we know best, and the one that had an enormous impact, was with the first western Greeks, who settled an international community in Pithekoussai, on the island of Ischia.[5] There, near the coast of Naples, they had easy access to the southern Etruscan cities and the valuable minerals these polities exported, but they were not so close as to threaten the wealthy Etruscan warrior elite, whose armed warriors were able to defend their coastlines and keep Greek settlers at arm's length.

The Etruscans found themselves at the center of the Mediterranean world at a fateful historical moment, the exuberant Orientalizing period, when the lands bordering the sea were in closer contact than they had been for a long time, a world much like the international one in which Odysseus had found himself in his wanderings. They enthusiastically adopted the Greek alphabet and the corpus of Greek myths, and immediately used these to express their language, customs, and beliefs. Their own peculiar non-Indo-European language, different from that of any other people of Europe, and their religion, different from that of the patriarchal Indo-European male weather gods, gave them their separate identity. But they were far from isolated.

As non-Greeks, the Etruscans were technically barbarians, but their literacy, technical advances, and aristocratic society, their civilized, city-centered, luxury-filled way of life, and the pull they exerted on Greek traders and immigrants at various moments of Greek history made them more similar to the Homeric Phaeacians than the western Cyclopes.[6] In the course of the Orientalizing and the early Archaic periods the Etruscans' international, cosmopolitan character put them in a favorable position as intermediaries; they participated fully in the cultures of the Mediterranean, and interacted with the other two great civilizations of the time, the Greeks and the Phoenicians.

Their favorable geographical location was an important reason for their success and for their role as mediators (Map 8.1). Italy's position in the center of the Mediterranean and its configuration as a long, narrow, boot-shaped peninsula running more or less north–south have always affected its history and involved it in the Mediterranean as much as in Europe. In antiquity Italy acted as a kind of funnel, transmitting aspects of Mediterranean culture from the South to the North: the Alps were as much a bridge as a barrier. Furthermore, Italy is blessed with some of the best harbors in the Mediterranean, always tempting for foreign merchants and travelers, and its rivers are remarkably efficient for trafficking goods and people northward as well as downstream into the Mediterranean.

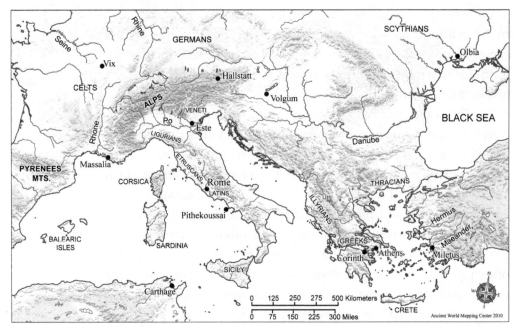

Map 8.1. Etruria in the Mediterranean, eighth century BC. (Courtesy Ancient World Mapping Center, copyright 2010, www.unc.edu/awmc.)

Huge quantities of amber from the Baltic in the graves of eighth-century Etruscan elite women or princesses testify to the importance of their long-lasting commerce with Northern Europe,[7] while in the Mediterranean, the Etruscans' vast metal resources played a critical role in making them wealthy and giving them a central role in the Orientalizing Revolution.[8] Their great wealth and international contacts are reflected in the luxurious tombs of the eighth and seventh centuries BC, furnished with exotic goods, Phoenician bowls and Egyptianizing faience, tridacna shells from the East, and decorated vases from Greece.

In Italy, Greek colonies soon occupied the southern coasts, while the Etruscan cities controlled the north. There was much movement and interaction between south and north, as well as between east and west, as Greeks continued to come westward from mainland Greece and from the Ionian coast. As members of this international community, Etruscans sent gifts to Delphi and Olympia,[9] while the permanent presence of Greeks in Etruscan cities is attested early on in the sanctuary of Gravisca and elsewhere. In the sixth century BC, Ionian Greeks came west and established ceramic workshops like those of the Caeretan hydriae at Cerveteri (Caere). Phoenicians frequented the sanctuary of Pyrgi, where archaeologists found bilingual inscriptions written on gold tablets around 500 BC, with the dedication of the king of Caere or Cisra in both the Etruscan and Phoenician languages.[10]

The Etruscans were at all times highly literate. Their language was written in the alphabet familiar to us today and still learned by schoolchildren in the original order of the Phoenician script brought into Greece and Etruria. Some 13,000 to 9,000 Etruscan inscriptions have come down to us, 700 of them dating from the early period; the number compares respectably to the number of the earliest Greek inscriptions, which come from a much wider area. Only a half dozen longer Etruscan inscriptions, relating to religion and ritual, survive, however. Most are very short. They are alphabets, statements of ownership, dedications of gifts to the dead or to the gods, and brief epitaphs. Etruscan literature has not survived, except for occasional fragments of rituals of the *etrusca disciplina* that the Romans used and preserved.[11]

Writing was always a status symbol, which was no doubt one reason for the frequent presence of writing materials and objects inscribed with the alphabet and the names of the elite men and women in whose graves they were placed.[12] The Etruscans had their models near at hand. The earliest metrical Greek inscription, from the eighth century BC, was found in Italy, on the Nestor cup from Pithekoussai. It refers to the cup of Nestor mentioned in the *Iliad* (11.632–637) and so parallels Homeric scenes in early Etruscan art of the adventures of Odysseus in the far-off lands of the West.[13] Yet writing is never mentioned in the *Odyssey*. When Homer refers to it (only once, in *Iliad* 6.168–170), it has a dreadful, magical power. As Glaukos tells the story of his ancestor Bellerophon, he describes a folding tablet on which were written "life-destroying signs": the message instructed the recipient to kill the messenger. Homer was probably referring to Phoenician writing tablets used in his own time, which looked much like the seventh-century Etruscan miniature ivory tablet from Marsiliana (Fig. 8.1). In early times writing was considered to be magical, and it has even been suggested that the inscription on the Nestor cup was an incantation, designed to give magical power to the cup of wine and turn it into a love potion.[14]

When they used it in inscriptions, the Etruscans modified the alphabet they had adopted from the Greeks and Phoenicians to take account of their own pronunciation.[15] So too various aspects of classical

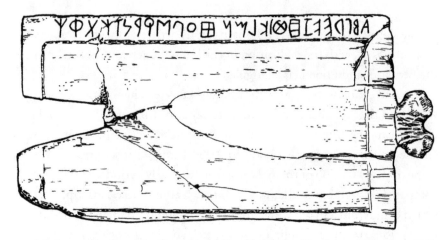

8.1. Ivory tablet from Marsiliana. Model (Greek) alphabet (Bonfante and Bonfante 2002, 132, Source 1).

"civilization," in the sense of the culture of cities, were transformed on Etruscan soil: monumental architecture and sculpture, narrative art, the image of the kouros and nudity in art, gods and heroes of Greek myth, the symposium. Adopted as external signs of culture, these innovations served to express the Etruscans' customs, ideas, and religious beliefs without changing them to any great extent. They had their own culture: "Their genius was to express it with whatever means came to hand ... those means were often, but not exclusively, Greek...."[16]

The following survey focuses on images of human beings, the favorite subject of Greek art, adopted in Etruria along with the Greek alphabet, Greek art, and Greek myths. Just as the Etruscans used the Greek alphabet to write their own peculiar language, they made their ideas, beliefs, and customs visible by means of the Greek imagery and myth they had adopted along with the script. The Etruscans, in turn, influenced the art and customs of peoples farther north, in Italy and beyond the Alps, including situla art treated in the following chapter by Otto-Herman Frey.

There is abundant evidence for the Etruscans in the form of archaeological monuments, mythological imagery, and inscriptions. The language of Etruscan images is easier to read and to understand than that of other peoples we have been dealing with; just as we recognize the alphabet with which they wrote down their language, we recognize the visual language of classical iconography.[17] Their monuments, imagery, and inscriptions show that they were familiar early on with Greek mythology. Much of this narrative art and myths they had learned as early as the eighth century BC from the Greek vases they imported and placed in their graves, and from the stories they heard in poems, songs, and plays.[18] Images of Greek myth decorated Etruscan temples and tombs to make religious and political statements, and to add a sense of luxury, luster, and culture to their private houses.[19]

In the early graves, however, elite Etruscan society celebrated the cult of ancestors in a native imagery that did not depend on Greek myth. Their funerary art represented the heroized ancestors of aristocratic families, often being entertained at banquets in the afterlife as they had been in their own lifetimes.[20] Examples of such imagery are the large-scale statues of male and female ancestors on the roof of the early sixth-century BC building at Murlo, near Siena (Fig. 8.4), the male and female terracotta images of ancestors forever seated at a banquet in the tomb of the Five Chairs at Cerveteri, and the human-shaped "canopic" Orientalizing ash urns of Chiusi (Fig. 8.2 and Plate XX), with figures both male and female, some of them shown wearing golden earrings and dressed in purple mantles.[21] Other examples of couples representing the generations of the family are large-scale reliefs of a couple at Ceri,[22] the stone statues of the Warrior of Capestrano with his wife (Fig. 8.20),[23] and perhaps the earliest monumental funerary sculpture, from the Orientalizing site of the necropolis of Casale Marittimo near Volterra.[24]

The sumptuary laws that marked the history of the Greeks and Romans do not seem to have been at work in the Etruscan cities, whose art reflects the luxurious *truphe* that the Greeks, and later the Romans, attributed to barbarian foreigners, tyrants, and women.[25]

An example of this Etruscan luxury is the fancifully decorated, colorful patterned textiles that appear in Etruscan tomb painting and that no doubt adorned the homes of Etruscans and the northern peoples.[26] The actual manufacturing processes of these textiles, so important in their life and commerce, were the province of women, in whose tombs were found spindles, spindle whorls, loom weights, spools, and even looms. In fact, spinning and weaving implements are the most plentiful evidence for our understanding of the scale of production and the technology of the textile industry in ancient Italy,[27] since the actual textiles have for the most part disappeared, with one remarkable exception, as we shall see.

8.2. Canopus from Dolciano. 650–600 BC. Chiusi, Museo Archeologico Nazionale. (Photo courtesy Soprintendenza per i Beni Archeologici della Toscana.)

Several monuments picture women working wool and weaving it on elaborate looms.[28] A bronze axe-shaped amulet or tintinnabulum, once worn at the neck of a wealthy lady who took it to her grave in Bologna (Frey, Chapter 9 in this volume, Fig. 9.12), has engraved scenes showing well-dressed, aristocratic ladies involved in various stages of working wool.[29] The style is close to that of the northern situla art described in the following chapter. Two women are carding and spinning the thread, while one is seated at the upper level of a high, two-story loom. The height of the loom had a practical aspect, for it allowed her to weave a longer piece of cloth: once she had gone to the trouble of setting up the loom and the loom weights, it was more economical to weave as large a cloth as possible. Farther north, on the somewhat earlier vase from Sopron (Frey, Chapter 9 in this volume, Fig. 9.14), we see the same purpose served by the pit into which the heavy cloth falls as it is woven. The ladies working at the tall, elaborately decorated loom pictured on the Verucchio Throne (see Fig. 8.8b) are raised up on supports under their chairs, allowing them to weave a longer piece of cloth.[30]

Recent scholarship has drawn attention to the relationship of weaving patterns in textiles and poetic composition and singing. With this idea in mind, it is possible to think of the musician on the vase from Sopron (Frey, Chapter 9 in this volume, Fig. 9.14) as "singing the web," participating in the activity by providing the pattern for the weaver, rather than only entertaining the women at their work.[31] The reasons for the relationship between weaving, women, and writing, also a recent area of research, are not yet entirely clear. Certainly weaving was an activity characteristic of aristocratic ladies, and as such was a mark of status.[32]

The remarkable finds of textiles, amber, wood, and other organic materials from eighth-century BC Verucchio, on the Adriatic coast near Rimini, include at least two rounded mantles or *tebennas*, ancestors of the much later Roman toga. There are wooden thrones of a shape usually reserved for Etruscan women of rank, perhaps originally wedding presents. One of these bears a decoration incised in the wood, with detailed scenes of men and women engaged in the process of woolworking, as well as a ritual scene with two women protected by armed warriors (Figs. 8.8a–c).[33] The rich graves of the women contained great quantities of bronze, amber, and glass paste jewelry. The precious amber spindles, far too delicate to have been used in real life, evidently served as signs of status.

Later, during the fifth and third centuries BC, specialized Etruscan craftsmen made gleaming bronze mirrors for elite women, who received them as wedding presents and took them to their graves when they died. These were brightly polished on the reflecting side and often bore on their backs mythological or other scenes; the inscriptions identifying the characters imply that their upper-class, aristocratic owners were literate.[34]

Also a sign of status, starting in the seventh century BC, were the monumental stone statues that demonstrate the route and transformation to the West, and eventually to the North, of the typically Greek image of the completely nude male kouros. In Greece, the statue of the beautiful, aristocratic youth, the kouros, appears around 700 BC in a religious context probably related to the initiation of young men. The image was publicly displayed and used in a variety of ways: as a representation of the beautiful, youthful Apollo, as a gift for the gods, and as a funerary marker. Its nudity was eventually understood as a civic costume, or a sign of citizenship.[35] The impressive form and monumentality of the kouros inspired local artists outside Greece to invent strange transformations of the original models. Non-Greek barbarians, including Etruscans, shared a reluctance to represent nudity, except to signify divinity or for its apotropaic, protective magical powers. They accepted Greek male nudity in art but not in real life. In accordance with local customs, they therefore translated the original Greek model into their own idiom when they used monumental standing statues to honor the graves of dead warriors.

In Italy the greater than life-size Capestrano Warrior created a sensation when it was excavated in 1934 in the mountain region of Picenum, near the Adriatic coast (Figs. 8.20a-b). Though its monumentality is Greek, its provincial style is a far cry from the archaic stylization of the Greek kouros. This remarkable sixth-century BC limestone statue, today in the Chieti Museum, is not naked. It represents a warrior, fully armed with sword and axe and body armor, wearing a hat or helmet with an enormous brim. He is endowed with powerful thighs, and wears a *perizoma*, or short pants. A fragment of a much smaller female statue was found under his helmet; it shows that in Italy these representations were not reserved for men, as we have seen.[36]

From Etruria proper come a number of large-scale seventh-century BC human figures representing ancestors. Among them, the earliest are a number of fragmentary statues from the seventh-century Pietrera tomb in Vetulonia: here too the men are not naked, but wear a *perizoma*.[37] Even earlier are the two life-size statues of ancestors from Casale Marittimo near Volterra.[38] A surprising find in Sardinia revealed for the first time the existence of large-scale stone sculptures on the island. Like the Capestrano Warrior, they seem to have been modeled on small bronze statuettes, enlarged to life size. But they are not related to the statues from Italy and the North.[39]

Etruscan art illustrates a custom shared by the peoples of Europe and the Mediterranean in pre-Roman times: the practice of human sacrifice. Evidence from literature, art, and archaeology indicates that the religion of the Etruscans required such rituals at particular times. Ancient historians record two occasions when the Etruscans carried out a massacre of war prisoners as a human sacrifice. The first occurred after the Battle of Alalia, in about 540 BC, fought in the waters of the Sardinian sea by Carthaginians and Etruscans of Cerveteri against the Greek Phocaeans. According to the story, the men of Cerveteri led the Greek prisoners out and stoned them to death. This action evidently did not please the gods, for soon afterward a pestilence arose, and when the Etruscans inquired of the oracle of Delphi how they could stop this plague, they were told to atone for their offense by establishing religious rites and games.[40] A similar episode took place at the time of the wars between Tarquinia and Rome (358–351 BC), when the men of Tarquinia took 307 Roman soldiers prisoner and massacred them as an act of sacrifice. Much later, at the time of the Punic Wars, Livy tells us, sacrifices were carried out in the Roman Forum.[41]

The cult of ancestors and the related burial practices of the Etruscans required blood for the dead, though artistic representations might have supplied this at some point and substituted for actual sacrifices.[42] Stories of human sacrifice from Greek myth, such as those of Polyxena or Iphigeneia, were favorite subjects on funerary monuments, along with scenes of bloody battles and murders. The most impressive funerary monument is the François Tomb from Vulci, built in the fourth century for the family of an aristocratic general whose triumphal mantle indicates that he has been successfully involved in the fighting against Rome. Its carefully planned painted decorative program includes the scene of the sacrifice of twelve Trojan prisoners by Achilles at the funeral of Patroclus, a scene frequently represented in Italy. It was only briefly described in the *Iliad* (23, 175–176) and was absent from the art of the Greek mainland.[43] On the opposite wall is depicted a story picturing in vivid detail the slaughter of the enemy by local heroes; this scene involves someone identified as "Tarquin of Rome," as well as Mastarna, the Etruscan name of Servius Tullius, so that it seems to have taken place in the sixth century BC in the context of a war against Rome.

Evidently foundation rites, like funerary rituals, required human sacrifices.[44] The excavation of the habitation site of the Civita at Tarquinia has provided remarkable new evidence about the earliest, eighth-century phase of the city, and the first archaeological evidence for Etruscan human sacrifice: the skeleton of a sailor or soldier shows that he was intentionally and brutally killed. Also buried in this area were an epileptic boy and several newborn babies, one of them beheaded. Special circumstances surrounded their burial in what was clearly a sacred area in the earliest occupation level of the city and point to their having been buried as foundation sacrifices.

These, then, were the cities of the Etruscans, a people involved in both Europe and the Mediterranean, international, sophisticated, curious about other peoples, events, and innovations, yet content with their own world until they could no longer maintain it.

Etruscan Influence in the North

New discoveries and new studies shed light on the manifold aspects of 800 years of contacts between the Etruscans and their northern neighbors, and bring out evidence of the important role that Etruscan influence and interaction had for the development of the Iron Age cultures of Europe.[45] Much of the evidence comes from monuments of northern art dating from the fifth and fourth centuries BC, which reflect aspects of the art of an earlier period, with its Orientalizing monsters and monumental sculpture.[46]

Many customs that were adopted by peoples beyond the Alps came by way of Italy in the eighth and seventh centuries BC: they include literacy, the use of wine for ceremonial and social occasions, and monumental sculpture in funerary art to exalt deceased ancestors and great warriors. The taste for narrative, for using images to tell a story, which was evident from the start in Etruscan art, soon influenced the art of the Celts, situla art, and the art of other neighbors to the north.

Most important for this interchange between North and South, aside from their proximity, was the fact that the people of Etruria shared a wider common culture and a number of artistic habits and religious customs with many of the more northern regions, including a feudal society, a reluctance to represent nudity in art except for its apotropaic, protective magical powers, the importance of prophecy, and the practice of human sacrifice.[47] The aristocratic nature of Etruscan society that had informed their own culture and transformed classical motifs provided a repertoire more easily adapted to the social structure of their northern neighbors than did that of the Greeks. The customs, images, and artistic motifs of Etruscan "princes" and their taste for luxury suited the chieftains of the North, who used them to assert their rank, status, and authority.[48] In the end, the social structure of the Etruscans was far closer to that of the Alpine peoples, the Celts, the Thracians, the Scythians, and other peoples of Europe than was the culture of mainland Greece, which was already following a different direction from that of its contemporaries.

Etruscan influence brought the alphabet, arguably the most momentous innovation of the Orientalizing period, to the peoples beyond the Alps as well as to the many diverse regions of Italy. The Etruscan alphabet, a modified form of the script that the Greeks had adapted from the Phoenicians, spread throughout the whole of Italy. By the fourth century BC, it was used for all the languages spoken on the peninsula with the exception of Greek, Messapic, and the native languages of Sicily. The peoples of central and northern Italy eventually all used alphabets that derived directly from the Etruscan to record the Umbrian, Oscan, Venetic, Lepontian, Gallic (Gaulish, of northern Italy), Picene, Rhaetic or Raetian, and Latin languages.[49] The script also traveled north, opposite the flow of amber. The east Alpine amber route in fact became the main way of communication between northeast Italy and the North.[50] There is some controversy about the origin of the Germanic runes, but it is generally agreed that their form derives from that of the writing of the people of Veneto and northeast Italy.[51] Like early Etruscan and probably Greek writing, runes were at first magic signs, carved as protection on helmets, spearheads, and other objects to make them more powerful (Fig. 8.3).[52]

Runes were also used for divination. Tacitus describes the way the Germans carried out this divination by means of marks carved on wooden slivers (*Germania* 10.1.3). The northern runes were probably written on pieces of wood long before the appearance of the earliest

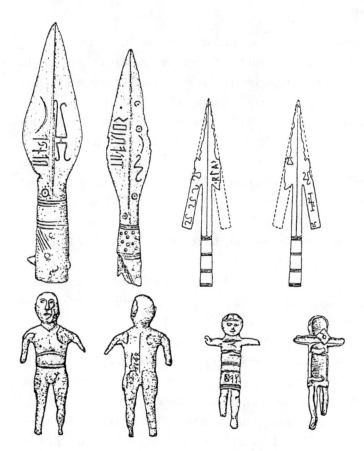

8.3. Germanic runes on statuettes and weapons. (Bonfante and Bonfante 2002, 118, fig. 9.)

surviving runes on Roman marble inscriptions.[53] The importance of wood as a material in the North, with its rich forests, is confirmed by recent finds of wooden furniture from Verucchio, wooden constructions of roads or graves (Fig. 8.11), wooden shields, and wooden statuettes from ritual water deposits. Trees had special properties in the religions of the northern Celts and Germans, and the wood of the slivers on which the signs were carved also could have had special significance.[54] In archaic Rome, too, wood was used to record oracular sayings, treaties, and priestly records.[55] Wooden objects of daily use rarely survived, but they must have been ubiquitous.

In his contribution on the Germans, Peter Wells shows how trade with neighboring regions is evident in the presence of luxury goods, such as bronze fibulae, bracelets, and belt hooks imported from the south and placed in the graves of wealthy elite warriors of Europe and their families.

In exchange for fine pottery, metal vessels, and other luxury items from the South, the communities of Northern Europe exported slaves, fur, leather, hides, wool and textiles, salt, preserved meat, and other goods – materials hard to trace in the archaeological record.[56] From the shores of the Baltic and North seas came the raw amber made into beads for necklaces and other decorations and status symbols, and used together with glass paste beads made by Phoenician craftsmen or in local workshops set up along the amber routes.

Amber had long been prized for its commercial, magical, and therapeutic value. Exchanges along the amber routes began in the middle of the second millennium BC and lasted down to Roman times, a remarkably long span of time, allowing us to follow trade and cultural contacts that took place along far-reaching distances, from the Baltic regions in the North to southern Italy (Rolle, Chapter 4 in this volume, Map 4.2). Verucchio, a frontier town between Italy and the North, was part of a north–south thoroughfare from which Etruscan luxury goods headed north to the homes of the chieftains who used these imported objects at the banquets they hosted and buried them in their tombs as signs of their wealth and power. The amber found in the rich graves of Verucchio was only part of the great quantities of amber from the Baltic brought across the Apennines to the great Etruscan cities of the Tyrrhenian coast. An amber route continued along the Adriatic, by way of the Picene region, down to the southern tip of the Amber Route in the Basilicata, where, from the sixth through the fourth centuries BC, skilled craftsmen carved amulets that were miniature amber sculptures, using a Greek archaic style mediated by Italic and Etruscan art and culture.[57]

In the Orientalizing period, much of the Etruscan influence going north to the Alpine regions of situla art went by way of Chiusi, in central Italy. The Chiusi connection was part of a network that is still not completely understood. In modern times, Chiusi is still the hub for train travel in Italy. In antiquity it was open to river traffic, wealthy from its rich agricultural resources, and secure because of its location high on a hill and well guarded on all sides. Porsenna, an early king of Chiusi, was known to the Romans as a powerful enemy.

During the Orientalizing period, Chiusi's wealth and central location allowed it to play a central role as a link between the cities of Etruria and Northern Europe, connecting the great harbor cities with those of the

Po, Este, and beyond. It was from Chiusi that the alphabet spread north to Este and beyond.[58] The Chiusi district acted as a center of diffusion of Orientalizing figurative motifs that reached Bologna and the Po Valley by way of imported objects, as well as by traveling craftsmen working for rich clients eager to own beautifully crafted bronzework modeled on the lively narrative north Etruscan artistic fashions.[59] In art and language Chiusi was conservative, keeping alive older features along with the new.[60]

Chiusi provided the Alpine artists who crafted the situlas with Orientalizing models, like the Plicasnas situla. This silver-gilt vase was inscribed with the name of the owner, Plikasnas, and has the narratives arranged in registers. It has been ascribed to an Oriental craftsman working in a southern city, perhaps Caere, who decorated it in a style that is a mixture of Egyptianizing, Phoenician, Cypriote, and Greek elements and motifs.[61]

The Chiusi connection is confirmed by its artistic ties with Murlo (Poggio Civitate), near Siena. We do not know the name of this important site in antiquity, one of the rare excavations of a nonfunerary Etruscan site. In the art of Murlo, the figures have no mythological reference; instead, the fantastic animals and impressive array of figures of men and women were designed to exalt the power and status of the lord and lady of the place.[62] On the ridgepole of the roof of an early archaic building (ca. 600 BC) were aligned many large-scale figures (Fig. 8.4),[63] with Orientalizing monsters and animals alternating with images of male and female ancestors. The series of terra-cotta plaques that decorated the lower part of the roof (Figs. 8.5a–d) illustrated four aspects of the life and rituals of the aristocracy. There is a horse race, shown with the prize, a precious cauldron (Fig. 8.5a); a banquet, with men and women reclining, musicians and attendants (Fig. 8.5b); a procession frieze, with two figures in a carriage (Fig. 8.5c); and the married couple, enthroned in front of a group of seated lords and ladies (Fig. 8.5d), indicating family continuity.[64] These remarkable terra-cotta sculptures and reliefs show an affinity with situla art in the primitive, expressive style of the figures and in the nonmythological repertoire of aristocratic activities.

Evidence of similar ritual customs and images of power and status of the feudal lords of the Alpine regions farther north is illustrated in

8.4. Terra-cotta statue akroteria from the ridgepole of the roof of an archaic building complex at Poggio Civitate (Murlo). Female figure, "Cowboy," and winged centaur. Ca. 600 BC. Murlo, Antiquarium. (Photo by Anthony Tuck.)

Otto-Herman Frey's survey of situla art, which shows how representations of ceremonial dress and of sports – often as conservative in form as religious rituals – reflect cultural contacts with Etruria. The fact that the beginning of situla art took place in the seventh century BC accounts for the popularity and persistence in the northern situla art of Etruscan Orientalizing decorative motifs such as the plants coming out of the mouths of animals, or the limb in mouth motif illustrated by countless panthers and lions that parade with human legs hanging out of their mouths.[65] These and other early features survived as fossilized motifs in situla art of the fifth and fourth centuries, whose images still reflect an Orientalizing influence from the south.

The little figures going about their rituals and ceremonies on these bronze embossed situlas of northern Italy and the Alpine region wear typical seventh-century BC Etruscan dress – plaid mantles, hats, and hairstyles, such as the long braids of women. Their wide mantles, pointed shoes, and wide hats (Fig. 8.6; Frey, Chapter 9 in this volume, Figs 9.2–9.6, 9.8, 9.11) are particularly close in style to those of the large-scale seated figures at Murlo. In certain cases it is clear that Etruscan influence was not merely artistic and external, but provided models that affected real, actual aspects of the local culture. Such scenes, realistic in their contexts

8.5a–c. Terra-cotta frieze plaques from the roof of an archaic building complex at Poggio Civitate (Murlo). a. Horse race. b. Banquet scene. c. Procession. Ca. 600 BC. Murlo, Antiquarium. (Courtesy of Poggio Civitate Excavations.)

8.5d. Terra-cotta frieze plaque from the roof of an archaic building complex at Poggio Civitate (Murlo). d. Seated figures. Ca. 600 BC. Murlo, Antiquarium. (Courtesy of Poggio Civitate Excavations.)

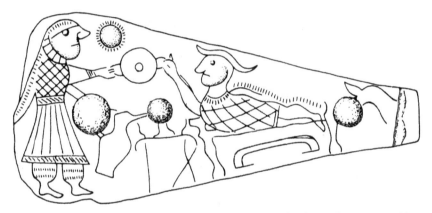

8.6. Reclining banqueter and female attendant. Bronze belt plaque from Este. Fifth century BC. Este, Museo Nazionale Atestino (Frey 1960, plate 67, 18.)

as well as in their details, are inspired by images of Etruscan aristocratic life rather than by Greek myths.

Realistic motifs include sporting events. The horse races depicted on these terra-cotta plaques have been compared to the Palio horse races at Siena, and indeed they seem to represent a similarly competitive sport, with the prize, a large cauldron, prominently displayed.[66] Representations of chariot races include a particularly lively one on the situla from Kuffarn (Frey, Chapter 9 in this volume, Fig. 9.5).[67] Charioteers and jockeys wear high, pointed caps like those of riders on an Etruscan terra-cotta frieze from Murlo (Fig. 8.5a; Frey, Chapter 9 in this volume, Fig. 9.5).[68] Chariots, which were special symbols of prestige

8.7. Military parade, erotic symplegma, and other scenes. Details of decoration of a terra-cotta jug from Tragliatella (Cerveteri). Ca. 600 BC. Rome, Capitoline Museum, Palazzo dei Conservatori. (Giglioli 1929, pl. 26.)

in Etruria, were a specialty of Celtic craftsmen, who made a great variety of them and exported them abroad.[69]

Representations of organized military forces in parades of heavily equipped warriors led by officers on horseback, on both the Certosa situla (Frey, Fig. 9.3) and the seventh-century BC Etruscan Tragliatella urn from Cerveteri (Fig. 8.7),[70] seem to reflect the well-organized Greek phalanx that was developed in the Orientalizing period and eventually adopted in Etruria.[71] Some helmets resemble those on the Villanovan funerary canopic ash urns of Chiusi; others are of the seventh-century local northern type with metal plates.[72]

Like Etruscan funerary art, the situlas emphasize the luxurious fur-nishings that surround the lords at their banquets as they are served by handsome servants and entertained by musicians. Their symposium ware is exhibited on situla holders testifying to their wealth and generos-ity. (Frey, Chapter 9 in this volume, Figs. 9.5, 9.11).[73] These heroic chief-tains or ancestors are seated on throne-like chairs. Only once, on the belt plaque from Carceri (Este), the lord is reclining in the modern fash-ion, as a woman prepares to pour wine into his two-handled cup from a typically Etruscan bronze beaked jug, or *Schnabelkanne* (Fig. 8.6).[74]

Early Etruscan images of ancestors are often seated on throne-like chairs (Fig. 8.2 and Plate XX), following a fashion that predates the

8.8a. Wooden throne from Verucchio (Rimini). Eighth century BC. Verucchio Museum. (Photo Courtesy Soprintendenza per i Beni Archeologica dell' Emilia Romagna.)

Etruscan adoption of the Ionian habit of reclining at banquets in the early sixth century BC, as on the banquet frieze from Murlo (Fig. 8.5b).[75] The rounded throne-like chair is a long-lived symbol of honor; it was probably the form of the throne donated at Olympia by the Etruscan king Arimnestos, said to have been the first barbarian to bring a votive offering to Olympia.[76] It is found as early as the eighth century BC in a carved wooden throne from Verucchio decorated with scenes of wool working, including women weaving at a tall loom, and a ritual scene involving two women flanked by armed guards (Figs. 8.8a–c).[77] Seven hundred years later, in late Republican times, the type was preserved by the archaizing Corsini Chair, a Roman marble throne decorated with motifs from situla art (Fig. 8.9).[78]

This round-backed shape was used in Etruria by women, like the ladies at their woolworking on the seventh-century tintinnabulum from Bologna (Frey, Chapter 9 in this volume, Fig. 9.12) and by both

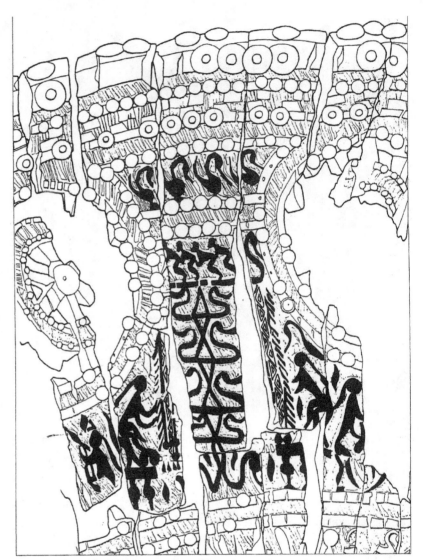

8.8b. Scene of women weaving at a tall loom. Detail from the Verucchio Throne.

male and female canopic figures (see Fig. 8.2 and Plate XX). Such chairs were extremely popular in the north, where they were used by the well-dressed lords shown on the situlas.[79] A rounded shape characterizes the back of the remarkably luxurious bronze couch found in the princely Celtic burial of Hochdorf, which could be rolled on casters and had eight female caryatids serving as supports (Fig. 8.10).[80] A similar couch is illustrated on the Certosa situla: it is decorated with statues of nude athletes reminiscent of Lucretius's description of the golden statues of

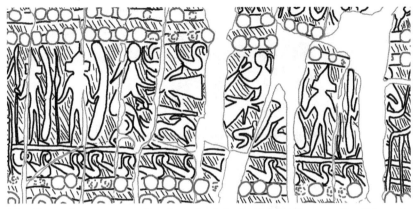

8.8c. Scene of two women performing a ritual, flanked by armed guards. Detail from the Verucchio Throne.

youths holding lit torches in their right hands at decadently luxurious Roman banquets.[81]

Clearly, northern craftsmen were much influenced by the classical forms of Etruscan art.[82] But the influence was not a one-way street. At least some visiting Etruscans were clearly intrigued by northern customs and illustrated them in a completely different context. The strange barbell-shaped objects represented on the situlas being used by boxers and hunters are clearly a local northern custom, illustrated on the situlas (Fig. 8.11; Frey, Chapter 9 in this volume, Figs. 9.2, 9.4–9.5, 9.11).[83] But they make a surprising appearance abroad, on two sixth-century Etruscan Pontic amphoras showing mythological Gorgons holding such objects (Fig. 8.12), while farther east, Gorgons are again shown holding this type of object on the architrave of the archaic Greek temple of Apollo at Didyma (ca. 540–520 BC).[84] The exotic objects held by the monstrous Gorgons on these sixth-century BC Greek and Etruscan monuments may have been meant to represent barbarian weapons that seemed appropriate for the fierce, exotic images of the mythological Gorgons.[85] We can imagine that travelers might have come to know these objects from representations that they had seen on the northern situla art, or perhaps they had actually seen them being used during a stay among some of these peoples who lived along an amber route.

A sixth-century BC traveler brought back to Athens a report of a different sort of exotic Western image, the strikingly primitive ancestor busts on Villanovan anthropomorphic ash urns, still being used in conservative Chiusi (Fig. 8.2 and Plate XX). Such an image must have provided

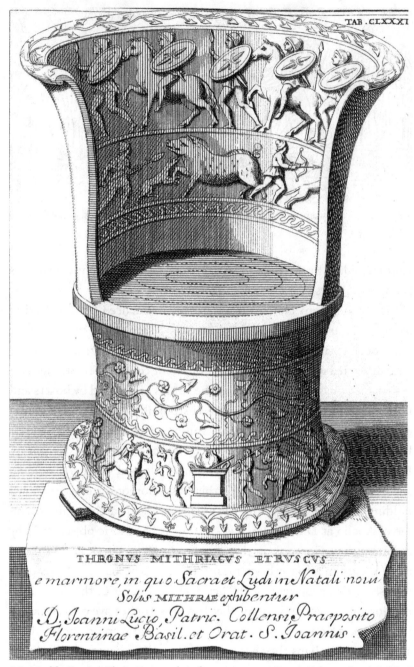

8.9. Marble Corsini Chair. Roman, late first century BC. Rome, Palazzo Corsini. (Gori 1737, pl. CLXXXI.)

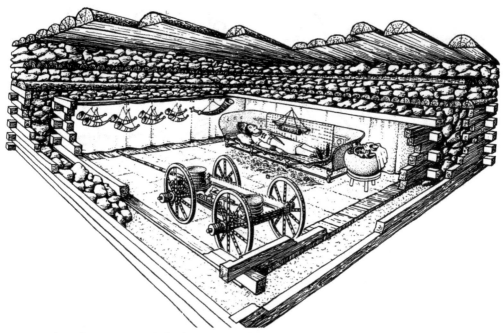

8.10. Drawing of a reconstructed chieftain's grave, Eberdingen-Hochdorf, with bronze couch. Hallstatt period. (Frey 1991, 86.)

the inspiration for the artist of a sixth-century Attic black-figure "head vase" who represented a similar round body, with a pointed beard like that of male Etruscan canopic urns.[86]

The Role of Women

Etruscan art reflects the public role of women in the life of the aristo-cratic society of the oligarchic Etruscan cities, showing them together with their husbands as married couples at banquets, spectacles, and a variety of events as well as together in death, on sarcophagi, urns, and funerary statues. At Murlo, recent publications have made it clear that both the large-scale figures on the roof and the smaller figures on the terra-cotta plaques represent groups of male and female figures together.[87] (Figs. 8.4, 8.5b–d). Female ancestors could receive equal honors with men, given the wealth of the graves of elite women. The wall paintings in the Tomb of the Monkey at Chiusi show an aristocratic lady, the owner of the tomb, being entertained by jugglers, dancers, and musicians.[88] That the ritual role of women was important is also clear from the scene

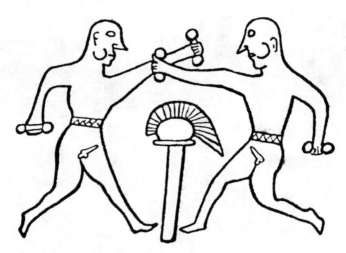

8.11. Boxers with "barbells" from a belt buckle from Magdalenska Gora. Detail (Bonfante 1999a, 505, fig. 2).

on the Verucchio Throne of two women carrying out some kind of ritual or sacrifice in a sacred space protected by armed guards (Fig. 8.8c).[89]

Scenes of married couples, with parallel images of husband and wife, so ubiquitous in Etruscan art, are rare both in Greek art and in the iconography of the art of the Etruscans' neighbors, beyond the Alps. In the Northern climate, as Otto-Herman Frey notes, women do not seem to have the same privileged position as in the Etruscan cities. Instead of attending the banquet with their husbands, they are shown serving the lords, who loll on their rounded thrones, wearing splendid mantles, fancy shoes, and hats that mark their special status. (Frey, Chapter 9 in this volume, Figs. 9.2, 9.4, 9.5, 9.11).

Women do appear together with men in erotic "symplegmata," the polite archaeological term for scenes of sexual intercourse or embrace. Several monuments of situla art represent such explicitly erotic scenes, which signified the consummation of a marriage and the continuing generations of the aristocratic families. These scenes and the contexts in which they appear involve a remarkable point of contact between situla art and Etruscan art.[90]

On the Tragliatella jug from Cerveteri[91] (Fig. 8.7), an Etruscan scene of explicit lovemaking appears within the context of episodes of an aristocratic style of life. Around the erotic couples are depicted a parade of armed soldiers, horseback riders, and hunting scenes. Other aspects of the jug's decoration are obscure. Why are there two couples, one above

8.12. Gorgons with "barbells." On the neck is a double-bodied panther. Etruscan Pontic amphora, provenance unknown, 530–510 BC. Detail. (Formerly J. Paul Getty Museum, Inv. 96. AE. 139. Repatriated, now in Rome. Courtesy of the Ministero per i Beni e le Attività Culturali. Soprintendenza per i Beni Archeologici dell'Etruria Meridionale.)

the other, as on bunk beds?[92] Though their images suggest a mythological reference, perhaps the story of Theseus and Ariadne, the personal names of the three figures standing together – a man, a woman, and a child – identify them as Ammarce (Mamarce), Thesathei (a theophoric name referring to Thesan, the Dawn), and Velelia. They are to be seen as a family group. The inscriptions preclude a mythological interpretation and show that the vase was created on commission; the meaning of its images was purely Etruscan, though we can no longer understand the particular references.

On the monuments of situla art, several explicit artistic representations of sexual intercourse also appear within the context of scenes of an aristocratic style of life, where they serve to express important and

8.13. Symplegma on a swan bed and other scenes of aristocratic life. Bronze mirror from Castelvetro. Fifth century BC. Innsbruck, Museum Ferdinandeum (Lucke-Frey 1962, pl. 21).

symbolic messages, documenting aristocratic marriages and the legitimacy of the heirs.[93] These erotic scenes do not represent casual sex, like those on Attic symposium ware. Rather than illustrating genre-like scenes of courtship or other social customs like those on contemporary Greek vases,[94] they indicate the importance of the marriage relationship within the context of a feudal society.

On a mirror from Castelvetro (Fig. 8.13) the couple lies on a beautifully decorated bed with swan finials. A situla from Sanzeno also shows the couple in bed.[95] On a belt fragment from Brezje (Fig. 8.14), the woman is fully dressed and seated on a round-backed throne, while the man standing before her has raised his garment. He is exposing his genitals in a gesture of *anasyrma*, whose sexual implications are familiar from Near Eastern art, though there it usually appears on female figures.[96] A large wine vessel on a stand beside them shows that the scene

8.14. Symplegma: male figure with seated female figure; wine crater on a stand. Bronze belt from Brezje. Fifth century BC. Vienna, Naturhistorisches Museum. (Lucke-Frey 1962, pl. 32.)

takes place in the context of a banquet – or perhaps it underlines the ritual importance of the action. This fifth-century BC scene has much in common with an erotic scene on a fourth-century silver-gilt plaque from Letnitsa, a nearly contemporary monument of the Thracian art of Bulgaria (Fig. 8.15 and Plate XXI). Here too the setting is the banquet: a servant girl brings wine in a decorated vessel and holds a huge leafy fan over the head of the woman. The seated position of the man, rather than the woman, contrasts with the scene on the Brezje belt, but it agrees with the representations of similar scenes in Greek erotic art, where the man is sitting.[97]

Other fourth-century BC monuments of Thracian art also reflect the influence of Etruscan art. The imagery of a richly decorated, painted tholos tomb recently discovered at Alexandrova, in southern Bulgaria, exhibits close ties to the art of Italy of this same period,[98] while the Thracian plaques from Letnitsa decorated with scenes in relief are, as we have seen, especially rich in local adaptations of classical motifs. On one of them, the image of a female figure confronting a triple-headed snake (Fig. 8.16)[99] may derive from Etruscan art, for it resembles a female

8.15. Symplegma: female figure on the lap of a seated male figure, with a standing attendant holding a decorated vase and tree branch. Thracian silver-gilt plaque from Letnitsa. Fourth century BC. Lovech Museum of History. (Marazov 1998, 162–163, no. 92.)

figure, perhaps Medea, dealing with a triple-headed snake on a seventh-century BC painted Etruscan vase now in Amsterdam (Fig. 8.17).[100]

The mirror held by the heroine or divinity on the Thracian plaque is a common Etruscan attribute of women, and an object regularly found in their tombs. These portable luxury objects were an Etruscan specialty from the fifth through the third or second centuries BC, when they circulated widely and were evidently appreciated in the north. The artists of the situlas imitated the decoration of Etruscan mirrors as well as their form (Fig. 8.13),[101] while the Celts put some of their most beautiful

8.16. Female figure holding a mirror, confronting a triple-headed serpent. Thracian silver-gilt plaque from Letnitsa. Fourth century BC. Lovech Museum of History. (Marazov 1998, 162, no. 91.)

decorative patterns on the backs of their bronze mirrors.[102] The plain handled mirrors held by the figure on the Letnitsa plaque, as well as by other Thracian female figures of divinities, were Etruscan rather than Greek mirrors, for the latter were usually represented in art with decorated frames.[103]

8.17. Female figure confronting a triple-headed serpent. Etruscan Orientalizing vase in Amsterdam, Allard Pierson Museum. Provenance unknown. Seventh century BC. (Museum photo.)

The Kouros Abroad

Related to the large-scale statues from Italy discussed previously are some spectacular stone statues discovered beyond the Alps, in modern Germany,[104] which were influenced by the Greek kouros by way of Etruscan models. The Hirschlanden Warrior, dating from around 500 BC (Fig. 8.18), represents a Hallstatt prince armed with a belt and a knife and wearing a torque and a small conical hat or helmet. Though

8.18. Stone statue of a life-size warrior from Hirschlanden. Sixth century BC. Stuttgart, Württembergisches Landesmuseum. (Museum photo.)

he is naked, his nudity is not the conventional Greek "heroic nudity." It has been translated into something very different from that of the beautiful, youthful Greek kouroi who are his distant artistic models, for he is ithyphallic.[105] His is an apotropaic and magically protective nudity, appropriate for a statue standing on top of a burial mound, guarding the grave of a warrior (Fig. 8.19). Here and elsewhere, non-Greek barbarians made use of the classical Greek motif of male nudity and gave it their own special symbolic meaning: the nudity of a male figure wielding

8.19. Reconstruction of the original placement of the Hirschlanden Warrior on top of a funeral mound. (Frey 1980, 99.)

an axe in the late fourth-century BC tomb of Alexandrova, for example, was most probably a sign of divinity (Plate XII).[106]

Also harking back to an Etruscan model is the fifth-century BC Glauberg statue excavated in 1988,[107] an impressive figure standing 2 meters high. Its crown of leaves, a sign of divinity or high status, give the impression of wings or gigantic ears, and quickly gained for it the nickname Mickey Mouse. It was found in situ beside a huge funeral mound, together with southern imports providing evidence of South–North interchange.[108] Like the Capestrano Warrior (Fig. 8.20a–b),[109] the figure was not naked, but fully armed, and served a funerary purpose, like the warror from Hirschlanden.

From southern France comes a different type of statue, a fragmentary life-sized torso of a limestone sculpture originally representing a kneeling warrior holding a bow or a spear. Discovered at Lattes, a Celtic seaport in southern France, where there apparently lived a resident settlement of Etruscans, it reflects a stronger cultural influence of Etruscan civilization throughout the western Mediterranean region than was previously realized.[110]

The preceding brief survey of North–South connections serves to remind us of how much material has been lost forever. Though many

8.20a–b. Capestrano Warrior from the Picenum. Ca. 550 BC. Chieti, Museo Archeologico Nazionale d'Abruzzo. (Photo Courtesy Soprintendenza per i Beni Archeologici dell'Abruzzo – Chieti.)

stone and ceramic objects, statues and bucchero vases and bronze *Schnabelkannen*, or beaked jugs, that were favored imports from Etruria still remain, the organic materials that constituted much of the wealth of the North – wool, textiles, wood, leather, skins, slaves – have left very few archaeological traces of their existence. Yet even the indirect evidence of artistic representations shows how important all these materials were in the lives and commerce of these peoples, and records the lively exchange across the Alps and beyond that flourished from the time when the Etruscans first established relations with the peoples of Europe that would eventually be united by Rome.

At that time, the Etruscans brought writing to Europe, and made the barbarians of ancient Europe visible by bringing the human figure and monumental architecture north. While the Greeks brought much symposium equipment and wine into Gaul from their coastal base at Marseilles, much of it also came from across the Alps. When the Gauls had tasted the wine and fruits of Chiusi, Livy tells us, they came down and settled in northern Italy,[111] adding to the splendid diversity of the peninsula. Thus the Etruscans, who almost united Italy before Rome, translated and introduced into Europe many aspects of the classical tradition, which would henceforward merge with the barbarian heritage to develop into what we know as Western civilization.

Notes

1. Bickerman 1952, 65–81.
2. Pallottino 1975, 78–79.
3. Ridgway and Serra Ridgway 1995, 271–277. "… by the beginning of the first millennium, the indigenous nuragic communities of Sardinia were technologically far more advanced than their contemporaries on the Italian mainland." Hellenism never permeated Sardinia, directly or indirectly: Ridgway 1992, 28.
4. Torelli 1986, 51–52; Turfa 1986, 74; Haynes 2000, 195, 197; Bonfante 2003b, 43–58.
5. Ridgway 1992.
6. Bonfante, 2011.
7. Baltic amber: Todd 2003; Palavestra and Krstic 2006; Nava and Salerno 2007. Verucchio: von Eles 1994. The huge quantities of amber in Etruscan women's tombs primarily played the role of social distinction (Bonfante 2009a,220–233; Negroni Catacchio 2009, 190–219), while the small pieces of amber in children's tombs had a magical, protective purpose, perhaps medicinal. Amber was always special, like the gold of Thracian kings and Scythian warriors: see Ivantchik, Chapter 3, and Marazov, Chapter 5, in this volume.
8. Burkert 1992.
9. Naso 2000, 193–207; 2006, 325–358.
10. Bonfante and Bonfante 2002, 64–68.
11. Bagnasco Gianni 1999, 85–106; Bonfante and Bonfante 2002; Bonfante and Swaddling 2006, 9–10; de Grummond 2006; de Grummond and Simon 2006.
12. Pandolfini and Prosdocimi 1990; Bonfante and Bonfante 2002, 55, 132–135. Etruscans, like Phoenicians, usually wrote from right to left. The writing on the inkwell, which came from a site near Viterbo in the south, was left to right, as

often occurred in the early period in Cerveteri and the southern cities, probably due to Greek influence.

13. See, e.g., Martelli 1987, 263–265, No. 40.
14. Faraone 1996, 77–112.
15. Bonfante and Bonfante 2002, 75–81.
16. Ridgway 2002, 28.
17. In the absence of their literature, their own myths and legends are harder to understand, but see de Grummond 2006.
18. Lowenstam 2008, 124–176.
19. Nielsen 2002b, 171–198.
20. On representations of ancestors, see Serra Ridgway 2001, 353–354; Højte 2002; Elsner 2004, 478–479.
21. Canopi: Torelli, 2000, Nos. 132, 135–136.
22. Statues from Ceri: Colonna and von Hase 1984, 13–59; Prayon 1998, 193; Bonfante 2003a, 219, fig. B5.
23. Capestrano: Cianfarani et al. 1978, 116–118, 185, 309, 314, fig. 12, Plate VI; Colonna 1992, 103, 110, 113–115, figs. 14–15, Plate II; Brendel 1995, 100–102; *Eroi e regine* 2001; Cherici 2003, 538–553.
24. Casale Marittimo: Esposito 1999, 33–39. Possibly a couple, male and female, Bonfante 2003a, 219–221; 2006, 34, fig. 4. But see Serra Ridgway 2001, 354: "their interpretation as ancestors... remains debatable."
25. For sumptuary laws, see Bonfante, Chapter 1, in this volume; Ogden 2002, 210.
26. Barber 1991; Bonfante 2003a, 11–17; Harris 2003, 43–84.
27. Gleba 2008, 36; 2009, 69–84. A belt loom was found in the grave of the Regina di Sirolo: Landolfi 2001, 350ff.; 2007, 171.
28. Barber 1991, 1994; von Eles 2002; Bonfante 2003a, 11–17; 2005, 3–11; Gleba 2008.
29. Morigi Govi 1971, 211–235; Barber 1991, 116, fig. 3.32, and 269, fig. 12.2; Bonfante 2003a, fig. 2.
30. I am grateful to Elizabeth Barber for this explanation.
31. "Singing the web": Tuck 2006, 539–550.
32. Ridgway 1996, 87–97; Bagnasco Gianni 1999, 85–106. Texts and textiles: Wagner-Hasel 2002, 25–28; Edmunds et al. 2004; Bergren 2008.
33. Von Eles 2002; Bonfante 2005, 3–11.
34. De Grummond 1982 and volumes of the Corpus of Etruscan Mirrors, the *Corpus Speculorum Etruscorum* (CSE).
35. Bonfante 1989, 543–570.
36. See note 23.
37. Brendel 1995, 92–93; Bonfante 2003a, 25, fig. 28.
38. Casale Marittimo: see note 25.
39. Bonfante 1986b, 73–83; Tronchetti 1986, 41–59.
40. Herodotus 1.167. Torelli (1981, 2) suggests that a huge temple founded outside Cerveteri at the end of the sixth century BC may have been related to the ritual practices of expiation for this crime. Caere, the ancient name of the city, had a treasury at Delphi; Naso 2006, 330.
41. Livy 7.15.10. See Dio Cassius 43.24.4, and Justin (Pompeius Trogus) 18.6.11–12. I am grateful to David Levene and Francesco de Angelis for references.
42. Etruscan human sacrifice: Bonfante 1978, 147–148; 1984a, 531–539; 1984b, 143–150; Torelli 1981, 1–7; Scheffer 1994, 203–204, 209, n. 60. Steuernagel 1998, who deals with such scenes represented on Hellenistic cinerary urns,

denies the reality of Etruscan human sacrifice. We do not know when it ceased to be practiced.

43. Buranelli 1987, with earlier bibliography.

44. Bonghi Jovino and Chiaramonte Treré 1997, 165–166, 186–189, 218–220; Bonghi Jovino 2010, 165–166.

45. Bibliography can be found in the following: Bonfante 1981a; Adam et al. 1992; Aigner Foresti 1992a, 1992b, 2001; Capuis 1992, 27–44; 2004, 130–145, 309; Pallottino 1992; Swaddling et al. 1995. For Etruscan influence in the Hallstatt sphere, see Cunliffe 1997, 61–63. The extent of my debt to Otto-Herman Frey will be clear throughout the following section.

46. For the monsters see Gran-Aymerich 2004, 15–158; Warden 2004, 51–56.

47. Bouzek 2003a, 197–207. For the importance of prophecy, see de Grummond 2006, 23–40; Briquel 1997. For human sacrifice, see Chapter 1 in this volume.

48. Bonfante 1981b. See Bouzek 1998 on the "tribal aristocracy" of the northern chieftains; cf. Capuis 1992, 27–44, for the Veneto.

49. Morandi 1982.

50. See Bouzek 2003a, 201, on the Golasecca culture, where a Celtic dialect was spoken, as responsible for much of the mutual exchange. For the amber route see Bouzek 2003c, 155–163; Cunliffe 2008, 44.

51. Elliott 1989; Bonfante and Bonfante 2002, 117–120. For the various theories, see Page 1987, 9; Rix 1992, 411–441.

52. Bonfante and Bonfante 2002, 118.

53. Page 1987, 7–8; Scardigli 1992, 206–209.

54. Sievers et al. 1991, 436. On the sacred groves of the Celts, see Finlay 1973, 68–69. Over 5,000 wood figures and other carvings were found around a spring in Auvergne dating from the early Gallo-Roman period: Piggott 1985, 80–81, fig. 63; Megaw and Megaw 1989, 172–173. Wooden furnishings from Verucchio: von Eles 2002, 74–80, 290–299. Compare the wooden furniture from Gordion, Simpson et al. 1999, figs. 13–21, 24–31, 61–80 Wooden shields: Wells 2001, 72.

55. For oracles, see Cicero, *de divinatione* II, 41: *in robore sculptas priscarum litterarum notis*. For treaties and records see Livy 1, I, 24, and Livy 1, 32.2.

56. Briggs 2003, 243–259; Wells, Chapter 7, in this volume. For the trade in slaves see Cunliffe, Chapters 6 and 13, in this volume.

57. Warden 1994, 134–143; Nava and Salerno 2007; Bonfante 2009a, 220–233; Negroni Catacchio 2009, 190–219; Palavestra 2009.

58. See Cristofani 1979, 373–412, fig. 2, for a distribution map of the Etruscan alphabet in Italy; Maggiani 1998, 227–234. Chiusi provided more inscriptions than any other Etruscan city in the later period, and the language shift from Etruscan to Latin took longer there than elsewhere: Kaimio 1972, 206–210; Bonfante and Bonfante 2002, 30.

59. Sassatelli 1999, 469; Minetti 2004, 554. An exhibit on Orientalizing Vetulonia and Verucchio illustrated the flow of amber between North and South and across the Apennines: Rafanelli and von Eles 2009.

60. Bartoloni and Morigi Govi 1995, 161; Brendel 1995, 177–179.

61. Florence, Archaeological Museum; Haynes 2000, 108–110; *Principi Etruschi* 2000, 230, No. 256; Minetti 2004, 454–455.

62. Bonfante 1981a, 37, 55; Edlund-Berry 1992, 189–191.

63. A tradition inherited from Villanovan times: Edlund-Berry 1992, 18.

64. Family continuity: Nielsen 2002a, 89–126; Steingräber 2002, 127–158. For the frieze plaques, see Haynes 2000, 120–126. For the banquet, see Rathje 1994, 95–99, and Small 1994, 85–94; for the horse race, see Root 1973; for the carriage procession and seated figures, see Sinos 1994, 100–117.
65. The motif is an Etruscan invention: Szilágyi 1992, 42–43, figs. 2b–c; Gran-Aymerich 2004. Banti (1973, 256, plate 64a; 258, plate 65a) sees the volute issuing from the jaws of winged quadrupeds as a stylization of this motif.
66. Haynes 2000, 120.
67. Bronson 1965, 89–106.
68. Root 1973, 121–137.
69. For Etruscan chariots see Emiliozzi 1997; Haynes 2000, 101–102. For Celtic chariots see Sievers et al. 1991, 436; Egg and Pare 1997, 45–51. For chariots in situla art see Camerin 1997, 40–41.
70. For the jug from Tragliatella see Säflund 1986, 471–478; 1993, 47–51; Martelli 1987, 271–272, No. 49.
71. For the phalanx see, e.g, Turfa 1986, 72. The fact that it was represented does not necessarily mean that it was actually put into practice.
72. For Villanovan helmets see Haynes 2000, 12. For the local type, from Verucchio, see *Principi Etruschi* 2000, 359, 367, Cat No. 529; Sassatelli 2004, 182.
73. The situla holders on the Benvenuti and Kuffarn situlas (see Frey, Chapter 9, this volume, Figs. 9.6 and 9.12; Steingräber 1979, Typenkatalog, p. 16): these pieces of furniture can be compared to the *kylikeia* that displayed Greek and Etruscan drinking cups and the vases exhibited in Etruscan tomb paintings: Steingräber 1986, No. 123, cf. No. 34.
74. Frey 1969, 105, No. 18, plate 67, and plate 28, 10–19 (tomb group); Bonfante 1981a, fig. 46; Boardman 1994, 300, fig. 8.8; Frey, Chapter 9, in this volume. For the distribution of the *Schnabelkanne* see Bouloumié 1973; 1985, 167–178; Shefton 1995, 9–39.
75. On the seventh-century urn from Montescudaio (Steingräber 1979, Cat. No 573, plate 31.3) and the Tomb of the Five Chairs at Cerveteri (Haynes 2000, 92–94), the images of ancestors are seated at a banquet. For the custom of reclining on couches, see Haynes 2000, 93–95, 122–124.
76. Pausanias 5.12.5. Naso 2000, 198, lists fragments of metal coverings for such thrones.
77. Von Eles 2002, 235–248, plates II–V, for the throne; 248–272, figs. 120–128, for the decoration. Bonfante 2005, 3–11.
78. Bonfante 1977, 111–122; 2005, 3–11; Torelli 1990, 355–367, with previous bibliography.
79. Steingräber 1979, Type 1a.
80. Moscati 1991, 86; Cunliffe 1997, 60–61.
81. Steingräber 1979, Type Catalogue, p. 3, Klinentyp 2S. Lucretius, *de rerum natura* 2.24–26: *si non aurea sunt iuvenum simulacra per aedes/lampadas igniferas manibus retinentia dextris,/lumina nocturnis epulis ut suppeditentur.* For statues of golden boys holding torches, see *Odyssey* 7.100.
82. Celtic craftsmen created stylized bronze works in abstract forms, often reacting to classical forms of Etruscan bronzes: see, e.g., Frey 1969, 62–63, figs. 67–68, for a Praenestine cista handle and the Celtic forms it inspired. Frey 2004, 107–129, discusses the important new finds since the work of Jacobsthal.

83. Lucke-Frey 1962, plate 42; Bonfante 1981a, fig. 97; 1999a, 503–510, with bibliography. Two pugilists use these barbells on the base of the Roman Corsini throne: Bonfante 2005, 3–11.

84. Pontic vase, formerly in the Getty collection, returned to Italy 2009. Bonfante 1999a, 505–506, plate I; de Puma 2000, 23–24, No. 20, plates 489–493. Greek relief in Istanbul: Boardman 1978, 218.2; Stewart 1990, plate 164.

85. Bonfante 1999a, 503–506. I owe this suggestion to Giovanni Colonna.

86. Mertens 1993, 5–11; Bonfante 2003b, 43–58.

87. Edlund-Berry 1992; Rathje 1994, 95–99. For women in Etruria see Rallo 1989. For couples see Bonfante. 1981b, 323–343; 2006, 31–36.

88. Steingräber 1986, No. 25; Haynes 2000, 247.

89. Von Eles 2002, 251–253, 262–264, fig. 121. On the Queen of Sirolo, see also Landolfi 2001; 2007, 171–173.

90. Bonfante 1999b, 20–25.

91. Martelli 1987, 271–272, No. 49; Säflund 1993, 47–51, 143, figs. 33–36s.

92. Haynes 2000, 97–99.

93. See Marazov, Chapter 5, in this volume, for images of marriage as visual confirmation of legitimacy.

94. As Boardman (1971, 123–140) once suggested. See Johns 1982, 123.

95. Lucke-Frey 1962, 69–70, Cat. No. 15, plate 31; Bonfante 1999b, 20–25.

96. Brezje belt fragment: Lucke-Frey 1962, 70, Cat. No. 17, plate 32. Böhm 1990, 89–90: the gesture was originally Near Eastern. Also known as the "Baubo gesture," the *anasyrma* gesture appeared on both male and female figures in Etruscan art; in Roman art it was used for hermaphrodites and for the god Priapus. Bonfante 2009b, 158–170, with previous bibliography.

97. Letnitsa plaque: Marazov 1998, 162–163, No. 92. On an oinochoe by the Shuvalov Painter, an Attic artist of the end of the fifth century BC, the man is sitting. Brendel 1970, 39–40, figs. 25, 26; von Blanckenhagen 1976, 37–41.

98. Kitov 2001, 15–29; Kitov and Theodossiev 2003, 41.

99. Marazov 1998, 160–161, No. 90. The short hair and lack of breasts have led some to assume that the figure is male (Theodossiev 1994, 317–319); according to Marazov, they indicate that it is a virgin.

100. Martelli 1987, 265, No. 41, with previous bibliography; Menichetti 1994, 49–50, fig. 31a-b; Torelli 2000, 420, 607, Cat. No. 211.

101. Castelvetro mirror: Montelius 1895, cols. 449–450; Bonfante 1981a, fig. 56. See also the Arnoaldi mirror: Bonfante 1981a, figs. 57, 58; *Rasenna* 1986, fig. 532.

102. Finlay 1973, 86–88; Megaw and Megaw 1989, 9, 115, 206, 210–215.

103. Trendall 1989, 92, figs. 171, 214.

104. Frey 2002, 47–107. Male torsos from Nesactium, Istria: Frey 2002, 214, 216, Cat. Nos. 129.2–3, figs. 205, 206.

105. See Brendel 1995, 92–93, for the contrast between early monumental Etruscan funerary statues and the more abstract concept of the early Greek kouroi. On their nudity, see Bonfante 1989, 549–570.

106. Kitov 2001, 15–29; Frey 2002, 216; Kitov and Theodossiev 2003, 41.

107. Herrmann 2002, 104–107, figs. 69–71; 261–263, Cat. No. 3.1. Now in the Hessisches Landesmuseum, Darmstadt. Four statues were found; the other three are fragmentary.

108. *Glauberg* 2002, figs. 69–71. Frey 2002, 208–211; 2004, 107–129; Hermann 2002, 104–107. See also Wells 2001, 63–67.

109. Capestrano: see note 23.

110. Dietler and Py 2003, 780–795; *EtrNews* 4, 2004, 12.
111. Livy 5.33.1–3.

Bibliography

Adam, Richard, Dominique Briquel, Jean Gran-Aymerich, David Ridgway, Ingrid Strøm, and Friedrich-Wilhelm von Hase. 1992. "I rapporti transalpini." In Pallottino 1992, 166–183.

Aigner-Foresti, Luciana. 1992a. "Relazioni protostoriche tra Italia e Europa centrale." In Pallottino 1992, 120–153.

ed. 1992b. *'Etrusker Nördlich von Etrurien. Etruskishe Präsenz in Norditalien und nördlich der Alpen sowie ihre Einflüsse auf die einheimischen Kulturen.* Vienna.

2001. "'Europa' e gli Etruschi." In *Studi sull'Europa antica* II, ed. Marta Sordi, 37–50. Alessandria.

Bagnasco Gianni, Giovanna. 1999. "L'acquisizione della scrittura in Etruria. Materiali a confronto per la ricostruzione del quadro storico e culturale." In *Scritture Mediterranee tra il IX e il VII secolo a.C.*, ed. G. Bagnasco Gianni and F. Cordano, 85–106. Milan.

Banti, Luisa, 1973. *The Etruscan Cities and Their Culture.* Berkeley, CA. (Originally published in Italian, 1968.)

Barber, E. J. W. 1991. *Prehistoric Textiles: The Development of Cloth in the Neolithic and Bronze Ages with Special Reference to the Aegean.* Princeton, NJ.

1994. *Women's Work: The First 20,000 Years: Women, Cloth, and Society in Early Times.* New York.

Bartoloni, Gilda, and Cristiana Morigi Govi. 1995. "Etruscan Craftsmanship in Italy: Etruria and Situla Art: The Certosa Situla – New Perspectives." In Swaddling et al. 1995, 159–176.

Beck, C.W., I. B. Loze, and J.M. Todd, eds. 2003. *Amber in Archaeology.* Proceedings of the IV International Conference on Amber in Archaeology, Talsi, 2001. Riga.

Bergren, Ann. 2008. *Weaving Truth: Essays on Language and the Female in Greek Thoughts.* Cambridge, MA, and London.

Bickerman, Elias J. 1952. "Origines gentium." *CPh* 47 (1952) 65–81 = *Religions and Politics in the Hellenistic and Roman Periods*, ed. Emilio Gabba and Morton Smith, 401–417. Biblioteca di Athenaeum 5. Como 1985.

Boardman, John. 1971. "A Southern View of Situla Art." In *The European Community in Later Prehistory: Studies in Honour of C. F. C. Hawkes*, ed. J. Boardman, M. A. Brown, and T. G. E. Powell, 123–140. London.

1978. *Greek Sculpture: The Archaic Period.* London.

1994. *The Diffusion of Classical Art in Antiquity.* Mellon Lectures in the Fine Arts 1993, 225–291. Princeton, NJ.

Böhm, Stephanie 1990. *Die Nackte Göttin: Zur Ikonographie und Deutung unbekleideter weiblicher Figuren in der frügriechischen Kunst.* Mainz.

Bonfante, Larissa. 1977. "The Corsini Throne," *Essays in Honor of Dorothy K. Hill. The Journal of the Walters Art Gallery* 36:111–122.

1978. "Historical Art: Etruscan and Early Roman." *American Journal of Ancient History* 3:136–162.

1981a. *Out of Etruria: Etruscan Influence North and South*. Oxford.

1981b. "Etruscan Couples and Their Aristocratic Society." *Reflections of Women in Antiquity*, ed. H. P. Foley, 323–343. New York.

1984a. "Human Sacrifice on an Etruscan Urn." *AJA* 88:531–539.

1984b. "Un'urna etrusca a New York con têtes coupées." In *Studi di antichità in onore di G. Maetzke*, Archaeologica 49: 143–150. Rome.

1985. "Amber, Women, and Situla Art." *Journal of Baltic Studies* 16:276–291.

ed. 1986a. *Etruscan Life and Afterlife*. Detroit.

1986b. "The Etruscan Connection." In *Studies in Sardinian Archaeology II, Sardinia in the Mediterranean*, ed. Miriam Balmuth, 73–83. Ann Arbor, MI.

1989. "Nudity as a Costume in Classical Art." *AJA* 93: 543–570.

1994. "Excursus: Etruscan Women." In Fantham et al. 1994, 243–259.

1999a. "Abiti e abitudini nell'arte delle situle." *Protostoria e storia del venetorum angulus*. Atti del XX Convegno di Studi Etruschi, Istituti Editoriali Poligrafici Internazionali, Este – Adria 1996, 501–511. Pisa.

1999b. "Marriage Scenes, Sacred and Otherwise: The Conjugal Embrace." *Art Studies Quarterly* 4:20–25. (Sofia, Bulgaria.)

2003a. *Etruscan Dress*. Baltimore. (Originally published 1975.)

2003b. "The Greeks in Etruria." In *The Greeks Beyond the Aegean: From Marseilles to Bactria*, ed. Vassos Karageorghis, 43–58. New York.

2005. "The Verucchio Throne and the Corsini Chair: Two Status Symbols of Ancient Italy." In *Terra Marique: Studies in Art History and Marine Archaeology in Honor of Anna Marguerite McCann on the Receipt of the Gold Medal of the Archaeological Institute of America*, ed. John Pollini, 3–11. Oxford.

2006. "Etruscan Couples Once More" In *Italo-Tusco-Romana. Festschrift für Luciana Aigner-Foresti*, ed. Petra Amann, Marco Pedrazzi, and Hans Taeuber, 31–36, plates 9, 10 and figs. 1–6. Vienna and Holzhausen.

2009a. "Observations on Amber Artifacts in Italy and the 'Orientalizing' Period." In Palavestra 2009a, 220–233.

2009b. "Some Thoughts on the Baubo Gesture in Etruscan Art." In *New Perspectives on Etruria and Early Rome*, ed. Sinclair Bell and Helen Nagy, 158–170. Madison, WI.

2011. "What Role for the Etruscans?" ΑΜΙΛΛΑ: *The Quest for Excellence. Studies in Honor of Guenter Kopcke. Festschrift for Guenter Kopcke*, Robert Koehl, ed. Philadelphia.

Bonfante, Larissa, and Giuliano Bonfante. 2002. *The Etruscan Language: An Introduction*, 2nd ed. Manchester.

Bonfante, Larissa, and Vassos Karageorghis, eds. 2001. *Italy and Cyprus in Antiquity 1500–450 BC*. Nicosia.

Bonfante, Larissa, and Judith Swaddling. 2006. *Etruscan Myths*. London.

Bonghi Jovino, Maria. 2010. "The Tarquinia Project: A Summary of 25 Years of Excavation." *AJA* 114:161–180, with previous bibliography.

Bonghi Jovino, Maria, and Cristina Chiaramonte Trerè. 1997. *Tarquinia: Testimonianze archeologiche e ricostruzione storica, Scavi sistematici nell'abitato: campagne 1982–1988. (Tarchna 1)*. Rome.

Bouloumié, Bernard. 1973. *Les oenochoés en bronze du type "Schnabelkanne" en Italie*. Rome.

1985. "Les vases de bronze étrusques et leur diffusion hors d'Italie." In *Il commercio etrusco arcaico*, Atti dell'Incontro di Studio 1983. Quaderni del centro di studio per l'archeologia etrusco-italica 9, CNRS, 167–178. Rome.

1986. "Vases de bronze étrusques du service du vin." In Swaddling 1986, 63–79.

1992. "La diffusione del vino in Europa centrale e nord-occidentale." In Pallottino 1992, 184–189.

Bouzek, Jan. 1998. "Some New Aspects of the Amber Route Studies." *Atti del XIII Congresso UISPP Forli, 1996*. Workshop 6,1. Forlí.

2003a. *Etruskové. Jini nez vsechny ostatni narody* ("The Etruscans: Different from All Other Nations"), 197–207. English summary. Prague.

2003b. "Etruscan Art and Etruscan Mind." *Eirene* 39:150–173.

2003c. "The Central European Amber Route during the La Tène and Early Imperial Times." In *Amber in Archaeology*, ed. Curt Beck, Ilze B. Loze, and Joan M. Todd, 155–163. Proceedings of the IV International Conference of Amber in Archaeology, Talsi, 2001. Riga.

Brendel, Otto J. 1970. "The Scope and Temperament of Erotic Art in the Greco-Roman World." In *Studies in Erotic Art*, ed. T. Bowie and C. V. Christenson. New York.

1995. *Etruscan Art*. New Haven, CT. (Originally published 1978.)

Briggs, Daphne Nash. 2003. "Metals, Salt, and Slaves: Economic Links Between Gaul and Italy from the Eighth to the Late Sixth Centuries B.C." *Oxford Journal of Archaeology* 22:243–259.

Briquel, Dominique. 1997. *Chrétiens et haruspices: La religion étrusque, dernier rempart du paganisme romain*. Paris.

Bronson, R. C. 1965. "Chariot Racing in Etruria." In *Studi in onore di Luisa Banti*, G. Camporeale, ed., 89–106. Rome.

Buranelli, Francesco, ed. 1987. *La Tomba François di Vulci*. Rome.

Burkert, Walter. 1992. *The Orientalizing Revolution: Near Eastern Influence on Greek Culture in the Early Archaic* Age. Cambridge, MA.

Camerin, Nicoletta. 1997. "L'Italia antica: Italia settentrionale." In Emiliozzi 1997, 33–44.

Capuis, Loredana. 1992. "Il Veneto nel quadro dei rapporti etrusco-italici ed europei dalla fine dell'età del bronzo alla romanizzazione." In Aigner-Foresti 1992b, 27–44.

2004. "The Etruscans in the Veneto." In *The Etruscans Outside Etruria*, G. Camporeale, ed., 130–145. Los Angeles.

Cherici, Armando. 2003. "Armi e società nel Piceno, con una premessa di metodo e una nota sul Guerriero di Capestrano." In *Piceni e l'Italia Medio-Adriatica*, 538–553. Pisa and Rome.

Cianfarani, V., L. Franchi Dall'Orto, and A. la Regina. 1978. *Culture Adriatiche antiche d'Abruzzo e di Molise*. Rome.

Civiltà picena nelle Marche. 1992. Ripatransone (AP). Marche.

Colonna, Giovanni. 1989. "Etruschi e Umbri a nord del Po." In *Gli Etruschi a Nord del Po*, 11–26. Mantua.

1992. "Apporti etruschi all'Orientalizzante 'piceno': il caso della statuaria." In *Civiltà picena nelle Marche* 1992, 92–127.

1999. "La scultura in pietra." In *Piceni* 1999, 104–109.

Colonna, Giovanni, and Friedrich-Wilhelm von Hase. 1984 [1986]. "All'origine della statuaria etrusca: La Tomba delle Statue presso Ceri." *Studi Etruschi* 52:13–59.

Cristofani, Mauro. 1979. "Recent Advances in Etruscan Epigraphy and Language." In Ridgway and Ridgway 1979, 373–418.

Cunliffe, Barry. 1997. *The Ancient Celts*. Harmondsworth.
   2001. *Facing the Ocean: The Atlantic and Its Peoples 8000 BC–AD 1500*. Oxford.
   2008. *Europe Between the Oceans: 9000 BC–AD 1000*. New Haven, CT.

D'Agostino, Bruno, and Luca Cerchiai. 1999. *Il mare, la morte, l'amore: Gli Etruschi, i Greci, e l'immagine*. Rome and Donzelli.

de Grummond, Nancy T. 1982. *A Guide to Etruscan Mirrors*. Tallahassee, FL.
   2006. *Etruscan Myth, Sacred History, and Legend*. Philadelphia.

de Grummond, Nancy T., and Erika Simon. 2006. *The Religion of the Etruscans*. Austin, TX.

Dehn, Wolfgang, and Otto-Herman Frey. 1979. "Southern Imports and the Hallstatt and early La Tène Chronology of Central Europe." In Ridgway and Ridgway 1979, 489–511.

de Min, Maurizia. 2007. "L'Ambra nel Veneto Protostorico." In Nava and Salerno 2007, 112–115.

De Puma, Richard. 2000. *Etruscan Painted Pottery* = CVA J. Paul Getty Museum 9. USA 34 23–24, No. 20, plates 489–493. Los Angeles.

De Puma, Richard, and Jocelyn Penny Small, eds. 1994. *Murlo and the Etruscans: Art and Society in Ancient Etruria*. Madison, WI.

Dietler, Michael, and Michel Py. 2003. "The Warrior of Lattes: An Iron Age Statue Discovered in Mediterranean France." *Antiquity* 77:780–795.

Edlund-Berry, Ingrid M. E. 1992. *The Seated and Standing Statue Akroteria from Poggio Civitate (Murlo)*. Rome.

Edmunds, Susan, Prudence Jones, and Gregory Nagy. 2004. *Text & Textile: An Introduction to Wool-Working for Readers of Greek and Latin*. Video. New Brunswick, NJ, Department of Classics, Rutgers University. http://classics.rutgers.edu

Egg, Marcus, and Christopher F. E. Pare. 1997. "Il mondo celtico." In Emiliozzi 1997, 45–51.

Eibner, Alexandra. 2007. "Thron – Schemel-Zepter. Zeichen der Herrschaft und Würde." In *Scripta* 2007, 435–451.

Elliott, Ralph W. V. 1989. *Runes: An Introduction*, 2nd ed. Manchester.

Elsner, Jas. 2004. Review of Højte 2002. *AJA* 108:478–479.

Emiliozzi, Adriana. 1997. *Carri da Guerra e Principi Etruschi*. Rome.

Eroi e regine. 2001. *Eroi e regine. Piceni popolo d'Europa*. Rome.

Esposito, A. M., ed. 1999. *Principi guerrieri: La necropoli orientalizzante di Casale Marittimo*. Exhibition Catalogue, Cecina. Milan.

Fantham, E., H. P. Foley, N. B. Kampen, S. B. Pomeroy, and H. A. Shapiro, eds. 1994. *Women in the Classical World*. Oxford.

Faraone, Christopher A. 1996. "Taking the Nestor's Cup Inscription Seriously: Conditional Curses and Erotic Magic in the Earliest Greek Hexameters." *Classical Antiquity* 15:77–112.

Finlay, Ian. 1973. *Celtic Art*. Park Ridge, NJ.

Fogolari, Giulia, and Aldo Luigi Prosdocimi. 1988. *I Veneti antichi: Lingua e cultura*. Padova.

Frel, Faya Causey. 1984. "Studies on Greek, Etruscan, and Italic Carved Ambers." PhD dissertation. Santa Barbara, CA.

Frey, Otto-Herman 1962 = Lucke-Frey. Lucke, Wolfgang, and Otto Herman Frey. 1962. *Die Situla in Providence*. Berlin.

1969. *Die Entstehung der Situlenkunst*. Berlin.

1991. " 'I primi principi celti' nel VI secolo a.C." In Moscati 1991, 74–92.

1992. "Beziehungen der Situlenkunst zum Kunstschaffen Etruriens." In Aigner-Foresti 1992b, 93–101.

2000. "Keltische Grossplastik." *Reallexikon der germanischen Altertumskunde* 16:395–407. Berlin and New York.

2002. "Wer waren die Kelten?", "Glaube, Mythos, Wirklichkeit," and "Menschen oder Heroen?" In *Glauberg* 2002, 47–57, 172–205, 208–222.

2004. "A New Approach to Early Celtic Art." *Proceedings of the Royal Irish Academy* 104C (5): 107–129.

Frey, Otto-Herman, and Fritz-Rudolf Herrmann. 1997. "Ein frühkeltischer Fürsterngrabhügel am Glauberg im Wetteraukreis, Hessen." *Germania* 75 2: 459–550.

Giglioli, G. Q. 1929. "L'oinochoe della Tragliatella," *StEtr* 3:111–159, plates 23–26.

Glauberg 2002. *Das Raetsel der Kelten vom Glauberg. Glaube – Mythos – Wirklichkeit. Catalogue of the Glauberg Exhibit*. Stuttgart.

Gleba, Margarita. 2008. *Textile Production in Pre-Roman Italy*. Llandysul, Wales.

2009. "Textile Tools in Ancient Italian Votive Contexts: Evidence of Dedication or Production?" In Gleba and Becker 2009, 69–84.

Gleba, Margarita, and Hilary Becker, eds. 2009. *Votives, Places and Rituals in Etruscan Religion: Studies in Honor of Jean MacIntosh Turfa*. Leiden.

Gori, A. F. 1737–1743. *Musaeum Etruscum*. Florence.

Gran-Aymerich, Jean. 2004. "Le fauve carnassier dans l'art étrusque et son influence sur le premier art celtique." *In Le Tarasque de Noves: Réflexions sur un motif iconographique et sa postérité*, ed. Odile Cavalier, 15–27. Musée Calvet, Avignon.

2009. "Gli Etruschi fuori d'Etruria. Dons et offrandes étrusques en Méditerraneé occidentale et dans l'Ouest de l'Europe." In Gleba and Becker 2009, 15–41.

Harris, Susanna. 2003. "Representations of Woven Textiles in Alpine Europe during the Copper Age." In *Inhabiting Symbols. Symbol and Image in the Ancient Mediterranean*, ed. J. Wilkins and E. Herring, Accordia Specialist Studies in the Mediterranean 5:43–84. London.

Haynes, Sybille. 2000. *Etruscan Civilization: A Cultural History*. Los Angeles.

Herrmann, Fritz-Rudolf. 2002. "Fürstensitz, Fürstengräber und Heiligtum." In *Glauberg* 2002, 90–107.

Hodos, Tamar. 1998. "The Asp's Poison: Women and Literacy in Iron Age Italy." In Whitehouse 1998, 197–208.

Højte, Jakob Munk, ed. 2002. *Images of Ancestors*. Aarhus.

Jacobsthal, P. 1944. *Early Celtic Art*. Oxford. Reprint 1969.

Johns, Catherine. 1982. *Sex or Symbol: Erotic Images of Greece and Rome*. Austin, TX.

Kaimio, J. 1972. "The Ousting of Etruscan by Latin in Etruria." *Acta Instituti Romani Finlandiae* 5:85–245.

Kitov, G. 2001. "A Newly Found Thracian Tomb with Frescoes." *Archaeologica Bulgarica* 2:15–29.

Kitov, G., and N. Theodossiev. 2003. "I colori dei Traci." *Archeo* 222:34–47.

Kruta, Venceslas. 2004. *I Celti e il Mediterraneo*. Milan.

Landolfi, Maurizio. 2001. "La Tomba della Regina nella necropoli picena 'I Pini' di Sirolo-Numana." *In Eroi e regine* 2001.

  2007. "Ricchezza e ostentazione tra i Piceni: La Regina di Sirolo." In Nava and Salerno 2007, 171–173. Milan.

LIMC. Lexicon Iconographicum Mythologiae Classicae. Zurich and Munich.

Llewellyn-Jones, Lloyd, ed. 2002. *Woman's Dress in the Ancient Greek World*. Swansea.

Lowenstam, Steven. 2008. *As Witnessed by Images: The Trojan War Tradition in Greek and Etruscan Art*. Baltimore.

Maggiani, Adriano. 1998. "Sulla paleografia delle iscrizioni di Spina." In *Spina e il Delta padano: Riflessioni sul catalogo e sulla mostra ferrarese*, ed. Fernando Rebecchi, 227–234. Rome.

Marazov, Ivan, ed. 1998. *Ancient Gold: The Wealth of the Thracians: Treasures from the Republic of Bulgaria*. New York.

Martelli, Marina. 1987. *La ceramica degli Etruschi*. Novara.

Megaw, Ruth, and Vincent Megaw. 1989. *Celtic Art: From Its Beginnings to the Book of Kells*. New York.

Menichetti, Mauro. 1994. *Archeologia del potere*. Milan.

Mertens, Joan R. 1993. "Reflections on an Italian Journey on an Early Attic Lekythos?" *Metropolitan Museum Journal* 28:5–11.

Minetti, Alessandra. 2004. *L'Orientalizzante a Chiusi e nel suo Territorio*. Rome.

Montelius, O. 1895. 1910. *La civilisation primitive en Italie depuis l'introduction des métaux*. 2 vols. Stockholm.

Morandi, Alessandro. 1982. *Epigrafia Italica*. Rome.

Morigi Govi, Cristiana. 1971. "Il tintinnabulo della Tomba degli Ori." *ArchClass* 23:211–235.

  ed. 2000. See *Principi Etruschi* 2000.

Moscati, Sabatino, ed. 1991. *The Celts*. Venice and New York.

Naso, Alessandro. 2000. "Etruscan and Italic Artefacts from the Aegean." In *Ancient Italy in Its Mediterranean Setting: Studies in Honour of Ellen Macnamara*, ed. D. Ridgway, Francesca R. Serra Ridgway, Mark Pearce, Edward Herring, Ruth D. Whitehouse, and John B. Wilkins, 193–207. London.

  2006. "Etruschi (e Italici) nei santuari greci." In *Stranieri e non cittadini nei santuari greci,* ed. Alessandro Naso. Atti del Convegno Internazionale. Studi Udinesi sul Mondo Antico, 325–358. Florence.

Nava, Maria Luisa, and Antonio Salerno, eds. 2007. *Ambre: Trasparenze dall'Antico*. Milan.

Negroni Catacchio, Nuccia. 2009. "Amber as Prestige and Social Indicator in Late Prehistoric Italy." In Palavestra 2009, 190–219.

Nielsen, Marjatta. 2002a. "'… stemmate quod Tusco ramum millesime ducis …' (Family Tombs and Genealogical Memory among the Etruscans)." In Højte 2002, 89–126.

2002b. "Greek Myth – Etruscan Symbol." In *Myth and Symbol I: Symbolic Phenomena in Ancient Greek Culture*. Papers from the First International Symposium on Symbolism at the University of Tromso, June 4–7, 1998, 172–198. Bergen.

Ogden, Daniel. 2002. "Controlling Women's Dress: *gynaikonomoi*." In Llewellyn-Jones 2002, 203–225.

Page, R. I. 1987. *Reading the Past: Runes*. London and Berkeley, CA.

Palavestra, Aleksandar. 2009. *Amber in Archaeology*. Proceedings of the Fifth International Conference on Amber in Archaeology. Belgrade.

Palavestra, Aleksandar, and Vera Krstic. 2006. *The Magic of Amber*. Exhibition. Archaeological Monographs 18. Belgrade.

Pallottino, Massimo. 1975. *The Etruscans*, ed. David Ridgway. Bloomington, IN. ed. 1992. *Gli Etruschi e l'Europa*. Milan.

Pandolfini, M., and A. Prosdocimi 1990. *Alfabetari e insegnamento della scrittura in Etruria e nell'Italia antica*. Florence.

Piceni 1999. *Piceni, Popoli d'Europa*. Exhibition Catalogue, Frankfurt and Ascoli Piceno.

Piggott, Stuart 1985. *The Druids*. New York. (Originally published in London 1968.)

Prayon, Friedhelm. 1998. "Die Anfänge grosssformatiger Plastik in Etrurien. Archäologische Untersuchungen zu den Beziehungen zwischen Altitalien und der Zone nordwärds der Alpen während der Frühen Eisenzeit Alteuropas." Kolloquium, Regensburg 1994. *Regensburger Beiträge zur Prähistorischen Archäologie* 4:191–205.

Principi Etruschi 2000. *Principi Etruschi tra Mediterraneo ed Europa*. Bologna and Venice.

Rafanelli. Simona, and Patrizia von Eles. 2009. *Sovrani etruschi dei due mari. Tesori d'oro e d'ambra da Vetulonia e Verucchio*. Vetulonia.

Rallo, Antonia. 1989. *Le donne in Etruria*. Rome.

Rasenna 1986. *Rasenna: Storia e civiltà degli Etruschi*. Milan.

Rathje, Annette. 1994. "Banquet and Ideology: Some New Considerations About Banqueting at Poggio Civitate." In De Puma and Small 1994, 95–99.

Richardson, Emeline. 1964. *The Etruscans: Their Art and Civilization*. Chicago.

Ridgway, David. 1992. *The First Western Greeks*. Cambridge.

1996. "Greek Letters at Osteria dell'Osa." *Opuscula Romana* 20:87–97.

1997. "Nestor's Cup and the Etruscans." *Oxford Journal of Archaeology* 16 (3): 334–335.

2002. *The World of the Early Etruscans*. Jonsered.

Ridgway, David, and Francesca R. Serra Ridgway, eds. 1979. *Italy Before the Romans*. London.

1995. "Su Tempiesu and the Ceri Effect: Two Nuragic Notes." In *Ancient Sicily*, ed. Tobias Fischer-Hansen. Acta Hyperborea 6:263–278.

Rix, Helmut. 1992. "Thesen zum Ursprung der Runenschrift." In Aigner-Foresti 1992b, 411–441.

Root, Margharet C. 1973. "An Etruscan Horse Race from Poggio Civitate (Murlo)." *AJA* 77:121–138.

Säflund, G. 1986. "'Hieros Gamos' Motive in der Etruskischen Sepulchrakunst." In Swaddling 1986, 471–478.

1993. *Etruscan Imagery: Symbol and Meaning.* Jonsered.

Sassatelli, Giuseppe. 1999. "Nuovi dati epigrafici e il ruolo degli Etruschi nei rapporti con l'Italia nord-orientale." In *Protostoria e storia del 'venetorum angulus.*' Atti del XX Convegno di Studi Etruschi, Este-Adria 1996, 453–475. Pisa and Rome.

2004. "The Etruscans on the Po Plain." In G. Camporeale, ed., *The Etruscans Outside Etruria*, 168–191. Los Angeles.

Scardigli, Piergiuseppe. 1992. "Sulla derivazione della scrittura runica dalla scrittura etrusca settentrionale." In Pallottino 1992, 206–209.

Scheffer, Charlotte. 1994. "The Arched Door in Late Etruscan Funerary Art." In De Puma and Small 1994, 196–210.

Scripta 2007. *Scripta Praehistorica in Honorem Biba Terzan: Situla* 44, ed. Martina Blecic et al. 535–555. Ljubljana.

Serra Ridgway, Francesca R. 2001. "Near Eastern Influences in Etruscan Art." In Bonfante and Karageorghis 2001, 351–359.

Shefton, Brian. 1995. "Exports North of Italy. Leaven in the Dough: Greek and Etruscan Imports North of the Alps – The Classical Period." In Swaddling et al. 1995, 9–39.

Sievers, Susanne, Radomir Pleiner, Natalie Venclova, and Udo Geilenbrügge. 1991. "Crafts." In Moscati 1991, 436–450.

Simpson, Elizabeth, and Krysia Spirydowicz. 1999. *Gordion: Wooden Furniture.* Ankara.

Sinos, Rebecca Hague. 1994. "Godlike Men: A Discussion of the Murlo Procession Frieze." In De Puma and Small 1994, 100–117.

Small, Jocelyn Penny. 1994. "Eat, Drink, and Be Merry: Etruscan Banquets." In De Puma and Small 1994, 85–94.

Steingräber, Stephan. 1979. *Etruskische Möbel.* Rome.

1986. *Etruscan Painting.* New York.

2002. "Ahnenkult und bildliche Darstellungen von Ahnen in etruskischen und unteritalischen Grabgemälden aus vor römischer Zeit." In Højte 2002, 127–158.

Steuernagel, Dirk. 1998. *Menschenopfer und Mord am Altar: Griechische Mythen in Etruskischen Gräbern.* Wiesbaden.

Stewart, Andrew. 1990. *Greek Sculpture.* New Haven, CT.

Swaddling, Judith, ed. 1986. *Iron Age Artefacts in the British Museum.* London.

Swaddling, Judith, Susan Walker, and Paul Roberts, eds. 1995. *Italy in Europe: Economic Relations 700 BC–AD 50.* London.

Szilágyi, Janos G. 1992, 1998. *Ceramica etrusco-corinzia figurata I–II. Monumenti Etruschi* NS 7–8. Florence.

Theodossiev, Nikola. 1994. "The Thracian Ithyphallic Altar from Polianthos and the Sacred Marriage of the Gods." *Oxford Journal of Archaeology* 13:313–323.

Torelli, Mario. 1981. "Delitto religioso: qualche indizio sulla situazione in Etruria." In *Le délit religieux*. Table Ronde, Rome, 1978. Collection de l'École Française de Rome 48:1–7. Rome.

1986. "History: Land and People." In Bonfante 1986a, 47–65.

1990. "La 'Sedia Corsini,' monumento della genealogia etrusca dei Plautii." In *Mélanges Pierre Lévêque*, ed. M. M. Mactoux, E. Gerry, and M. Garrido-Hory, vol. 5, 355–367. Paris.

ed. 2000. *The Etruscans*. Catalogue of Exhibit at Palazzo Grassi, Venice. London.

Trendall, A. D. 1989. *Red Figure Vases of South Italy and Sicily*. London.

Tronchetti, Carlo. 1986. "Nuragic Statuary from Monte Prama." In *Studies in Sardinian Archaeology II: Sardinia in the Mediterranean*, ed. Miriam Balmuth, 41–59. Ann Arbor, MI.

Tuck, Anthony S. 2006. "Singing the Rug: Patterned Textiles and the Origins of Indo-European Metrical Poetry." *AJA* 110:539–550.

Turfa, Jean MacIntosh. 1986. "International Contacts: Commerce, Trade, and Foreign Affairs." In Bonfante 1986a, 66–91.

von Blanckenhagen, Peter 1976. "Puerilia." In *In Memoriam Otto J. Brendel*, ed. Larissa Bonfante and Helga von Heintze, 37–41. Berlin.

von Eles, Patrizia, ed. 1994. *Il dono delle Eliadi: Ambre e Oreficerie dei principi etruschi di Verucchio. Studi e documenti di archeologia*. Quaderni 4. Verucchio. Rimini, Museo Civico Archeologico.

ed. 2002. *Guerriero e Sacerdote. Autorità e comunità nell'Età del Ferro a Verucchio: La Tomba del Trono*. Quaderni di Archeologia dell'Emilia Romagna 6. Florence.

von Hase, Friedrich-Wilhelm. 2000. "Culture mediterranee e mondo celtico tra VII e VI secolo a.C." In *Principi Etruschi* 2000, 79–90.

Wagner-Hasel, Beate. 2002. "The Graces and Colour Weaving." In Llewellyn-Jones 2002, 17–32.

Warden, P. Gregory. 1994. "Amber, Ivory, and the Diffusion of the Orientalizing Style Along the Adriatic Coast: Italic Amber in the University Museum (Philadelphia)." In De Puma and Small 1994, 134–143.

2004. "Men, Beasts, and Monsters: Pattern and Narrative in Etruscan Art." In *Greek Vase Painting: Form, Figure, and Narrative: Treasures of the National Archaeological Museum in Madrid*, ed. Gregory P. Warden, 51–56. Dallas, TX.

Wells, Peter S. 2001. *Beyond Celts, Germans and Scythians*. London.

Whitehouse, Ruth, ed. 1998. *Gender and Italian Archaeology: Challenging the Stereotypes*. London.

CHAPTER NINE

THE WORLD OF SITULA ART

Otto-Herman Frey

"Situla art" refers to the figured scenes on the bronze repoussé work of bucket-shaped wine containers called "situlas" made by the inhabitants of the Northern, Alpine regions of Italy, Switzerland, Austria, and Slovenia. These peoples spoke different languages, Venetic, Keltic, Rhaetic, and Illyrian, all of which – except Illyrian, which was never written – were written in a script derived from the Etruscan alphabet.[1] But their art and archaeology reflect a similar way of life: their feudal societies, ruled by tribal chiefs, seem to have had a lot in common with those of the Homeric kings. Figured representations on bronze vessels, pottery, and rock engravings of the Hallstatt period from this area of the eastern Alps give insights into the conceptual framework of the people living there, as well as their lifestyle, many details of which correspond to those of Mediterranean cultures. Examples from the Veneto region of northern Italy, especially from Este, show how earlier dress styles, weaponry, and activities, like those of the Benvenuti situla of about 600 BC, continue to be reflected in the later situlas of the fifth and fourth centuries BC. The cultural groups represented by situla and Este art, whose style and content were indebted to Etruscan art, acted as intermediaries with the classical world for Central Europe and transmitted elements to the Celtic art of the fifth century BC.

This chapter deals with connections between the "barbarians" on the northern border of Italy not yet known from ancient literary sources and the Greek world mediated by Italic and Etruscan culture, as shown in situla art.[2] It is divided into four parts. First, I will speak about situla art in the traditional, strict sense;[3] second, about the Veneto/Este style; and third, about older examples or predecessors of this art. Finally, I will explore some contacts with and distinctions from the figural style found in early Celtic contexts.

Situla Art in the Traditional Sense

The friezes of human figures on these decorated bronze-handled buckets, or situlas (Fig. 9.1), can help us visualize a chapter of European history whose development ended in the fourth century BC because of the turbulence and new ideas brought in by Celtic migrations, which affected large areas. The most important situlas had been discovered in the second half of the nineteenth century.[4] Apart from these situlas, other types of vessels and a number of belt plates with similar decoration were found. Altogether they amount to about sixty items, some only in small fragments. They were excavated from tombs and other find-complexes of the late Hallstatt period of the fifth and early fourth centuries BC in the east Alpine zone, between Tyrol – with the upper Adige Valley – to the west and Slovenia to the east. They thus belong to a prehistoric context, in regions that were later inhabited by Raeti and groups of Veneti, and perhaps also by Illyrians and others, by the beginning of Roman occupation.

I will not digress into a discussion of the ethnicity of these peoples; it is enough to recognize that we already encounter these same peoples in previous centuries. They spoke different languages, but they had acquired a similar lifestyle.[5] It has long been supposed that the figural friezes of the situlas reflected the activities of these local populations, because their figured decoration depicts objects that were actually placed in the graves as funerary gifts. The images on the situlas almost certainly represented ideas belonging to the sacral sphere or determined by a vision of an otherworldly existence, but the artistic realization of such ideas was based on a reality, a common way of life – specifically, of course, the style of life of the upper class.

To the finds from the Alpine sites should be added several examples from a different context, that of the Etruscan cities in the southeast Po Valley. These cities must have been open and attracted other foreign peoples, apart from the Greeks – Umbrians, Veneti, and others, as the

9.1. Situla from Magdalenska Gora, Slovenia. Naturhistorisches Museum, Vienna. Late Hallstatt (ca. 400 BC). (Lucke and Frey 1962, plate 34.)

finds show. It is an interesting phenomenon, which, however, can only be touched on briefly in this chapter.[6]

Hardly any finds of this art have been made in the central Veneto area, with its pre-urban centers such as Este, Padua, and so on. In this region, spreading far into the Alpine valleys and to the Etruscan centers farther to the south, we see a slightly different art style, with different subjects; until the late sixth and early fifth centuries BC these were predominantly representations of animals, with few anthropomorphic pictures.[7] This Venetian style harks back to the seventh century and continues into Roman times, mostly with votive tablets from the Venetian sanctuaries that show, for example, the dedicators. Statuettes are also known from the sanctuaries. This mixed style overlaps with that of the situlas, so that

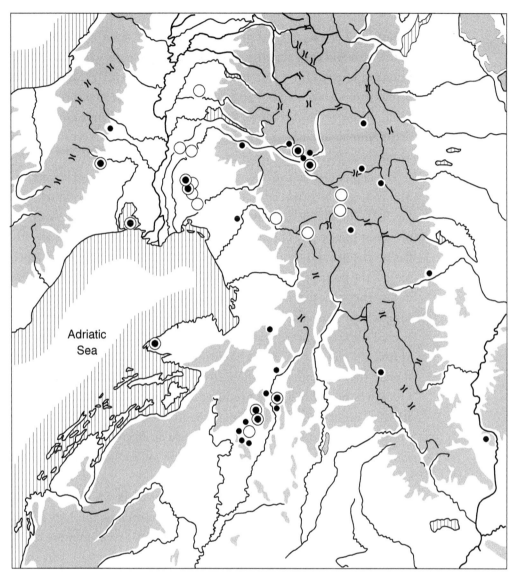

Map 9.1. Distribution map of finds of situla art in the strict sense, together with contemporary examples in the Venetian/Este style. (After Frey 1999, fig. 3.)

in spite of the differences, many scholars include this Veneto art style under the heading of situla art. The distribution map shows the finds of situla art in the strict sense, together with contemporary material in the Veneto/Este style (Map 9.1).[8]

Besides these two main groups there exist further contemporary works, with related decoration, in the southern Alps and the adjacent areas.[9]

Nearly all dated pieces of situla art in the strict sense belong to graves of the fifth and early fourth centuries BC. Only two much earlier exceptions are known: the situla Benvenuti from Este and a fragment of a helmet from Magdalenska Gora in Slovenia.[10] These two earlier pieces could, however, be claimed as Este/Venetian works from a comparison of the animals and plants represented with those on late seventh-century works from Este.[11] I will return to this question later.

The depictions on the later situlas are relatively primitive in comparison to Greek or Etruscan examples of the late Archaic period (cf., e.g., Fig. 9.2). The shields and clothing of the men cover their bodies without revealing their pose. Often no arms are shown at all. The feet are still flat on the ground. In the boxing matches, which are frequently represented, the pugilists with their widely swinging arms look different, but in fact they repeat a single scheme. Such a boring repetition of motifs suggests the existence of a kind of pattern book.[12] The animals in the animal friezes are nearly identical and are distinguished only by antlers or horns. Fantastic creatures like winged lions and sphinxes are rarely shown: they do appear on the Certosa situla from Bologna (Fig. 9.3), which was probably locally produced and has closer links to Etruscan art than other items.[13] The depictions in the Este style often present winged beings.[14] On the other hand, situlas from the Alpine region sometimes depict typical local game of the mountains, such as ibexes or a chamois.[15]

The figure style is modeled on Etruscan or other Middle Italic prototypes. This is clearly seen in such typical motifs as the legs shown dangling from the jaws of beasts of prey (Fig. 9.3) or, even more often, plants growing out of the mouths of herbivores (Fig. 9.4).[16] In some scenes a derivation from ancient models is obvious. The uniformly repeated gesture of the boxers, with one arm outstretched, the other swinging back, and between them the prize for the winner in the form of a precious vessel or a helmet, resemble early Greek and Etruscan representations, though their attitude is a bit different, and they wear a special kind of hand guard instead of boxing bandages.[17] A fragment (insufficiently restored) of a situla from Novo Mesto in Slovenia presents a duel between two warriors: they are armed with their local battle-axes, but fight, like the heroes on Greek vases, over the body of a fallen man stretched out at their feet.[18]

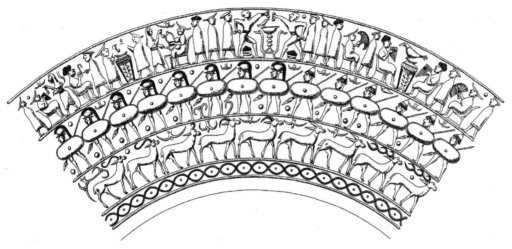

9.2. Figure friezes of situla in the Providence, Rhode Island, School of Design. 550–500 BC. (Lucke and Frey 1962, Suppl. plate 1.)

9.3. Figure friezes of the Certosa situla from Bologna. Ca. 500 BC. (Lucke and Frey 1962, plate 64.)

On the other hand, many details correspond closely to the east Alpine pattern. In addition to the items already enumerated, several weapons, especially the battle-axes, are significant for local traditions. The unusual musical instruments also fit in this context.[19] Certain forms of hats worn by seated men at banquets (Figs. 9.2–9.6, 9.8, 9.12; Bonfante, Chapter 8 in this volume, Fig. 8.6)[20] characterize them as persons of rank. The local aspect of the narrative scenes is suggested not only by such objects, but also by the activities represented. Of the various hunting

Fig. 9.4. Figure friezes of a situla from Vace (Watsch), Slovenia. Ca. 500 BC. (Lucke and Frey 1962, plate 73.)

scenes that appear, stag hunting on horseback[21] must have been typical for this area: the only parallels from the South are distant East Greek monuments.

A central subject of situla art is the feast or symposium,[22] which is represented in a particular manner. We see men of high status, sometimes holding scepters or fans in their hands and wearing their characteristic hats, being served drinks. Some of them play musical instruments. No single person is particularly emphasized; obviously, the scenes refer to an aristocratic society of persons of equal rank. They are not reclining on couches like symposiasts in the South, but are sitting on chairs,[23] as was still the custom in seventh-century BC Etruria. Only once, in situla art of the Este style, is a man shown stretched out on a *kline* as he is served a drink[24] (Bonfante, Chapter 8 in this volume, Fig. 8.6). Nearby, intoxicating drinks are mixed in large cauldrons placed on elaborate stands, reserved for these notables. Male and female servants carry on these and other activities. There are some scenes of couples making love, but women of rank do not participate in the festivities.[25] They are shown serving drinks to the men, but they do not take part in the symposium on equal terms with the men, and their status is not comparable to that of women in Etruscan art.

An important question is whether certain classical images that appear in this art were merely adopted as artistic conventions or instead referred to an external reality. To what extent was life in the Alpine region in fact influenced and transformed by the culture reflected in the art that

9.5. Scenes of competitive sports: "boxing match" with prize, horse race, and chariot race. Banquet scene (upper left). Situla from Kuffarn, Lower Austria. Ca. 400 BC. (Lucke and Frey 1962, plate 75.)

developed in this period under the stimulus of the South? To answer this question, we will examine more closely some representations of sport in situla art.

First of all, it is interesting to note that, as in Greece or early Etruria, we recognize actual sporting events. Local features appear in the boxing matches and in the horse races and biga- or two-horse chariot races. The boxing scenes, for example, show the typical hand-guards, shaped like dumbbells, secured by a strap over the back of the hand; these are also shown on statuettes of boxers from the same region.[26] The wrists are bandaged. These pugilists are naked, apart from a belt, which may mark the line below which low punches are not allowed. Judges are sometimes on hand, carrying rods or staffs to make sure that the combatants keep to the rules (Fig. 9.5). All these athletic contests are generally closely connected with the banquets.

Most of the prizes are helmets,[27] the insignia of a free elite. In the depiction of a boxing match on the situla in the Museum of the Rhode Island School of Design in Providence, the clothes of the pugilists lie neatly folded at their feet, with the typical hats on top, showing that the fighters belong to the upper class (Fig. 9.2). Undoubtedly, these bouts were not a barbarous scuffle, but competitions in which free aristocrats pitted their strength and dexterity according to rules set by society. The contests do not seem to take place in honor of gods, however, with a laurel branch or a similar token as the sole reward.[28] Instead, someone from the elite, or an organized community, must have been responsible for the presentation of such luxurious prizes as the precious weapons or bronze vessels that were given to the winners.

A slightly different situation is reflected in the chariot races (Fig. 9.5), whose representation is clearly inspired by Etruscan motifs, such as the scene of the lead charioteer, who turns to look back to see whether he is being overtaken, or the judge on the Arnoaldi situla from Bologna (Fig. 9.7), who meets the chariots and holds out the victory fillet in his hand.[29]

Yet other details seem to derive from local ideas and customs. The funny coattail of the short chiton of the charioteers on the situla from Kuffarn (Fig. 9.5) is a motif that also turns up on statuettes from the Tyrol.[30] The high pointed caps on this situla, a special costume of the charioteers and of the jockeys in the horse race, have a close parallel in the depiction of riders on a terra-cotta frieze from Murlo in northern Etruria[31] (Bonfante, Chapter 8 in this volume, Fig. 8.5a). Another clear link with Etruria – and not with Greece – is the way the charioteers tie the reins in a knot around their waists, a dangerous trick the Romans also learned from the Etruscans.[32] Typical of local types are the light chariots with metal fittings in spiral form on the railing, for which good comparisons are found in two chariot graves of Sesto Calende near the Lago Maggiore, dating from about 600 BC.[33] Pictures of such early vehicles are known from central Italy as well.[34] Distinguishing local and imported motifs in the representations of sports can serve to clarify both the cultural contacts of the situla area with Etruria and local developments illustrating what the Alpine peoples made of such links.

Military scenes offer further examples.[35] On a belt plaque from Vace in Slovenia two mounted warriors, accompanied by their shield-bearers on foot, are fighting a lively duel with spear and battle-axe (Fig. 9.6). It looks like a picture of two noblemen in single knightly combat. But is it a representation of a contemporary event or of a mythical episode from long ago? In favor of an interpretation as a contemporary event is the fact that no other scenes suggest mythical themes. The parades that are often shown, divided into different formations of heavily equipped

9.6. Mounted warriors fighting, with spear bearers on foot. Belt-plate from Vace (Watsch), Slovenia. Ca. 500 BC. (Lucke and Frey 1962, plate 54.)

9.7. Procession of soldiers: military parade with trumpeter and military standard. Detail. Figure frieze from the Arnoaldi situla, Bologna. Ca. 400 BC. (Lucke and Frey 1962, plate 63.)

warriors, reflect well-organized military forces led by officers on horseback, with commands given by trumpets and *signa* (Figs. 9.3, 9.7).[36] As a whole, the armor is local, with only a few resemblances to early Etruscan or Italic outfits.

Of special interest are the great round shields without a middle boss with which one of the units on the Certosa situla is equipped (Fig. 9.3). These are typical hoplite shields, carried on the arm by an armband, the *porpax*, and with the *antilabé*, the handle for the hand at the rim. Such weapons are characteristic for men on an equal level, fighting shoulder to shoulder in close-packed ranks. This detail reflects the widespread phalanx tactic developed in Greece and adopted in Etruria in the course of the seventh century BC; and it perhaps suggests that actual Greek or Etruscan military standards were imitated. The efficient armies represented on the situlas would presuppose a certain basic social structure that may correspond with the great citylike centers of northern Italy as far as the southern Alps.

9.8. Ritual procession. Detail. "Situla" from Welzelach, Tyrol. (Lucke and Frey 1962, plate 76.)

Finally, we have representations of rituals. On the Certosa situla is depicted a procession (Fig. 9.3).[37] Several men of rank carry various objects, some of them half-covered by their cloaks. Two carry a big bucket – an urn, or more likely a container for a special drink; another shoulders a bundle of spits to roast meat. Following are servants and women carrying vessels, baskets, and firewood. A notable leads a bull on a rope and a servant leads a ram, almost certainly to be slaughtered. All the details are very similar to ancient scenes of sacrifices. An interpretation as a sacred ritual is strengthened by another cortège on the situla from Welzelach in Tyrol, where notables with helmets walk along playing the syrinx, accompanied by women again carrying vessels (Fig. 9.8).[38] For whom was the ritual meant? This the iconography cannot tell us.

The scenes depicted on the situlas do, however, allow us to understand that they represent the men of rank of that world in the way they wanted to be seen. Their noble qualities and privileges are highlighted in the actions and narratives depicted, but also their power, and thus their responsibilities as heads of society. They are responsible for the rites, and they defend the community as well as organizing the military forces: so, we encounter them killing dangerous beasts of prey that are attacking livestock or other peaceful animals. In the same way, the significance of the image of the plowman can be interpreted apart from

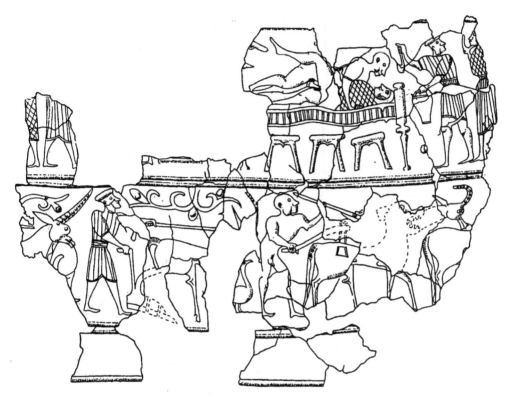

9.9. Symplegma (upper register) and scenes of plowing and hunting (lower register). Fragment of cista from Sanzeno, Trento province. (Lucke and Frey 1962, plate 67.)

his actual function, in his original meaning as a part of fertility or other rites (Fig. 9.9).

No myths are depicted, as they are on Greek vases. Obviously, the scenes do not reflect mythical events recalled to mind. Instead they mirror typical scenes in the life of the aristocrats and, we suppose, in their desired existence after death.[39] All have a timeless quality.

Perhaps the find contexts can give a hint of their relative importance and their meaning. In Slovenia, and around the Etruscan centers in upper Italy, the buckets are funerary gifts. In Tyrol, on the other hand, they are often offerings in hoards and sacred places, frequently damaged and preserved only in fragments. Particularly interesting for their evaluation is the fact that several belt-plaques from Slovenia, likewise known only from fragments, suggest that the plaques were riveted together without considering the decoration at all, while other items were tightly bent, leaving the figures unrecognizable; yet such objects served as magic gifts for the graves.[40] They clearly must have had a significance beyond that

9.10. Armed warriors on a sheath with a dagger from "predio Franchini," Este, tomb 18. (Frey 1969, plate 66.17.)

of the object itself, or of the figures pictured in the scenes that decorated it. Various attempts have been made to find a symbolic background for several depictions, but they are only suggestions and have not yet been convincingly proven.

Situlas in the Veneto/Este Style

In the related, contemporary Venetian/Este works, apart from the animals and fabulous creatures, we have images of warriors (Fig. 9.10), boxers, and other persons.[41] But here there is no narrative, scenic representation. From the fifth or even the late sixth century BC, we also have a great many figural votive offerings from sanctuaries with local images.[42] Most interesting are some of the new subjects that appear on later works. From a rich female tomb from Este of the first half of the third century BC comes a bronze bench, so reduced in size that it functions only as a symbolic throne. On its back are depicted four harnessed horses driven by a wolf. The scene is thought to be mythical, the oldest one that can be linked to a literary Venetic tradition.[43] From the same period come Venetic inscriptions with references to offerings and to gods,[44] but it is open to question whether we already have any anthropomorphic representation of local gods or goddesses.[45]

Predecessors of the Situla and the Venetian/Este Style

On the Certosa situla, a regiment of soldiers wears helmets reinforced with round plaques and nails (Fig. 9.3), the so-called *Schüsselhelme*, which are also known from a number of earlier tombs in the region.[46] These and other items pictured on the Certosa situla all belong to an earlier phase of the Hallstatt period, separated by over 100 years from the Certosa find, which is dated by the Attic *lekythos* of 490/480 BC it contained. Other details represented show a similar time difference. Could the Certosa situla be an heirloom in a later tomb context?[47] But other works too show that situla art in the traditional strict sense is a relatively late outcome of a much longer development of pictorial creations. The figure style of the situlas does not reflect late archaic models; its roots reach much further back.[48] We can suppose an initial phase at least as early as the end of the seventh century BC, since woodcarvings or designs in other materials could have transmitted older motifs to the engravers of the situlas. The richly decorated finds of carved wooden furniture from Verucchio, not far away, seem to confirm such an idea (Figs. 8.8a–c).[49]

Very important in this context is the Benvenuti situla from Este previously referred to, of typical Venetian shape (Fig. 9.11);[50] its find context points to a time around 600 BC. In spite of some differences, its decoration gives the impression of being a predecessor of that of the later situlas. Depicted in the upper zone is a man, again with a wide-brimmed hat, as well as a patterned coat and pointed shoes. He sits on a real Etruscan throne[51] – not its derivation, as shown on the later situlae – and, as in early Etruria, his feet rest on a footstool. In one hand he holds

9.11. Figure friezes of the Benvenuti situla from Este. Ca. 600 BC. (Lucke and Frey 1962, plate 65.)

a drinking vessel, in the other long reins, which are attached to a horse that is being cared for by a groom. Clearly he is a nobleman, the owner of well-treated horses. Probably the motif in the second zone, with a herdsman and his dog tending a cow, signifies that the nobleman also possessed a herd of cattle.

Is this man an outstanding chief, or does he belong to the more or less oligarchic society that is so obviously presented on the later situlas? Nearby are other persons, also wearing wide-brimmed hats, and on the side of the boxing match is what looks like an empty throne, on which is placed a bundle of garments with such a hat on top. Do these persons belong to the same rank? The naked pugilists have a slightly different stance from those we saw earlier, but they have, once again, the local hand-guards shaped like dumbbells.

Contrasting with these scenes are the series of animals and fantastic creatures in the Orientalizing style: sphinxes, a dressed centaur,[52] a real lion, winged, and a griffin of Etruscan shape. The lower zone is not, as usual, reserved for an animal frieze, but is used instead to represent successful military events. The warriors, armed with spears and helmets, wear oval shaped belts and short pants, or *perizomata*, as in early Etruria. One of them is protected by a corselet whose shoulder-pieces, the *epomides*, are clearly visible,[53] and he attacks another man blowing a horn, who falls back over a plant. There is also a chariot, showing the typical railing with curved terminals, driven by a single man of higher rank who is supervising the events. Of special interest are the soldiers leading away prisoners whose hands are bound in front of them. They carry their shields on a sling, the *telamon* of the heroic age, a feature that had at this time already been completely abandoned in the South.

The warriors have large round shields without middle bosses, though perhaps not as large as the later shields of real hoplites on votive tablets from Este.[54] A contemporary fragment of a helmet from Slovenia also depicts warriors with heavier shields.[55] These warriors in heavy armor and probably of equal status attacked in closed ranks, according to their shields. They may be compared with soldiers of the Greek and Etruscan urban centers, and fit in the context of the large, densely populated communities in the North, such as Este.

These two monuments, the helmet and the Benvenuti situla, are closely related to the later situla art; they tell the story of contacts between the region under consideration and the south, especially Etruria, at the time of the Orientalizing and early archaic style. Yet a third work can be mentioned in this context,[56] a pendant from a rich late seventh-century BC grave in Bologna (Fig. 9.12). This typically local pendant in the form of an axe, a so-called tintinnabulum, was made from two sheets of bronze fastened together: it was originally a kind of locket, or rattle, as shown by the bead designed to rattle in the hollow space between the bronze sheets. Its design, worked in repoussé, was revealed by the cleaning of the surface. It shows women of rank in a domestic setting, dressed like the contemporary female figures from northern Etruria or on the later situlae. They are spinning, weaving, and combing wool, sitting on real Etruscan chairs. The decorative filling motifs of plants are very similar to those on the Benvenuti situla. Is it possible that it was an Etruscan artist from Bologna who engraved all these works, which exemplify the birth of the Orientalizing style in the north?

Several bronzes decorated with similar representations of plants and animals, also close to the Benvenuti situla,[57] are found over a large area, from the Picenum in the Southeast up to Slovenia, to the Lombard lakes and to Hallstatt in the North, showing that the impetus of Orientalizing culture was very strong outside Etruria.

Orientalizing Influence and Local Production

This willing and active adoption of Etruscan and Greek culture trends so far in the North, and their transformation in a local lifestyle, show

9.12. Scenes of women carding and spinning wool and weaving on a double-story loom. Bronze tintinnabulum from Bologna, Arsenale Militare. Ca. 600 BC. (Bonfante 2003, fig. 2.)

that the influence of the Orientalizing culture here was considerable. Such influence can be found even farther on in the eastern Alps, where a number of other works of imagery tell a similar story. On the bronze buckets from Kleinklein in Styria, decorated in a much more primitive technique, the stylized hunting scenes are very vivid (Fig. 9.13).[58] A scene of the hunt for an Alpine bear shows the hunter with a huge dog; he may be holding a rope loop. His equipment, which is that of a noble warrior, with shield, helmet, and battle-axe, is out of context. There are also what are probably scenes of feasts, even with pugilists, but the musical instruments are different from those on the situlas. The schematic nature of some of these representations is shown by the appearance of human legs dangling beneath the bellies of horses, although the bodies of the riders do not appear. There are other vessels and statuettes from this area, the most famous monument of which is the cult-wagon from Strettweg in Styria, with its clear Etruscan/Italic connections.[59]

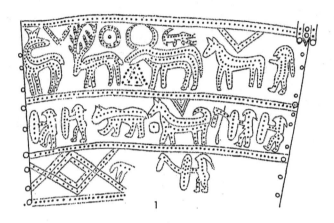

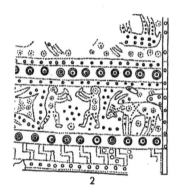

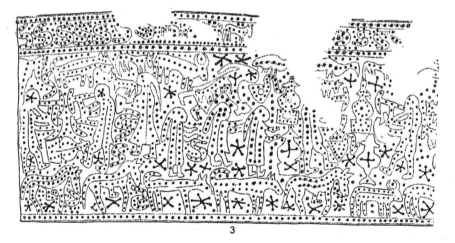

9.13. 1–3. Hunting scene, pugilists, feast, and various animals. Details of buckets from Kleinklein, Styria. (Frey 1999, fig. 2.)

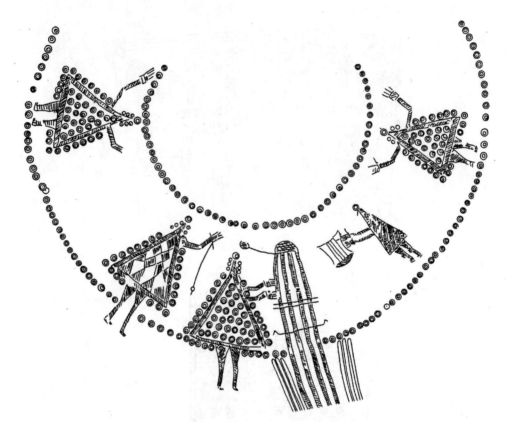

9.14. Aristocratic ladies spinning and weaving, accompanied by a musician playing a lyre. Terra-cotta vase from Sopron, west Hungary. Hallstatt period. (Frey 1980, 99.)

It is impossible to examine here more thoroughly such early evidence of the Northern Orientalizing style. We will only briefly consider some primitive designs scratched on pottery of the same period found still farther north.[60] Their relationship of the style to the Basarabi culture in Southeast Europe is perceptible in the stylization of various elements. The contents, however, are local, and show Mediterranean influence as well.

Local Production

A vessel from Sopron, in the frontier region between Austria and Hungary, shows a stag hunt on horseback.[61] Still more interesting is a scene in a domestic setting, on the urn of another burial (Fig. 9.14),[62] showing richly dressed, high-ranking ladies skillfully spinning and weaving. Next to them stands a man with a lyre in his hands, apparently singing. But what is he singing for the ladies?[63] Tales of gods or love songs? That it was possible for a singer to have a high status is suggested by comparison with Homer (*Odyssey* 3, 267f.), who relates that before leaving for Troy, Agamemnon entrusted his wife to the care of an ancient bard. Simple as the design is, it offers a clear glimpse of the highly cultured life, or imagined life, of the people in the east of the Hallstatt area. All these finds show that the earlier art of this area provided fertile ground for the rise of the phenomenon of situla art in a strict sense nearby, with its picture language allowing such a remarkable insight into an increasingly developed society on the fringe of the ancient world.

Of course, the documentation available to us is one-sided and leaves many questions open. We have an insufficient idea of the religious thought of these people. No gods are represented, as on Greek vases, unless the huge middle figure on the Strettweg wagon is a goddess.[64] And only a few scenes on the situlas seem to have a ritual character, as we have seen, with the possible exception of an urn from the early Hallstatt period with a depiction that may signify a sacrifice.[65] These are isolated instances of this kind of representation, and they give no real insight into religious ideas. In spite of such gaps in our knowledge, the substantial positive evidence we have provides as a whole a wealth of information.

Early Celtic Contexts

Finally, we must ask whether this culture area in the eastern Alps and upper Italy is a typical example of the spread of ancient, classical culture outside Greece and Etruria to the "barbaric" regions in the North. Perhaps it is a peculiar phenomenon, itself perhaps influencing development in the adjacent regions. The distribution map of situla art also shows finds north of the Alps and underlines the fact that such products were appreciated in the neighboring Celtic lands. Does this mean something more than a mere importing of art objects?

A noted related work is the famous La Tène A sword from Hallstatt.[66] On the scabbard are engraved various scenes, including a cortège of warriors. This decoration has long been regarded as evidence that a foreign, "Venetian" artist had depicted Celts.[67] The artist must also have been very familiar with Celtic artistic products, because the horses of the riders, for instance, show unmistakably La Tène ornaments on the hindquarters.

More pieces adorned only with animals could be mentioned. A pottery flask from Matzhausen in Bavaria offers not only a sequence of animals, but also the heraldic composition so typical of the La Tène style.[68] A fragment of a pottery bowl from Libkovice in Bohemia shows a stamped decoration of arcs, and in between them hares closely resembling the hares on belt-plates and other works in the Este style.[69] Further examples could be described. All these pieces have been explained as direct copies of east Alpine or Venetian works.

Even more interesting is the decoration of a Celtic *Schnabelkanne*, or beaked flagon, from Dürrnberg in the Salzburg region.[70] As on Etruscan prototypes, the handle-arms along the rim are in the form of lions, out of whose jaws surprisingly emerge long tendrils similar to the plants emerging from the mouths of herbivores in situla art. Is this motif misunderstood or is it intentionally changed and interpreted in a Celtic manner? A similar connection can be supported by another example, the engraving on a girdle clasp from the Glauberg in Hesse[71] with the end of its hook in the form of a typical Celtic wild beast threatening a human head. On its plate are engraved two symmetrically arranged predatory animals with tendrils emerging from their mouths (Fig. 9.15, top). A number of works from the Veneto also offer comparisons for such a motif, for example a herbivore on the lid of a bronze bucket from Este (Fig. 9.15, bottom).[72]

The same Glauberg tomb from which the girdle clasp came produced a richly ornamented sword (Fig. 9.16 [4–5]).[73] On the back of its scabbard are depicted – among other motifs – a pair of horses looking back, a composition that we can compare to that of roes and hares in the same attitude on bronze vessels and girdle plates from the Veneto (Fig. 9.16, 9.1–9.3). On the front of the scabbard is found a similar composition of animals; these, with their big round eyes and more rigid legs, have a considerably more Celtic look. A second sword from a nearby tomb (Fig. 9.16, 9.6) shows terrifying dogs or other wild animals in the same attitude, deriving from the same models that were transformed into the dreadful products of the Celtic imagination.[74]

There is little doubt that apart from direct Etruscan/Italic connections, influences of the art of the east Alpine region were also at work

9.15. Top: plate of a girdle hook from Glauberg, Hesse. Bottom: herbivorous animal on a lid from Este, Villa of Benvenuti tomb 124. (Frey 1969, 29.12; 64; 65.)

in early Celtic design, as can be shown by many more examples.[75] Yet the resulting Celtic works are quite different. Situlas as well as other products of the art of Este, with their scenic descriptive depictions, are lively, cheerful, and human, and they mirror a civilized society with local coloring. Though the pictures seem to describe no specific single events, but only classes of peoples, the whole effect is very close to the imagery of the ancient classical world. The early La Tène Celts relied on the same

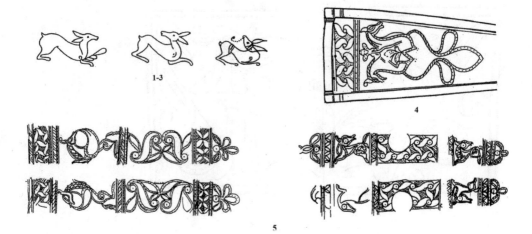

9.16. 1–3. Animals of situlas from Este. 4. Detail on the back of a scabbard from Glauberg, Hesse, tomb 1. 5. Decoration on front of same scabbard. 6. Decoration on scabbard, Glauberg, Hesse, tomb 2. (Frey 2007, fig. 15.)

art patterns, but they chose for their depictions decorative ornamental designs, distorted human faces, and weird magic beasts, figures whose roots were in their own religious traditions and served as symbols for their specific mentality.

Conclusion

In this survey of situla art, the art of handled buckets of the east Alpine region decorated in repoussé with human figures, I have examined the kinds of scenes depicted on objects of situla art in the traditional, strict sense. I have also looked at related phenomena in neighboring regions, specifically the Veneto/Este style, and at older examples or predecessors of this art, as well as local variants. Finally, contacts with and distinctions from the early Celtic figural style have been explored.

Most interesting in the context of this volume are the connections this material illustrates between "barbarians" on the northern border of Italy, not known from ancient literary sources, and the Greek world mediated by Italic and Etruscan culture. Figured representations on bronze vessels, pottery, and rock engravings of the Hallstatt period from the area of the eastern Alps give insights into the conceptual framework of the people living there, as well as into their lifestyle, many details of which correspond to those of Mediterranean cultures. Examples from the Veneto region of northern Italy, especially from Este, show how earlier dress styles, weaponry, and activities, as depicted on the Benvenuti situla of approximately 600 BC, continue to be reflected in the later situlas of the fifth and fourth centuries. The cultural groups represented by situla and Este art were indebted to Etruscan art for their style and content. They, in turn, acted as intermediaries with the classical world for Central Europe and transmitted many elements to the richly imaginative decorative Celtic art of the fifth century BC.

Notes

1. Bonfante 1981, 111–134.
2. I am very much indebted to Larissa Bonfante and to the late Stuart Wheeler for their invitation to participate in the conference in Richmond, Virginia, in the spring of 2003. For publication I have left my text nearly unchanged; the notes therefore contain not only the necessary references, but also some further comments that I could not include in my original lecture. I am extremely thankful to Mrs. Catherine Errington, Marburg, who very kindly corrected my poor English.
3. See especially the extensive documentation in the old book by Lucke and Frey 1962 (abbreviated L.-F.). Since this book gives a full interpretation of the representations, I only occasionally quote more recent studies. The latest comprehensive publication, with an ample bibliography and a detailed attempt to explain the scenes, Huth 2003, was published too late to be incorporated into the discussion. My last article about situla art provides a list of new finds together with a distribution map: Frey 1992, especially note 21 with fig. 2. For further supplements, see Dal Ri 1992; Gleirscher 1994, with fig. 3; Sydow 1995, No. 329; Kris 1997, 24ff. T. 37–39, appendixes 3 and 4; Egg 1999, especially 339f.; Tomedi and Appler 2001; Zeller 2001, 79f., fig. 51.
4. For the research history, see Frey 1969, chapter 1.
5. Of course, to present a more complete picture, we would have to analyze other material aside from the objects of figurative art. However, in this brief contribution, only these could be treated.
6. The same ideas are expressed by Torelli 1984, 189ff.; see also, e.g., Malnati and Manfredi 1991.
7. Frey 1969. Rather than including a long list of publications and important studies by our Italian colleagues, I cite the summarizing work of Capuis 1993 and the more recent two volumes by Chieco Bianchi and Ruta Serafini 2002, both with ample bibliographies.

8. After Frey 1999, fig. 3.
9. I cannot refer to them in this limited chapter. Some have been included in the catalogue of the exhibition, *Mostra dell'arte delle situle* (1961), which started the modern discussion of this art style.
10. The Benvenuti situla: Frey 1969, No. 4. An improved drawing can be seen in Fogolari and Prosdocimi 1988. For the find of Magdalenska Gora, see Egg 1980a.
11. Frey 1969.
12. The problem is briefly stated in Frey 1966b. For the bucket of Treviso, see Gerhardinger 1991, No. 46.
13. Apart from the Certosa situla, L.-F. No. 4, compare L.-F. No. 2: Appiano/Eppan.
14. Frey 1969; Chieco Bianchi and Ruta Serafini 2002.
15. L.-F. No. 1.
16. See the lions with human legs in their mouths, lower register of figs. 4 and 5; and see the deer with plants in fig. 5, lower register. For the motif, see Bocci 1965 and Bonfante, Chapter 8, in this volume.
17. Cf. here and further on Lucke and Frey 1962. Thuillier 1985, 261ff., thinks of a *caestus*, reinforced with metal. But I share the opinion of Lucke that the hand-guards are made of light material to soften the blows and not to shed the blood of the contestants.
18. Frey 1976, 584f., from Tumulus III in Kandija, grave 33. There exists no drawing. For the find see Knez 1986, 87.
19. See Eibner 1980, 1987, 1994, and, e.g., Lawergren 1993, 75.
20. For the hats, and also for the way of dressing, see Bonfante 1981, 18ff.
21. L.-F. No. 39.
22. Several authors want to integrate the whole scenario of situla art in such a feast, for example Hoernes 1894; Kromer 1980; see also Frey 1986, 203ff.
23. E.g., Zuffa 1965; Bonfante 1981, 21f.
24. L.- F. No. 5, or Frey 1969, No. 18.
25. The limited role women play in situla art – in contrast to their presence in wealthy tombs – confirms that the scenario depicted represents not daily life, but only a section from the life or the desired world of aristocratic men; see Frey 1976. For a more cautious evaluation of the role of women cf. Bonfante 1981, 40ff., and see Bonfante, Chapter 8, in this volume.
26. Von Merhart 1932; Egg 1980b. [Note: For a different interpretation, see Bonfante, Chapter 8, in this volume, text and Figure 8.11.]
27. The only exception is offered by the situla in Providence L.-F. No 1, with a basin on a stand between the contestants. A parallel is to be found in a clay relief from Este: Callegari 1925.
28. It is difficult to know how strong the religious background of such contests would have been at that time. The scenes on the situlas do not offer any clues. The comparisons often made with foreign cultures are problematic, for example Eibner 1981.
29. Lucke and Frey 1962, No. 3. Compare the judge of a running match on a stone relief from Chiusi: Jannot 1984, No. 198. On the Arnoaldi situla the detail may be damaged by a crack in the metal.
30. Kromer 1974.
31. Root 1973, 121–137.
32. Bronson 1965, 89; Thuillier 1996.

33. Ghislanzoni 1944, 26ff.
34. Woytowitsch 1978; Emiliozzi 1997.
35. Frey 1973.
36. Pauli 1973, 96ff.
37. L.-F. No. 4.
38. L.-F. No. 44. Cf. also the situla fragment from Nesactium. L.-F. No. 30e; Mihovilič 2001, plate 16,5.
39. I am not so sure about this in the unique battle scene with a ship from Nesactium. Other pictures from the same situla, however, offer the ordinary repertoire: Mihovilič 2001, 113ff. figs. 108, 109.
40. See Brezje: L.-F., No. 17–18, with Barth 1999 and *Jahrb. RGZM* (Molnik) 1987, 787f.
41. Frey 1969, No. 16–18, 22, 31, 36, 49. Further examples are found in Callegari 1925; Fogolari and Prosdocimi 1988, figs. 54 and 121; Capuis and Ruta Serafini 2002; and others.
42. Pascucci 1990; Chieco Bianchi and Ruta Serafini 2002.
43. Capuis and Ruta Serafini 2002, 39ff. For the whole grave find, see Chieco Bianchi 1987.
44. A summary view is given by Capuis 1993, 178ff.; see especially Prosdocimi in Fogolari and Prosdocimi 1988, 221ff.
45. Giulia dei Fogolari 1956 called the female figures on the discs from Montebelluna goddesses. The oldest disc may belong to the late fourth century BC. This attribution has not been challenged so far. Other figures, such as the ones with the "sun disc" above the head, are often supposed to be priestesses. Cf. also Dämmer 1986, 48ff, 100ff.
46. Frey 1990, 231f.
47. Frey 1966a; 1969, 88ff. W. Lucke had already commented on the animal frieze of the Welzelach bucket, where the beast of prey is not only facing the herbivores but is hiding – in the manner of a hunter – between the trees (L.-F. No. 44). Again, on the Certosa situla (fig. 4), the depiction of the plowman has also become a genre scene: the man is driving his oxen home after work with his plow, no longer being used, on his shoulder. Such developments of situla art can be only briefly commented on here; they have not yet been thoroughly studied. Discernible are not only the gradual formation of the art style and the modification of older traditional motifs and of others more recently adopted but also, more importantly, changes of ideas and of the way of life as a background of the representations. Most of our pictures are of relatively late date, and when we interpret them we have to consider the time differences. We must differentiate between the probable reflections of earlier themes related mostly to religious ideas (cf. Kossack 1999), which were first expressed in our art under the influence of the Etruscan Orientalizing style, and the elements that have become a more or less conventional background within the conditions of the later period.
48. See Bonfante 1981, 15ff., for the reflection of seventh-century Etruscan dress in situla art.
49. Cf. Kossack 1992; von Eles 2002.
50. Frey 1969.
51. See, e.g., Zuffa 1965.
52. Compare, here and for the following, Bonfante 2003.
53. The last publication is Hansen 2003.
54. Frey 1973.

55. Egg 1980a.
56. Morigi Govi 1971.
57. Frey 1969.
58. Schmid 1933; Reichenberger and Dobiat 1985; Prüssing 1991; Frey 1999.
59. Aigner Foresti 1980; Egg 1996.
60. See Dobiat 1982; Nebelsick 1992; Reichenberger 2002; Huth 2003. For Basarabi connections cf. Metzner-Nebelsick 1992.
61. Eibner-Persy 1980, 63ff., 142ff. Taf. 28–29 Beil. 5.
62. Eibner-Persy 1980, 63ff., 133ff. Taf. 16–17 Beil. 4.
63. See Bonfante, Chapter 8, in this volume.
64. Aigner Foresti 1980; Egg 1996.
65. See, e.g., Reichenberger 2000, 118ff. plates 43 and 44.
66. Kromer 1959, 182f., plate 201a-b, 202; Krieger und Salzherren 1970, plates 78–81; the best photographs are in Kruta et al. 1978/1979, figs. 23 and 25; Frey 2004.
67. See, e.g., Jacobsthal 1969, 1f.
68. Torbrügge and Uenze 1968, 218ff., figs. 260 and 261; Jacobsthal 1969, No. 402; Schwappach 1974, 117ff.
69. Schwappach 1974, 123ff.
70. Jacobsthal 1969, No. 382; Moosleitner 1985.
71. *Ausstellung Frankfurt* 2002, No. 1.13.1: 196f. 242ff., figs. 246 and 247.
72. Frey 1969, No. 14.
73. *Ausstellung Frankfurt* 2002, No. 1.16: 154ff., 196f., 253, figs. 118, 176.
74. *Ausstellung Frankfurt* 2002, No. 2.9: 156f., 196f., 258f., figs. 121, 176.
75. See, e.g., Schwappach 1974, 116ff.; *Ausstellung Frankfurt* 2002, 194f., fig. 173.

Bibliography

Aigner Foresti, L. 1980. *Der Ostalpenraum und Italien: ihre kulturellen Beziehungen im Spiegel der anthropomorphen Kleinplastik aus Bronze des 7. Jh. s v. Chr*. Diss. Istituto di Studi Etruschi ed Italici 3. Florence.

Ausstellung Frankfurt 2002. *Das Rätsel der Kelten vom Glauberg. Glaube – Mythos – Wirklichkeit*. Stuttgart.

Barth, F. E. 1999. "Zu den im Situlenstil verzierten Gürtelblechen aus Brezje." *Slowenien. Arch. Korrbl*. 29:57–59.

Bocci, P. 1965. "Motivi etruschi sui bronzi atestini e alpini." In *Studi in onore di Luisa Banti*, ed. G. Camporeale, 69–79. Rome.

Bonfante, L. 1981. *Out of Etruria: Etruscan Influence North and South*. BAR International Series 103. Oxford.

   2003. *Etruscan Dress*. Updated edition, Baltimore and London. (Originally published 1975.)

Bronson, R. C. 1965. "Chariot Racing in Etruria." *Studi in onore di Luisa Banti*, G. Camporeale, ed., 89–106. Rome.

Callegari, A. 1925. "Este. – Ritrovamenti casuali di antichità paleo-venete." *Not. Scavi*, 333–337.

Capuis, L. 1993. I Veneti. *Società e cultura di un popolo dell'Italia preromana*. Milan.

Capuis, L., and A. M. Chieco Bianchi. 2006. *Este 2: La necropoli del Villa Benvenuti*. *MonAnt* 64, Serie monografica 7. Rome.

Capuis, L., and A. Ruta Serafini. 2002. "L'uomo alato, il cavallo, il lupo: tra arte delle situle e racconti adriatici." In *L'alto e medio adriatico tra VI e V secolo a. C.* Atti Convegno Internaz. Adria. *Padusa* n.s. 3 (2002): 35–55.

Chieco Bianchi, A. M. 1987. "Dati preliminari su nuove tombe di III sec. da Este." In *Celti ed Etruschi nell'Italia centro-settentrionale dal V secolo a. C. alla romanizzazione*, ed. D. Vitali, 191–232. Colloquio Internazionale, Bologna 1985. Bologna.

Chieco Bianchi, A. M., and A. Ruta Serafini, eds. 2002. "Il museo di Este: passato e futuro." In *Este preromana: una città e i suoi santuari*, 2 vols. Treviso.

Dal Ri, L. 1992. "Etruskische Einflüsse im Etschtal." In *Etrusker nördlich von Etrurien*. Akten Symposium Wien – Schloß Neuwaldegg 1989. L. Aigner Foresti, ed. *Österr. Akad. d. Wiss., phil.-hist. Kl. Sitzungsber. Wien* 589:71–91.

Dämmer, H.-W. 1986. *San Pietro Montagnon*. Mainz.

Dobiat, C. 1982. "Menschendarstellungen auf ostalpiner Hallstattkeramik. Eine Bestandsaufnahme." *Acta Arch. Hung* 34:279–322.

Egg, M. 1980a. "Zum Helmfragment von Magdalenska gora. Zbornik posvecen Stanetu Gabrovcu ob sestdesetletnici." *Situla* 20/21:241–249.

1980b. "Ein Caestuskämpfer im Römisch-Germanischen Zentralmuseum." *Arch. Korrbl.* 10:55–59.

1996. "Das hallstattzeitliche Fürstengrab von Strettweg bei Judenburg in der Obersteiermark." *Monogr. RGZM* 37. Mainz.

1999. "Waffenbrüder? Eine ungewöhnliche Bestattung der Frühlatènezeit in Novo mesto in Slowenien. Jahrb." *RGZM* 46: 317–356.

Eibner, A. 1980. "Musikleben in der Hallstattzeit. Betrachtungen zur *Musiké* anhand der bildlichen Darstellungen." *Mitt. Österr. Arbeitsgem. Ur- u. Frühgesch.* 30:121–148.

1981. "Darstellungsinhalte in der Kunst der Hallstattkultur." In *Die Hallstattkultur. Ber. Symposium Steyr 1980*, 261–296. Linz.

1987. "Musikleben in der Hallstattzeit. Betrachtungen zur "Musiké" anhand der bildlichen Darstellungen." In *Musik in Antike und Neuzeit. Quellen und Studien zur Musikgeschichte von der Antike bis in die Gegenwart* 1, 271–381. Frankfurt.

1994. "Music during the Hallstatt period. Observations on *Musiké* as Depicted on Iron Age Circumalpine Vessels." In *La pluridisciplinarité en archéologie musicale de L'ICTM*, Saint-Germain-en-Laye 1990. Asnières-sur-Oise 1994, 301–320.

Eibner-Persy, A. 1980. *Hallstattzeitliche Grabhügel von Sopron (Ödenburg)*. Eisenstadt.

Emiliozzi, A., ed. 1997. *Carri da guerra e principi etruschi*. Catalogo della mostra, Viterbo 1997–1998. Rome.

Fogolari, G. dei. 1956. "Dischi bronzei figurati di Treviso." *Boll. d'Arte* 41:1–10.

Fogolari, G. dei, and A. L. Prosdocimi. 1988. *I Veneti antichi. Lingua e cultura*. Padova.

Frey, O.-H. 1966a. "Der Ostalpenraum und die antike Welt in der frühen Eisenzeit." *Germania* 44:48–66.

1966b. "Eine figürlich verzierte Ziste in Treviso." *Germania* 44:66–73.

1969. *Die Entstehung der Situlenkunst. Studien zur figürlich verzierten Toreutik von Este*. Berlin.

1973. "Bemerkungen zur hallstättischen Bewaffnung im Südostalpenraum." *Arh. Vestnik* 24:621–636.

1976. "Bemerkungen zu figürlichen Darstellungen des Osthallstattkreises." In *Festschrift Richard Pittioni I. Arch. Austriaca*, Beih. 13:578–587. Vienna.

1980. "Die Westhallstattkreis im 6. Jahrhundert v. Chr." In *Die Hallstattkultur. Frühform europäischer Einheit*, 80–116. Schloss Lamberg, Steyr.

1986. "Les fêtes dans l'art des situles." *Ktema* 11:199–209.

1990. "Ein tönerner Kammhelm aus Populonia: Überlegungen zur Verbreitung früher Helme in Italien." *Gedenkschr. Jürgen Driehaus*, 225–234. Mainz.

1992. "Beziehungen der Situlenkunst zum Kunstschaffen Etruriens." In *Etrusker nördlich von Etrurien*, ed. L. Aigner-Foresti. Akten Symposium Wien – Schloß Neuwaldegg 1989. *Österr. Akad. d. Wiss., phil.-hist. Kl., Sitzungsber, Wien*. 589:93–101.

1999. "Il Veneto e il mondo di Hallstatt-La Tène." In *Protostoria e storia del 'venetorum angulus.'* Atti XX Convegno Studi Etruschi ed Italici, Portogruario – Quarto d'Altino – Este – Adria 1996, ed. O. Paoletti, 17–27. Pisa and Rome.

2004. "Zur Kampfesweise der Kelten." In *Ad fontes. Festschrift Gerhard Dobesch*, ed. Gerhard Dobesch, Herbert Heftner, and Kurt Tomaschitz, 645–651. Vienna.

2007. "Keltische Kunst. Celtic Art." *Die Kunde* N.F. 58:197–220.

Gerhardinger, M. E. 1991. *Reperti paleoveneti del Museo Civico di Treviso*. Rome.

Ghislanzoni, E. 1944. "Una nuova tomba di guerriero scoperta a Sesto Calende." In *Munera, raccolta di scritti in onore di Antonio Giussani*, A. Giussani, ed., 1–55. Milan.

Gleirscher, P. 1994. "Ein Schalenstein in einem späthallstattzeitlichen Häuptlingsgrab in Waisenberg (Gem. Völkermarkt, Kärnten)." *Arch. Österreichs* 5:46–50.

Hansen, L. 2003. *Die Panzerung der Kelten: Eine diachrone und interkulturelle Untersuchung eisenzeitlicher Rüstungen*. Kiel.

Hoernes, M. 1894. "Über die Situla von Watsch und verwandte Denkmäler." In *Verhandl. 42 Versammlung der deutschen Philologen und Schulmänner in Wien 1893*, 300–309. Leipzig.

Huth, Ch. 2003. *Menschenbilder und Menschenbild: Anthropomorphe Bildwerke der frühen Eisenzeit*. Berlin.

Jacobsthal, P. 1969. *Early Celtic Art*. Oxford. (Originally published 1944.)

Jahrbuch RGZM 34, 1987, 787f. (Molnik).

Jannot, J.-R. 1984. *Les reliefs archaïques de Chiusi*. Coll. Ecole Française de Rome 71. Rome.

Knez, T. 1986. *Novo Mesto I: Halstatski grobovi/Hallstattzeitliche Gräber*. Novo Mesto.

Kossack, G. 1992. "Lebensbilder, mythische Bilderzählungen und Kultfestbilder. Bemerkungen zu Bildszenen auf einer Thronlehne von Verucchio." In A

Festschrift zur 50jährigen Bestehen Inst. Ur- und Frühgeschichte Innsbruck. Univ. Forsch. Prähist. Arch. A. Lippert and K. Spindler, eds., 8:231–246. Bonn.

1999. Religiöses Denken in dinglicher und bildlicher Überlieferung Alteuropas aus der Spätbronze- und frühen Eisenzeit. (9.-6. Jahrhundert v. Chr. Geb.). Abhandl. Bayer. Akad. d. Wiss. phil.-hist. Kl. N. F. 116. Munich.

Krieger und Salzherren. 1970. Hallstattkultur im Ostalpenraum. Ausstellung Naturhist. Mus. Wien im RGZM. Mainz.

Kris, B. 1997. Novo Mesto IV. Ljubljana.

Kromer, K. 1959. Das Gräberfeld von Hallstatt. Florence.

1974. "Ein Votivfigürchen aus Südtirol." In Opuscula Iosepho Kastelic sexagenario dicata, Joze. Kastelic, Aleksander Jelocnik, ed. Situla 14/15:53–59.

1980. "Das Situlenfest. Versuch einer Interpretation der Darstellungen auf figural verzierten Situlen. Zbornik posvecen Stanetu Gabrovcu ob sestdesetletnici." Situla 20/21:225–240.

Kruta, V., M. Szabo, and E. Lessing. 1978/1979. Die Kelten: Entwicklung und Geschichte einer europäischen Kultur. Freiburg, Basel, and Vienna.

Lawergren, B. 1993. "Lyres in the West (Italy, Greece) and East (Egypt, the Near East), ca. 2000 to 400 B.C." Opuscula Romana 19:55–76.

Lucke, W., and O.-H. Frey. 1962. Die Situla in Providence (Rhode Island). Ein Beitrag zur Situlenkunst des Osthallstattkreises. Berlin. (Abbreviated L.-F.).

Malnati, L., and V. Manfredi. 1991. Gli Etruschi in Val Padana, Milan.

Merhart, G. von. 1932. "Venetoillyrische Relieffigürchen aus Tirol." Mannus 24:56–63.

Metzner-Nebelsick, C. 1992. "Gefäße mit basarabischer Ornamentik aus Frög." In Festschrift zur 50jährigen Bestehen Institut Ur- und Frühgesch.ichte Innsbruck. Univ. Forsch. Prähist. Arch., ed. A. Lippert and K. Spindler, 8:349–383. Bonn.

Mihovilič, K. 2001. Nezakcij: Prapovijesni nalazi 1900–1953. (Nesactium: Prehistoric Finds 1900–1953). Monogr. Kat. 11 Arheol. Muz. Istre. Pula.

Moosleitner, F. 1985. Die Schnabelkanne vom Dürrnberg: Ein Meisterwerk keltischer Handwerkskunst. Salzburg.

Morigi Govi, C. 1971. "Il tintinnabulo della 'tomba degli ori' dell'Arsenale Militare di Bologna." Arch. Classica 23:211–235.

Mostra dell'Arte delle situle dal Po al Danubio (VI–IV secolo a. C.). 1961–1962. Padova, Ljubiana, Vienna and Padova 1961–1962. Florence 1961.

Nebelsick, K. 1992. "Figürliche Kunst der Hallstattzeit im Spannungsfeld zwischen alteuropäischer Tradition und italischem Lebensstil." In Festschrift z. 50jährigen Bestehen Inst. Ur- und Frühgeschichte. Innsbruck Universität Forschung Prähistorische Archäologie, ed. A. Lippert and K. Spindler, 8:401–432. Bonn.

Pascucci, Paola. 1990. I depositi paleoveneti per un'archeologia del culto. Società archeologica veneta. Padua.

Pauli, L. 1973. "Ein latènezeitliches Steinrelief aus Bormio am Stilfser Joch." Germania 51:85–120.

Prüssing, G. 1991. "Die Bronzegefäße in Österreich." Prähistorische Bronzefunde II, 5. Stuttgart.

Reichenberger, A. 2002. "Bildhafte Darstellungen der Hallstattzeit." *Beiträge Vorgeschichte Nordostbayern. Naturhistorische Gesellschaft Nürnberg* 3. Fürth.

Reichenberger, A., and C. Dobiat. 1985. "Kröll-Schmiedkogel. Beiträge zu einem 'Fürstengrab' der östlichen Hallstattkultur in Kleinklein (Steiermark)." *Kleine Schr. Vorgesch. Seminar Marburg* 18.

Root, M. C. 1973. "An Etruscan Horse Race from Poggio Civitate." *AJA* 77:121–137.

Schmid, W. 1933. "Die Fürstengräber von Klein Glein in Steiermark." *Prähistorische Zeitschrift* 24:219–282.

Schwappach, F. 1974. "Zu einigen Tierdarstellungen der Frühlatènekunst." *Hamburger Beiträge zur Archäologie* 4:103–140.

Sydow, W. 1995. *Der hallstattzeitliche Bronzehort von Fliess im Oberinntal. Tirol.* Fundberichte Österreich, Materialh. A 3. Horn.

Thuillier, J.-P. 1985. *Les jeux athlétiques dans la civilisation étrusque.* Bibl. Ecoles Françaises. d'Athènes et de Rome 256. Rome.

   1996. *Le sport dans la Rome antique.* Paris.

Tomedi, G., and H. Appler. 2001. "Neue Zeugnisse der Situlenkunst aus Nordtirol." In *Archeo Tirol. Kleine Schriften* 3:113–122. Wattens.

Torbrügge, W., and H. P. Uenze. 1968. *Bilder zur Vorgeschichte Bayerns.* Konstanz, Lindau, and Stuttgart.

Torelli, M. 1984. *Storia degli Etruschi,* 2nd ed. Rome and Bari.

Von Eles, P., ed. 2002. *Guerriero e sacerdote: Autorità e comunità nell'età del ferro a Verucchio: La Tomba del Trono.* Florence.

Woytowitsch, E. 1978. "Wagen der Bronze- und frühen Eisenzeit in Italien." In *Prähistorische Bronzefunde XVII, 1.* Munich.

Zeller, K. W. 2001. *Der Dürrnberg bei Hallein: Ein Zentrum keltischer Kultur am Nordrand der Alpen.* Hallein.

Zuffa, M. 1965. "Trono miniaturistico da Verucchio." In *Studi in onore di Luisa Banti,* G. Camporeale, ed., 350–355. Rome.

CHAPTER TEN

A BARBARIAN MYTH? THE CASE
OF THE TALKING HEAD

Nancy Thomson de Grummond

This chapter is concerned with a methodological problem: what can the exami-nation of comparative mythological iconography tell us about the different ways in which Greeks and barbarians viewed a particular religious ritual element? A test case is presented here in a specific mytheme found both in Greece and in barbarian lands: a head that seems to talk, most likely uttering a prophecy. Scholars who recognize the motif as a prophetic head usually associate it with Orpheus, but in some cases there are serious discrepancies for such an identifica-tion, and we should not automatically assume that this well-known Greek myth is the only possible interpretation. In this chapter are recognized three different types of talking heads: the head standing for a voice heard coming from some unknown source (The Head as a Voice); the head emerging from the earth, often with part of the body visible (The Chthonic Head); and the decapitated head that seems to continue to function (The Severed Head), the only type that properly applies to Orpheus. The chapter also deals more generally with the baf-fling figure of Orpheus (was he Thracian or Greek?), who dies a brutal, violent death, which the Greeks represented in art frequently and with relish, while the Etruscans and Thracians seemed more interested in the ritual significance of the talking head.

This chapter originated as part of my research on Etruscan mythology and how to separate it meaningfully from Greek mythology, with par-ticular attention to images in art that appear to show a head with or without a portion of the body, emerging from earth, sky, or a container and making a prophecy.[1] This motif in art may be used as a test case to compare and contrast the way in which the Greeks and non-Greek barbarians such as the Etruscans used this kind of mytho-ritual element. This inquiry also considers the presence of the motif in other barbarian cultures appropriate for the present volume, especially Thracian, but also Roman, Scythian, and Celtic contexts.

The discussion abandons the traditional mythographic dichotomy of Indo-European versus non-Indo-European[2] in favor of the dialectic of this book, in which Greeks are contrasted with barbarians, that is, everybody else. The Etruscans, widely believed to have been non-Indo-European,[3] are seen to have much in common with the Indo-European Thracians and Scythians, who share their existence as a "peripheral" culture. There are several reasons for their similarity. As observed elsewhere in this volume, these peoples sometimes responded in a parallel fashion to the culture of Greece. Further, they experienced both direct and indirect contacts with one another, especially in the fourth and third centuries BC, a period critical for my study, and thus may have been mutually influential. Also applicable here is an idea articulated by Ivan Marazov in regard to the Thracians. He notes that the Thracians, though contemporary with the Greeks, belonged to a different epoch in the process of history. He goes on to state that the barbarians "perceived reality with different cognitive patterns."[4] An interesting corollary to Marazov's insight is that Etruscans and Scythians, partaking of a different historical epoch, often show social, political, and religious patterns that fit best with pre-Classical Greece.

In this chapter, I shall probe the implications of the dichotomy between Greeks and barbarians by studying the motif of the head represented in art without a body or with the body deemphasized. While this subject has been much investigated in regard to the "severed head" motif, which has been regarded as a distinctively barbarian motif,[5] more important for the analysis here is the recognition that the head is often depicted as speaking or singing and, most likely, making a prophecy. The severed head will certainly be included in this study, insofar as it may be related to prophecy. But here it will also be suggested that there are two other types of heads that prophesy: the head coming from the clouds or some vaguely defined landscape element, which evidently stands for an oracular voice of unknown provenance, and the chthonic head, coming from the earth or underworld, which sometimes shows some of the body. I shall argue that the Etruscans and other barbarians who utilized these motifs had in common a perception of the talking head as a ritual means of expression but that the Greeks had little interest in using the theme for this purpose.

The Head as a Voice

Let us examine examples of the head as a voice first, because it is rarely discussed in connection with the artistic representation of the talking head,[6] and recognition of its existence may affect our interpretation of some of the other specimens of this motif. This type of prophetic head may be represented as coming out of clouds or the side of a hill or out of the ground (Figs. 10.1–10.4), depicting, I believe, the idea found commonly in Greek and Roman literature that prophetic voices were suddenly heard speaking, whether in a grove or on the battlefield or in town. The best example is provided by the story told by Cicero, *De divinatione* 1.101, of the Roman deity Aius Loquens: "… we are told that Fauni have often been heard in battle and that during turbulent times truly prophetic messages have been sent from mysterious places. [For example], not long before the capture of the city by the Gauls, a voice, issuing from Vesta's sacred grove, which slopes from the foot of the Palatine Hill to the new road, was heard to say, 'The walls and gates must be repaired; unless this is done, the city will be taken.' Neglect of the warning, while it was possible to heed it, was atoned for after the supreme disaster had occurred; for adjoining the grove, an altar, which is now to be seen enclosed with a hedge, was dedicated to Aius Loquens."[7]

The name Aius Loquens is clearly made up of two verbs relating to speaking in Latin, *aio* and *loquor*, and seems a logical personification of the prophetic voice. It is interesting that Cicero notes here the habits of Fauni, and one may compare Virgil, *Aeneid*, 7. 120, when Latinus goes to the grove of Faunus to hear his prophetic message: "A sudden voice was sent from that thick forest."[8] Closely related to Faunus was Silenus, a Bacchic follower dear to the Romans, who on occasion would get drunk and prophesy.[9] It is possible that the many instances of masks of Silenus with an open mouth appearing in Roman art are actually meant to portray the voice of this prophetic figure rather than a scene from the theater.[10]

10.1. Fragment of an Etruscan krater (*ceramica argentata*). Scene of prophecy with a head of Silenus. From Gazzetta (near Bolsena). Fourth century BC. (L. Pernier, *NotSc* 1903, 590, fig. 2.)

Etruscan imagery has numerous parallels. Quite common is the head of a Silenus or satyr involved in prophecy, and I believe these to be equivalent to the Fauni or Sileni in Latin literature. The scene on an Etruscan krater from the necropolis of Gazzetta, near Orvieto, dating to the fourth century BC (Fig. 10.1),[11] shows a rustic, oracular, bearded head emerging from a wooded, rocky setting populated by a group of divinities. The group consulting the oracle includes a nude couple who stand next to the head. The female pulls up her mantle in the bridal gesture of *anakalypsis*, suggesting that the couple is to be married, and that therefore they must be hearing a prophecy relating to their wedding. The male figure leaning on his staff with his hand under his chin is very likely the interpreter of the oracle.

Similarly, a bronze Etruscan mirror in Berlin shows the prophetic bearded head, this time with the identity as Silenus clearly evident (Fig. 10.2).[12] The theme here is universally recognized as an adornment of the bride (Malavisch in Etruscan), and again it is likely that the voice of the Silenus is delivering a prophecy about marriage. This time the talking head comes from the sky and is surrounded by clouds.

The prophetic head may also appear in a scene of birth, as on an Etruscan mirror showing Fufluns, the Etruscan counterpart of Dionysos, as he emerges from his father's thigh (Fig. 10.3).[13] Here, situated on high,

10.2. Etruscan bronze mirror with adornment of Malavisch. Berlin, Staatliche Museen. (After *ES* II, 212.)

is the head of a satyr with wild hair who declares the oracle, indicated by streaming lines coming from his mouth.

Finally, the head of a Silenus may come up from the ground (Fig. 10.4),[14] and this time the scene is one of dire significance, for Aritimi (=Artemis) is carrying a small female figure named Esia who seems to be wrapped as a soul, and the bow and arrows carried by Aritimi may well be the cause of her death. Though the head comes up from the ground,

10.3. Etruscan bronze mirror with the birth of Fufluns. Naples, Museo Archeologico Nazionale. (After *ES* I. 82.)

I believe it is a different kind of thing from the chthonic heads discussed next. I believe that here the Silenus head simply reflects the idea that a voice is heard, but it is not certain exactly whence it issues.

These scenes, I propose, all show key moments in life – birth, marriage, death – somehow predicted or impacted by a prophecy declared by a voice coming from some unknown source.

10.4. Etruscan bronze mirror with Artumes carrying Esia. Brussels, Musées Royaux d'Art et d'Histoire. (After Lambrechts 1978, p. 71.)

The Chthonic Head

A rather different situation is that in which a distinctly identified personage comes up from the ground or underworld and utters a message. In this chthonic framework, sometimes only the head is shown, but part of the body may be included as well. An Etruscan gem in the Museo di Villa Giulia shows a boy emerging from the ground as a tall, robed man bends over toward him (Plate XXIIA); the scene is probably to be identified as a representation of the story about Tages, the archprophet of the Etruscans, told by Cicero (*De divinatione* 2.23).[15] He relates that one day at Tarquinia, while a peasant was at work in the fields, he plowed an unusually deep furrow, and suddenly a child with the features and wisdom of an old man rose up from the earth and began to sing, revealing the whole of the *Etrusca disciplina*, the Etruscan teachings about the relationships between gods and men. The Etruscan hero Tarchon was summoned, and he wrote down all of the revelations and interpreted them for the other Etruscans. A gem in the British Museum is thought to show a variant representation of the myth, depicting the peasant pointing down at the prophetic head, and the figure of Tarchon leaning over and listening intently[16] (Plate XXIIB).

Yet another Etruscan myth in which a figure rises from the ground is seen on an Etruscan red-figure stamnos from Vulci depicting Turms, the Etruscan counterpart of Hermes.[17] Or rather, we should say that it depicts two figures of Turms, reflecting the Etruscan recognition of Turms as twinned,[18] according to which there were two manifestations of the god; one Turms, beardless, with winged sandals and from the upper world, is paying a visit to the Turms of the underworld. The latter, bearded but recognizable by his typical hat, rises up from the ground and seems to be giving a consultation for a young warrior standing nearby.

This type of chthonic apparition in the form of a head or a head and part of a body occurs rarely in Greek art. Of particular interest is a red-figure calyx krater[19] on which Odysseus, seeking admission to the underworld, sits beside the pit in which he has put his offering of a ram as he awaits the appearance of Teiresias, as in *Odyssey* 11.90–137. The prophet is represented as rising out of the ground, with his head sticking up, mouth open and eyes closed. His shoulder and right hand are also visible. This is the only Greek representation known of this Homeric theme, and it is worth noting that it comes from Lucania, and thus represents an area where the Greeks were in the orbit of traditions of Italy. Furthermore it is quite close in date to the many representations of chthonic heads in Etruria of the fourth century BC.[20]

The Severed Head

We may now consider the subject of the Severed Head, which is of interest here only insofar as it had a role in prophesying. The heads that I shall discuss belong in the classifications of Stith Thompson in his *Motif-Index of Folk Literature* described as the "vital head." (No. E783, "Vital head. Retains life after being cut off," and No. E783.5, "Vital head speaks"). Perhaps the best-known example of the talking Severed Head from the Classical world is that of Orpheus.[21] It is interesting that this archetypal figure of Greek religion and philosophy is normally conceived of as being a Thracian poet and king, at least partly non-Greek, born from the river god Oiagros, who presided over the rising of the Hebrus River in Thrace. An alternate tradition, not as common, is that he is the son of Apollo. His mother is sometimes called a "Muse," most frequently the Muse Kalliope.[22] Whatever his parentage, the story of the murder of Orpheus and his decapitation by Thracian women is, of course, situated by the Greeks in a foreign context. The dismemberment theme is shocking and barbaric, and thus it made sense that it was attributed to barbarians. It is somewhat surprising that the vicious attack of the Thracian women was actually the part of the Orpheus myth that most interested the Greeks. In the catalogue of images of Orpheus by Garezou are listed twenty vase paintings of the charming scene in which Orpheus sings for an audience of Thracians (both men and women or, more often, just men), whereas the count for the attack of the women is forty-two.[23] The Thracian women, often recognizable from their tattoos and their Thracian dress, throw rocks and brandish swords and spears, and sometimes run Orpheus through or saw at his neck with a sword; two specimens show a Thracian woman triumphantly brandishing the head.[24]

An even more interesting statistic for this study pertains to the theme of the severed head of Orpheus as a prophetic element. It is in fact very rare in Greek art, with only three possible instances, and these all have an ambiguous quality, to be discussed later. Perhaps even more important, the literary evidence for the story of the head as oracular does not occur until late antiquity, in Philostratos's *Life of Apollonios of Tyana*, 4.14, probably early third century AD. Ovid (*Met.* 11.1–59) and Konon (*Fab.* 45), in the period of Augustus, both narrate well the story of the Thracian women tearing the body limb from limb and the severed head floating down the Hebrus, still singing. One tradition is that it came to be buried on the island of Lesbos. But not until Philostratos do we have the account that *oracles* were given at the sacred site.

Otherwise, the Greek evidence for the oracular quality of the head of
Orpheus rests on three vase paintings, all dated to the second half of
the fifth century BC. It is odd that they all come from Athens; so far, no
representations of a prophetic head of Orpheus have been confirmed
among the Greeks of southern Italy,[25] where the cult of Orpheus and
the afterlife was extremely important. It is also worth noting that none
of these paintings has an inscription to identify the head as Orpheus,
and that the context is vague enough to raise doubts that the Thracian
bard is in fact the subject. Many scholars have treated the theme, usually
taking it for granted that these three scenes do represent Orpheus.[26] In
the end they may be right, but it is worthwhile to review the scenes to
observe some of the differences among the Greek scenes themselves, as
well as among some representations from Etruria that are often brought
in for comparison. I believe that if we avoid forcing the evidence into a
mold, we will catch some of the nuances of these scenes that have not
been noticed before.

An Attic red-figure kylix in Cambridge, dated to about 410 BC
(Fig. 10.5),[27] shows an enlarged head on the ground, with a male figure thought to be Apollo holding a laurel in one hand and extending
his other hand over the head in a commanding gesture. A third figure
writes something on a tablet, presumably the words being spoken by
the head, implying that the head is emitting an oracle. The reverse of
the kylix shows two female figures, one with a lyre and one with a ribbon, sometimes identified as Muses, sometimes as the women of Lesbos
finding the lyre of Orpheus.[28] It has long been assumed that the head
is Orpheus, but as noted, there is no inscription. In fact, there is little
here to indicate that the story is anything more than Apollo delivering
a prophecy, in the presence of Muses, as a visitor to the oracle (note the
traveler's hat) writes it down. The head emerging from the ground need
not be severed, but could simply be used here as a convention to indicate
that a voice is announcing the oracular message delivered by Apollo.
That is, it may simply be the convention of the Head as a Voice.

There are similar problems with the image on an Attic red-figure
hydria in Dunedin dated 420 BC,[29] which shows a head on the ground[30]
and a male figure with lyre and laurel branch standing by and looking
down, perhaps even striking the ground next to the head. Two female
figures stand by – one, on the left, tightly wrapped in clothing, and the

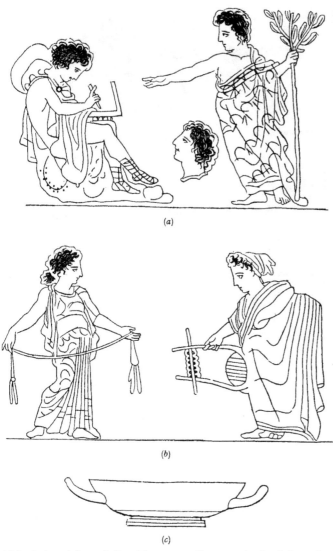

(a)

(b)

(c)

10.5. Attic red-figure kylix with a scene of an oracular head. Loan Ant.103.25, Corpus Christi College, Cambridge, Massachusetts, and the Fitzwilliam Museum. (G. Minervini, *Bull. Arch. Nap.* 6, 1858, plate 4.)

other, on the right, gesturing gently toward the head as if to elicit a reaction. Again, the male figure must be Apollo, though the identity of the female figures is elusive.[31] And again, there is no inscription to tell us that this is Orpheus; furthermore, no story is preserved from this period that would help to explain the theme.

An Attic red-figured hydria in Basel, dated 440–430 BC (Fig. 10.6), shows a rather different scene. A head is upon the ground, again

10.6. Attic red-figured hydria with a scene of an oracular head. Antikenmuseum Basel und Sammlung Ludwig. (Photo: Museum.)

enlarged, seemingly lodged in a rocky depression, and Muses are present with pipes and three lyres (the scene continues all the way around the vase).[32] The tending male figure is bearded and manipulates what has been identified alternatively as two lances, two shafts of wood, or a cord folded double, perhaps supporting him as he hangs over the head. His hand reaches down toward the head, again a gesture that may refer to an attempt to elicit a response from it. While the identification of the Muses has been generally accepted, it must be admitted that there are no identifying inscriptions. The scene is so different from the others that there cannot even be any certainty that it relates the same story as the other two. Where is Apollo now, and just who is the man who interacts with the oracle?[33] And since there are three lyres, should we still refer to the lyre of Orpheus?

Strange to say, scholars have enlisted Etruscan art to make their identification of these scenes as showing Orpheus by referring to a bronze engraved mirror from Chiusi dating to the late fourth century BC, about 100 years later than the vessels in question (Fig. 10.7).[34] It is unfortunately damaged but shows sufficiently well a head on the ground, with hair streaming as if in inspiration, labeled Urphe.[35] This is the word we would expect for the Etruscan version of the name Orpheus. A female

10.7. Etruscan bronze mirror with a prophecy of Urphe. Siena, Archaeological Museum. (After Maggiani 1992, fig. 2.)

figure on the right, labeled Alpunea, seems to be in charge of display-ing a written message, while a beardless male figure stands on the left. Alpunea is definitely an Italic component, for her name is the same as that of the Sibyl of Tibur, called Albunea in Latin.[36] The male figure is labeled Umaele, a character so far not successfully equated with any figure in Greek or Latin mythology.[37] Also in the scene is a couple, evi-dently a bride and groom: the female, nude, holds up her mantle in the gesture of *anakalypsis* appropriate for brides. She is labeled Ethurpa or possibly Euturpa, a name that suggests a Greek Muse, but the nudity and bridal pose are quite inappropriate for a Muse. The other inscriptions are too disputed to offer much help for the interpretation of this mirror.[38]

Umaele is evidently the custodian of the head. I say "custodian" because other examples of this scene, such as one of the same date from Castelgiorgio, near Orvieto (Fig. 10.8), show more clearly that the figure

10.8. Etruscan bronze mirror with an oracular head. Paris, Musée du Louvre. (After Emmanuel-Rebuffat 1988, 1.2a.)

on the left holds a tubelike bag with a reticulate pattern on it and a ribbon attached to the sack.[39] It has been suggested that when the head is not in use, it is kept in the container.[40] There are no names inscribed on the mirror, but the elements are virtually identical, with the oracular head with its streaming hair below, the bride with her groom, and the scribe who displays the oracle (in this case, a male). These need not be the same individuals as those on the previous mirror, but this may be a representation of the same ritual act.

Another scene with a talking head has recently been brought into the dialogue about the series of Etruscan mirrors that have prophetic heads (Fig. 10.9).[41] A bronze mirror in a collection in Switzerland, dated to the fourth century BC, shows a very different story, for the oracular head is here bearded, quite unlike any seen before in either the Greek oracular scenes or the Etruscan ones. The group gathered round for the

37a

10.9. Etruscan bronze mirror with an oracular head. Private collection, Switzerland. (After Jucker 2001, fig. 37.)

oracle consists of the Etruscan deities known as Turms, Menrva, and Aplu. That much of the scene seems very different from the examples previously examined. We see further that there is no married couple, no writing, and no streaming hair. But the presence of the youth with the bag makes the comparison more compelling; he extends his right hand down toward the head, using again the gesture that may show an attempt to elicit a response from the head. Given the differences between this mirror and those in the other group, I suspect that these are not all the same myth; but the presence of a head and a bag suggest that they are nevertheless images of a similar ritual. That is, we have the same mytheme – the talking head in a bag – but not the same mythologem of a complex of motifs related to a particular story.

It is very important to recognize the significance of the bag. This motif implies, first of all, that the head is truly severed (i.e., it is not a Chthonic Head or a Head as a Voice), else it would be impossible to put it in a bag. The container also may be a crucial link in identifying at least one of the Greek scenes as truly Orphic. Mauro Cristofani has argued[42] that the scene on the Basel amphora (Fig. 10.6) shows a quiver ("una sorta di turcasso") on the ground next to the feet of the consultant and that the man is actually holding up the cord that was used to tie it up ("nastro ripiegato").[43]

The theme of the prophetic Severed Head occurs on numerous carved Etruscan sealstones as well, beginning in the fourth century BC.[44] There is one in the British Museum that does not yet seem to have been linked with the head in the bag, but that I believe shows the head actually emerging from the container (Plate XXIIB).[45] Here only one figure is present for the consultation, and it is Turms, easily identified by his attributes. The bag is recognizable since it shows the same kind of reticulate pattern on it, and the gesture of Turms, which seems to be drawing the answer out of the head, is familiar. The stance of Turms, with one leg raised (it would be the left leg in a sealing made from the stone), is one quite familiar in prophetic scenes.

One is reminded of another head in a bag in classical myth: the head of Medusa. She is represented often in Etruscan art, sometimes as a head in a bag. On one mirror of the fourth century BC, Perseus runs away with the head in a bag, its hair streaming, as commonly shown in Etruscan scenes of prophecy and inspiration, and another mirror, slightly later in date,[46] shows the head not in its bag, but held up openly by Menrva (Fig. 10.10).[47] Here we have fascinating evidence that in Etruria, the head of Medusa can prophesy. On this mirror, the head, in enlarged form, seems to be reflected in the ground below, where it takes on a three-dimensional

10.10. Etruscan bronze mirror with the oracular head of Medusa. Brussels, Musées Royaux d'Art et d'Histoire. (After Lambrechts 1978, p. 25. Courtesy Musées Royaux d'Art et d'Histoire.)

quality and looks rather like the heads of Urphe we have observed. Etruscan Pherse observes and assumes the role of an interpreter, with left leg raised and didactic finger pointing.

I cannot leave the subject of the prophetic Severed Head in Etruria without mentioning an article by Laura Ambrosini that proposes a startling new identification of the head of Orpheus in Italy.[48] She argues that two mirrors found at Corchiano, near Civita Castellana, dating to the third century BC,[49] feature a scene with a prophetic head of unusual type. The better preserved of the two mirrors, reproduced here (Fig. 10.11),[50] shows the well-known Etruscan adornment spirit referred to by the conventional designation of "Lasa."[51] This divine figure is normally nude, often winged, usually female, and frequently carries an attribute of adornment or anointing, such as a perfume bottle and/or dipper.[52] The spirit may wear a head covering, either a diadem or, in the case of the Corchiano mirrors and many others, a "Phrygian" cap.

10.11. Etruscan bronze mirror with Lasa and an oracular head. Civita Castellana, Museo Archeologico dell'Agro Falisco. (After Ambrosini 1996, fig. 1.)

She is also most often alone, though she may be joined by a twin figure that faces her.[53] These two mirrors are unique in that they show not a twin, but a similar head, set near the bottom of the field, facing in the same direction as the spirit and wearing an identical cap. Ambrosini points to comparisons with a stock motif occurring in the decoration of some twenty-five Apulian vase paintings, showing a head adorned with a Phrygian cap, emerging from a calyx of rich vegetation.[54] That head, realized as a decorative motif rather than as part of a mythological scene, has been identified with a number of figures, including Attis, Adonis, Bendis, Paris, Perseus, and Orpheus. A similar motif appears on a number of Etruscan mirrors and also occurs on antefixes from sites in Italy.[55]

While the new evidence from Corchiano is not conclusive, it could strengthen the case for recognizing the head motif from southern Italy as Orpheus. To Ambrosini's argument we may add the observation that in fact the Phrygian cap is equally "Thracian," as may be seen from helmets found in Thrace that seem to imitate a type of leather cap worn there.[56] Also, on the other Corchiano mirror,[57] the Lasa figure dangles her arm down toward the head, with a motion very similar to the "eliciting" gesture noted in other prophetic representations.

On the other hand, there are no other prophetic motifs on the Apulian vases to reveal that the context there is oracular. Further, on the Apulian vases, the head does not seem to be severed, but rather to emerge from the vegetation. Also, the heads are sometimes winged, for which there does not seem to be a precedent in the iconography of Orpheus. Finally, it is important to note that there are other heads in vegetation, some of them clearly female, in both southern Italy and Etruria, that are not the same as the head with the Phrygian cap.[58] None shows that the head is severed, and I suggest that rather than conclude that they or the Phrygian heads show a decapitated prophet, it is more logical to interpret these as the Head as a Voice.

How do the prophetic heads of Etruscan art compare with the Greek examples? I note, first of all, that the use of the prophetic head in a mytho-ritual scene seems to be far more common in Etruscan art than in Greek. Against the dozens of examples in Etruria,[59] Greek art so far has the three examples I have cited of disembodied heads that may be truly prophetic, and none of these is actually labeled. It is also interesting to note that the Etruscans, stereotyped as loving gory scenes, did not always live up to this reputation. They discreetly kept the frightening head of Urphe in a bag and brought it out for special mantic occasions. Further, the Etruscans show no interest whatsoever in the vicious dismemberment of Orpheus: there does not seem to be a single representation of this act in Etruscan art.

The Etruscan story of the prophetic head also involves a different range of characters. The Greek versions twice have the figure of Apollo, and perhaps three times have women identifiable as the Muses, while in the Etruscan versions a figure equivalent to Apollo occurs only with the bearded oracular head, and not on any of the mirrors with marriage oracles.[60] Some of the nude female figures occurring in the Umaele mirrors could be Muses, but they have no attributes to make such an identity firm. The consultants of the oracle on the Etruscan mirrors in some cases seem to be couples, suggesting that the theme of the oracles was marriage. For the three Greek versions, we do not have specific clues as to the subject of the oracles. Finally, we may ask whether the Greeks indeed had the head in a bag; it is not impossible, but the evidence so far is modest.

Yet another paradox is posed by the thought that the prophetic ritual with the severed head of Orpheus does not appear in southern Italy, where Orphic doctrine was most widespread. Ambrosini's theory would certainly help to fill the gap, though the image she identifies as Orpheus emerging from vegetation does not seem to be severed. The Etruscans surely were acquainted with Orphic ideas,[61] but there is not enough space here to probe this question. I will only remark that the Etruscan depictions of the severed heads of Orpheus and Medusa provide a vivid illustration of the Orphic idea that at death the individual really comes to life.[62] Probably because of the Orphic belief that the head is the repository of the soul, the head can operate after being separated from the body, and is able to draw on its divinity and prophesy. [63]

After this brief review of the three categories of the talking head – the Head as a Voice, the Chthonic Head, and the Severed Head in Greece and Etruria – I will turn to a few possible examples of the speaking head motif in Thracian, Scythian, and Celtic art. It has been pointed out that Orpheus does not appear in Thracian mythological art.[64] Nevertheless, I argue that there is evidence of Thracian prophetic heads. The most convincing examples of these may be found in the Rogozen Treasure and the Letnitsa Treasure, both dated to the fourth century BC, firmly within the chronological orbit of the many Etruscan examples. Jug No. 159 from the Rogozen Treasure (Fig. 10.12), made of gilded silver,[65] depicts a narrative of a boar hunt with two hunters attacking the beast; turning the jug, one sees beneath the handle a bust of a female figure that seems to be part of the narrative. Marazov explained the head as that of a goddess, who is there to support her hero in the trial and initiation represented by the boar hunt. Without disagreeing, I suggest that she may also have spoken a prophecy of the outcome, and for this reason, instead of an image of the whole deity, the artist represented only her head and a bit of the shoulders. The head is enlarged, as in some other mytho-ritual scenes, but it does not seem to be severed; rather, I think it likely that we have here the Head as a Voice, heard in the heat of the hunt.

10.12. Thracian gilded silver jug with a boar hunt and an oracular head (Rogozen Treasure). Sofia, National Museum of History. (After Marazov 1996, p. 160.)

From the Letnitsa Treasure come the tiny silver gilt plaques thought to be part of the decoration of a horse's harness, which show the theme of the hero horseman riding, spear in hand, as if to the attack (Figs. 10.13, 10.14).[66] On five of the plaques there is in the field a head, always larger than life size. Two of the heads are male, one is female, and two others are of horses. These heads have been interpreted in the past as representing the sacrificial victims offered before battle, and without necessarily rejecting that hypothesis, I suggest that prophecies come from the heads.

There are two reasons to think of the heads as prophetic: one is the extraordinary size of the heads in comparison with that of the hero, and the other is that in all of them the mouth is quite conspicuously open. The stylistic convention in the Letnitsa Treasure is to show the mouth as a small semicircle, and the hero's mouth does display that convention. But the mouth of the hypothesized talking heads is noticeably larger. The heads twist and turn in space and are always behind the hero, in a good position to speak to him. Since these are all battle scenes, it is quite appropriate to think that a prophecy was expected before each battle.[67]

The selection of horses to declare a prophecy is not surprising. There are many parallels in ancient myth and ritual for the idea that horses have special knowledge of the future. Indeed, the horses of Achilles talk to him as he goes into battle (*Iliad* 19.405 ff), and his horse Xanthos prophesies: "Xanthos, as he spoke, bowed his head, so that all the mane fell away from the pad and swept the ground … the goddess of the white arms, Hera, had put a voice in him: 'We shall keep you safe for

10.13. Thracian gilded silver plaque with a rider and an oracular head (Letnitsa Treasure). Lovech, Museum of History. (After Marazov 1998, fig. 98.)

10.14. Thracian gilded silver plaque with a rider and an oracular horse's head (Letnitsa Treasure). Lovech, Museum of History. (After Marazov 1998, fig. 100.)

this time, o hard Achilleus, And yet the day of your death is near, but it is not we who are to blame …' Achilles of the swift feet answered him, 'Xanthos, why do you prophesy my death?'"[68] Similarly, Julius Caesar's horses wept when they had foreknowledge of his death (Suetonius, *Julius Caesar* 18), and Tacitus relates how a German chief might yoke white horses and walk them around, listening carefully to their neighs and snorts (*Germania* 10). A remarkable parallel for the use of a speaking horse's head is found in the *Rig Veda* 1.117.22, in the adventure of the Aśvin twins in which they seek knowledge from Dadhyañc, the son of the Atharvan, the priest in charge of fire and the magic drink *soma*. Because Indra had threatened Dadhyañc with beheading if he revealed the secret of *soma*, the twins removed his head and replaced it with the head of a horse through which he could then make the revelation.[69]

When we turn to the Scythians, we find that great attention has been given to the presence in their customs and in their art of the grim severed heads of enemies killed in battle.[70] Often cited is the famous passage in Herodotus (4.64-66) that tells of their habit of taking the scalps of enemies and making them into handkerchiefs or using the skulls as drinking cups, sometimes with gilding added. This information is combined with archaeological evidence from the habitation of settled Scythians at Bel'sk in the forest steppes of Ukraine, where an actual workshop for making the skull cups has been discovered.[71] More recently, the spotlight has been turned on the exciting discovery of a new monument of Scythian/Bosporan art, the battle relief from Yubeljenoe now in the Pushkin Museum, Moscow, dating to the fourth century BC.[72] It shows the remarkable custom of hanging the severed heads of enemies on the saddle or neck of the horse. The practice was described by Strabo in regard to Gauls (*Geography* 4.4.5), but it seems to fit the Scythians and Thracians as well. To my knowledge, none of these heads of enemies decapitated in battle is prophetic.

I offer here one image of a severed head in Scythian art that very probably has a prophetic nature; recognition of that aspect may open a window for the understanding of other Scythian representations. Very suggestive is a gold clothing plaque from Kul' Oba, of the fourth century BC, known in five exemplars showing a goddess figure, recognizable as such by her unusual hybrid body made up of a mix of vegetation and animal parts. She holds up a Silenus head in her left hand and seems to hold a knife in the right.[73] The goddess has been identified with a mythological Scythian figure mentioned by Herodotus (4.9),[74] but it is not possible to associate her with any capabilities for prophecy. The main reason for seeing a prophetic connection, I suggest, relates to the head of Silenus – who, as we have seen, was a prophetic figure for the Etruscans, appearing in the guise of a Head as a Voice. Here he seems to have changed categories, and for some reason is depicted as a Severed Head, a motif for which it is hard to find parallels. He also appears on the spectacular phiale found at Kul' Oba,[75] where twenty-four Silenus heads ring the outer surface of the bowl, sharing space with two sets of twelve Medusa heads. The phiale (patera) is demonstrably a prophetic vessel used in *lekanomanteia* (divination from a liquid surface) by Greeks and Etruscans[76] and may well have been used thus by Scythians.

The Celts are perhaps most renowned for observing rituals with the vital Severed Head,[77] with evidence coming from art, from excavations, from Greek and Roman literary texts, and from surviving myths of ancient Britain written down at a much later date. Livy (23.24) tells us of the Gallic practice of drinking from skulls, and the excavations at the great *oppidum* at Manching (Bavaria, Germany) have also yielded evidence of the working of skulls into cups.[78] Excavation of a shrine at Roquepertuse (Provence) dating to the third-second centuries BC revealed the practice of displaying the actual heads of victims in a sanctuary, and sculptures from Entremont, also in southern France, show a number of severed heads immortalized in stone.[79] An intriguing connecting point for the themes of this chapter is found at Roquepertuse, where the ensemble included sculptures of heads, niches for the placement of real severed heads, and a frieze carved with simple outline drawings of horses' heads, with several showing a line across the neck to indicate that they were cut off. Similarly, at Nages (Provence), severed heads of humans were represented in alternation with galloping horses – admittedly not heads in this case.[80]

Evidence that any of these heads, whether human or equine, could prophesy is scarce. There is a good bit of evidence concerning the Celtic practices of divination, but so far there is no clear statement from Classical antiquity that such severed heads had an oracular character.[81] There is certainly reason to believe that the victims of human sacrifice could be used in divination, as indicated by Diodorus Siculus (5.31.2–5)

and Strabo (7.2.3), who referred to the custom of Celtic priests observing the death throes of the murdered victims and interpreting the
omens.[82] But for the idea that the heads could speak we must resort
to the evidence of medieval Irish and Welsh literature,[83] which sometimes contains material predating the arrival of Christianity in Britain.
The legend of Each Labra, the horse that would rise out of a mound
on Midsummer's Night and prophesy about events to come, must
date back to the pre-Christian sacrifice of the horse at midsummer.[84]
But while there is abundant evidence of horse cults in the Celtic world,
including the shrines at Roquepertuse and Nages noted earlier, there is
little evidence for the beliefs that went along with the cults.[85]

Of particular interest also is the story of the giant Bran the Blessed,
who, when dying, asked his own men to decapitate him and keep his
talking head around for advice and good luck.[86] The head of the over-
sized hero did not proclaim prophecies, however, but rather acted out
the ones made by Bran before his decapitation; it eventually served as
a kind of talisman, for it was buried, as he had asked, in the Tower of
London, where it safeguarded the realm from outside invaders. Thus,
our search for prophetic heads in Celtic culture remains inconclusive
for the present.

We have come quite a long way in surveying the material from various
cultures. The division of the material into three different categories of
the talking head is basic, it is argued here, and should help in the future
to organize discussion of the meaning of the images of the talking head.
Certain surprises have emerged from the discourse, such as the Orphic
head in the bag and the prophetic nature of the head of Medusa, as
well as the usage of horses for prophecy recorded in literature and now
hypothesized in art. What other generalizations or new observations can
be made that will help to provide a perspective on this material? Is it
possible to say, for example, that there are any aspects of the talking
heads that are decidedly barbarian or any that are emphatically Greek?

Bonfante and Knauer have stressed the idea that most evidence for the
brutally severed heads of military conquest and human sacrifice come
from a barbarian context.[87] But this generalization is in need of some
nuances. It should be remembered that plenty of beheading was done
by Greeks in the *Iliad*. Probably nothing in ancient literature can surpass
the gory slaughter and decapitation of the enemy by the Greek Peneleos

as he killed Ilioneus: "Peneleos caught [him] underneath the brow, at the bases of the eye, and pushed the eyeball out, and the spear went clean through the eye socket ... drawing his sharp sword [Peneleos] hewed at the neck in the middle, and so dashed downward the head, with helm upon it, while still on the point of his spear the eyeball stuck. Lifting it high like the head of a poppy, he displayed it and spoke vaunting over it" (*Iliad* 14.493ff.).[88] Here, and in many passages of the *Iliad*, it is clear that the early Greeks so much studied and admired for all the centuries of Greek culture were in fact quite "barbaric."

Further, some of the "barbarian" relish of gore may also be detected in Greek tragedy – for example, the *Bacchae* of Euripides, in which Pentheus is torn up in a manner similar to Orpheus and the act is justified by reference to outsiders who are conducting the cult activities. The murder of Orpheus itself seems to have been treated similarly in the *Bessarides* of Aeschylus,[89] and as already noted, the depictions of this ghastly act were very popular in Attic red-figure vase painting. Edith Hall has argued convincingly that the Greeks began to distinguish themselves from barbarians only in the fifth century BC,[90] and thus their sense that they were different from barbarians may have been of limited duration. Besides, she makes it clear that even at the height of barbarian-bashing in the fifth century, there were important exceptions of "barbaric Greeks" and "noble barbarians."[91]

Thus, there is no reason to believe that barbarians were interested in the head motif through a barbaric fixation on dismemberment any more than the Greeks themselves. With the motif of the talking head, the division between Greeks and barbarians, I submit, lies in another direction. What is remarkable is that there is so little evidence for *ritual* with the head in Greek art, literature, and religion and so much in the religious activities of the barbarians. With the Etruscans, in particular, the theme of the speaking, prophetic head is abundant and diverse.[92] They practiced divination rituals quite freely in a wide variety of contexts, both public and private, and with a number of methods.[93] For the other barbarian peoples discussed in this chapter, while attempts to identify prophetic motifs remain tentative, it is certain that the Thracians, Scythians, and Celts showed an awe and fascination with the head severed from the body, and that they mediated their fear of it in contexts of religious and social ritual. The heads of enemies were deposited in sacred places or kept for display on special, formal occasions, revealing a profound motivation to keep their power under control. If the evidence of art adduced here may be accepted, they also respected the heads, whether of humans or horses, as capable of or symbolic of prophetic activity.

This chapter leaves much to be discussed. As I prepared it, I omitted many worthwhile directions for the examination of the prophetic head, and the conviction grew in me that the topic deserves a much longer study.[94] For now I hope that I have provided a helpful introduction to the spectrum of reactions of barbarians and Greeks to the intriguing phenomenon of the potent, vital, speaking head.

Notes

1. De Grummond 2006, 12–15, 32–40.
2. Puhvel 1987, 33–42, addresses the concept of Indo-European.
3. Bonfante and Bonfante 2002, 50.
4. Marazov 1998, 34.
5. See especially Bonfante 1984a and 1984b and Knauer 2001.
6. Cristofani 1982, 9, refers to the head that stands for a voice.
7. *De divinatione*, 1.101, trans. Falconer 1922; Briquel 1993; Wardle 2006, 349–350, for other instances.
8. Mandelbaum 1971, 166.
9. Virgil, *Eclogues* 6; de Grummond 2002, 73–74, 80.
10. De Grummond 2002, 74 and fig. 21 (fresco in the Villa of the Mysteries).
11. Cristofani 1982, 9 and 12 (note 70, with previous bibliography); Maggiani 1986, 25 and 39, note 113, with bibliography.
12. Dated ca. 325–300 BC. De Grummond 2000, 46.
13. Dated ca. 350–325 BC. De Grummond 2000, 46–48; 2002, 65.
14. Dated 425–400 BC. Lambrechts 1978, 67–73; de Grummond 2000, 43–45.
15. For the gem, see Torelli 2000, 529 and 637 (no. 325). On Tages, see de Grummond 2006, 23–27, and the ancient literary sources Ovid, *Met.* 15.553–559, Johannes Lydos, *De ostentis* 2.6.B, and Festus 492.6.8.
16. I see no reason to identify either of these scenes as a consultation of the head of Orpheus (the theme is discussed later), as is often done. The Orpheus myth involves only the head, not other parts of the body; the slightly rough form of the emerging figure is consistent with the story in Ovid, in which clods of earth slowly formed into a recognizable figure. Further, as regards the British Museum gem, there is no known Orpheus motif in which two men, one a rustic, consult a soothsaying head. A gem quite similar to the British Museum gem has been published by Furtwängler 1900, I, plate 22.15 and II, 108.
17. Museo Gregoriano Etrusco, Vatican Museum. Dated to the first half of the fourth century BC. Harari 1997, 106 (No. 97).
18. Harari 1997, 107 (Nos. 105 and 115).
19. Zimmerman 1997, 1190.
20. Zimmerman 1997, 1190, dates the vase to the first quarter of the fourth century BC.
21. The bibliography is vast. I have found the following quite useful: Nagy 1990; Bremmer 1991; Schmidt 1991; Guthrie 1993; Garezou 1994; Wright 2003. I am

grateful to Svetla Slaveva-Griffin for assistance with the topic of Orpheus and Orphism and for many useful criticisms of this study.

22. Guthrie 1993, 27; Garezou 1994, 81.
23. Garezou 1994, 84–88. All of these scenes date to the fifth or early fourth century BC.
24. Garezou 1994, Nos. 25–67. See esp. Nos. 35 and 36 (cutting at the neck) and 66 and 67 (brandishing the head).
25. For a possible exception to this statement, see note 48 and related text.
26. Guthrie 1993, esp. 35–39. Schmidt 1972 is essential for the history of scholarship on all three vases discussed here. For other bibliography, see De Puma 2001, 28, note 6; see also Cristofani 1982; Maggiani 1986.
27. Schmidt 1972, 130; Guthrie 1993, 36; Garezou 1994, 88 (No. 70); de Puma 2001, 26.
28. Muses: Doerig 1991, 63; Guthrie 1993, 36, calls them women of Lesbos but cites no literary evidence for this identification.
29. Garezou 1994, 88 (No. 69).
30. I have not been able to ascertain from photographs if the head is enlarged here.
31. Guthrie 1993, 36, attempts to identify the female figures with varying suggestions: the figure with the eliciting hand could be the Pythia (but she has nothing to do with Orpheus); the wrapped woman on the left could be the mother of Orpheus (but she does not dress like a Muse) or Eurydice (but Orpheus's wife has nothing to do with the oracle at Lesbos).
32. Schmidt 1972, plate 39; Garezou 1994, 88 (No. 69).
33. Schmidt 1972, 152, proposes that he may be Terpander of Lesbos, as a follower of Orpheus. Etruscan scholars have noted that his role is similar to that of Umaele in Etruria, discussed later; see note 36 and related text. Cristofani 1982, 7; van der Meer 1995, 86.
34. De Grummond 2000, 39 (note 22 with bibliography); De Puma 2001, 20–22.
35. The name is written upside down and from right to left. For all of the inscriptions on this mirror see Rix 1991, Cl S. 11 and Cl 0.7. There is much to discuss about these inscriptions, but this is not the appropriate place. I shall attempt to honor the least controversial conclusions.
36. The reading of this name, established by Maggiani 1986, 16–17, with the meaningful equation with the prophetic figure Albunea, is completely convincing. The acerbic debate launched by Emmanuel-Rebuffat 1984, over a character thought to be (wrongly) labeled Aliunea, can now be brought to a close.
37. Maggiani 1986, 11, suggests that the name is derived from Apollo Maloeis, whose cult was on Lesbos, but this time his argument is strained. Cf. Cristofani 1982, 8, for other attempts and Camporeale 1997, 158, for rejection of the idea that he should be equated with Eumelos, son of Alkestis and Admetos. I thank Giovanna Bagnasco Gianni for informing me of her theory for a new identification of a counterpart for Umaele in Greece, discussed by Bagnasco Gianni 2009, 48–56, published too late for inclusion in this volume.
38. Cf. note 34.
39. Camporeale 1997, 159 (No. 3). There is a total of six mirrors that seem to relate to the theme of the consultation of the head in the bag. In addition to the two cited here, there is a fragmentary inscribed mirror formerly in the Borgia collection (De Puma 2001, 22, and Fig. 6, with bibliography, note 13) and one newly presented example in Princeton (De Puma 2001). In addition, there are two mirrors that show the bag but no head: Cristofani 1982, 7–8.

40. Cristofani 1982, 7–8.
41. De Puma 2001, 23; Jucker 2001, No. 37. As will be seen from my description of this mirror, I consider it to be very different from the others listed in note 38.
42. Cristofani 1982, 7.
43. It is not possible to confirm the existence of the bag from viewing photographs, but the suggestion is appealing.
44. Emmanuel-Rebuffat 1984, 501, figs. 11–14, lists her candidates. But her fig. 13 cannot be the same story since parts of the body are included, and thus the image fits better the Etruscan story of Tages. De Puma 2001, 29 (note 25), also lists a selection of gems from Martini 1971, of which the following seem to me to be the best candidates for an Orphic story: Cat. Nos. 37, 49, 111, 133, 192, and 255. It is worth noting that Martini often shows his discretion about a final identification of these gems by using quotation marks around the designation "Weissagendes Haupt des Orpheus." There are certainly other themes of the talking head on gems, and like the mirrors, the gems must be studied carefully to sort out which ones are truly Orphic. Unfortunately, there is not space here for such a review, but I will mention at least one type that is obviously not Orpheus: a warrior stands over a decapitated body and holds up the severed head of his adversary so that their heads seem to regard each other and converse (Martini 1971, 137, No. 69, plate 14.6). For a wide range of soothsaying heads on gems, see Furtwängler 1900, I, plate 21, 27–72; 22, 1–15; II, 104–108; and III, 245–252.
45. Zazoff 1968, 168, 167 (No. 134). Harari 1997, 108 (No. 117), floats the suggestion that Hermes is freeing "Laran" from a pithos, but in fact the shape and decoration of the container fit much better with the idea of the bag.
46. Lambrechts 1978, 23–27; de Grummond 2000, 51–52; 2006, 35–36.
47. ES 5.68; de Grummond 1981, 121. The scene is strange and worth discussing as being related to prophecy, since not only Medusa, but also Perseus himself and another male figure, Purciuś, have streaming hair. But further consideration of it here would take us far from the main theme.
48. Ambrosini 1996, 1998.
49. Civita Castellana (ancient Falerii) is located about halfway between Orvieto and Rome. The site is Faliscan and thus technically not Etruscan, but it is widely acknowledged that Faliscan culture is closely related to Etruria geographically and culturally. For the dating of the mirrors, see the careful review of chronology of mirrors of this general type in Ambrosini 1996, 76–88.
50. Ambrosini 1996, 64–65 (Civita Castellana, Museo Archeologico dell'Agro Falisco, inv. 6131).
51. See Ambrosini's 1996 useful survey of the problem of Lasa terminology, 63–64.
52. There are also Lasa figures that vary from this pattern, by wearing clothing or not having wings or not being female or not carrying the adornment attributes. See Lambrechts 1992.
53. De Grummond 1991, 20–22; ES I, 42.1–5, 43.1–4.
54. Ambrosini 1996, 71; Garezou 1994, 104.
55. Ambrosini 1996, 71; Garezou 1994, 104. The head on the antefixes is sometimes identified as Athena.
56. Hoddinott 1981, 107.
57. Ambrosini 1996, fig. 2.
58. Cristofani 1967, esp. 194–196.

59. It would be interesting to have a complete inventory. There are numerous mirrors and gems. See Ambrosini 1996, 72, for the long bibliography. Cf. note 43 on gems. On mirrors, see de Grummond 2000, 42–49, 51–54, 66–67.

60. Aplu does appear with Umaele in a scene with quite different content: a mirror from Castelgiorgio shows Umaele reading a liver as he is watched by Turms, Alpnu, and Aplu. De Puma 2001, 24; van der Meer 1995, 86. This mirror does not have to do with Orpheus, despite van der Meer's incorrect statement that the inscription *urφe* is written on the rock beneath the foot. Cf. de Grummond 2000, 42 (note 24).

61. Ambrosini 1996, 75, with previous bibliography.

62. Guthrie 1993, chapter V, discusses the Orphic afterlife.

63. The Orphic (and also Pythagorean) belief that the soul enters the body through the breath immediately marks the head as an area of the greatest significance and vitality. Guthrie 1993, 94.

64. Marazov 1998, 33; Chapter 5, in this volume. Cf. the analysis of Greek myths of Orpheus vis-à-vis Thracian realities in Archibald 1998, 208–209.

65. Marazov 1996, 160–179; 1998, 154.

66. See Marazov 1998, 160–171, on the Letnitsa Treasure and 167–169 on the five plaques discussed here.

67. We are reminded that on the eve of battle Xenophon and his army regularly sacrificed a victim, and from the victim obtained the omens that determined whether to go to battle the next day (e.g., *Anabasis*, 6.4.20, 6.5.2, 6.5.25).

68. Lattimore 1951, 403.

69. Indra duly decapitated Dadhyañc, but the twins were able to replace his real head, which they had saved. The horse's head later "hidden in the mountains" made a revelation to Indra himself. O'Flaherty 1975, 56–58; Nagy 1990, 218. A further intriguing parallel is found in a Bronze Age burial at Potapovka on the Volga River, where the Sintashta-Petrokva culture shows links with the Rig Veda. A burial was found in which a decapitated human victim lay on top of the grave, his head replaced with that of a horse. Anthony and Vinogradov 1995, 40–41. I thank Jean MacIntosh Turfa for this reference.

70. Knauer 2001 brings together the bibliography and the evidence.

71. Rolle 1989, 83.

72. Savostina 2001. I am most grateful to Maya Muratov for providing me with a copy of this publication. Knauer 2001. (A variant of this article appears in Savostina 2001, 186–213, in both English and Russian.)

73. Artamonov 1969, 70 and text, fig. 230; Jacobson 1995, 174; Knauer 2001, 288 (note 17).

74. Corcella et al. 1993, 281. Many thanks to John Marincola for providing me with a copy of this work.

75. Jacobson 1995, 215–216; Knauer 2001, 288 (note 17).

76. De Grummond 2000, 48–50; 2002, 69, 80.

77. MacCulloch 1911, 240–242; Wait 1985, 199–200; Green 1992, 114–117; Cunliffe 1997, 127–128.

78. Knauer 2001, 291 (note 28 with bibliography). On Manching in general see Wells 1999, esp. 28–31. Other literary allusions to Celtic head hunting: Livy 10.26, Diodorus Siculus 5.29.4, and Strabo 4.4.5.

79. Cunliffe 1997, 200, 202. Roquepertuse: Green 1992, 178–179. Entremont: Green 1992, 90.

80. Green 1992, 156–157.

81. MacCulloch 1911, 247–251; Wait 1985, 207.

82. Green 1992, 82.

83. Green 1992, 18–21, gives a helpful critical review of the limits of using this material.

84. MacCulloch 1911, 215.

85. Green 1992, 120–122.

86. Told in *the Second Branch of the Mabinogi* (ca. 1100 A.D.). MacCulloch 1911, 101–103; Green 1992, 42; Wright 2003, 183–184.

87. See note 5. Cf. the statement by Knauer 2001, 290, note 21, on "How much civilized Greeks abhorred the spectacle of severing the head of an enemy and impaling it."

88. Lattimore 1951. Cf. Vermeule 1979.

89. Garezou 1994, 82.

90. Hall 1989.

91. Hall 1989, 201–223.

92. There are more examples in Etruscan art than in the other cultures of the Voice as a Head and the Chthonic Head, as well as of the Severed Head.

93. It is of interest that oracular shrines are rare in Etruria. Curnow 2004, map 9, of sites in Italy, shows Etruria as virtually blank. He does list Veii, just north of Rome, as oracular, but in fact the temple of Juno there has been identified only as having a healing cult. There is a single literary reference to an oracle in Etruria: Plutarch, *Romulus* 2, mentions an oracle of Tethys consulted by the early Sabine king Tarchetius. The reference is quite baffling, and so far no trace of such an oracle has been found. Maggiani 1986, 7. There is some evidence of the use of *sortes*, prophetic lots, at Etruscan sites: Bagnasco Gianni 2001, and Colonna 2006, 135.

94. In particular, I did not deal with the problem of the *anodos*, the emergence of a being from the earth or underworld, studied by Bérard 1974, which I see as overlapping with the Chthonic Head but probably lacking in the prophetic theme. I also did not include a discussion of Ambrosini 1998, another excellent article on the head motif in Etruria and Italy, deserving fuller attention than I could have justified in the context of the issues about barbarians emphasized here. She deals with *anodos* heads and with a number of other suggestions that have been made to explain various head motifs. I think there is a good chance that a number of her examples may be categorized as the Head as a Voice. In addition, I would like to investigate the presence of Silenus heads more fully, especially in relation to the use of the prophetic phiale. There are surprising and numerous representations of Silenus figures in Thracian, Scythian, and Celtic art. Finally, I would like to explore more fully the spiritual component of the vital head, and attempt to understand better its relation to Orphism and other philosophical and religious concepts of the soul.

Bibliography

Ambrosini, L. 1996."Una coppia di specchi del gruppo "delle Lase" con un nuovo tipo di raffiguranza." *Studi Etruschi* 62:63–94.

    1998. "Il Pittore di Micali: Nota iconografica sulla raffigurazione di due teste isolate." *Archeologia Classica* 50:343–361.

Anthony, D. W., and N. B. Vinogradov 1995. "Birth of the Chariot." *Archaeology* 48:36–41.

Archibald, Z. H. 1998. *The Odrysian Kingdom of Thrace: Orpheus Unmasked.* Oxford.

Artamonov, M. I. 1969. *The Splendours of Scythian Art.* New York.

Bagnasco Gianni, G. 2001. "Le *sortes* etrusche." In *Sorteggio pubblico e cleromanzia dall'antichità all'età moderna*, ed. Federica Cordano and Cristiano Grottanelli, 197–219. Milan.

   2009. "The Importance of Being Umaele." In Swaddling and Perkins 2009, 48–56.

Bérard, C. 1974. *Anodoi, Essai sur l'imagerie des passages chthoniens.* Bibliotheca Helvetica Romana 13. Neuchâtel.

Bonfante, G., and L. Bonfante. 2002. *The Etruscan Language: An Introduction*, 2nd ed. Manchester.

Bonfante, L. 1984a. "Human Sacrifice on an Etruscan Funerary Urn." *AJA* 88:531–539.

   1984b. "Un'urna chiusina con 'têtes coupées' a New York." In *Studi di antichità in onore di Guglielmo Maetzke* I, 143–150. Rome.

Bremmer, J. 1991. "Orpheus: From Guru to Gay." In *Orphisme et Orphée, en l'honneur de Jean Rudhardt. Recherches et Rencontres*, ed. P. Borgeaud, 3:13–30. Geneva.

Briquel, D. 1993. "Les voix oraculaires." In *Les bois sacrés*, ed. O. de Casanove and J. Scheid, 77–90. Naples.

Camporeale, G. 1997. "Umaele." *LIMC* VIII:158–159.

Colonna, G. 2006. "Sacred Architecture and the Religion of the Etruscans." In *The Religion of the Etruscans*, ed. N. T. de Grummond and E. Simon, 132–168. Austin, TX.

Corcella, A., S. M. Medaglia, and A. Fraschetti. 1993. *Erodoto, Le Storie, Libro IV, La Scizia e la Libia*. Vicenza.

Cristofani, M. 1967. "Ricerche sulle pitture della tomba François di Vulci. I fregi decorativi." *Dialoghi di Archeologia* 1:186–219

   1982. "Faone, la testa di Orfeo e l'immaginario femminile." *Prospettiva* 42:2–12.

Cunliffe, B. 1997. *The Ancient Celts.* Oxford.

Curnow, T. 2004. *The Oracles of the Ancient World.* London.

de Grummond, N. T. 2000. 'Mirrors and Manteia: Themes of Prophecy on Etruscan Mirrors." In *Aspetti e problemi della produzione degli specchi figurati etruschi*, ed. M. D. Gentili, 27–67. Rome.

   2002. "Mirrors, Marriage and Mysteries," *JRA,* Suppl. 47:63–85.

   2006. *Etruscan Myth, Sacred History and Legend.* Philadelphia.

de Grummond, N. T. ed., 1981. *A Guide to Etruscan Mirrors.* Tallahassee, FL.

   1991. "Etruscan Twins and Mirror Images: The Dioskouroi at the Door." *Yale University Art Gallery Bulletin,* 10–31.

De Puma, R. D. 2001. "An Etruscan Mirror with the Prophesying Head of Orpheus." *Record, Princeton University Art Museum* 60:18–29.

Doerig, J. 1991. "La tête qui chante." In *Orphisme et Orphée, en l'honneur de Jean Rudhardt. Recherches et Rencontres*, ed. P. Borgeaud, 3:61–64. Geneva.

Emmanuel-Rebuffat, D. 1984. "Aliunea n'a jamais existé." *Latomus* 43:501–516.
1988. *CSE* France 1. Paris, Musée du Louvre I. Rome.

ES, ed. E. Gerhard, A. Klügmann, and E. Körte. *Etruskische Spiegel*, 5 vols. 1840–1897. Berlin.

Falconer, W. A. 1922. Cicero, *De senectute, de amicitia, de divinatione*, trans. W. A. Falconer. Cambridge, MA.

Furtwängler, A. 1900. *Die Antiken Gemmen*. 3 vols. Munich.

Garezou, M.-X. 1994. "Orpheus." *LIMC* VII:81–105.

Green, M. J. 1992. *Dictionary of Celtic Myth and Legend*. London.

Guthrie, W. K. C. 1993. *Orpheus and Greek Religion*. Princeton, NJ. (Reprint of the 1952 edition.)

Hall, E. 1989. *Inventing the Barbarian: Greek Self-Definition through Tragedy*. Oxford.

Harari, M. 1997. "Turms." *LIMC* VIII:98–111.

Hodinott, R. F. 1981. *The Thracians*. London.

Jacobson, E. 1995. *The Art of the Scythians*. Leiden.

Jucker, I. 2001. *CSE Schweiz* 1. Berne.

Knauer, E. R. 2001. "Observations on the "Barbarian" Custom of Suspending the Heads of Vanquished Enemies from the Neck of Horses." *Archäologisches Mitteilungen aus Iran und Turan* 33:283–332.

Krauskopf, I. 1981. "Aliunea." *LIMC* I:529–531.

Lambrechts, R. 1978. *Les miroirs étrusques et prénestins des Musées Royaux d'Art et d'Histoire à Bruxelles*. Brussels.
1992: "Lasa." *LIMC* VI:217–225.

Lattimore, R. 1951. *The Iliad of Homer*, trans. R. Lattimore. Chicago.

MacCulloch, J. A. 1911. *The Religion of the Ancient Celts*. London.

Maggiani, A. 1986. "La divinazione oraculaire in Etruria." *Caesarodunum* Suppl. 56:6–48.
1992. "Iconografie greche e storie locali nell'arte etrusco-italica tra IV e III secolo a.C." *Prospettiva* 68:3–11.

Mandelbaum, A. 1971. *The Aeneid of Virgil*, trans. A. Mandelbaum. Toronto.

Marazov, I. 1996. *The Rogozen Treasure*. Sofia.
1998. *Ancient Gold: The Wealth of the Thracians*. New York.

Martini, W. 1971. *Die Etruskische Ringsteinglyptik*. RM, Erg. 18. Heidelberg.

Nagy, J. F. 1990. "Hierarchy, Heroes and Heads: Indo-European Structures in Greek Myth." In *Approaches to Greek Myth*, ed. L. Edmunds, 199–238. Baltimore.

O'Flaherty, W. D. 1975. *Hindu Myths: A Sourcebook Translated from the Sanskrit*. London.

Potter, D. 1994. *Prophets and Emperors: Human and Divine Authority from Augustus to Theodosius*. Cambridge, MA.

Pruciuc, A. 2003. "Orpheus – Name and Function." *Thracia 15, In Honour of Alexander Fol's 70th Anniversary*, 197–211. Sofia.

Puhvel, J. 1987. *Comparative Mythology*. Baltimore.

Rix, H. 1991. *Etruskische Texte*: Editio Minor. Tübingen.

Rolle, R. 1989. *The World of the Scythians*. Berkeley, CA.

Savostina, E., ed. 2001. *Bosporan Battle Relief: Amazonomachia?*. Moscow.

Schmidt, M. 1972. "Ein Neues Zeugnis zum Mythos vom Orpheushaupt." *Antike Kunst* 15:128–137.

———. 1991. 'Bemerkungen zu Orpheus in Unterwelts-und Thrakerdarstellungen." In *Orphisme et Orphée, en l'honneur de Jean Rudhardt. Recherches et Rencontres*, ed. P. Borgeaud, 3:31–50. Geneva.

Small, J. P. 1994. "Tages." *LIMC* VII:832–833.

Swaddling, J., and P. Perkins, eds. 2009. *Etruscan by Definition: Papers in Honour of Sybille Haynes*, MBE. London.

Torelli, M., ed. 2000. *Gli Etruschi*. Milan.

van der Meer, L. B. 1995. *Interpretatio Etrusca: Greek Myths on Etruscan Mirrors*. Amsterdam.

Vermeule, E. 1979. *Aspects of Death in Early Greek Art and Poetry*. Berkeley, CA.

Wait, G. A. 1985. *Ritual and Religion in Iron Age Britain*. Oxford.

Wardle, D. 2006. *Cicero on Divination: De Divinatione, Book 1*. Oxford.

Wells, P. 1999. *The Barbarians Speak: How the Conquered Peoples Shaped Roman Europe*. Princeton, NJ.

———. 2001. *Beyond Celts, Germans and Scythians: Archaeology and Identity in Iron Age Europe*. London.

Wright, G. H. R. 2003. "Orpheus with His Head." *Thracia 15, In Honour of Alexander Fol's 70th Anniversary*, 179–188. Sofia.

Zazoff, P. 1968. *Etruskische Skarabäen*. Mainz.

Zimmerman, K. 1997. "Teiresias." *LIMC* VIII:1188–1191.

CHAPTER ELEVEN

ROMANS AND/AS BARBARIANS

John Marincola

The Greeks' quandary of where to locate the Romans within the Greek/barbarian dichotomy was one that constantly presented itself to the Greeks over the long centuries in which their history was interwoven with that of the Romans. The problem was never "solved," so to speak, but the ways in which that relationship changed to suit alterations in the cultural and political context are illuminating for our understanding of Greek (and Roman) identity.

Thucydides reminds us that for Homer the distinction between Greeks and barbarians did not exist.[1] That distinction, we should remember, is a creation of the fifth century BC, and the catalyst for its creation was the Greek conflict - first in Asia Minor and then on mainland Greece - with the Persians. That is not to say that the Greeks may not have had a notion of themselves as different from others before then, but the dichotomy, in its classic form, came into existence only by slow steps in a specific historical context.[2] The distinction is, of course, already visible in Herodotus, although recent scholarship has also emphasized that for this author the boundary between the two peoples is fluid and permeable.[3] Herodotus has no trouble at all in attributing much

This contribution retains the form in which it was given at Richmond, although I have added a few new remarks and the appropriate bibliographical references. I am grateful to Larissa Bonfante for inviting me to participate in this stimulating conference. The literature on the Greco-Roman construction of the barbarian is now vast. My views here have been much influenced by (most recently) Timpe 2000, Saïd 2001, and Sourvinou-Inwood 2003.

of Greek religion and ritual to the Egyptians, and his work in general shows expectations of a kind of cultural osmosis rarely seen after him.[4] It was, however, fifth-century literature that developed the distinction in what we might call its classic form: the "Greek," on the one hand, as representative of order, liberty, self-determination, and reason, and the "barbarian," on the other hand, stereotypically described in terms of chaos, slavery, despotism, and unbridled passion.[5]

In the fourth century BC we can begin to see a change in the Greek/barbarian dichotomy. Isocrates and others begin to see Greek as a cultural, not an ethnic, category, and these authors suggest, if somewhat tentatively, that Greek *paideia* is open to all.[6] Xenophon, for his part, further complicated this distinction in his *Cyropaedia* by portraying the Persian Cyrus in the guise of a Greek wisdom figure (there were precedents in Herodotus for that, of course).[7] But both Isocrates and Xenophon could hold these beliefs while simultaneously either campaigning or encouraging a campaign against the barbarian Persians. Success in that campaign was left ultimately to Alexander, but his own inclination to form a Macedonian–Persian élite was not quite what his Greek and Macedonian supporters had been expecting. It is very likely that as a Macedonian, he was already familiar with marginalization.[8] However these individuals and their actions or writings are interpreted, it is important to keep in mind that the concept of barbarian was not fixed or immutable, even if certain aspects tend to be emphasized again and again.[9]

Among the peoples of this conference, that is, the barbarians of Europe, the Romans occupy a unique position for two very important reasons: first, we have for them, as we do not for any of the other peoples, an abundant dialogue between themselves and the Greeks, preserved not only in their art but also in their literature; and second, the Romans were for the Greeks no temporary barbarian invaders, like the Thracians or Celts, but a permanent presence in their land, which they conquered and then ruled for centuries.

It is a truism repeated often enough that Rome found itself between two much more advanced civilizations in Italy: the Etruscans to the north and the Greek city-states to the south. Rome was being founded at just about the time that the Greeks were planting their first westward colonies, and archaeology has revealed early and profound contacts between Greeks and Romans: Nicholas Purcell has recently reminded us that there is never a time when we can look at Rome and *not* see Greek influence.[10] Rome's growing contacts, sometimes aggressive, with the Greek cities of southern Italy constituted the first encounters in what was to be a centuries-long process of trial and error. But Greek influence doesn't make you Greek.

As Paul Keyser has noted, the Greeks were slow to turn their eyes westward.[11] Although Hellanicus of Lesbos mentioned Aeneas and Rome already in the late fifth century,[12] more substantial treatments of the Romans by Greeks had to wait another 150 years. It was Hieronymus of Cardia, the historian of Alexander's successors, who seems to have been the first to treat the Romans in detail, narrating their early history, probably in a digression in his treatment of Pyrrhus's wars in Italy.[13] After him, Timaeus of Tauromenium gave fuller and more detailed treatment, and was, before Polybius (and for some even after Polybius), the great authority on the West and Rome.[14] Timaeus, no doubt, saw a bit more clearly than the others because he came from Sicily. In general, however, the Romans long remained on the periphery of the Greek mental map.

Their move to the center of Greek consciousness corresponds with Rome's increased military aims and ambitions in the late third to mid-second century BC. It began in the same way it often did with the Greeks: one entity – in this case, the Aetolian League – called in an outside power to help it settle its disputes with another Greek state.[15] That turned out to be a mistake of grand proportions. It all happened so quickly: only fifty years separate Flamininus's proclamation of the "freedom of the Greeks" at the Isthmian games of 196 BC from the razing of the ancient city of Corinth in 146. It would have been hard at that moment for the Greeks to see this Western power as anything other than a barbarian menace – more Cyclops than Phaeacians, to use Larissa Bonfante's terms[16] – and it would have been a tall order to convince most of the Greeks otherwise. But at least one man decided to try it.

Polybius of Megalopolis, who had fought against the Romans when he was a member of the Achaean League and was later a political prisoner at Rome, took on this grand challenge, and it is clear from his work that it was not easy or uncontested or without its contradictions.[17] What made it particularly difficult was that when a Greek looked at the Romans, he saw much that was familiar: like most Greek settlements, Rome was a city-state, with an aristocracy distinguished by wealth and social standing. The Romans had temples to the gods very similar to the Greeks' own. They had a citizen army, and an oligarchic government with annual elections and rotation of magistrates. Polybius could even explain this government in terms the Greeks would understand, as a form of mixed constitution, and superior to any Greek one at that.[18] And the Romans had writing and even a written law code. To the Greeks the Romans looked different, in most senses, from the Thracians or Scythians or Celts.

But in some ways they looked very much like barbarians, particularly in the ferocity of their fighting and the intensity of their devotion to their military and their imperialism. Polybius's description of the Roman funeral is meant to convey just how deeply ingrained the militaristic strain in Romans was and how profound for their way of life their love of glory was.[19] His description of the Roman army is meant to explain how the Romans could have the ferocity of the Western barbarians and yet at the same time possess an admirable and thoroughly Greek devotion to order and method. Romans fought with the passion (*thymos*) of Celts but with the sensibility (*logismos*) of Greeks.[20] None of the Greeks' regular stereotypes about barbarians really fit the Romans.

Nor was Roman behavior toward Greece consistent at all periods of their interaction. Craige Champion has argued in fact that the Romans had no "fixed" position in Polybius's work, and at times they could be portrayed as Greeks, at times as barbarians. Much depended on their behavior at any given time, and this led to what he calls a politics of "cultural indeterminacy."[21] Such an approach has the benefit of helping us to understand the very different strands, sometimes contradictory, that made up the complex reaction to and evaluation of the Romans by the Greeks of the mid-second century BC.

A century after Polybius, with Greece long pacified and with a very different political landscape, the battle for Greek hearts and minds was still being fought. Dionysius of Halicarnassus needed twenty books to make an argument that built on Polybius's, namely, that the Romans were truly Greeks – and not late converts to Hellenism, but Greeks from the very outset, and achievers of deeds as glorious as any the Greeks had done.[22] Dionysius's message was perhaps meant as one of comfort as the Greeks settled in for the long haul of Roman rule: since the Romans really were Greeks, his argument goes, their achievements redounded to Greek credit and increased Greek glory. It was even, therefore, appropriate that they should rule Greeks, since that was doing no more than exercising command over one's fellow citizens.[23]

But let us turn aside for the moment from the Greeks and focus on the Romans themselves. For this process of cultural and political definition was not one-sided, nor was it dictated entirely by Greeks. There is no need to rehearse, of course, things long known, especially about Greek influence on early Roman culture: the first work of Latin literature is a translation of Homer's *Odyssey*, and the plays of Plautus and Terence, though written in Latin, are full of Greek characters and Greek situations. It is perhaps more to our point here to note that the first Roman historian, Quintus Fabius Pictor, wrote his history of Rome in Greek.[24] That means that he saw himself, at least in part, as trying to fit his country into a specifically Greek framework. How he did this exactly we cannot know, but even the meager fragments show that he spent a good deal of time on the foundation stories of Rome, and emphasized his city's Greek origins and character.[25] (Plutarch tells us that he even used Greek sources, including the little-known Diocles of Peparethus, for the history of his own city!)[26] We note, therefore, the reciprocal efforts of both Romans and Greeks to define the Romans in terms of the Greeks.

The Roman obsession with the Greeks finds expression in nearly every aspect of their culture: in their art, their philosophy, and their literature, they looked constantly to Greek models and vied with them to make their own. Even Cato the Elder, often held up as an enemy of the Greeks, needs to be included here. His criticisms of the Greeks are well known, yet his *Origines* begins with an unmistakable allusion to Xenophon's *Memorabilia*[27] (not really the kind of work you can imagine Cato reading), and the history itself, with its interest in the origins of Italian cities, is deeply influenced by Greek foundation narratives (the title *Origines* may be an attempt to render in Latin the Greek word *Ktiseis*) and even by Greek methods.[28]

The story changes, of course, as we move on. In the Roman Empire, there is a strong assimilation of the Greek elite into the Roman structure of government. No doubt the blessings of peace, something the Greeks were not particularly good at when left on their own, must have done something to make the Romans less "barbarian" than they might early on have been. Greek vanity was flattered by philhellene emperors such as

Nero and Hadrian. Nero, in particular, is a good case in point: portrayed in an unremittingly negative way in the Roman tradition, he was much praised and beloved in the Greek tradition,[29] and Dio of Prusa reports that there were those who, after his fall, believed that Nero was still alive and hoped fervently that he would come back to reoccupy his position as emperor.[30] Even Plutarch, usually a model of sober judgment, praises Nero for his love of things Greek.[31] And Plutarch's own work, the *Parallel Lives*, though an experiment (and perhaps a daring one for the time), is unimaginable without a framework in which it was possible to speak of Greeks and Romans as equals in important senses of that term.[32]

Space prohibits anything like a detailed treatment of the various stages in the relationship of Greeks and Romans, so it may be more useful to end with a few points that may not be wholly irrelevant to the topic of this conference. First, the concept of the barbarian, as we can trace it in the Greek tradition, was one that constantly evolved and needed to evolve as the Greeks' own situation changed. To give just one example: in the fifth and fourth centuries BC, monarchy was a form of government especially characteristic of barbarians; two centuries later in the Hellenistic world, most of the Greeks were living under kings. Greek writers who in an earlier time would doubtless have been quick to condemn monarchy as inherently wicked instead had to get busy to explain how the good king could benefit both cities and subjects.[33] That's not hypocrisy, that's pragmatism.

Second, the interaction between Greeks and Romans shows that at least for one "barbarian" people, the categories of definition were in continuous dialogue, both on the Greek side and on the barbarian one. Horace's famous remark that captive Greece conquered her savage conqueror[34] is the pithiest formulation of this process. Now it may not be the case that the other barbarians cared to define themselves in opposition to the Greeks, but we must at least recognize that cultural definition is a two-way street, and the tendency to have the Greeks as the sole speakers in what is, after all, a complex and varied dialogue must be resisted.[35] Here, if anywhere, it is imperative to help the barbarian people speak.

Finally, the Greeks' notions of themselves and others must be contextualized in the framework of the larger political events in which they came to birth and developed. Homer had no need of barbarians, but the fifth-century Greeks did, and there's a reason for it. It is very likely that before Roman involvement in Greece, the Greeks were content to see the Romans as merely a distant people with a tradition linking them to Troy.[36] At the time, it didn't really matter who the Romans were: only when they began to impinge on the Greeks did it become necessary to define or redefine or reconfigure them. The great Celtic invasion of Greece and Asia Minor in 280 BC and the years following had likewise made it necessary for the Greeks to fit these Gauls into their larger picture of the world, and we can trace in some detail how they were assimilated to earlier barbarians such as the Amazons while retaining some individual features of their own, as is clear from the description of them in Polybius and other writers.[37] The difficulties and contradictions, however, remained: how dearly we would love to know what it was like – and what the Greeks told themselves – when those same "Amazonian" Celts fought as mercenaries, side by side with Greek and Macedonian soldiers, under Hellenistic kings.[38]

Notes

1. Thuc. i. 3. 3: "Homer especially bears witness to this [i.e., that there was no united Hellas in early times]: for although he lived much later than the Trojan Wars, he nowhere has one name for them [sc. the Greeks], … but in his poems he calls them Danaans, Argives, and Achaeans. Nor does he ever refer to 'barbarians' because, I think, the Hellenes were not distinguished by one equally corresponding name." For the terms *Panachaioi* and *Panhellenes* in Homer, see S. Hornblower 1991, 17.
2. For the Persian Wars as crucial to the Greeks' consciousness of themselves as distinct from the barbarian see Momigliano 1975, Lévy 1984; E. Hall 1989, 56–62. Certain elements, however, that came to be part of the construction of the barbarian – their numbers, their incomprehensible speech, and their wealth – were already present before the fifth century BC, as Harrison 2002, 3–4, points out.
3. For the Greek/barbarian dichotomy in Herodotus, see the contributions in Nenci 1990; cf. Cartledge 1990; 2002, 8–17, 36–77; Lévy 1992. See, however, Pelling 1997, who demonstrates that the supposed characteristics of the barbarians are – at least at the end of the *Histories* and possibly even before – already being assumed by some of the Greek participants.
4. On Herodotus and foreign religion in general see Burkert 1990; Harrison 2000, 208–222; for his treatment of Egypt specifically, see Lloyd 1976, passim.
5. E. Hall 1989, 56–133.
6. Isocrates states this most clearly at *Paneg.* 50; for Isocrates's views see Saïd 2001.
7. For the *Cyropaedia* see Gera 1993; for Herodotus's use of foreigners to convey Greek wisdom see Fehling 1989, 193–194.
8. On the ethnic identity of the Macedonians, much debated even in antiquity, see J. Hall 2001.

9. On the change in definition of barbarian over time, see Timpe 2000.
10. Purcell 2003, 13–14.
11. Keyser, Chapter 2, in this volume. See also Alonso-Núñez 1987.
12. Hellanicus, *FGrHist* 4 F 31 = D. Hal. *A.R.* i. 45. 4–48. 1
13. Theopompus was the first Greek historian to actually mention the Romans (*FGrHist* 115 F 317), and Diocles of Peparethus was the first to write on the foundation of Rome (*FGrHist* 820 T 2a and n. 26 in this chapter), but Hieronymus was the first to give a detailed treatment of early Roman history: see *FGrHist* 154 FF 11, 13 with J. Hornblower 1981, 248–250.
14. On Timaeus and Rome see Brown 1958, 34–35; Momigliano 1959; Vattuone 1991, 265–301; 2002, 217–222.
15. For the events leading up to Rome's intervention in Greece see Gruen 1984, 437–480.
16. See Bonfante, Chapter 1, in this volume.
17. There is a vast bibliography on Polybius's attitude toward Rome: see (i.a.) Walbank 1963, 1974; Musti 1978; Derow 1979; Richardson 1979; Shimron 1979/1980; Dubuisson 1990; Eckstein 1995, 84–117, 194–236; Champion 2000 and especially 2004.
18. Much has been written on Polybius's account of the Roman constitution in Book 6. See most recently Champion 2004, 67–99. One should also point out that the Greeks had the capacity to make many of the peoples with whom they came into contact Greeks from a long way back: see the classic exposition of Bickerman 1952.
19. Polybius 6.53–54.
20. See Champion 2004, 117–143, 255–259.
21. Champion 2004.
22. For Dionysius's *Antiquitates* and their relationship to Rome, see Gabba 1991, 190–216.
23. See Gabba 1991, 195–200; some aspects of this way of thinking probably predate Dionysius: see Gabba 1991, 196–197, n. 22.
24. The fragments of Pictor's work are in Peter, *HRR* i. 5–39 and *FGrHist* 809; a fuller and more up-to-date collection is now in Chassignet 1996, 16–54; cf. Beck and Walter 2005, 62–136, for text, German translation, and historical commentary on the fragments.
25. *FGrHist* 809 FF 1–6, 29, 31.
26. *FGrHist* 809 F 4a = *HRR* F 5a = F 7 Chassignet *FRH* F 7a = Plut. *Rom.* 8.9. For Diocles of Peparethus see *DNP* 3 (1997) 613, s.v. "Diokles [7]."
27. *HRR* F 2 = Cato *FRH* F 1, 2 with the commentary of Beck and Walter 2005, ad loc.
28. A great deal has been written about Cato's attitude toward Greek culture; for recent treatments see Kienast 1979, 101–116; Gruen 1992, 52–83; Jehne 1999.
29. See Griffin 1984, 208–220.
30. Dio Chrys. *Orat.* 21.9–10.
31. Plut. *Mor.* 567F-568A; cf. Philostr. *Life of Apollonia* v. 41.
32. On the issues of identity inherent in Plutarch's use of Greeks and Romans in his *Lives* see Swain 1996, 135–186; Duff 1999, 287–309
33. For a survey of Hellenistic theories about kingship see most recently Hahm 2000.
34. Hor. *Epist.* ii. 1. 156–157: *Graecia capta ferum uictorem cepit et arti/intulit agresti Latio.*

35. For an example from a much earlier time period see Moyer 2002, who has argued that the Egyptians were hardly the passive constructs of the Greeks that they are often made out to be, but rather had a strong hand in shaping the view of themselves that is reflected in Herodotus.

36. For the difficulty of recovering the Greek view of Rome and Troy before the Augustan age see Erskine 2001, 23-43.

37. For the Celts as barbarians see Mitchell 2003; for the Coan decree of 279 (*SIG* 398) see Champion 1995; on their portrayal in art, see Smith 1991, 99-104; Kremer 1994.

38. For Celts in the service of Attalus I, see Pol. v. 77. 2; in the service of Nicomedes of Bithynia, see Memnon, *FGrHist* 434 F 11; in the service of Antiochus Hierax, see *OGIS* 280. It is sometimes unclear whether the Celts served as allies or mercenaries, though the latter is more likely; see Mitchell 2003, 290-293.

Bibliography

Alonso-Núñez, J. M. 1987. "Herodotus on the Far West." *AC* 56:243-249.

Beck, H., and U. Walter, 2005. *Die Frühen Römischen Historiker I: Von Fabius Pictor bis Cn. Gellius*, 2nd edition. Darmstadt.

Bickerman, E. J. 1952. "*Origines Gentium*," *CPh* 47:65-81, reprinted in E. J. Bickerman, *Religion and Politics in the Ancient World*, ed. E. Gabba and M. Smith, 399-417. Como, 1985.

Braund, D., and C. Gill, eds. 2003. *Myth, History and Culture in Republican Rome: Studies in Honour of T. P. Wiseman.* Exeter.

Brown, T. S. 1958. *Timaeus of Tauromenium.* Berkeley, CA, and Los Angeles.

Burkert, W. 1990. "Herodot als Historiker fremden Religionen." In Nenci 1990, 1-39.

Cartledge, P. 1990. "Herodotus and 'the Other': A Meditation on Empire," *EMC/ CV* 34:27-40.

2002. *The Greeks: A Portrait of Self and Others.* Oxford.

Champion, C. 1995. "The Soteria at Delphi: Aetolian Propaganda in the Epigraphical Record." *AJP* 116:213-20.

2000. "Histories 12.4b.1-c.1: An Overlooked Key to Polybius' Views on Rome." *Histos* 4 (http://www.dur.ac.uk/Classics/histos/2000/champion. html).

2004. *Cultural Politics in Polybius' Histories.* Berkeley, CA, Los Angeles, and London.

Chassignet, M. 1996. *L'Annalistique romaine. Tome I: Les annales des pontifes et l'annalistique ancienne. (Fragments).* Paris.

Derow, P. S. 1979. "Polybius, Rome and the East." *JRS* 69:1-15.

Dubuisson, M. 1990. "La vision polybienne de Rome." In *Purposes of History: Studies in Greek Historiography from the 4th to the 2nd centuries B.C. Studia Hellenistica*, ed. H. Verdin, G. Schepens, and E. deKeyser, 30: 233-243. Leuven.

Duff, T. 1999. *Plutarch's Lives: Exploring Virtue and Vice.* Oxford.

Eckstein, A. 1995. *Moral Vision in the* Histories *of Polybius.* Berkeley, CA, Los Angeles, and London.

Erskine, A. 2001. *Troy between Greece and Rome: Local Tradition and Imperial Power.* Oxford.

Fehling, D. 1989. *Herodotus and His "Sources": Citation, Invention and Narrative Art* (Leeds); revised and expanded trans. by J. G. Howie of *Die Quellenangaben bei Herodot*. Berlin and New York 1971.

Gabba, E. 1991. *Dionysius and* The History of Archaic Rome. Berkeley, CA, Los Angeles, and London.

Gera, D. L. 1993. *Xenophon's* Cyropaedia: *Style, Genre and Literary Technique*. Oxford.

Griffin, M. 1984. *Nero: The End of a Dynasty*. London and New Haven, CT.

Gruen, E. 1984. *The Hellenistic World and the Coming of Rome*. Berkeley, CA, Los Angeles, and London.

— 1992. *Culture and National Identity in Republican Rome*. Ithaca, NY, and London.

Hahm, D. E. 2000. "Kings and Constitutions: Hellenistic Theories." In *The Cambridge History of Greek and Roman Political Thought*, ed. C. Rowe and M. Schofield, 457–476. Cambridge.

Hall, E. 1989. *Inventing the Barbarian: Greek Self-Definition through Tragedy*. Oxford.

Hall, J. 1997. *Ethnic Identity in Ancient Greece*. Cambridge.

— 2001. "Contested Ethnicities: Perceptions of Macedonia within Evolving Definitions of Greek Ethnicity." In Malkin 2001, 159–186.

Harrison, T. 2000. *Divinity and History: The Religion of Herodotus*. Oxford.

— ed. 2002. *Greeks and Barbarians*. London and New York.

Hornblower, J. 1981. *Hieronymus of Cardia*. Oxford.

Hornblower, S. 1991. *A Commentary on Thucydides: Volume I, Books I–III*. Oxford.

Jehne, M. 1999. "Cato und die Bewahrung der traditionellen Res Publica: Zum Spannungsverhältnis zwischen *mos maiorum* und griechischer Kultur im zweiten Jahrhundert v. Chr." In *Rezeption und Identität: Die kulturelle Auseinandersetzung Roms mit Griechenland als europäisches Paradigma*, ed. G. Vogt-Spira and B. Rommel, 115–134. Stuttgart.

Kienast, D. 1979. *Cato der Zensor*. Darmstadt.

Kremer, B. 1994. *Das Bild der Kelten bis in augusteische Zeit: Studien zur Instrumentalisierung eines antiken Feindbildes bei griechischen und römischen Autoren*. Stuttgart.

Lévy, E. 1984. "Naissance du concept de barbare." *Ktèma* 9:5–14.

— 1992. "Hérodote *philobarbaros* ou la vision du barbare chez Hérodote." In *L'Étranger dans le monde grec*, ed. R. Lonis, 2:193–244. Nancy.

Lloyd, A. B. 1976. *Herodotus Book II: Commentary 1–98*. Leiden.

Malkin, I., ed. 2001. *Ancient Perceptions of Greek Ethnicity*. Cambridge, MA.

Mitchell, S. 2003. 'The Galatians: Representations and Realities.' In *A Companion to the Hellenistic World*, ed. A. Erskine, 280–293. Oxford and Malden, MA.

Momigliano, A. 1959. "Atene nel III secolo a.C. e la scoperta di Roma nelle storie di Timeo di Tauromenio." *RSI* 71:529–556 = 1966, 23–53 = 1977, 37–66. (In English.)

— 1966. *Terzo Contributo alla Storia degli Studi Classici e del mondo antico*. 2 vols. Rome.

— 1975. *Alien Wisdom: The Limits of Hellenization*. Cambridge.

1977. *Essays in Ancient and Modern Historiography*. Oxford.

Moyer, I. 2002. "Herodotus and an Egyptian Mirage: The Genealogies of the Theban Priests." *JHS* 122:70–90.

Musti, D. 1978. *Polibio e l'imperialismo romano*. Naples.

Nenci, G., ed. 1990. *Hérodote et les peuples non-grecs*. Vandœuvres-Genève.

Pelling, C. 1997. "East Is East and West Is West: Or Are They?" *Histos* 1 (electronic publication): http://www.dur.ac.uk/Classics/histos/1997/pelling.html).

Purcell, N. 2003. "Becoming Historical: The Roman Case." In Braund and Gill 2003, 12–40.

Richardson, J. S. 1979. "Polybius' View of the Roman Empire." *PBSR* 47:1–11.

Saïd, S. 2001. "The Discourse of Identity in Greek Rhetoric from Isocrates to Aristides." In Malkin 2001, 275–299.

Shimron, B. 1979/1980. "Polybius on Rome: A Reexamination of the Evidence." *SCI* 5:94–117.

Smith, R. R. R. 1991. *Hellenistic Sculpture: A Handbook*. New York.

Sourvinou-Inwood, C. 2003. "Herodotos (and Others) on Pelasgians: Some Perceptions of Ethnicity." In *Herodotus and His World. Essays from a Conference in Memory of George Forrest*, ed. P. Derow and R. Parker, 103–144. Oxford.

Swain, S. 1996. *Hellenism and Empire: Language, Classicism and Power in the Greek World, AD 50–250*. Oxford.

Timpe, D. 2000. "Der Barbar als Nachbar." In *Ideologie – Sport – Außenseiter: Aktuelle Aspekte einer Beschäftigung mit der antiken Gesellschaft*, ed. C. Ulf, 203–230. Innsbruck.

Vattuone, R. 1991. *Sapienza d'Occidente: Il pensiero storico di Timeo di Tauromenio*. Bologna.

2002. "Timeo di Tauromenio." In *Storici Greci d'Occidente*, ed. R. Vattuone, 177–232. Bologna.

Walbank, F. W. 1963. "Polybius and Rome's Eastern Policy." *JRS* 53:1–13 (reprinted in Walbank 1985, 138–156).

1974. "Polybius between Greece and Rome." In *Polybe*, ed. E. Gabba, 1–31. Vandœuvres-Genève. (Reprinted in Walbank 1985, 280–297.)

1985. *Selected Papers in Greek History and Historiography*. Cambridge.

CHAPTER TWELVE

THE IDENTITY OF LATE BARBARIANS: GOTHS AND WINE

Walter Stevenson

Wine, symbol of civilization in the Mediterranean for millennia and still a pro-found cultural marker in Europe today, is not often associated with the Goths.[1] But there is evidence allowing us to add this Northern European barbarian people to the tapestry of ancient wine production[2] at the same time that they were beginning to cultivate the first European barbarian literature with the translation of the Bible into the Gothic language.

The word "culture" is used as a metaphor of cultivation in our modern understanding of cultural identity. A classic ancient explication comes from Cicero's *Tusculan Disputations*. The character defending philoso-phy (M.) tries to explain why so many philosophers can live morally bad lives. "All cultivated minds do not bear fruit. To continue this metaphor, just as a field, however good the soil, cannot be productive without culti-vation, so the mind cannot be productive without teaching. So true it is that the one without the other is ineffective. The cultivation of the mind is philosophy (*cultura autem animi philosophia est*); this pulls out vices by the roots and makes minds fit for the reception of seeds and commits them to the mind and, so to speak, sows in the mind seeds of a kind to bear the richest fruit when fully matured" (2.13).[3] Had the Goths gone from literal cultivation of grapes to metaphorical cultivation of their unique culture?

Let us take up the question of the cultivation of wine first. Of the three "B's" of the barbarians – butter, britches, and beer – their use of dairy products earned the Scythians, and Northern barbarians in general, a reputation as "milk drinkers." We have seen that trousers, practical for cold climates and horseback riders, were considered by Greeks and Romans as stereotypically barbarian dress.[4] What about beer versus wine? From stories of the first Gallic invasions in Italy being driven by a novel wine thirst to Tacitus's puzzlement at "a sort of wine made from fermented barley,"[5] beer and the lack of wine characterized barbarian people in ways that even language did not. For instance, I would guess that a Celtic mercenary in a Hellenistic army, no matter how perfect his Greek, would raise eyebrows if he waxed eloquent to his Greek comrades on the virtues of ale.[6]

But as with many stereotypes, barbarian beer drinking does not hold up very well to the evidence for two reasons. On the one hand, recent archaeological work has warned us that there may have been a good deal more beer drinking going on in the eastern Mediterranean than literary sources admit. And on the other hand, even our Greek literary sources refer to barbarian wine production and drinking.[7]

A growing body of evidence for beer drinking has emerged over the last few decades.[8] Michael Homan argues from evidence in early Hebrew texts that the social prestige of wine drove the abundant pleasures of beer drinking out of literature. In fact, he asserts that even the editing of Hebrew texts reflects this bias, as the term *šēkār* (Greek *sikera*) has been translated as "strong drink" for centuries, while it could far more easily be understood as beer.[9] Homan adds archaeological evidence, from excavated pottery to painted reliefs, to demonstrate beer's wide sway in the eastern Mediterranean. Moving us nearer to the Greek-speaking world, Greenwalt quotes Archilochus to illustrate a Phrygian beer mug's use, and Mellink identifies beer drinkers in a wall painting in Gordion.[10] These references are usually interpreted to refer only to the highly civilized Asian barbarians of Lydia and Phrygia, but Paul McGovern has argued that Homer's discussions of *kykeon*, often simply translated as "potion," refer to a grog made from wine, cheese, and fermenting barley, which may well be depicted in Mellink's wall painting.[11] Though I am inclined to wait for more evidence before concluding that Greeks drank beer, recent work makes us hesitate before passing judgment.

The record for barbarian viticulture, however, is far stronger than for Greek beer. From the beginning of Greek literature we see in Homer's *Iliad* the Greeks fueling their Trojan siege with Thracian wine. My guess is that Western European peoples did not make much wine until they met the Romans, and surely they could not do so farther north than where grapes could grow. But in the Balkans and Black Sea area the issue becomes more complex, and more confused as time passes. Not only was Achilles drinking a fine Thracian vintage in his tent, but there seems to be good evidence that the Thracians were making wine at least as early as the Greeks. Even if Scythians preferred fermented milk, wine was being produced in the Black Sea area from a very early date.[12] By Hellenistic times we read of the Balkan barbarians, Macedonians and Molossians,[13] for example, making wine. Which brings us chronologically to the later barbarians.

Suddenly around AD 270, Greeks, Latins, and Persians simultaneously started using the word "Goth" for the people inhabiting the area of modern Bulgaria, Crimea, Romania, and Serbia. Barry Cunliffe has introduced us to the magic bag of the Celts. If I can borrow the image, the Gothic bag today seems to include all things distinct from classical Greco-Roman taste – ornate cathedrals, long-winded novels, and pale teenagers in black clothes. But the realities of ancient Goths remain elusive today. And yet they had what makes them unusual among European barbarians: they not only contrived a way to write their language down, but we still have a good deal of it, manuscripts from the sixth century BC and inscriptions from the late fifth century BC.[14]

There is also evidence that Goths made and drank wine, contrary to our stereotype of the Goth as a tall Nordic type in furs who only tasted wine after he had slaughtered everyone in the vineyard.[15] The Gothic translation of the Gospel of Mark 12, the parable of the vineyard, offers a different picture. The New International Version states: "A man planted a vineyard. He put a wall around it, dug a pit for the winepress and built a watchtower." It is hard to imagine our wild-eyed barbarian as someone who could understand this sentence, and even less as having the technical words in his language for the elements of wine production. (Even our modern translation struggles with the Greek *hypolenion*, or "vat for collecting juice under the winepress"; the King James Bible has "winefat"). But Gothic comes up with *dal uf mesa*. Gothic *dal* is cognate to German *Tal* and English "dale" or "dell"; *uf* with a dative refers to "under" as a position; and *mesa* seems to come from

Latin *mensa* – enough Latin in the Gothic term "winepress" to raise questions regarding sources of agricultural influence.

This could mean a very crude "ditch under the table." Or it could represent the standard Gothic term for a familiar part of the winemaking process. It is interesting to note that the translator did not just transliterate the Greek term, as he tends to do some 20 percent of the time, especially when stumped by the poverty of the Gothic language.[16]

Indeed, circumstances argue that the Goths were familiar with wine production and could have had winepresses. Our translators were those Goths living in the Roman province of Moesia (modern Serbia) in the mid-fourth century AD, where presumably wine had been made for some time. Some Goths were thought to have come from the west and north Black Sea area, where winemaking had been known for a millennium or longer. And, as Christians, they were using wine regularly in their liturgy. There is no reason to assume that they did not actually make their own wine.[17]

Some pertinent archaeological evidence comes from Volgum (modern Fenékpuszta), a trading city on the southern end of Lake Balaton in modern Hungary, where excavations have found numerous grape seeds and vine stakes (Map 1.1).[18] According to the excavation report, the style of the bells buried with children, the vessels and ornaments placed in the graves, and the type of grave construction attest to the presence of Sarmatians and eastern Germans.[19] The city walls were rebuilt around AD 350 in Roman style, but the contents of the graves indicate that the inhabitants were Sarmatians and Germans from the Black Sea area. Both ethnic groups were apparently Christian and partially Romanized. Considering that our oldest Gothic inscriptions were found in graves about 25 miles away (Hács), and that literary evidence shows that the Gothic tribes consisted of many ethnic groups, including Romans, however, one begins to suspect that these "Germans" and "Sarmatians" were actually Goths who had begun to make wine.[20] The Goths who wiped out the Romans at the battle of Adrianople in 378 might well have retired to their villas to enjoy the latest vintages.

Some consideration of this archaeological work and a critique of its interpretation may be helpful here. A team of Hungarian scholars excavated Volgum and its environs early in the twentieth century; sadly, some of their crucial finds were lost during World War II. When the excavations resumed after the war, Károly Sági first published interpretations of the site and its region for a non-Hungarian audience in the 1970s. Sági presents the details related to viticulture tersely: "We would like to point out that the influence of fourth-century Roman agricultural methods in this area is observable right through the invasion of the Magyars. Grape seeds and vine stakes from the graves and settlement areas of the time of the migration of peoples came to light."[21]

It would have been preferable if Sági had specified the contextual dating of these grape seeds and vine stakes. His own discussion implies that they were present continuously, from what he sees as a Roman foundation established by the emperor Constantius around AD 350 to the eventual invasion of Magyars at the end of the "migration of peoples." This latter term has become increasingly problematic since the time of Sági's writing. His narrative posits, as we have seen, Romanized Germans and Sarmatians in Constantius's fortified city, followed by the Alani, who damaged the site in 374. While recognizing agricultural continuity, he goes on to investigate an apparently planned and systematic destruction and rebuilding of the city in the mid-fifth century, after which we can be sure that it became a Gothic city. In fact, Volgum served in the 460s as the capital of the Ostrogoth king Thiudimir, whose son, born in Volgum, became the most celebrated Goth in history, Theodoric the Great.[22]

Two related points about this site are of particular importance for us: the agricultural continuity and the ethnic constituency. Not only are grape seeds and vine stakes found consistently throughout the period, but the excavations of the mid-fifth century destruction level revealed that a great number of Roman-style iron farming tools had apparently been systematically buried. The reason for this is obscure,[23] but the presence of these tools in the mid-fifth century adds weight to our assertion that whoever was living in this city from 350 to 450 cultivated in the Roman style and therefore probably produced wine. Thiudimir's violent takeover of the city around 455 does not force us to conclude that this meant that the Goths drove out any other ethnic group or an occasional isolated survivor of a Roman past.

The consistent agricultural practice, ethnic diversity of grave goods, and frequent disturbances seem rather to point to a period ripe for ethnogenesis.[24] We can read this as a place and period in which various members of Gothic armies who had been in close connection with the Roman Empire for generations had settled down to live an agricultural existence, as was most common for so-called federate Goths ever since the mid-fourth century. It would seem unlikely that Alani or Huns fresh from the East would have taken over the city and immediately settled down to Roman-style agriculture. It would seem equally unlikely that Constantius had settled a group of "real" Romans in this area in 350, and that they retained their distinct identity through a century of attacks by marauding armies of equally distinct ethnicity. Given the dominance of Goths in the region from about 370 on through the fifth century, it seems plausible that the people in the city called themselves Goths and that these Goths made wine.

At the same time, the Goths translated the Bible into their own language. Though many European barbarians had from antiquity left us evidence that they could represent their tongue with written symbols, only the Goths have left us a translation of a Greek text into their language. The motivation for this was very new: only Christianized barbarians would have felt the need to share a sacred Hebrew or Greek text with people of all classes and educational levels. The story is that Wulfila, the Gothic grandson of enslaved Greek ancestors, made this translation while in exile from the pagan Goths on the other side of the Danube.[25] This was the first European barbarian Bible.[26] And in fact, this Gothic Bible represented the first step of a Northern barbarian people toward what we term a "national identity."

An interesting parallel with another barbarian people can be seen in the Armenians. Around 400 a certain Mosrob created an Armenian alphabet and wrote a translation of the Bible into Armenian, as well as an Armenian version of the Syriac liturgy used at the time.[27] It can be argued that this literary language cemented the Armenian identity to a degree that no other ancient barbarian people achieved. The subsequent history of Armenians who survived every major invasion that swept across Western Asia, from the Umayyads right through Sovietization into the present, is almost unparalleled among ancient barbarians. Looking to parallels in early modern Europe, it is generally agreed that the Wycliff and King James bibles played a major role in the evolution of the English language, and of the idea of a nation.[28] Why should we be surprised that the Gothic Bible was beginning to play a similar role in late antique Gothia?

The answer may be that we have come to fear that Gothic myth lurking behind so many of Europe's nationalist excesses.[29] From Austria to Sweden the Goth became a symbol of national strength, a fresh, noble, unspoiled successor of the Roman Empire, the fearless warrior, bold ancestor of modern Europeans fated to dominate the world. This fear may be driving early medieval historians into the extreme position they have established, that is, that Gothic peoples had almost no sense of tribal identity or sense of loyalty to the crude kingdoms that they rigged up in the fifth century.[30] They were just a jumble of warriors looking for a good army, and when this army formed it would have made up a new name for itself.

To return to the Armenian parallel, two major differences may help to clarify the special case of the Goths. First, the Armenians never became part of the national mythology of a modern hegemonic state. Unlike the Goths, who were claimed by a wide variety of imperialist, even genocidal modern nations, the Armenians have preserved an unimpeachable record of victimization from Persian and Roman oppression in antiquity to Turkish genocide in modern times. If they had violently conquered and oppressed Europe and Western Asia in the modern period, as the Nazis and others did, we would be having a very different discussion about the early Armenian "myth" of being a nation.

Second, the Armenians enjoyed more than a millennium under relatively tolerant Islamic rule, during which time they were able to define their identity against the Umayyads, Abbasids, Seljuks, and Ottomans by cultivating the language and literature that early Christianity had given them. In short, the Armenians enjoyed excellent historical circumstances to elaborate an identity, and still today enjoy excellent political circumstances for an open discussion of it.

The Goths, of course, enjoyed neither. Through complex processes their cultural legacy was all but wiped out by the seventh century. The gradual disappearance of Gothic can mostly be attributed to waning political influence after the ascent of the Franks and Lombards, though the language may have lingered in pockets in the Iberian Peninsula, the Danube region, and Crimea. What slender legacy was revived in the modern period was so poisoned with moral repugnance that we are still reluctant to address it. But the differences between Goths and Armenians actually show that they were in a similar stage of cultural development in the fourth and fifth centuries. Both were cultivating an infant literature, and presumably an identity distinct from those of the dominant imperial cultures surrounding them. If the Goths had landed in a relatively consistent, tolerant, and yet culturally challenging imperial setting like the Islamic empires, and if modern hegemonic European states had looked elsewhere for a mythology of conquest, the Goths might well have headed toward an identity as stable as that of the Armenians. This shared fourth- and fifth-century experience is what I would call the first stages of defining cultural independence.

The local production of a fundamental commodity like wine could represent both a desire for economic independence from the Hellenized empire to its south and a process toward cultural independence; and though I am suggesting that the need to translate Christian texts and liturgy into Gothic triggered a process toward cultural independence, many other influences were at work. It seems clear, however, that while Roman historians speak of the empire's failure to assimilate the barbarian Goths, from the Balkan Gothic perspective we can see barbarian viticulture and literature as cultivated efforts to break away from their Greco-Roman neighbors.

Notes

1. I have not found any mention of wine in the many articles and books devoted to the Goths that are listed in my works cited.
2. The role of polyculture's triad of grain, wine, and olive oil in the development of Mediterranean civilization has been well discussed. A brief overview can be found in Greene 1990, 72–73. Drews 2001 also touches on agriculture in the origins of Indo-Hittite languages in Anatolia.
3. I modified the translation of King 1927, 159.
4. See Bonfante, Chapter 1, in this volume.
5. Livy 5.33; Tacitus, *Germania* 23.
6. For wine as a status symbol among barbarians, see an explanation of the respective value of the wine imported into Europe and bought by a Celtic chieftain: Cunliffe, Chapter 13, in this volume.
7. Homer, *Iliad* 9.72, speaks of Argives drinking Thracian wine.
8. See Nelson 2005 for a sweeping revision of the place of beer in history.
9. The first example in the Septuagint comes from Leviticus 10.9.1, which is translated in the New American Standard Bible: "Do not drink wine or *strong drink*, neither you nor your sons with you, when you come into the tent of meeting...." Homan 2004, 84, points out that though many translators of early Mesopotamian texts have chosen to use the word "wine," the word *šikaru* clearly refers to beer.

10. Mellink 1975, 92–93; Greenwalt 1997, 199.
11. *Iliad* 11.639–641 (description of a *kykeon* party) and *Od.* 10.233–236 (Circe's potion) present the only literary evidence from which McGovern argues that the presence of barley presumes that it was fermented along with the wine and cheese. See also the *kykeon* that Demeter drinks when she comes out of her mourning in *Homeric Hymn to Demeter*, 210.
12. Krapivina and Kudrenko 1986; Kryzhitskii and Krapivina 1994, 189. McGovern 2003 exploits the technique of chemical analysis of residues in excavated ceramics for historical results. For ancient wine see also McGovern et al. 1995; Murray and Tecuşan 1995; Witt 1997; Papadopoulos and Paspalas 1999.
13. *Hippiatrica Parisina* 376; Oder and Hoppe 1927, 29–114. See Xenophon, *Anabasis* 5.4.29, for an account of another Black Sea barbarian people making wine. Šceglov 1982 goes into some detail on local wine production, and on the relations between barbarians and Greeks in the Hellenistic Black Sea region.
14. See Scardigli 2000 for the current state of Gothic texts.
15. On the stereotype of the Northern barbarians see Keyser, Chapter 2, and Cunliffe, Chapter 6, in this volume.
16. For example, Gothic *aíwaggēljô* from Greek *euangelion*. Wolfram 1988, 90, calls for caution when using etymology to create historical judgments.
17. Schrenk and Weckbach 1997 and Scott 2002 present groundbreaking work on wine's place in medieval Central Europe.
18. Sági 1951, 1961, 1970 covers various interpretations of the site of Volgum and environs. Jacob 1997 vividly describes the archaeological problems involved in understanding late Roman and early medieval wine production.
19. Sági 1970, 152, recognizes that these Germans and Sarmatians were Romanized and were part of the Roman imperial defense system. Wolfram 1988, 91ff., discusses the integration of steppe horsemen like the Sarmatians into the Gothic territories on the Danube. According to Sági, the Christian-style burials within the city imply that the barbarians in Volgum were Christian; one might object that a few Christian burials do not necessarily prove that the Sarmatians and East Germans were in any significant way Christianized.
20. Wolfram 1988, 7, lists Finns, Slavs, Antes, Heruli, Rosomoni, Alans, Huns, Sarmatians, and probably Aesti as well in the Gothic kingdom of Ermanaric, along with a strong contingent of "former Roman provincials." Though this kingdom was situated north of the Black Sea, it coincides chronologically with our discussion of Goths in the late fourth-century Danube region.
21. Sági 1976, 396: "Wir möchten jedoch darauf hinweisen, daß sich der Einfluß der römischen Agrotechnik des 4. Jh. auf diesem Gebiet bis zu den landnehmenden Ungarn beobachten läßt. Traubenkerne und Rebestücke sind schon aus den Gräbern und Siedlungen der Völkerwanderungszeit zum Vorschein gekommen." (Read *Rebestöcke* for *Rebestücke*?)
22. Jordanes, *Get.* 52, explains Thiudimir's seat established *iuxta lacum Pelsois*, presumably Volgum, the only significant city on Lake Balaton in the fifth century. This settlement is generally dated to 455, at the time of Theodoric the Great's birth. See Sági 1976, 159.
23. This presents a mystery, for which Sági 1976, 153–156, gives an ingenious if somewhat elaborate explanation.
24. The literature on ethnic identification is vast; Pohl 2005 gives a recent overview focused on our period, while Roosen 1989 gives a clear, accessible explanation of the theory of ethnogenesis.

25. The essential sources for this story are Auxentius 307r (Gryson 1980, 244–251) and Philostorgius 2.6 (Winkelmann 1981).
26. Latin, Syriac, and various Egyptian dialects had their own Bibles earlier.
27. For Armenian early history, see Garsoian 1999.
28. See, e.g., Greenfeld 1992, 53ff.
29. Geary 2002, 99–103, and Wolfram 1988, 1–3, discuss European nationalist historiography. For discussion of the early history of nationalism, see in particular Hastings 1997, Smith 2000, and Marx 2003. See also Bonfante, Chapter 1, in this volume.
30. Wolfram 1988, Heather and Matthews 1991, Goffart 2006, Heather 2006, and Kulikowski 2006, present a variety of opinions on Gothic cohesiveness.

Bibliography

Drews, R. 2001. *Greater Anatolia and the Indo-Hittite Language Family: Papers Presented at a Conference at the University of Richmond, March 18–19, 2000.* Washington, DC.

Flobert, P. 1992. "Le vocabulaire de la vigne et du vin." *Bulletin de la société nationale des antiquaires de France* 1992:289–301.

Garsoian, N. 1999. *Church and Culture in Early Medieval Armenia.* Surrey.

Geary, P. J. 2002. *The Myth of Nations: The Medieval Origins of Europe.* Princeton, NJ.

Goffart, W. 2006. *Barbarian Tides: The Migration Age and the Later Roman Empire.* Philadelphia.

Green, D. H. 2007. "Linguistic and Literary Traces of the Ostrogoths." In *The Ostrogoths from the Migration Period to the Sixth Century: An Ethnographic Perspective*, ed. S. J. Barnish and F. Marazzi, 387–416. Oxford.

Greene, K. 1990. *The Archaeology of the Roman Economy.* Berkeley, CA.

Greenfeld, L. 1992. *Nationalism: Five Roads to Modernity.* Cambridge, MA.

Greenwalt, C. H. 1997. "A Lydian Canoe-Shaped Vessel from Sardis." *Anadolu* 23:195–220.

Gryson, R. 1980. *Scolies Ariennes sur le concile d'Aquilée.* Paris.

Hall, E. 2006. *The Theatrical Cast of Athens: Interactions between Ancient Greek Drama and Society.* Oxford.

Hastings, A. 1997. *The Construction of Nationhood: Ethnicity, Religion, and Nationalism.* Cambridge.

Heather, P. J. 2006. *The Fall of the Roman Empire: A New History of Rome and the Barbarians.* Oxford.

Heather, P. J., and J. F. Matthews 1991. *The Goths in the Fourth Century.* Liverpool.

Homan, M. M. 2004. "Beer and Its Drinkers: An Ancient Near Eastern Love Story." *Near Eastern Archaeology* 67 (2): 84–95.

Jacob, C. 1997. "Nachweise von Weinbau, Weinhandel und Weinverbrauch im Unterland in Römerzeit und Mittelalter aus archäologischer Sicht?" In Schrenk and Weckbach 1997, 77–84.

King, J. E. 1927. *Cicero: Tusculan Disputations.* London.

Krapivina, V. V., and A.I. Kudrenko 1986. "Vinodelni pervykh vekov nashei ery v Olvii (Winemaking in Olbia in the First Centuries of Our Era)." In

Antichnaya kultura Severnogo Prichernomorya v pervye veka nashei ery (Ancient Culture of the Northern Black Sea in the First Centuries of Our Era), 52–63. Kiev. (in Russian.)

Kryzhitskii, S. D., and V. V. Krapivina 1994. "A Quarter Century of Excavation at Olbia Pontica." *Echos du Monde Classique* 38:181–205.

Kulikowski, M. 2006. *Rome's Gothic Wars*. Cambridge.

Marx, A. 2003. *Faith in Nation: Exclusionary Origins of Nationalism*. Oxford.

McGovern, P. 2003. *Ancient Wine: The Search for the Origins of Viniculture*. Princeton, NJ.

McGovern, P., S. J. Fleming, and S. H. Katz, eds. 1995. *The Origin and Ancient History of Wine*. Langhorne, PA.

Mellink, M. J. 1975. "Archaic Wall Paintings from Gordion." In *From Athens to Gordion*, ed. K. de Vries, 91–98. Philadelphia.

Miller, N. F. 2008. "Sweeter Than Wine? The Use of the Grape in Early Western Asia." *Antiquity* 82:937–946.

Murray, O., and M. Tecuşan, eds. 1995. *In Vino Veritas*. London.

Nelson, M. 2005. *The Barbarian's Beverage*. London.

Oder, E., and K. Hoppe, eds. 1927. *Corpus hippiatricorum Graecorum*, vol. 2. Leipzig.

Papadopoulos, J. K., and S. A. Paspalas 1999. "Mendaian as Chalkidian Wine," *Hesperia* 68:162–188.

Pohl, W. 2005. "Aux origines d'une Europe ethnique: Identités en transformation entre antiquité et moyen âge," *Annales: Histoire, Sciences sociales* 60 (1): 183–208.

Reynolds, S. 1998. "Our Forefathers? Tribes, Peoples, and Nations in the Historiography of the Age of Migrations." In *After Rome's Fall: Narrators and Sources of Early Medieval History: Essays Presented to Walter Goffart*, ed. A. C. Murray, 17–36. Toronto.

Roosen, E. 1989. *Creating Ethnicity: The Process of Ethnogenesis*. London.

Sági, K. 1951. "La colonie romaine de Fenékpuszta et la zone intérieure des forteresses." *Acta Antiqua Academiae Scientiarum Hungaricae* 1:87–90.

———. 1961. "Die zweite altchristliche Basilika von Venékpuszta." *Acta Antiqua Academiae Scientiarum Hungaricae* 9:397–459.

———. 1970. "Das Problem der pannonischen Romanisation im Spiegel der Völkerwanderungszeitlichen Geschichte von Fenékpuszta." *Acta Antiqua Academiae Scientiarum Hungaricae* 18:147–196.

———. 1976. "Die Spätrömische Umgebung von Keszthely." *Acta Antiqua Academiae Scientiarum Hungaricae* 24:391–396.

Scardigli, P. 2000. "Neuentdeckte gotische Sprachreste." In *Die gotische Bibel*, bd. 3., 500–522. Heidelberg.

Šceglov, A. N. 1982. "L'interaction gréco-barbare sur la périphérie du monde hellénistique." In *The Black Sea Littoral*, 185–198. Tsqaltubo.

Schlumberger, D., L. Robert, A. Dupont-Sommer, and E. Benveniste. 1958. "Une bilingue gréco-araméenne d'Asoka." *Journal Asiatique* 246:1–48.

Schrenk, C., and H. Weckbach 1997. *Weinwirtschaft im Mittelalter: Zur Verbreitung, Regionalisierung und wirtschaftlichen Nutzung einer Sonderkultur aus der Römerzeit*. Heilbronn.

Scott, T. 2002. "Medieval Viticulture in the German-Speaking Lands." *German History* 20 (1): 95–115.

Smith, A. 2000. *The Nation in History*. Hanover, NH.

Valamoti, S. M., M. Mangafa, Ch. Koukouli-Chrysanthaki, and D. Malamidou. 2007. "Grape-Pressings from Northern Greece: The Earliest Wine in the Aegean?" *Antiquity* 81:54–61.

Winkelmann, F. 1981. *Historia ecclesiastica (fragmenta apud Photium): Philostorgius Kirchengeschichte*. Berlin.

Witt, C. 1997. *Barbarians on the Greek Periphery*. PhD dissertation, Charlottesville, VA http://www2.iath.virginia.edu/Barbarians/Essays/drink_main.html).

Wolfram, H. 1988. *The Goths*. Berkeley, CA.

CHAPTER THIRTEEN

SOME FINAL THOUGHTS

Barry Cunliffe

To sum up a book as rich and varied as this has been is no easy task, and indeed, with the papers now available here in printed form, it is hardly necessary. What can be offered, however, is some sense of the overarching themes that have emerged – themes that have given a welcome and enlightening coherence to our deliberations.

We have been exploring interfaces – interfaces between disciplines – Classical scholarship, iconography, language, and archaeology – and interfaces between peoples, in particular between the "civilized" peoples of the Mediterranean and the Black Sea, on the one hand, and those of the "barbarian" hinterland of Europe, on the other. This simple dichotomy, "us and the barbarians," was well established in the minds of the early Greek geographers – men like Hecataeus and Herodotus. To them the European barbarians could be divided into two broad groups: Scythians in the east and Celts in the west. As more knowledge of these nether regions was gained, further ethnic groupings were identified – Germans, Thracians, Dacians, Iberians, and others – and gradually the complexity of the human patchwork began to dawn. Today it is archaeologists who are showing us just how complex the palimpsest of peoples really is.

The geographical range of our conference has been, properly, wide. We have viewed many of the interfaces where Mediterranean cultures have come into active contact with neighboring hinterlands from the Mediterranean to the Baltic and from the Black Sea to the Atlantic. The zones where close interactions took place are many: the Black Sea littoral and the Scythians; the Balkan valleys and the Thracians; the Adriatic coasts and the Illyrians; the Bay of Naples and the Etruscans; the Golfe du Lion and the Celts; and the Spanish Levant and the Iberians. But the interface was never static, and as the Roman Empire expanded the zone moved northward through Europe, absorbing within the empire communities previously barbarian and engaging with peoples hitherto little known. Yet, at whatever period we are observing, the zone of contact is usually very narrow, and the social and economic interactions taking place there are usually articulated through specialized centers that archaeologists characterize as "ports of trade" or "gateway communities." These interface zones do not act as semipermeable membranes permitting only one-way movement; they allow – indeed, encourage – interchanges of materials, peoples, and ideas in both directions, and it is this dynamic that makes them all the more fascinating.

With his customary brilliance, Ferdinand Braudel grasped the core of the matter in his *Mediterranean in the Ancient World* (2001). Having stressed the vital importance of the sea "in the middle of the earth," he concludes, "So we find that our sea was from the very dawn of its prehistory a witness to those imbalances productive of change which would set the rhythm of its entire life." What Braudel is stressing here is, given that natural resources are unevenly spread throughout the world, the need for redistribution generates an underlying dynamic that binds disparate communities in networks of exchange. It is these networks that, in their different ways, bring the Mediterranean cities and states into direct relationship with less-developed barbarians around them.

I have deliberately used the phrase "Mediterranean cities and states" to dissociate us from the narrow-minded nineteenth-century legacy that only the Greeks, and just possibly the Romans, were of any significance. We are looking far more widely than that. The Etruscans, for example, working around the fringes of the Golfe du Lion in the late seventh century BC, were a formative influence in establishing contacts with the Celts of southern Gaul, and later in the fifth century, now acting through the Po Valley, with the Iron Age communities of the Moselle region where the first glimmerings of the Celtic art style developed. Nor should we forget the very considerable impact that Phoenicians had on the native communities of the western Mediterranean and, in particular, the south of Iberia. It was from their port of trade at Gadir (modern Cadiz) that they developed regular contacts with the Atlantic coastal population from Agadir in Morocco to the northwest corner of Iberia and possibly beyond.

It was the competitive trading impetus of the Phoenicians, Greeks, and Etruscans in the western Mediterranean that structured the geopolitics of the fifth to the second centuries BC and provided the opportunities for Rome to embark on its adventure of imperial expansion.

In an attempt to understand the nature of the peripheral interactions, economic historians and archaeologists have recently favoured simple core–periphery models. These stress the importance of a core region (like the Mediterranean) – a zone of innovation and escalating consumption – in creating the dynamic force needed to generate networks of exchange with peripheries. Stated in this way, the model is far too simple: it privileges the core over the periphery, implying that the core was the prime mover, the controller, and the chief beneficiary of the system. In reality it was seldom thus. For exchanges to take place, both parties must perceive there to be benefits. The exchange of a "slave for an amphora of wine," which Diodorus Siculus implies was the going rate between the Gaulish Celts and the Romans in the first century BC, might have seemed to the Roman entrepreneur to be a fantastic bargain, fleecing the poor, simple barbarians, because he could get six times the value for the same slave in Rome, but to the Celt the slave had little worth since he was just a by-product of raiding, whereas the amphora of wine was of considerable value in allowing the owner to provide the hospitality that enhanced his social standing and brought additional wealth. Similarly, when, in the late sixth century BC, the elite of Burgundy acquired the famous Vix krater and the other trappings of Mediterranean wine drinking, it is possible that they were merely the passive receivers of an "introductory offer" (Brian Shefton's phrase) sent by an entrepreneur wishing to ingratiate himself. A more likely scenario, however, is that the equipment was actively solicited by the lineage of the deceased woman, with whom it was buried as an act of prestation, so that they could display their power of acquisition and conspicuous consumption to competing elites. The value of an object, be it a Greek bronze vessel or a slave, would have varied significantly with the context. A Celtic chieftain in Gaul is unlikely to have regarded himself as inhabiting a periphery. In his world the core, or center, was where he was.

These dynamic relationships between core and periphery were therefore intricately complex in their competing value systems – a complexity that we can only dimly perceive – but overall, what emerges is a structure of mutual interdependence. Thus, we know that the Mediterranean world depended on barbarian Europe for a wide range of raw materials from metals, small grains, and hides to furs, hunting dogs, and smoked hams (all listed by Strabo). But dominating all of Strabo's lists were slaves. Without a constant inflow of manpower and raw materials, Rome would not have survived for long.

The impacts of these relationships on barbarian society were many. At an economic level, native systems of production had sometimes to be dramatically modified. In southwestern Iberia, the demand of Phoenician merchants for silver greatly encouraged the Tartessan communities to intensify the extraction of silver. What had been a sufficer level of production geared up to a maximizer level, because the surplus now had a market outlet. So, a similar process with grain growing in the lower Danube Valley would have satisfied the demands of the merchants who shipped the grain to the cities of Greece. It is also likely that the massive consumption of slaves by Rome exacerbated endemic systems of raiding among the Gaulish Celts, echoing the situation in West Africa in the seventeenth and eighteenth centuries.

There would also have been interaction at the more creative level. In what is now Bulgaria, the Thracian kingdoms flourished, borrowing extensively from neighboring Greece and Macedonia for their tomb architecture and tomb painting. Farther west, in the Moselle region of Germany and the Marne region of France, the elites of the Early La Tène culture benefited from luxury metalwork made by skilled craftsmen inspired by contemporary Etruscan styles. In this lay the beginnings of Celtic art, which played such a distinctive part in the life of Iron Age communities throughout Europe. In Iberia, too, the art of the potter and of the sculptor serving the emerging Iberian states owed much to inspiration emanating from the Greek world.

It is all too easy for archaeologists, writing of these matters, to forget that real people were involved, traveling as emissaries, traders, or simply explorers deep into unknown territory. In Germany the mud-brick architecture of the sixth century BC fortified residence at Heuneburg was surely overseen by an architect from the Mediterranean. Similarly, the superb sculptural composition found at Porcuna in Andalucía, though almost certainly made by a local sculptor, is so remarkable that he, or his teacher, is likely to have learned from an eastern Greek master. Nor should we forget the sheer curiosity that many a Mediterranean resident must have felt about the barbarian region – men like Pytheas of Massalia (Marseille), who in about 320 BC circumnavigated Britain and may even have ventured farther. The hints of these personal journeys are there in the historical and archaeological sources, but I suspect that we have grossly underestimated the degree of contact between the two worlds throughout the first millennium BC.

So, what have we learned from the diverse and fascinating papers presented at the conference and published here? Two things, I think, stand out. The first is that it is impossible to understand the peoples of barbarian Europe or of the Mediterranean region in isolation. The two worlds were so tightly bound together by intricate networks that they must be studied together. The second is to accept the fragility of our database, be it historical, linguistic, iconographic, or archaeological. No one approach will ever be satisfactory; a deeper understanding of the past comes only when the varied disciplines work closely together.

In bringing us all together and making us think about these matters, this conference has been a resounding success. We all owe a deep debt of gratitude to Larissa Bonfante for the inspired choice of subject and to her, Stuart Wheeler, and their colleagues at Richmond for their faultless organization. Where better than in the theater of Old Europe to study the subtleties of human interaction, to learn to respect those who differ from us, and to cherish the difference?

NOTE ON DELACROIX, "ENSLAVED AMONG THE BARBARIANS"

Ann E. Farkas

Ovid among the Scythians[1] (Plate XXIII) was commissioned in 1856 by Benoît Fould, a friend of the painter Ferdinand-Victor-Eugène Delacroix (1798–1863). As early as 1849 the artist had conceived of such an easel painting,[2] and he worked on the *Ovid* for almost three years, delivering it to Mme. Fould in 1859, after M. Fould's death in 1858. In an undated entry in his *Journal*, Delacroix set down the painting's title and his interpretation of the poet's state of mind. It depicts

> the feeling of a heart and of a sick imagination, that of a man who, after a worldly life, finds himself enslaved among the barbarians, or cast onto a desert island like Robinson, forced to fall back on the strength of his body and his own industry – which restores to him natural feelings and calms his imagination.[3]

In the catalogue for the Salon of 1859, Delacroix described the painting, one of several that he had submitted for that year's exhibition: "Ovid in exile among the Scythians. Some of them examine him with curiosity, others welcome him in their own way, offering him mare's milk, wild fruit, etc."[4] The figures are arranged in an arc before a barren, mountainous landscape framing a large body of water whose waves lap the shore: At the left, Ovid, clothed in togalike garments, reclines on the earth, his poetry scroll beside him;[5] before Ovid are two Scythian men,

The author thanks Lisa Lieberson, director, and the staff of the Village Library of Wrightstown, and Gene Constantine and the staff of the Interlibrary Loan Department, Bucks County District Library Center, Doylestown, Pennsylvania.

one of whom kneels and offers the poet a basket, as well as a woman holding a baby; at the far right are two seated Scythians; a walking figure and a man mounted on a horse climb a slope behind the poet; a young girl with a large dog walks toward Ovid; and in the right foreground, a Scythian man milks a large black mare.[6]

Delacroix has highlighted the contrast between the civilized poet and the barbarians: the area around Ovid is lit more brightly than the opposite part of the painting, and Ovid is dressed in white and blue (echoing the water, distant mountains, and sky), whereas the Scythians are partly naked and wear only earth-colored makeshift attire. The nomads are moving, sitting, or crouching; they are tense, muscular figures reacting in one way or another to the presence of the poet; even the black mare (the horse being one of Delacroix's favored motifs for suggesting untamed nature, though here used to draw attention to the mare-milker) tosses her mane and flings her tail to the side. But Ovid is motionless, partly turned away from his hosts, as befitting a man of thought rather than of action. Nevertheless, despite the subtle distinctions between the civilized poet and the barbaric nomads, the painting's most striking features are its serenity and abstract harmony, achieved through the arrangement of colors and shapes, and the wild grandeur of the landscape, which almost overwhelms the figures.

The painting is an expanded version of a motif that Delacroix had used in his decorations of the Palais-Bourbon in Paris. Beginning in late 1838, when the French government gave him the commission, Delacroix worked for almost ten years painting the upper parts (two half-domes and the cupolas over the five bays) of the library in the Palais-Bourbon. He described his subjects in a notice that he sent to the critic Théophile Thoré, which the latter quoted in his review of the decoration. Each of the five cupolas has four scenes referring to "categories adopted by all libraries, without following their exact classifications" – Science, History and Philosophy, Legislation and Eloquence, Theology, and Poetry.[7] In the Poetry cupola, *Ovid among the Scythians* forms one scene; the others are *The Education of Achilles*, *Hesiod and the Muse*, and *Alexander and Homer's Poems*. The half-domes are adorned with large paintings more expansive than those in the cupolas: in the south half-dome *Orpheus Civilizes the Greeks*, and in the north half-dome *Attila and His Hordes Overrun Italy and the Arts*. Thus the general theme of the library is the birth and death of ancient civilization, beginning with Orpheus's civilizing the Greeks and ending with the barbarian destruction of classical Rome, with civilization encompassing the various achievements in science, history, and so on as represented on the cupolas. At the same time, the scenes (and indeed, many other works of Delacroix) suggest a struggle between barbarism and civilization or an opposition between more and less civilized figures.

The painting does not show a historical event described by Ovid, nor does it distill Ovid's sentiments in exile as expressed in his last writings. Rather, Delacroix uses the subject to express his view of Ovid's emotional experiences in exile and alienation and thereby his own relation to art and society. For Delacroix, Ovid, like himself, was an isolated genius, tentatively accepted, if misunderstood, by a few rude barbarians and harshly criticized or ignored by others. In the library of the Palais-Bourbon, the paired themes of the artistic genius among ordinary people and the destruction of classical culture by barbarians are indeed not too different from Delacroix's own experiences.

Throughout his career, Delacroix was successful in the sense that the government purchased many of his major paintings and commissioned him to decorate public buildings, but he won the attention, negative and positive, of people whose opinions he did not always respect, and he distrusted critics like Baudelaire, who, according to David Scott, interpreted Delacroix's work so as to advance literature rather than accepting that Delacroix's ideas were those of a painter.[8]

On many occasions he was denied admission to the Institut de France and was elected only on his eighth attempt, in 1857, by which year he was almost fifty-nine years old, too old, he thought, to become a professor and form a school. Having seen inferior artists win seats at the Institut that should have gone to him, and always playing second fiddle to his competitor Jean-Auguste-Dominique Ingres (1780–1867), whom the French artistic hierarchy favored above all others, Delacroix had every reason to see himself as Ovid among the Scythians.

Thus Delacroix represented the Ovid that he, the painter, felt and understood. He achieved, one hopes, the intent, mentioned in his *Journal* entry, of using his artistry to overcome "the feeling of a heart and of a sick imagination" of a man who "finds himself enslaved among the barbarians" (*esclave chez les barbares*).[9] In short, he aimed to sublimate his emotions in his work and heal himself through his labors.

Showing that he could "master" Ovid by depicting a poetic idea by means of painting, Delacroix may also have been inspired to surpass the classical idylls of Nicolas Poussin (1594–1665), to demonstrate that he, more successfully than his predecessor, merged the artistic and intellectual aspects of his painting, thereby fulfilling the Renaissance reformulation of the classical ideal of art as painted poetry,[10] in a fitting tribute to the Roman poet. If something like this was Delacroix's intent, no critic aside from Baudelaire came close to grasping it, and Delacroix never exhibited at the Salon after the year of *Ovid*.

The year before his death, Delacroix had been involved in creating the Societé Nationale des Beaux-Arts with his friend Théophile Gautier; one of the first exhibitors was Édouard Manet. After Delacroix died, the Societé mounted a retrospective exhibition of the painter. The enormous success of the auction of his works brought Delacroix the acclaim he had been denied in life.

> When, after his death, in the auction rooms of the Hôtel Drouot, they saw that prodigious pile of drawings, studies, and sketches, which describe the master's daily, indefatigable labor, a cry of admiration arose from every heart. All at once we understood both the greatness of the man and of the work.... For their weight in gold, at any price, the least lines from this glorious pencil were disputed. Everything was bought, and carried away with an intoxicated fervor; one would have said that the public was taking revenge upon itself for its past disdain, making it a matter of honor to pay insane amounts.... The faithful ... greeted the higher bids with outbursts of frantic applause; it really was a magnificent sight, one of those one cannot forget.[11]

If he never formed a school, Delacroix's work inspired later artists, such as Manet, Degas, and Cézanne. Of him Cézanne wrote: "[A]ll this limpidity, I don't know how, it enters your eye like a glass of wine going down your throat, and you are immediately intoxicated.... And with Delacroix, there's nothing to say; he has something, a fever that you don't find among the older painters. It's the happy fever of convalescence, I think.... And he has a sense of the human being, of life in movement, of warmth. Everything moves. Everything shimmers. The light!"[12]

Notes

1. National Gallery, London; 88 by 130 centimeters; see Johnson 1981–1989, 3 and 4: nos. 334, 345. Another version, painted in 1862 and formerly in a private

collection in Bern, Switzerland, was recently acquired by the Metropolitan Museum of Art in honor of Philippe de Montebello. See *BMMA* 66, fall 2008, 38; Johnson 1981-1989, 3: no. 345, 155-159; no. 345, plate 143.

2. Delacroix 1981, 190, April 10, 1849; Sérullaz et al. 1998, 234.

3. Delacroix 1981, Supplement to the *Journal*, undated, 839; Sérullaz et al. 1998, 235.

4. Jobert 1998, 268, 325 n. 77; Sérullaz et al. 1998, 236.

5. Ovid's pose is reminiscent of that of Diogenes in Raphael's *School of Athens*. Delacroix often mentioned Raphael and his work in his *Journal* and wrote an article on Raphael, published in the *Revue de Paris*, 1830. (See Delacroix 1981, "Notes sur Raphael," Supplement to the *Journal*, undated, 829-830.) Although he never visited Rome, Delacroix was familiar with reproductions of Raphael's frescoes in the Vatican *stanze* and must have studied them when he laid out the scheme for the library in the Palais-Bourbon. Depicting Ovid after Raphael's Diogenes was perhaps Delacroix's homage to the artist he called a poet-painter.

6. Lee Johnson has noted that the small hut with a grass roof, at the far left of the painting, was probably inspired by James Cook's *Voyage to the Pacific Ocean*. One of the studies for the *Ovid among the Scythians* in the Poetry cupola in the Palais-Bourbon is inscribed by Delacroix *"un des paysages du voyage de Cook,"* and the cupola painting includes a thatched hut similar to the National Gallery version. Johnson 1981-1989, 3:151f.; 4: plates 142, 143, 151, 152.

7. Cited from Jobert 1998, 194.

8. David Scott, "Writing the Arts: Aesthetics, Art Criticism, and Literary Practice," in *Artistic Relations* 1994, 61-75, especially 67-69. Some writers who criticized *Ovid* carped at the horse; one called it "the mare of the Trojan horse," referring to its size (Johnson 1981-1989, 3:151). Everyone, even Charles Baudelaire (1821-1867), seemed not to see that Delacroix used the horse and the thatched hut as icons of barbarism, symbols of the wilderness beyond civilization. Nevertheless, Baudelaire – who wrote of the *Ovid* "Just as exile gave the brilliant poet that quality of sadness which he had hitherto lacked, so melancholy has clothed the painter's superabundant landscape with its own magical glaze" (Sérullaz et al. 1998, 237) – offered Delacroix's painting a lyrical tribute that is difficult to quarrel with. Perhaps Delacroix's distrust of literary criticism such as Baudelaire's has to do with the inevitable disparity between an artist's ideas about his work and the ideas of those who see it from the outside, with their own inherent biases.

9. Delacroix 1981, Supplement to the *Journal*, undated, 839; Sérullaz et al. 1998, 235.

10. Lee 1967, 3-4, 46.

11. La Madelène 1864, 8, cited from Jobert 1998, 303.

12. Gasquet 1921, 108, cited from Jobert 1998, 154-155.

Bibliography

Artistic Relations: Literature and the Visual Arts in Nineteenth-Century France, ed. Peter Collier and Robert Lethbridge. 1994. New Haven, CT.

Delacroix, Eugène. 1981. *Journal, 1822–1863*. H. Damisch, preface. A. Joubin, intro. and notes. Paris.

Gasquet, Joachim. 1921. *Cézanne*. Paris.

Jobert, B. 1998. *Delacroix*. Princeton, NJ.

Johnson, L. 1981–1989. *The Paintings of Eugène Delacroix: A Critical Catalogue, 1816–1831*. 6 vols. Oxford.

La Madelène, Joseph Henri de Collet, baron de. 1864. *Eugène Delacroix à l'exposition du Boulevard des Italiens*. Paris.

Lee, R. W. 1967. *Ut Pictura Poesis: The Humanistic Theory of Painting*. New York.

The Metropolitan Museum of Art Bulletin (BMMA), 66, 2. Fall 2008. "Recent Acquisitions: A Selection: 2007–2008." New York.

Sérullaz, A. 2004. *Delacroix*. Paris.

Sérullaz, A., et al. 1998. *Delacroix: The Late Work*. Philadelphia.

INDEX

Printed in the USA
CPSIA information can be obtained
at www.ICGtesting.com
LVHW080040291223
767614LV00002B/57